30 Eco-Trips in Florida

Wild Florida

Florida A&M University, Tallahassee
Florida Atlantic University, Boca Raton
Florida Gulf Coast University, Ft. Myers
Florida International University, Miami
Florida State University, Tallahassee
University of Central Florida, Orlando
University of Florida, Gainesville
University of North Florida, Jacksonville
University of South Florida, Tampa
University of West Florida, Pensacola

WILD FLORIDA

edited by M. Timothy O'Keefe

Books in this series are written for the many people who visit and/or move to Florida to participate in our remarkable outdoors, an environment rich in birds, animals, and activities, many exclusive to this state. Books in the series will offer readers a variety of formats: natural history guides, historical outdoor guides, guides to some of Florida's most popular pastimes and activities, and memoirs of outdoors folk and their unique lifestyles.

30 Eco-Trips in Florida: The Best Nature Excursions (and How to Leave Only Your Footprints), by Holly Ambrose (2005)

A Hiker's Guide to the Sunshine State, by Sandra Friend (2005)

30 Eco-Trips
in Florida

The Best Nature Excursions
(and How to Leave Only Your Footprints)

Holly Ambrose

Foreword by M. Timothy O'Keefe, series editor

University Press of Florida
Gainesville
Tallahassee
Tampa
Boca Raton
Pensacola
Orlando
Miami
Jacksonville
Ft. Myers

Copyright 2005 by Holly Ambrose
Printed in the United States of America on acid-free paper
All rights reserved

10 09 08 07 06 05   6 5 4 3 2 1

A record of cataloging-in-publication information is available from
the Library of Congress.
ISBN 0-8130-2850-7

The University Press of Florida is the scholarly publishing agency for the State
University System of Florida, comprising Florida A&M University, Florida Atlantic
University, Florida Gulf Coast University, Florida International University, Florida
State University, University of Central Florida, University of Florida, University
of North Florida, University of South Florida, and University of West Florida.

University Press of Florida
15 Northwest 15th Street
Gainesville, FL 32611-2079
http://www.upf.com

For Jim

So go unlock the door
And find what you are here for
Leave the great indoors

John Mayer

Contents

Part 1. Northwestern Florida

Part 2. Northern Florida

Part 3. Central Florida

Part 4. Southern Florida

Foreword

With Florida already ranked as one of the most populous states and hundreds of thousands more moving here every year, it seems impossible that truly wild places can remain anywhere in such a densely inhabited region.

Yet in spite of the tremendous influx of people wanting to enjoy the Sunshine state's warm climate and active outdoors lifestyle, significant sections of the original, natural Florida do still endure.

In fact the amount of Florida set aside for preservation surprises many people, especially first-time visitors and newly arrived residents. As this is written, Florida terrain is protected by three national forests, 11 national parks, 157 state parks, and 28 national wildlife refuges. In addition, individual Florida counties have designated their own protected public lands, providing for pristine rivers and sheltered coastline.

Yes, there is quite a lot of Florida that hasn't been paved over or badly disturbed by development—and it never will be.

The University Press of Florida celebrates the essential natural qualities of Florida, its environment, its creatures, and its people through the broad-ranging series Wild Florida.

30 Eco-Trips in Florida: The Best Nature Excursions (and How to Leave Only Your Footprints) by Holly Ambrose, the editor of *EcoFlorida*, is an excellent example of UPF's commitment to exploring, appreciating, and protecting wild Florida.

A thorough and comprehensive work, *30 Eco-Trips* provides many more possibilities than its title implies. The number 30 refers not to several dozen specific trips but to geographic regions that sometimes encompass several counties and extend for a hundred miles or more.

In reality, the guide covers scores of sites located in every region, from the western end of the Panhandle to the tip of the Florida Keys.

Expanding significantly beyond the scope of typical nature guides, *30 Eco-Trips* not only details where to go and what to see but also helps readers plan their own individualized trips with detailed guidelines and recommendations on where to stay.

Most significantly, Ambrose in her introduction distinguishes the various types of sightseeing available to those visiting wild Florida. There are subtle but important distinctions every traveler should bear in mind since, subconsciously, they help determine our conduct whenever we venture into the outdoors.

Nature travel, as Ambrose points out, is the most common and most obvious approach to outdoor tourism: we travel to immerse ourselves in nature.

Adventure travel, on the other hand, implies an element of risk. Without whitewater rapids and precarious mountain ascents, Florida has almost nothing to offer in this category.

But the milder form of tourism known as soft adventure certainly exists in many parts of Florida. Soft adventure, which is often family-oriented, includes such as activities as overnight trail riding or guided walking tours.

Ecotourism, however, is the most responsible form of nature travel. It expects us to be aware of our potential impact on the ecology or environment. It requires a respectful approach, as opposed to an unthinking, careless, or destructive one.

Ecotourism also imposes the burden of guardianship on us to guarantee those who follow in our footsteps will enjoy the same sights, sounds, and experiences and that we will not degrade these opportunities.

Ambrose suggests a uniquely simple way to minimize our impact on Wild Florida: *Know before you go.* Don't arrive at a destination haphazardly, but recognize precisely what it is you want to see and do, who can assist you, and your options on where to stay. This involves both advance planning and contacting knowledgeable people and organizations to learn current conditions, hours of operation and any admission fees or legal requirements.

With its comprehensive descriptions and meticulously researched contact information, *30 Eco-Trips in Florida* makes it convenient and effortless for all of us to be responsible ecotourists.

M. Timothy O'Keefe
Series Editor

1

Florida as an Ecotourism Destination

To the rest of the world, Florida has been a place to look for gold and treasure, a land of hope for better opportunities, an exotic beach escape, a swampy mosquito-ridden backwater, and even a place where voters don't know how to count ballots. Florida is seen as a place to grow oranges, see alligators, swim with dolphins, visit retired relatives, and drink tropical beverages by the pool in winter—many things you don't typically experience in other states. Florida may be all of these things, but the person who limits his or her view of Florida to just these alone is missing out on getting to know the real essence of Florida, its nature.

With its unique geography, geology, and climate, Florida and its preserved natural lands are perfect for a nature travel destination. The state's three national forests, 11 national parks, 28 national wildlife refuges, 157 state parks, and many other public lands make Florida a perfect place for nature travelers. Florida is already well-versed in traditional tourism and has the facilities and "system" set up for tourists. When a state that relies on tourism for its economy brings nature-based recreation into the mix, the state and nature travelers both can benefit.

According to Visit Florida, the state's official tourism bureau, nature tourism is the fastest-growing sector of world tourism, growing by 30 percent per year in the world. Nature tourism is strong in Florida, with other statistics from the bureau that seem to back this up: Florida state parks contributed $249 million to local economies for the fiscal year 1997–98. Florida canoe liveries bring in $38.5 million each year. Regional tourism development councils are spending more money to advertise their natural lands. More than half of Florida vacationers report participating in nature-based activities. All of these Visit Florida statistics point to a keen interest in nature travel and recreation.

The state of Florida is so proud of its suitability for nature travel that in 2000 it opened the Nature and Heritage Tourism Center (386-397-4461), a kind of information warehouse for this kind of tourism. If you arrive in Florida by car going south on I-75, stop by the center in White Springs for exhibits and kiosks about your travel interests.

The Nature of Florida

Florida is blessed with a distinctive location that makes it what it is. With a peninsula that stretches from the coastal plains of the south toward the Tropic of Cancer—with the Gulf of Mexico on one side, the Atlantic Ocean on the eastern side, and the Caribbean Sea to the south—Florida encompasses a variety of natural habitats from coastal dunes to limestone caverns, desertlike scrublands to wide open prairies, saltwater grassy marshes to dense subtropical forests, pine flatwood forests to rolling sandhills. Its mild winter climate makes Florida a target for more northerly tourists and seasonal residents during this time in particular.

Winter is known as the dry season, the half of the year when tropical storms and hurricanes don't threaten the state and the summer rains have passed. Cooler temperatures and reduced humidity from roughly November through April make this time of year more pleasant, particularly for nature travelers who will be outdoors.

Northwestern Florida, also known as the panhandle or the Emerald Coast, is less developed than other parts of Florida. Coastal resorts and preplanned communities are springing up along the Gulf of Mexico, and some inland towns are growing larger. However, this is where you'll find the largest national forest (the Apalachicola) and pristine rivers.

Northern Florida, in some places considered the Original Florida because of its role in the state's history, has pine forests and beautiful coastal marshes. As far as nature goes, though, it may be best known for its hundreds of freshwater springs and underground caves.

Central Florida is dotted with lakes of all sizes, interspersed with hills and prairies. Swamps feed rivers whose water empties into Florida's coastal waters in all directions. The eastern side's Indian River Lagoon and the western side's Tampa Bay are popular recreational areas and important estuaries.

Southern Florida is dominated by wetlands—most notably the Everglades—marl prairies, and hardwood hammocks. Both coasts are heavily populated, but there are pockets of preserved lands.

Ecotourism/Nature Travel/Adventure Travel/Soft Adventure: What's the Difference?

The book title uses the word eco-trip to describe visiting a place while keeping the ecology or environment in mind. Most of the time, the book will use the term "nature travel" to describe visiting parks, forests, refuges, preserves, conservation areas, and the like to enjoy their beauty and recreational opportunities. Travel agencies, tourism brochures, and magazines use many different terms to describe the different kinds of trips people take:

Nature Travel

Nature travel is pretty much what it sounds like—traveling to be in nature. This usually means an overnight stay in or near the natural area you're visiting. But nearby residents can get as much out of a day trip to a local area as a foreign visitor can.

Adventure Travel

Appealing to people who are looking for a vacation with an edge or an element of danger, adventure travel usually includes a sport or is heavy on gear. If a traveler's goal is an adrenaline rush, he or she is probably after adventure travel. Examples include multiday mountain treks and whitewater rafting tours.

Soft Adventure

Not quite as risky or grueling as adventure travel, a soft adventure trip is a good choice for active people like family groups. This might be a weekend of riding horseback or a guided walking tour through the country.

Ecotourism

Often used when referring to nature travel in developing countries, this term seems to have been given special reverence by those who consider themselves experts on the subject. Yet ecological tourism doesn't have to be reserved just for remote places that require a large travel budget and an interpreter. Ecotourism is nature travel with more emphasis on promoting the welfare of the destination's resources and residents.

Many people are concerned about ecotourism's impact on the environment, pointing out the irony that those who explore a region's natural areas can end up making those areas worse for the wear. There is some validity to this concern. For example, studies have shown that wildlife can be stressed in the presence of people. More people coming into an area usually means more waste and more use of resources. Some visitors don't take care to avoid trampling vegetation. Proponents of ecotourism and nature travel typically say that the benefits—namely, education—outweigh the downsides. There is truth to this statement, too, as people tend to protect what they understand and love.

There may be no definitive answer or solution to the impact question. Learning about an area and its environment before traveling—like reading this book—can help nature travelers be aware of a region's sensitivities. Nature tour guide certification is another step that some areas are taking to "educate the educators" so they don't pass mistakes on to their guests. As more people pour into natural areas, we may see some environmentally sensitive natural areas limiting the number of visitors allowed, in an attempt to reduce traffic.

Nature Travel Tips

The best advice is often the most simple. It seems so elementary that it's often overlooked or avoided. But with travel, the best advice is to *know before you go*. Even if you like to make decisions about what to do on the spur of the moment, you're going to need to know a few basics.

The first tip for planning anything from a week-long vacation to an overnight stay is to call ahead, especially when it comes to visiting natural areas that are public lands. Many people have gotten used to navigating the Web for travel information, and it certainly has made *know before you go* a lot easier. However, many public agencies are underfunded, understaffed—and simply may not make the best use of the Internet to do all they can to inform visitors. Months may go by before a national wildlife refuge Web site is updated, for example. Some information available on the Internet is just plain wrong. So although it seems too simple, call each natural area you plan to visit before you leave.

When you call, ask about the things you most want to know. For example, are you likely to see a roseate spoonbill, and where? Is fishing allowed? Do you have to bring your own gear, or can you rent it? Are restroom facilities available? Also ask questions about the basics: When does the park open? How much is the entrance fee? Do you need a permit? How long can you stay? This book has tried to provide this information, but change is constant. Phone numbers change, companies go out of business, campgrounds close for renovation, and prices increase. Calling ahead to ask questions is almost like taking out insurance against disappointment.

When you arrive at a natural area with a ranger station or visitor center near the entrance, always request a park map or guide. (If you don't want to keep it, you can always return it before you leave so someone else can use it—reduce, reuse, recycle.) If you want to explore the trails there, ask if a separate trail map is available. If you are interested in wildlife, inquire about lists of birds, reptiles, or mammals found in the park. Many natural areas provide such literature if you ask. If the natural area doesn't have a ranger station or visitor center, look for a kiosk. This may be just a two-sided board with legs where you can pick up a park guide or review information about the area on the board.

As a nature traveler, let the businesses you patronize know that you are spending money there because of the local natural lands. This will show the economic community and voters these lands are worth protecting, not only because your presence proves people are using the land, but also because nature travel can be good business. The more that nature travelers make their presence and intentions known, the more that natural lands and nature travel will continue to prosper.

Hours and Entrance Fees

National Parks

Whether they're called parks (like the Everglades), seashores (like Canaveral), or something else, National Park Service lands' hours and entrance fees vary. Some entrance fees are good for a whole week.

Frequent visitors may want to purchase one of the service's special passes to save money:

The National Parks Pass costs $50.00 and covers the cost of admission to parks for one year. You can buy a pass from the National Park Foundation (888-GO-PARKS; www.nationalparks.org).

The Golden Age Passport is available to U.S. citizens or permanent residents who are at least sixty-two years old. The $10.00 fee gives passholders a lifetime of entrance fees and 50 percent discounts on some activities like camping and tours. These passes must be purchased in person at a federal area entrance.

Golden Access Passports are for U.S. citizens or permanent residents who are blind or permanently disabled. Like the Golden Age Passport, this pass is for a lifetime, includes a half-price discount on some recreational fees, and must be purchased in person on site.

National Forests

Generally, national forests are open around the clock because the community uses roads that go through them. Some recreation areas may be open only during daylight hours, however.

Again because of access issues, national forests generally don't charge fees; you can drive right through them. But if you want to enter certain recreation areas or camp, you may be charged a fee, either at an entrance station or at an honor box.

National Parks Pass holders can add a $15.00 Golden Eagle hologram to a pass for access to national forests and wildlife refuges.

Individual forests also sell annual passes for entrance to certain recreation areas; contact each forest about these passes if you are going to return several times throughout the year.

National Wildlife Refuges

Wildlife refuge hours vary from location to location. Refuge visitor centers and ranger stations keep regular hours.

Entrance fees also vary. Some refuges are free, others accept donations, and others charge for access, usually not more than $5.00.

National Parks Pass holders can add a $15.00 Golden Eagle hologram to a pass for access to national forests and wildlife refuges.

State Parks

State parks are open every day from 8 a.m. until sundown, unless otherwise stated. Entrance fees are usually between $2.00 and $5.00 per vehicle for up to eight people; each extra individual pays $1.00. People who enter parks on foot or bicycle usually pay $1.00.

State parks offer entrance passes like the national parks. A Real Florida Vacation Pass is good for seven days and costs $10.00 to $12.50. The Annual Entrance Pass for a family of up to eight people in one vehicle ($60.00) or for an individual ($30.00) allows admission into state parks for a year. A Special Recreational Use Pass is like the Annual Entrance Pass, but includes the cost of activities fees (not camping), for a family of up to four people ($80.00) or individuals ($40.00).

State Forests

State forests generally are open all hours.

Some state forests are free, and others charge an entrance fee, usually $1.00 per person. Frequent visitors can buy an Annual Day Use Pass for $30.00 from any forest office. Camping requires an extra fee.

Trail Tripping

If you are new to using trails for hiking, bicycling, horseback riding, or pad-dling, learn about any equipment and techniques you need to know before leaving the trailhead. Books on some of these subjects are listed in the Resources section of this book (appendix 1).

Before heading down the trail, find out how long the trail is and about how long it might take to complete it. Unless a natural area allows open access, stay on trails to protect habitats and to avoid getting lost. Many times, even though signs are posted to remind people to stay on a trail or to stay off dunes, park visitors ignore these warnings to the detriment of the natural landscape and habitat. By staying in designated areas, nature travelers can help preserve these areas for future generations.

If you are planning an overnight trip along a trail—or if you are exploring a wilderness area for the day—be sure to tell someone what your plans are. Even if you don't file a formal trip report with a ranger (required in some places and on certain trails), someone you know should have an idea of your plans. Leave information about the time you left, the route you're taking, and when you expect to return, as well as an emergency phone number to call if you don't come back at your expected time. This person also should be responsible enough to actually watch for your return. No one expects to encounter danger while having fun outdoors, but it's best to be prepared.

Most natural areas in Florida require horseback riders to carry proof of a negative Coggins test (which shows that a horse doesn't carry the virus causing an equine anemia).

If you enjoy using trails in different places, you should know the Florida Division of Forestry offers programs for hikers and horseback riders. The Trailwalker program awards patches to people who hike a certain number of miles on specific state forest trails. The more trails you hike, the more patches you can earn. The similar Trailtrotter program rewards equestrians who ride specific state forest trails. For information on these programs, contact the Florida Division of Forestry or any state forest office.

Camping

Not every nature traveler is a camper, and not every camper is a tent camper. Whatever way you choose to spend the night on your eco-trip is simply a matter of personal preference. Just try to honor other nature travelers' preferences.

It's always best to make a reservation for a campsite because campgrounds can fill up months ahead of time, especially during Florida's peak tourist seasons. (Typically, northern Florida gets more tourists during the summer while central and southern Florida receive more visitors in the winter.) Most campgrounds (and outfitters) encourage or even require reservations. There are few things more frustrating about traveling than to drive for hours, only to arrive at a place and find there's nothing left for you. Some places take campers on a first-come, first-served basis. Others, like some county parks, take reservations only in person to aid local residents in getting campsites. A good tip is to travel with a campground directory (like *Florida Camping* by Marilyn Moore) and also a directory or two from nationwide chain hotels you like, just in case something happens (your reservation is lost, the campground closes unexpectedly because of extreme weather, you decide you don't like your campground, etc.).

Florida state parks have consistently well-maintained campgrounds. Most state park campgrounds have a central restroom area with showers. Individual campsites usually have a picnic table and fire grill; some have water and electricity, and others do not. State park campgrounds are detailed on the ReserveAmerica Web site. ReserveAmerica is a company in charge of taking reservations for Florida state park campgrounds and most state park cabins. (It also takes reservations for many other campgrounds in the United States.) You can make a reservation online or by phone; see the Resources section of this book for contact information (appendix 1).

ReserveAmerica usually doesn't take reservations for primitive campsites. So if you really like to rough it—pack in and out everything you need, forgo facilities, and sometimes hike a few miles to get to the campsite—contact the natural area itself. Primitive campsites vary in their "primitiveness," with some offering portable toilets close to a road, and others providing little more than a cleared space on the ground for a tent. Find out all you can about the primitive site when you call to make your reservation.

Check out books on camping in Florida listed in the Resources section of this book (appendix 1).

Wildlife Watching

Wildlife enjoy Florida's climate and variety of habitats, from the temperate to the subtropical. Wildlife watching, especially bird-watching, is such a big part of nature travel that the topic has its own tips section at the end of the book (appendix 2).

Pets

Many Florida natural areas allow pets as long as they are controlled and on a leash. Some places require proof of rabies vaccination. Other areas forbid pets. Before you arrive with your pet, call ahead to the place you want to visit to check on the pet policy.

Getting Around

Many people arrive in Florida by plane at a number of airports around the state. Most airports are magnets for rental car companies, so once you arrive, you should be able to find transportation from the airport to your destination.

Urban areas provide public transportation, but these lines may not reach natural areas. On the other hand, ferries are required or provide the best way to reach certain remote islands. Check with the county of the place you are visiting to find out bus routes and the like.

The major interstates will take you to most areas in Florida, but several spots in this book are in locations far from these well-traveled roads. I-95 runs north and south in the eastern part of Florida, ending in Miami; I-75 runs north and south through central, then western, then southern portions, turning east and also ending in Miami; I-10 crosses Florida east and west, ending in Jacksonville; I-4 cuts across the state diagonally from Tampa to Daytona Beach. In addition, there are several toll roads, most notably the Florida Turnpike (which begins at I-75 south of Ocala and ends north of the Keys) and the east/ west portion of I-75 known as Alligator Alley, which spans the Everglades area between Naples and Fort Lauderdale.

The Florida Department of Transportation (FDOT) can provide maps, locations of rest areas, toll amounts, and other useful information. FDOT also has placed signs near most natural areas to show the way to places that are off the main road or to indicate areas that are Great Florida Birding Trail sites. In both cases, these signs are brown. If you are traveling and looking for a natural area, watch for the brown signs along the road to show the way.

How to Use This Book

This is not a book that will tell you how to see the state in ten days or make use of organized commercial tours. If you want to ride in a bus full of people to a natural area where everything is arranged for you, this book is not for you.

However, if you want to get to know a specific spot in Florida and allow nature to reveal itself to you on your own schedule, this book aims to provide details that will help.

Arranged in thirty general geographic locations around the state, this book tells you about the land and habitats, what to do and see, the history, the wildlife, notable nearby attractions, and suggestions on places to stay. Each chapter takes a holistic approach to its region so you can begin planning your trip— even if you don't want to go everywhere, do everything, and see it all. Because of this arrangement into geographical clusters, not every notable natural area could be included. If, when you are traveling, you find a natural area you particularly like, ask a ranger or volunteer about other similar places to visit nearby. Most will be happy to tell you about their favorite places—many of which are likely to be in this book.

You can "shop" for a weekend getaway or a weeklong vacation by looking at the highlights for each chapter or choosing a portion of the state you want to visit. If you are interested in wildlife or particular outdoor activities, you might want to search for areas based on these interests. (Suggestions for activity-based locations are in appendix 3.)

Be sure to check the Resources section of the book for contact information of agencies, companies, and organizations that are mentioned frequently throughout the book, like the Florida Fish and Wildlife Conservation Commission, ReserveAmerica, and the Florida Trail Association (appendix 1).

Whether you're a resident wanting to get better acquainted with your state or a first-time visitor looking for the best introduction to Florida, hopefully you will find useful information here.

2

The Panhandle's Pitcher Plant Prairies

About as far west and north as you can go in Florida, there's a more Southern than distinctly Floridian atmosphere that predominates, as experienced by residents' accents and hospitable gestures. Here, you're less than an hour's drive from Alabama, after all, and Georgia is close by. Southern Mississippi isn't too far away, and you're about the same distance from New Orleans as you are from Orlando. As in much of the South, here you'll find farms, pine forests, and swamp-fed creeks that surround mostly small towns.

But it's still Florida, and the area presents its own unique character. One aspect that sets it apart: carnivorous plants. There are more species of carnivorous plants in Florida than in any other state, according to the Florida Fish and Wildlife Conservation Commission, and most of them are in the northwestern part of the state. There are six species of pitcher plants alone right here. Growing in wet to moist soil, carnivorous plants have captured our imagination as strange meat-eating creatures (theater fans may be thinking of Audrey II demanding, "Feed me!" in *Little Shop of Horrors*), but from late March to June, pitcher plants and others like it produce colorful blooms that rival other wildflowers.

Blooming pitcher plants may be one reason to visit the area, but not the only one. Large expanses of preserved land and numerous rivers and creeks give nature travelers a lot to explore.

Blackwater River State Forest is the largest in the state forest system with almost 190,000 acres. It connects with Conecuh National Forest to the north in Alabama and Eglin Air Force Base lands to the south. Nearby is Apalachicola National Forest, to the east. These connections create a large wildlife corridor that's important habitat for several species, including the threatened Florida black bear and red-cockaded woodpecker.

Blackwater River State Park (similar in name to the forest but run by a different state government department) seems to be one of those places that locals like to boast about. The main attraction is Blackwater River, for which both the park and forest are named. The river attracts paddlers and tubers to

Figure 1. Light rain falls on a bend of Blackwater River.

its clear water and swift current. It's also one of the best places to camp in the area.

Visiting both of these natural lands is a great way to get acquainted with Florida's great northwest.

What to Do There

The forest, state park, and connecting lands create a vast natural wooded area veined with rivers and creeks—a wonderful place to explore for the person who really likes to get out into the backcountry or someone who wants to get away from urban life. The closest large city is Pensacola, although there are a couple of towns around, so visitors should be prepared for the mostly rural lifestyle here and prepare their supplies and overnight stays accordingly.

Trail Tripping

The forest's expanse is crisscrossed mainly with dirt back roads, but there are still miles of trails to explore.

The longest is Jackson Red Ground Trail at 21 miles, which begins at the Karick Lake North recreation area and cuts southwest through the forest to Juniper Creek at Red Rock Road. Two hiking shelters are located along the trail.

Two other forest trails connect with Jackson Red Ground Trail. The Wiregrass Trail (6 miles) trailhead is located at the Hurricane Lake North recreation area, going east around the lake and crossing Blackwater River. You can pick up a guide to the native plants of Wiregrass Trail at the forest headquarters in the town of Munson south of State Road 4. Bear Lake Loop Trail (4 miles) begins at the Krul recreation area but can also be accessed at the Bear Lake recreation area, completely encircling the lake before heading east to Jackson Trail.

The Florida National Scenic Trail traverses the forest. Contact the Florida Trail Association (see appendix 1) for maps and information.

A series of equestrian trails in the western portion of the forest wander between the Coldwater recreation area and Red Rock Bridge on Juniper Creek. One of the trails crosses Pittman Creek.

Visitors can pick up a forest map showing roads, trails, and recreation areas at the forest headquarters, or request one in advance via postal mail.

Blackwater River State Park has two short nature trails. One meanders from the campground near the river in a loop. The other is also a loop, located south of the campground near a separate parking area on the riverbank.

Paddling and Boating

Blackwater River is famously known as one of the purest sand-bottom rivers in the world. Its tributaries also run clean and clear. Despite their clarity, these waters are infused with tannins from leaves, like tea, so they have a dark brown or black color. This normally doesn't prevent paddlers from seeing the sandy bottom with its serpentine patterns, however, because the rivers and creeks are shallow. The natural beauty of Blackwater River and its tributaries earned the area the title of Canoe Capital of Florida. With a designation like that, paddlers know they are in for an experience.

Blackwater River begins in Conecuh National Forest in Alabama. For 31 miles, the river is a Florida state canoe trail, flowing through Blackwater River State Forest and Blackwater River State Park. The trail begins at the Kennedy

Bridge Road bridge east of Hurricane Lake in the forest and ends at the Deaton Road bridge in the state park. After that, the river flows past the town of Milton into Blackwater Bay, the upper reaches of Pensacola Bay.

Nearby Shoal River, Yellow River, Sweetwater Creek, Juniper Creek, and Coldwater Creek also are recognized as state canoe trails. For details about these trails, contact the Florida Greenways and Trails office (see appendix 1). Paddlers should contact local outfitters about river levels before beginning a trip.

The Shoal River trail begins at County Road 285 northwest of the town of Defuniak Springs and flows southwest for 27 miles to the trail's end at CR 85, just south of the town of Crestview. The river continues on to join Yellow River.

The Yellow River trail begins at SR 2 north of Crestview and flows southwest for 56 miles to SR 87 near Eglin Air Force Base. Beyond this, the river runs toward Blackwater Bay. This trail is within the large Yellow River Water Management Area, maintained by the Northwest Florida Water Management District, which apparently allows riverside camping anywhere you please. The river is also a state aquatic preserve considered critical habitat for fish, wildlife, and birds, particularly ospreys.

For 11 miles, the Sweetwater/Juniper Creeks trail takes paddlers closer to Blackwater River. It begins at SR 4 near the state forest headquarters and continues on to Indian Ford Road, outside the western boundary of the state park.

The Coldwater Creek trail begins at SR 4 west of state forest headquarters and continues south for 18 miles to Munson Road (CR 191). Shortly thereafter, the creek joins Blackwater River.

Guided Tours

In a place considered the Canoe Capital of Florida, where there are several state canoe trails, it's a good thing that you find several outfitters and tour guides on the water.

Action on Blackwater River (850-537-2997; *www.actiononblackwater.com*) northeast of Milton offers day trips and overnight trips starting at $15.00 per person, with a minimum of two people per canoe. Kayak trips are also available.

Adventures Unlimited (800-239-6864; *www.adventuresunlimited.com*) north of Milton leads day trips and overnight paddling trips on Coldwater River, Juniper Creek, and Blackwater River. Trips start at $20.00 per person, with a minimum of two people per canoe or kayak.

Blackwater Canoe Rental and Outpost (800-967-6789) south of Blackwater

River State Park provides day and overnight canoe trips and kayak day trips. Prices start at $13.00, with a two-person minimum.

Bob's Canoe Rental and Sales (800-892-4504) is located in Milton on Coldwater River. One- to three-day canoe trips or one-day kayak trips are available, starting at $15.00 per person, two people to a canoe.

All of the above companies also offer tubing down the rivers. Reservations are always recommended.

Aside from water-oriented tours, there's Nature Tours by Alan Knothe (850-862-3498). Based in Fort Walton Beach, the guide leads bird-watching tours throughout most of the panhandle area. Tours can be designed around specific species you want to see and start at $175.00 for a one-day tour. Contact the company for details.

Nearby Natural Areas

Tarkiln Bayou Preserve State Park (850-492-1595) west of Pensacola is a recent acquisition for the state park system. The state bought the land for the park in stages to preserve pitcher plant areas and other sensitive habitat. Because the park is so new, there aren't any facilities available. However, there is a trail to the bayou, which can be flooded after heavy rains. Admission is free, at least while the state park is in "starter kit" phase (which most new state parks go through). Just a few miles north of the entrance to Big Lagoon State Park, Tarkiln Bayou is 1.5 miles south of US 98 on SR 293.

Sticking out into Pensacola Bay on a peninsula west of Blackwater Bay, Garcon Point (850-539-5999) is a good side trip for visitors to the area. Covering more than 3,200 acres, the natural area is good for hiking, wildlife-watching, and viewing pitcher plants. Garcon Point literature even boasts that a botanist once called the land "the Serengeti of carnivorous plants," and all plants and wildlife are protected. Maintained by the Northwest Florida Water Management District primarily to filter stormwater runoff, it still is worthwhile to visit for its views of coastal marsh and variety of birds. There are a couple of entrances, which are connected by a 1.2-mile trail through the prairie and flatwoods. An additional 1.5-mile loop trail leads from the southern entrance. Admission is free. To get there, follow CR 191 south from Milton. The entrances are on the eastern side of the road, with the southern entrance right before the toll bridge across the bay to the Gulf Breeze area and beaches.

Clear Creek Nature Trail (850-623-7181 ext. 18) offers a nice 1.5-mile round-trip walk through sandhill territory and swamp along Clear Creek, a quaint brook lined with moss. Halfway down the trail past turkey oaks and magnolias, there's an observation deck to view the creek before going through the swampy portion on a boardwalk. The trail is known for its wildlife and bird viewing, but these activities could be affected by the sounds from nearby Whiting Field, a U.S. Naval air station; the land is owned by the U.S. Navy. Admission is free. To get there, take CR 87 north from Milton to 87A and turn right (east). Then turn left just before the checkpoint gate into a parking lot. The trailhead is toward the back of the parking lot.

More than twice as large as Blackwater River State Forest, Eglin Air Force Base (850-882-4164) near Niceville allows the public some recreational access. A $5.00 permit is necessary to access the base for hiking or camping. It's best to call ahead for maps and other important tips because of the security-heavy nature of this military base. The Florida Trail cuts through the base's natural lands; contact the Florida Trail Association for information and requirements about exploring this portion of the trail. Also note that regular training exercises take place here; during the war in Iraq in spring 2003, the MOAB ("Massive Ordnance Air Blast" or "Mother Of All Bombs") was tested here.

Blackwater Heritage Trail State Park (850-245-2052) in Milton is an 8.5-mile rail trail that used to be the Whiting Naval Railway. The paved trail is open to any kind of trail user—bicyclist, equestrian, skater, or walker. Admission is free. The trailhead is at US 90 and SR 87.

Nearby Attractions

Milton's downtown historical district preserves the town's quaint atmosphere. Once called "Scratch Ankle"—because of the brambles along the Blackwater River's banks—Milton claims to be one of the oldest cities in Florida, dating back to 1844 with a history in timber. Shops, restaurants, and a restored 1912 theater are part of the downtown scene.

To the south, beaches of famed white sand dunes lie along the Gulf of Mexico.

Wildlife

Exploring Blackwater River State Forest or Blackwater River State Park is sure to uncover some of the area's wildlife. The forest's longleaf pine tracts are great for finding white-tailed deer and red-cockaded woodpeckers. In the forested sandhills, look for wild turkeys and migrating warblers. Roadsides might reveal bobwhite quail and gopher tortoises. In the pitcher plant bogs, you might hear the Florida bog frog, which sounds sort of like the pig frog but is much smaller, about two inches. Roaming around the area are Florida black bears, considered a threatened species in Florida.

Look for . . .

One of the area's more unique residents is the fox squirrel. Fox squirrels seem to be more common in northwestern Florida than in other parts of the state, although gray squirrels still outnumber them.

Larger than the gray squirrels of most backyards—and colored like a fox with red, brown, or black with white—it's easy to mistake fox squirrels for foxes with their long, bushy tails. They also spend less time in trees than gray squirrels, so they might run away from you on the ground if you happen upon them, as a fox would. But their face is distinctly squirrel-like, so that's one way to identify them. The oaks and hickories of the area give fox squirrels food and shelter.

Habitats

The area's distinction as a carnivorous plant haven and a longleaf pine forest means the soil here is generally poor in nutrients. Longleaf pines have the ability to grow well in sandy soil that doesn't offer much in the way of minerals, yet they can grow to 150 feet by some accounts. Carnivorous plants get nutrients from insects that they can't get from the earth; these include plants like sundews, butterworts, bladderworts, and pitcher plants.

Pitcher plants grow in wet areas like bogs, wet prairies, wet pine flatwoods, and ditches. When an insect is attracted to the flower, it can end up sliding down the plant's "tube," unable to get out because of fine hairlike extensions that point down and prevent the insect from escaping. The insect eventually drowns and decomposes, enriching the plant's soil. Other carnivorous plants capture insects with a sticky substance or by using a sort of trap door.

The state of Florida considers five species of pitcher plants to be threatened or endangered (white-top pitcher plant, decumbent pitcher plant, hooded pitcher plant, parrot pitcher plant, and red-flowered pitcher plant), so they are protected. Sometimes even the law cannot prevent loss, however.

Fire suppression, draining, and habitat destruction affect pitcher plants and other species that depend on pine flatwoods. Despite the region's natural areas preserving the largest system of longleaf pine trees in the world (according to the state forestry department), it's a fraction of what once stood. The U.S. Fish and Wildlife Service claims the longleaf pine ecosystem blanketing the southeastern United States is only 3 percent of what it used to be, which has affected some thirty plant and animal species that live in this ecosystem. Besides carnivorous plants, red-cockaded woodpeckers, Florida black bears, Florida pine snakes, flatwoods salamanders, and gopher frogs are protected species that depend on longleaf pine forests. Fortunately, state and federal agencies are restoring this habitat, working with private landowners and in places like Eglin Air Force Base.

Where to Stay

Campgrounds

Blackwater River State Park's campground has thirty campsites, all with water and electricity. A dump station is available for RVs. The campground is located in the main area of the state park, north of the parking areas for the trailheads. Contact ReserveAmerica for a reservation or information (see appendix 1).

In the state forest, several recreation areas offer camping: North Karick Lake, South Karick Lake, North Hurricane Lake, Bear Lake, and Krul. All campsites offer electricity; the Karick Lake sites also offer water. South Hurricane Lake offers primitive campsites for $5.00 per night.

At Adventures Unlimited (mentioned above), you'll find primitive campsites, RV sites, and group camping. Action on Blackwater River (also above) offers tent and RV sites.

Lodging

The northern portion of Escambia, Santa Rosa, and Okaloosa Counties have fewer lodging options than in the south near the beaches of Destin and Fort Walton Beach. Most lodging is located along I-10, like chain hotels (Milton's Holiday Inn Express: 850-626-9060; Crestview's Jameson Inn: 850-683-1778). Adventures Unlimited (mentioned above) offers various rental cottages and an inn; there is a minimum of a two-night stay, and sometimes three nights.

How to Get There

Blackwater River State Forest spans Santa Rosa and Okaloosa Counties just south of the Alabama state line. The headquarters is located just south of SR 4 on CR 191. Take I-10 Exit #26 (CR 191) and go north through the town of Milton. Continue north on this road about 20 miles to the forest office.

To get to Blackwater River State Park, take 1-10 Exit #31 (SR 87) north for a half-mile. Turn right (east) on US 90. At Deaton Bridge Road, turn left across the railroad tracks and follow the road to the park. The first parking areas are day-use fee station areas, but the main entrance is farther down the road.

      ✐   ✐   ✐

Blackwater River State Forest
11650 Munson Highway
Milton, Florida 32570
Phone: 850-957-6140
Entrance to the forest is free, but some recreation areas charge fees. The forest headquarters office is open 7 a.m. until 4 p.m., Monday through Friday.

Blackwater River State Park
7720 Deaton Bridge Road
Holt, Florida 32564
Phone: 850-983-5363
Entrance fee is $3.00 per vehicle for up to eight people, or $1.00 for pedestrians and bicyclists. Hours are 8 a.m. until dusk every day.

There are miles of pine forests in this relatively undeveloped area, where there are more types of carnivorous plants than in any other state. Several pure rivers run throughout the region and have earned it the title of "Canoe Capital of Florida." The region's mass of preserved lands enables nature travelers to plan a deep-woods wilderness experience.

Nearby

Emerald Coast (chapter 3)

3

Emerald Coast

Along the Florida panhandle, a stretch of shoreline is rutted with inlets, a region of water, all rivers and bays and ocean, dominated by the Gulf of Mexico. Creeks flow into bayous that flow into one another and finally open up to the great gulf.

Here, the coast is thinly sheltered by strips of barrier islands, capricious protectors that can shift and change shape with the wind. The coastline is a delicate place. Dunes typically rise above the shore several feet in some places, tethered by sea oats, Florida rosemary, and sometimes wax myrtle and stunted sand pines. Nearly white as snow—the dunes seem more like snow drifts during the cool winter months—the sand is pale quartz carried from the Appalachian Mountains by glaciers when they receded long ago.

This crystal sand is the perfect reflector for the gulf's water, whose varying green hue lends the region the name Emerald Coast. Depending on sunshine and underwater plant life for its palette, the water doesn't always appear green. But the beaches and dunes are always beautiful. Unfortunately, Hurricane Ivan washed away dunes here in September 2004, but given time they likely will rebuild.

Exactly which parts of the shoreline the Emerald Coast encompasses seems to be debated even among the region's promoters. Within the area, cities and towns stand distinctly different from each other; Panama City Beach has a completely different feel from Pensacola, and Destin is distinct from Seaside. But for more than 100 miles all of these communities share in common the Gulf of Mexico, with bright beaches and a series of bridges that cross lagoons to join islands with the mainland. To get acquainted with Emerald Coast nature, visit key natural lands in a sweep across the region: Gulf Islands National Seashore, Topsail Hill Preserve State Park, Grayton Beach State Park, and St. Andrews State Park.

Gulf Islands National Seashore preserves coastal wetlands and uplands in western Florida, skips Alabama and starts up again in Mississippi for a 160-mile span. The Florida portions of the seashore are scattered from Perdido

Figure 2. Walking on dune crossovers helps to protect the fragile dune environment along the Emerald Coast.

("Lost") Key to Fort Walton Beach. Visitors can simply take in miles of beach, or explore maritime forest trails and tour historic forts.

The 2,228-acre Grayton Beach State Park preserves a marshy lake and pine flatwoods right on the beach next to dunes. Trails connect the park to a state forest—an important connection in an area that has seen increased development. Visitors can camp on the lakeshore or stay in a cottage in a separate portion of the park.

Not too far away, 1,640-acre Topsail Hill Preserve State Park is named for the tallest dune on the beach, which looks like a boat's topsail. Visitors get the preserved sand pine scrub and coastal lake environments along with a top-rated campground.

At the far eastern end of the Emerald Coast, St. Andrews State Park conserves 1,260 acres on the tip of a barrier island with its marsh, pine flatwoods, and sand pine scrub. The park focuses on recreation, especially in the water. Visitors snorkel and fish along the jetty, and paddle or take a day shuttle to nearby Shell Island, an undeveloped barrier island, to look for shells. A campground on a lagoon invites nature travelers to stay the night.

Throughout the Emerald Coast, shorebirds, wading birds, and migratory songbirds enjoy the mild climate along with bald eagles, ospreys, owls, and animals that are suited to the sandy, salty habitats. For a Florida nature traveler who enjoys the ocean, this is a top destination.

What to Do There

Trail Tripping

The Florida National Scenic Trail begins (or ends) at Gulf Islands National Seashore's Fort Pickens area—the only part of the trail on the ocean. This part of the trail is about 8 miles long, and any seashore visitor may hike it. This trail is noted as a bicycle trail on the seashore map/brochure. Get a map of the trail from the visitor center or the Florida Trail Association.

Fort Pickens also has trails of its own. About a mile down the park road from the ranger station are Blackbird Marsh Nature Trail and Dune Nature Trail. The half-mile Blackbird Marsh trail is a loop through a maritime forest, located behind campground loops A and E. On the ocean side of the island, the dune trail is a short boardwalk through the dunes to the beach.

Behind Naval Live Oaks Visitor Center, trails start from an observation deck overlooking Santa Rosa Sound. The short Brackenridge Nature Trail shows off the live oaks that are the visitor center's namesake (and that provided the U.S. military with wood to make ships) and some of the largest magnolia trees anywhere. The trail is so close to US 98, however, that the road noise can be distracting. More trails are located on the other side of the street, north of US 98, where visitors can hike farther from the road. Take 1-mile Beaver Pond Trail to Brown's Pond, where you might actually see a beaver. Walk 2.2-mile Andrew Jackson Trail, which used to be the road from Pensacola to St. Augustine before Florida became a state. Or follow other interconnecting trails, using a free map from the visitor center.

At Fort Barrancas Visitor Center, Fort Barrancas Woodland Trail is a short loop near Pensacola Bay. Down at Perdido Key, the short Perdido Key Discovery Trail leads from the boat launch to salt marsh views and into maritime forest.

Topsail Hill Preserve State Park has two nice trails from the Topsail Road entrance, which is west of the main entrance. One is a short trail to Campbell Lake, and the other—Morris Lake Nature Trail—takes hikers 2.5 miles along the lake to dunes. The Topsail Road entrance provides better beach access than the main entrance does and seems more intimate. If you choose to enter the park at the main entrance, however, a 1-mile paved trail leads from the parking lot to the beach. A tram takes visitors to and from the beach along this trail (no other vehicles are allowed), but it runs only every two hours, starting at 9 a.m. Bicyclists and walkers are welcome on this trail.

Grayton Beach Nature Trail at Grayton Beach State Park provides interpretive signs along the way; pick up a trail guide if you like, to follow along and learn about the barrier island ecosystem. The trail begins at the end of the main park road in the parking lot and winds through dunes, along Western Lake and into pine flatwoods. The trail can be flooded after heavy rain.

Across the street from the park entrance, more trails connect Grayton Beach to Point Washington State Forest. The trails wander through an old pine turpentining area—once an important industry in the region. Bicyclists are also welcome on these trails. Ask for a trail map at the ranger station, or request one from the Florida Division of Forestry.

In St. Andrews State Park, Gator Lake Trail creates quite a sight—and smell—in February and March when several great blue herons nest on trees in the lake. From the lake overlook, the trail takes hikers up a cozy sand-pine-covered dune and around the side of the lake. Heron Pond Trail near the lagoon side of the island leads from a reconstructed turpentine still in a short loop.

Paddling and Boating

From Pensacola Bay to St. Andrew Bay, there is a lot of water to explore, whether sea kayaking around barrier islands or boating in the protected lagoons. Rent a canoe at Grayton Beach State Park and explore Western Lake, a rare coastal dune lake. At St. Andrews State Park, the park concession rents kayaks, which you can launch from the boat ramp on Grand Lagoon.

On nearby Shell Island, Shell Island Boat Rentals and Tours (800-227-0132; *www.shellislandshuttle.com*) rents kayaks from $35.00 a day. Paddlers are ferried to Shell Island, then provided with kayaks there. The service also rents snorkeling equipment and various kinds of motorboats.

If you don't have your own way of getting around on the water in other parts of the Emerald Coast, there are some outfitters and marinas in the area.

Key Sailing (877-932-7272; *www.keysailing.com*) in Pensacola Beach rents kayaks for paddling in Santa Rosa Sound. Here, you can also rent sailboats and powerboats, and arrange for a parasailing adventure or dolphin-watching boat tour.

The Kayak Experience (850-837-1577; *www.kayakexperience.com*) in Destin rents kayaks from $30.00. Paddle out of sheltered Destin Harbor into

Choctawhatchee Bay, looking for ospreys and pods of Atlantic bottle-nosed dolphins. Guided tours are offered by request.

Eco-Beach Store (850-936-7263; *www.eco-beach.com*) in Navarre Beach rents canoes as well as surf boards, snorkeling gear, bicycles, and other items beachgoers might want. Boat tours and sailing charters are available on request.

Snorkeling and Diving

The Emerald Coast area, Panama City in particular, is popular with divers and snorkelers. A coral reef lies close to shore near the Bay County Pier at M. B. Miller Park, about 5 miles northwest of St. Andrews State Park. Several artificial reefs, too, are offshore. Shipwrecks like *Grey Ghost*, SS *Tarpon*, and *Empire Mica* have helped Panama City become known as the Wreck Capital of the South. For a listing of all the reefs and wrecks and their locations, contact Bay County at 850-784-4024 or visit *www.co.bay.fl.us/community/reefs.html*.

Snorkelers at St. Andrews State Park should try the jetty on the eastern end of the island. Shell Island, across the inlet from the park, is another popular place to snorkel. The park concession rents snorkeling equipment, along with other beach items like lounge chairs, air mattresses, and shell nets.

For snorkel and dive charters or equipment, try Panama City Dive Center (850-235-3390; *www.pcdivecenter.com*) or Dive Locker (850-230-8006; *www.knology.net/~divelocker*) not far from the park, or Hydrospace Dive Shop (888-874-3483; *www.hydrospace.com*) on US 98.

Scenic Driving

With the Gulf of Mexico, forested areas, and so many bays around, merely getting from point A to point B can be a pretty drive in the Emerald Coast. There is a bridge over some kind of body of water almost everywhere you go. There are also designated scenic routes here for those who like to drive for reasons other than just getting around.

Pensacola Bluffs Scenic Highway, a designated state scenic highway, winds for 11 miles along Escambia Bay. Drive past wetlands and areas marked by Florida's Native American and Spanish history. For a map and more information, contact the Florida Department of Transportation.

Scenic Highway 30A follows the shore and provides a good view of the beach for most of the way. Just south of US 98, 30A connects to it directly about 10 miles east of Destin and again about 10 miles west of Panama City

Beach, with other access points in between. For a map and more information, see *www.30-a.com/discover/discover.asp.*

Guided Tours

The St. Andrews State Park concession offers a shuttle across the inlet to Shell Island in spring and summer. Tours run every hour or every half hour, depending on the schedule; contact the concession at 850-233-0197. The ten-minute trip is $9.50 for adults and $5.50 for children.

Blue Dolphin Kayak EcoTours (850-939-7734) in Navarre takes paddlers to see birds and other wildlife. Full moon and sunset paddling tours are popular and start at $25.00. Custom tours are available.

Gulf Islands National Seashore rangers sometimes provide tours and talks. Contact the seashore for a schedule of these events before you arrive if you'd like to take part.

Tours are available through kayak and boat rental companies listed above under "Paddling and Boating."

Nearby Natural Areas

Perdido Key State Park (850-492-1595) near the Alabama state line is the westernmost park in the state park system. It also has the distinction of being one of the few places where the endangered Perdido Key beach mouse lives. Visitors come pretty much for the beach, which is more of the beautiful white sand dunes across the panhandle. From downtown Pensacola, take County Road 292/Gulf Beach Highway southwest to the barrier island of Perdido Key and watch for park signs. Admission is $2.00 per vehicle.

Big Lagoon State Park (850-492-1595) in Pensacola is a good all-around park for just about anything you'd want to do. With beaches, a boat ramp on Big Lagoon, nature trails, and a campground, the park is a nice stop on the far end of the Emerald Coast. An observation tower on the beach provides a great view of the park and Perdido Key across the lagoon. To get there, take US 98 to CR 293 and head south. The road ends at the park entrance. The entrance fee is $4.00 per vehicle.

Near Choctawhatchee Bay, Fred Gannon Rocky Bayou State Park (850-833-9144) in Niceville is named for an Air Force colonel who was responsible for turning the area into a park after its previous use as a World War II bombing practice range. (Eglin Air Force Base is nearby.) Visitors come to launch fishing boats at the ramp on Rocky Bayou, a delicate seagrass area that leads directly into Choctawhatchee Bay. Nature travelers will also enjoy the park's three nature trails—Red Cedar Trail, Sand Pine Trail, and Rocky Bayou Trail—to explore 4 miles of the different bay environments. Look for migratory waterfowl in the winter, and dolphins, ospreys, and river otters all year round. To get there, take I-10 Exit #56 (State Road 85) south to SR 20 and go east. Rocky Bayou State Park is about 5 miles down on the left. Admission is $3.00 per vehicle.

Point Washington State Forest (850-747-5639) between Panama City Beach and Destin preserves more than ten natural communities in 15,000 acres. Gopher tortoises and flatwoods salamanders are at home here, along with white-topped pitcher plants, according to the Florida Division of Forestry. The best way to explore the forest is by hiking or biking the Eastern Lake Trail System that connects with Grayton Beach, Topsail Hill Preserve and Deer Lake State Parks. Take the 3.5-, 5-, or 10-mile loop through sand pine scrub and sandhills. Access the trails at the trailhead parking lot on CR 395 north of Grayton Beach State Park. Trails are for day use only.

Pine Log State Forest (850-535-2888) in Ebro was Florida's first state forest, purchased in 1936. With almost 7,000 acres and more than 14 miles of trails—including 8 miles of the Florida National Scenic Trail—there's a lot to explore here. Hike, bike, or ride your horse through pine flatwoods and sandhills and past cypress swamps; contact the forest or the Florida Trail Association for maps and information, including hunting seasons. Look for Florida black bears and migratory songbirds on your visit. To get there, take SR 79 north from Panama City Beach or south from I-10 (Exit #112) to just south of SR 20 and look for entrances on SR 79.

Deer Lake State Park (850-231-0337) in Santa Rosa Beach is new to the state park system, so there's not much there yet besides the beach. Its long boardwalk through the dunes leads from the parking lot to the Gulf of Mexico. To get there, take 30A west from Panama City to Santa Rosa Beach and watch for the park sign. Admission is free.

Nearby Attractions

The National Museum of Naval Aviation (800-327-5002; www.naval-air.org) in Pensacola is one of the best museums to visit in the area, with more than 170 aircraft on exhibit. Military history buffs, aviation hobbyists, and cloud-minded children will all enjoy viewing the planes and other displays. Visitors can ride a flight simulator and walk through a World War II aircraft carrier replica. To get there, take I-10 Exit #7A (CR 297) south to Blue Angel Parkway.

Continue on to the Naval Air Station. Admission is free, but museum IMAX movies and the simulator ride charge fees. The museum is open from 9 a.m. until 5 p.m., closed on New Year's Day, Thanksgiving Day, and Christmas Day.

Historic Pensacola Village (850-595-5985 ext. 100; *www.historicpensacola. org*) preserves a collection of museums and buildings in the city's historic district, which is on the National Register of Historic Places. Tour the Museum of Commerce, the Museum of Industry, and original estates. Look for re-enactors dressed in period clothing. Admission is $6.00 for adults, $2.50 for children four to sixteen, and $5.00 for senior citizens and active military personnel. The village is located one block north of US 98 on Zaragoza Street. From I-10, take Exit #4 to I-110, heading south. Exit at 1C (Garden Street), then turn left at Tarragona Street. Head toward the village on Zaragoza Street.

Unlike some butterfly attractions, Panhandle Butterfly House (850-939-0085; *www.thebutterflyhouse.com*) in Navarre focuses on native butterflies and native plants, taken care of by volunteers. Located on Santa Rosa Sound, Panhandle Butterfly House is open every day from 11:00 a.m. until 4:00 p.m. from late April until early September. Admission is free, but donations are welcome. The butterfly house is located on US 98 just west of the Navarre Beach Causeway bridge and just east of the intersection with SR 87.

Eden Gardens State Park (850-231-4214) in Point Washington showcases the ornamental gardens and home of a late timber company owner. Roses, camellias, and azaleas bloom at certain times of the year, peaking in March or April. A trail leads past Tucker Bayou back through the gardens. Visitors can take a guided tour through antique-filled Wesley House Thursday through Monday every hour from 10 a.m. until 3 p.m. Admission is $3.00 per vehicle; tours are $3.00 for adults and $1.00 for children. To get there, take US 98 to the Point Washington area (between Destin and Panama City Beach) and go north on CR 395, watching for the park sign.

Gulf World Marine Park (850-234-5271; *www.gulfworldmarinepark.com*) in Panama City Beach features alligators, dolphins, sharks, sea turtles, and other marine animals, along with shows and programs that aquariums are usually known for. To get there, take US 98 west from Panama City to Alt 98 (Front Beach Road) and follow it about 5 miles along the beach to the marine park. Admission is $19.51 for adults and $13.47 for children five to eleven. The park opens at 9 a.m. and closes at different times depending on the seasons.

Panama City Beach is the current college spring break hotspot in Florida. Students (and other visitors) flock here for the beaches but also try out the roadside mini golf, bumper boat, and arcade attractions up and down US 98.

Wildlife

The Emerald Coast's dune-rich white beaches attract many kinds of wildlife. Several kinds of shorebirds and wading birds live along the coast year-round. More birds arrive for the winter or for a quick stop on their way to and from South America during spring and fall. Gulf Islands National Seashore boasts 280 species of birds that live in or visit the park at some time during the year. Beaches also attract nesting sea turtles like loggerheads, greens, and leatherbacks, which usually lay their eggs around May or June. Atlantic bottle-nosed dolphins may fish for mullet or play in the waves just yards from shore. Dolphins also frequent the interior bays.

In the region's uplands, look for gopher tortoises, migratory songbirds, and snakes—including venomous snakes like the diamondback rattlesnake, pygmy rattlesnake, coral snake, and cottonmouth. White-tailed deer roam the pinelands, and you might see them from the park roads at St. Andrews State Park.

Look for . . .

Unique to the area are several species of beach mice that live in the sandy dunes. Some of these species are federally endangered and threatened with extinction as a result of beachfront development, storms, and other causes of dune degradation (a great reason to follow signs that tell beachgoers not to walk all over the dunes but to use the boardwalks instead). House cats also have affected beach mouse populations by hunting.

The Choctawhatchee beach mouse found at Grayton Beach and Topsail Hill Preserve State Parks and at Shell Island; Santa Rosa beach mouse at Fort Pickens, Opal Beach, and Eglin Air Force Base; and Perdido Key beach mouse at Johnson Beach are all endangered species that depend on sea oats and other dune plants for food. By day, they live in burrows—which crabs and snakes might sneak into—and by night, they look for food and mates. Their nocturnal lifestyle and shy nature make it hard to spot a beach mouse.

Although there are threats to their environment, beach mice have a good reproduction rate. Once mature, one female beach mouse can produce from nine to twenty-four offspring each year, according to studies performed by Auburn University in neighboring Alabama (which is also home to distinct beach mice species).

The Perdido Key beach mouse made news in early 2004 when the U.S. Fish and Wildlife Service notified nearby developments they might have to set aside land for the mouse. After the mouse population was hit hard by 1990s hurricanes, the population rebounded to about 800 individuals—when wildlife biologists claimed the mouse had run out of room at Gulf Islands National Seashore and Perdido Key State Park.

Habitats

Coastal barrier islands and coastal scrub may be what most people call to mind when they think of Florida. The Emerald Coast's white quartz beaches and towering dunes draw out-of-state and out-of-country visitors year-round, but especially in summer. Some of them may spend so much time near the beach that they won't notice the pine flatwoods, sand pine scrub, sandhills, marshes, and wet prairies that are also important elements of the region's ecosystem. Gulf Islands National Seashore, Topsail Hill Preserve State Park, Grayton Beach State Park, St. Andrews State Park, and other nearby natural lands preserve these habitats. This is important in a region that is seeing more development and planned communities, especially along the coast.

A concern of environmentalists and area residents is runaway growth as they've seen in other parts of Florida. While some residents welcome growth that they hope will bring more jobs, others want to maintain the small beach town feel for which portions of the Emerald Coast are known.

Some are wary in particular of the development plans of the St. Joe Company, the largest private landowner in the state. St. Joe Co. used to be primarily a timber corporation but has been converting its land holdings into towns like WaterColor. St. Joe Co. plans call for moving a portion of US 98 inland to accommodate a construction project and building an airport near Panama City, among other developments. In early 2004, the company got approval from the state Department of Environmental Protection to forego the usual permitting process for developments near wetlands, receiving blanket approval to fill in wetlands within certain guidelines of the agreement. According to the Associated Press news service, the state and proponents of the agreement said it was "a model for regional growth that will preserve, rather than destroy, wetlands." But critics fear St. Joe Co. will fill in 20 percent of the wetlands in the 38,500-acre area in Bay and Walton Counties under the agreement. Time will show whether the St. Joe Co. permitting agreement was successful. Passing years also will see how development will have affected the Emerald Coast and its natural environments.

Where to Stay

Campgrounds

Beach-loving campers should be pleased with the number of campgrounds close to the beach here.

The Big Lagoon State Park campground offers seventy-five campsites with water and electric hookups and a dump station. There is also a small playground. Contact ReserveAmerica for information and reservations.

At Gulf Islands National Seashore, the Fort Pickens Campground has 200 sites in five loops. All sites have water and electric hookups. A camp store and laundry are near the campground. There is also a group campground here for ten to forty people who are part of an organized group. The group campground has unheated showers and doesn't offer electricity, but grills and picnic tables are at the site. The seashore's Naval Live Oaks area also offers group camping for organized youth groups of ten to forty people. Amenities are the same as at Fort Pickens's group campground, with the addition of a fire circle. For information and reservations, contact the American Park Network (800-365-CAMP; *www.americanparknetwork.com*).

Fred Gannon Rocky Bayou State Park has forty-two shady sites on the bayou with water and electricity. A laundry facility is also on site. Get information and reservations from ReserveAmerica.

Pine Log State Forest has a twenty-site campground on a lake with restrooms, water, electricity, and a dump station. Pine Log also offers a youth group campground and three primitive campsites. Sites are filled on a first-come, first-served basis using a self-service pay station, so the forest doesn't take reservations.

Grayton Beach State Park offers a thirty-seven-site campground with electric and water hookups. The scrubby campground is situated on Western Lake. Even-numbered sites 12 through 22 are situated right on the lake. For information and reservations, contact ReserveAmerica.

The Topsail Hill Preserve State Park campground was once a private RV resort. There are 156 sites with water and electric hookups and sewer service. The campground boasts a laundry facility, heated swimming pool, and tennis courts. Make reservations through ReserveAmerica.

St. Andrews State Park's campground features 167 campsites with electric and water hookups. Tent campers may want to ask for sites 142 through 144 because they are clustered and placed somewhat away from RV sites. Information and reservations are available from ReserveAmerica. For information about the primitive youth campground, contact the park directly.

Lodging

The major cities of the Emerald Coast—Pensacola, Gulf Breeze, Fort Walton Beach, Destin, and Panama City—offer the most lodging options, from small motels to large chain hotels. Beach house rentals (try Emerald Coast Vacation Rentals: 888-232-3224; *www.ecvr.com*) are available in some areas, usually by the week.

Topsail Hill Preserve State Park offers cottages by the week ($575.00) or month ($1,100.00). Contact the park directly for information and reservations. Grayton Beach State Park also rents cottages, for $110.00 a night, at a separate park entrance about 1 mile west of the main entrance. Contact ReserveAmerica for reservations. Cottages in both parks are fully furnished.

Bed-and-breakfast inns are around, as in Seaside east of Grayton Beach (Josephine's Inn: 800-848-1840; *www.josephinesinn.com*) and in Fort Walton Beach west of Topsail Hill (Aunt Martha's Bed and Breakfast: 850-243-6702; *www.auntmarthasbedandbreakfast.com*).

How to Get There

The Florida portions of Gulf Islands National Seashore are spread out from almost the Alabama state line on Perdido Key to Fort Walton Beach, so it's a good idea to get an official map/brochure from the National Park Service to find all locations. You can pick one up for free at seashore visitor centers. From I-10, try the exit for I-110 (Exit #12), which takes you to downtown Pensacola, where you can access US 98—an important road for the Emerald Coast. Fort Pickens Visitor Center is in Pensacola Beach on CR 399. To get there, take US 98 to Gulf Breeze, then watch for the beach exit and take the toll bridge ($1.00) south across Santa Rosa Sound. Turn right at Fort Pickens Road and follow it to the ranger station. Naval Live Oaks Visitor Center is on US 98 in Gulf Breeze about 2 miles east of Pensacola Bay Bridge. Fort Barrancas Visitor Center is near Pensacola Naval Air Station. To get there, take CR 292/Gulf Beach Highway southwest from downtown to CR 295 and go south, following signs to the center.

Topsail Hill Preserve State Park is about 10 miles east of Destin in Santa Rosa Beach on 30A, the road that follows the beach along this stretch of shoreline. From I-10, take Exit #85 (US 331) and go south to US 98. Head west for about 5 miles to 30A, then turn left and look for the park entrance.

For Grayton Beach State Park, take US 98 to CR 283 and head south to 30A. The park entrance is 1 mile to the east, about halfway between Destin and

Panama City Beach. From I-10, take Exit #85 (US 331), go south to US 98 and follow directions from there.

St. Andrews State Park is on the eastern end of the Panama City Beach barrier island. From I-10, take Exit #120 (SR 77) or Exit #130 (US 231) south to Panama City. At US 98, turn west and head across the bay. Take Thomas Drive south from US 98 and turn left at the fork in the road, heading east and following signs to the end of the road where the entrance is.

ꙮ ꙮ ꙮ

Gulf Islands National Seashore
1801 Gulf Breeze Parkway
Gulf Breeze, Florida 32563-5000
Phone: 850-934-2600
Naval Live Oaks Visitor Center is open all year from 8:00 a.m. until 5:30 p.m. Fort Pickens Visitor Center is open from 8:30 a.m. until 4:00 p.m. from November through February, and from 9:30 a.m. until 5:00 p.m. the rest of the year.

Fort Barrancas Visitor Center is open from 8:30 a.m. until 3:45 p.m. from November through February, and from 9:30 a.m. until 4:45 p.m. the rest of the year.

Only Fort Pickens, Rosamond Johnson Beach on Perdido Key, and Opal Beach on Santa Rosa Island charge entrance fees. Admission is $8.00 per vehicle or $3.00 per individual pedestrian or bicyclist, both good for seven days.

Topsail Hill Preserve State Park
7525 W. Scenic Highway 30A
Santa Rosa Beach, Florida 32459
Phone: 877-232-2478
Entrance fee is $2.00 per vehicle.

Grayton Beach State Park
357 Main Park Road
Santa Rosa Beach, Florida 32459
Phone: 850-231-4210
Entrance fee is $4.00 per vehicle.

St. Andrews State Park
4607 State Park Lane
Panama City, Florida 32408
Phone: 850-233-5140
Entrance fee is $5.00 per vehicle.

The Emerald Coast is known for its white quartz sand beaches and delicate, rolling sand dunes. It's also a place where scenic bays, bayous, and lagoons are abundant throughout the region. From barrier islands to coastal dune lakes to pine forests, nature travelers have a variety of habitats to explore in an area seeing coastal development growth.

Nearby

Pitcher Plant Prairies (chapter 2), Forgotten Coast (chapter 4), Apalachicola River Lands (chapter 6)

4

Forgotten Coast

So called because it apparently once was overlooked in a feature on Florida travel, the Forgotten Coast does prove to live up to its name as a place to forget life's hustle and bustle. This string of small towns on the Gulf of Mexico in Gulf and Franklin Counties plays up its slower pace and its remoteness. (A local restaurant's menu lightheartedly reminds diners that the closest Wal-Mart is 60 miles away.) It also plays up its best feature, its location on the gulf with its beautiful white sand beaches. This is a place for the quiet beachcomber looking for solitude.

Beyond the shore are swamps and forests that separate the coastal towns of Apalachicola and Port St. Joe from farmland. Apalachicola is named for the river at whose mouth it sits. Looking out at Apalachicola Bay, it's interesting to think that water came from Georgia's Appalachian Mountains, flowing through Atlanta down the Chattahoochee River into Lake Seminole, where the Apalachicola River begins at the Florida state border. From the lake, the Apalachicola River winds through pinelands and sandhills to empty into Apalachicola Bay. Across the water is St. George Island, a long, quiet strip of sand dominated by beachfront homes. On the eastern end of the island is Dr. Julian G. Bruce St. George Island State Park, which preserves almost 2,000 acres and 9 miles of beach along with sand pine scrub and marshes. The park is a true representation of the Forgotten Coast.

The other main town here, Port St. Joe, faces St. Joseph Bay, protected by the St. Joseph Peninsula, which appears on maps like the curled-up toe of a jester's boot. At the point where the toe just begins to curl upward is Cape San Blas. Although the cape is just a small geographical feature (which is part of an Eglin Air Force Base holding), residents and business owners on the entire peninsula tend to call all of it Cape San Blas.

Like St. George Island State Park, another state park rests at the edge of the land. T. H. Stone Memorial St. Joseph Peninsula State Park covers more than 2,500 acres on the northern tip of the peninsula and spans 10 miles of beach

Figure 3. Tall dunes make the beach at St. Joseph Peninsula State Park one of the most beautiful in the state.

where dunes pile up along the gulf. Inland—just barely, because the peninsula is so narrow—coastal pine forests remain. Beyond is St. Joseph Bay.

Between these two areas just offshore is St. Vincent Island, an undeveloped barrier island preserved as a national wildlife refuge. The largest of the barrier islands in the Forgotten Coast with more than 12,000 acres, St. Vincent National Wildlife Refuge is home to several endangered species like bald eagles, wood storks, sea turtles, and red wolves. The natural dune, forest, scrub, and marsh habitats of the region are conserved here.

Altogether, the parks and refuge give nature travelers several opportunities to enjoy the best of the Forgotten Coast.

What to Do There

The main thing to do in the Forgotten Coast is to enjoy the Gulf of Mexico, Apalachicola Bay, or St. Joseph Bay, along with the beaches.

In 2002, St. Joseph Peninsula State Park was called the No. 1 beach in the United States by "Dr. Beach" Stephen Leatherman, a geologist and professor at Florida International University, who makes an annual top-ten list each Memorial Day weekend. The beaches of the park and the surrounding Cape San Blas area are clean and white, lined with high dunes in some places. The dunes were whipped in September 2004 by Hurricane Ivan, but they will likely pile up again in time.

The shallow, clear St. Joseph Bay is a good place to see starfish and sand dollars. From July to the beginning of September, scalloping season draws seafood lovers to the bay. The bay is also great for snorkeling and paddling.

Apalachicola Bay is well known as a top oystering location, providing a reported 90 percent of all Florida oysters and 10 percent of all American oysters. You might see small, handmade-looking oyster boats gathering in the bay.

Trail Tripping

The grand presence of the beach, gulf, and bays don't mean there aren't places to hike, though. There are three trails at St. Joseph Peninsula State Park: Wilderness Preserve Trail, Maritime Hammock Trail, and Bayview Trail. The park requires Wilderness Preserve Trail hikers to sign in before hiking this 7-mile trail that leads to the end of the tiny St. Joseph peninsula. Maritime Hammock Trail near the entrance and Bayview Nature Trail near Eagle Harbor pass through coastal hammocks along the bay.

At St. George Island State Park on St. George Island, a 2.5-mile trail leads from the campground to Gap Point on the island's northern sand pine scrub section. Look for nesting bald eagles, great horned owls, and other birds. Don't be fooled by the sign near the campground road that reads, "Registered campers only." That just means if you want to camp, you need to register first (and hopefully have a reservation). If you're not camping during your visit, but just hiking, go down the road to the campground and use the trailhead parking area near the campground's playground.

Remote St. Vincent Island has a grid of dirt roads where anyone may hike. (Off-road bicycling is an option, too, but be aware of the potentially soft sand in some areas.) Use the roads to get from the bay side of the island to the gulf side, or from the western tip near Indian Pass to the wet eastern end. Mosquito swarms can be thick on the trails during warm months, making beach walking the more tolerable option.

Paddling and Boating

Forgotten Coast visitors can't help but find themselves near the water, where canoes, kayaks, and boats of all kinds are accommodating.

At St. George Island State Park, rent a canoe or kayak (or bring your own boat with a shallow draft) and launch from two boat ramps on Apalachicola Bay. Head out to the bay's Goose Island or explore Rattlesnake Cove.

Paddlers and boaters are welcome at the Eagle Harbor marina in St. Joseph Peninsula State Park. The marina has room for fifteen to eighteen small boats. Only overnight guests may leave their boats here past sunset. The boat launch fee is $3.00. To rent a kayak or motorboat, contact The Entrance (850-227-7529; *www.escapetothecape.com*) just outside the entrance to the state park. The Entrance also rents bicycles, arranges charters, and sells beach items.

Some Cape San Blas–area inns and vacation rental houses offer use of watercraft; ask about availability when making a reservation.

St. Vincent Island is only about 500 yards from the mainland at the tip of Indian Peninsula, so paddling to and around the island is usually easy. (As a barrier island, however, St. Vincent's distance from the mainland could change over time or because of extreme weather.)

Guided Tours

Broke-a-Toes Outdoor Service (850-899-7433) in Port St. Joe offers tours of St. Vincent Island, Apalachicola River, and Little St. George Island. Fishing charters also can be arranged. Many Cape San Blas visitors go to Broke-a-Toes just for guided horseback rides on the cape beach, however.

Happy Ours Kayak and Canoe Outpost (866-229-1991; *www.happyours kayak.com*) leads guided paddling, snorkeling, fishing, and scalloping tours starting at $100.00 for a half-day tour. Kayak rentals start at $25.00 for a half day.

EcoVentures (850-653-2593; *www.apalachicolatours.com*) in Apalachicola leads two-hour boat tours of the Apalachicola River estuary starting at $20.00 for adults and $10.00 for children.

Journeys of St. George Island (850-927-3259; *www.sgislandjourneys.com*) leads paddling trips to Little St. George Island, St. Vincent Island, Apalachicola River, and area creeks starting at $60.00 for adults and $40.00 for children. Other boat tours for bird-watching, oystering, shelling, and fishing are available. Journeys also rents kayaks, canoes, and snorkeling and fishing equipment.

St. Vincent National Wildlife Refuge staff lead tours during National Wildlife Refuge Week, usually every October. Contact the refuge in September for upcoming events.

To get to the island refuge, you can take the ferry service operated by St. Vincent Island Shuttle (850-229-1065; *www.stvincentisland.com*), which operates a pontoon boat from a ramp right on Indian Pass. The shuttle service also arranges private tours and fishing charter trips.

Nearby Natural Areas

North of St. Joe on State Road 71 in the town of Wewahitchka is Dead Lakes (850-639-2702), a recreational area on the Chipola River. The lakes formed when sandbars blocked the river flow, flooding the surrounding forest and killing its trees. Dead Lakes is popular with local anglers. ("Wewa" is also known for its pure, ungranulating tupelo honey, which you can buy just about anywhere here. The movie *Ulee's Gold*, about a Wewa beekeeper played by Peter Fonda, was filmed here.)

The 2,145-acre St. Joseph Bay State Buffer Preserve (850-670-4783) protects the bay area watershed and provides a home for several protected species, such as gopher tortoises, sea turtles, and red-cockaded woodpeckers. Visitors can hike through the uplands. The preserve is one site of the Florida Panhandle Birding and Wildflower Festival held every fall, usually in October. The preserve is about 5 miles south of US 98 between routes 30 and 30A.

The boundaries of Apalachicola National Forest and Tate's Hell State Forest are just north of the town of Apalachicola, along SR 65. See chapter 5, Apalachicola National Forest.

Nearby Attractions

John Gorrie Museum State Park (850-653-9347) in Apalachicola commemorates the invention of the first ice machine, which led to modern air conditioning. John Gorrie was an Apalachicola physician in the 1800s who developed the ice machine as a way to help his patients through a yellow fever epidemic. A replica of his ice machine is on display in the museum. Town history is also part of the museum. The visitor center is open from 9 a.m. until 5 p.m. Thursday through Monday. Admission is $1.00 for each visitor over six years old. To get there, take US 98 to Apalachicola and turn east on 6th Street, watching for the sign.

Before Tallahassee was the capital of Florida, when Florida was just a territory of the United States, statehood supporters completed a draft of the state constitution in Port St. Joe in 1839. Although Florida wasn't admitted to the Union until 1845—by which time Port St. Joe had been destroyed by yellow fever and a hurricane—residents remembered the meeting. Constitution Convention Museum State Park (850-229-8029) in Port St. Joe marks the site and preserves the memory of Florida's early history. Hours are 9 a.m. to noon and 1 p.m. to 5 p.m. Thursday through Monday. Admission is $1.00 per person. The park is on Cape San Blas Road off US 98 about a mile south of SR 71.

Apalachicola itself is an attraction for those who enjoy antiques shopping and architectural history. The town's historic district includes riverfront buildings and several restored homes.

Wildlife

With so much of the Forgotten Coast relatively undeveloped, it's a good place for viewing wildlife. White-tailed deer, raccoons, and Atlantic bottle-nosed dolphins are common sights. Sea turtles nest on the beach in the summer, with hatchlings appearing from late summer into early fall. Sea turtles are in good company because the region is home to the highest density of reptile and amphibian species in the United States and Canada, according to government studies.

There are more than 300 species of birds that live in or visit the region: shorebirds on the beach, wading birds in the salt marshes, raptors (like bald eagles and peregrine falcons) above, and songbirds in the uplands.

Bird-watchers may want to time a visit during fall, usually in October, for the Florida Panhandle Birding and Wildflower Festival (*www.birdfestival.org*). The festival features guided field trips to natural lands throughout the region.

On St. Vincent Island, the refuge is home to the large sambar deer, an exotic species from Asia. The deer remain from the time when the island was a private hunting reserve. Other introduced animals once included zebras, elands, and ring-necked pheasants.

Look for . . .

Another unusual species on St. Vincent Island is the red wolf. Once ranging from the Mid-Atlantic states down into Florida and over to central Texas, the red wolf was nearly wiped out by predator-control programs based on protecting cattle. Now the red wolf is considered extinct even in the wild. However, the red wolves that live on St. Vincent are part of a captive-breeding program that aims to re-establish them.

Red wolves usually mate for life. Weaned wolf pups on the island are relocated to places where the U.S. Fish and Wildlife Service is managing experimental red wolf populations, like Alligator River National Wildlife Refuge in North Carolina.

While the name indicates the wolf is red, an individual wolf's color may be black or gray. Larger than a coyote but smaller than a gray wolf, the red wolf can weigh up to eighty pounds.

The St. Vincent wolves—usually no more than six—are outfitted with radio collars so refuge staff can track them. They are free to hunt small mammals and may even prey on white-tailed deer. The wolves are usually more active at night, but may be more inclined to be active in the daytime during winter. If you want to catch a glimpse of one before it shyly darts away, that may be your best time to try.

Habitats

Dunes and coastal scrub dominate the beaches. Covered by protected sea oats and home to endangered St. Andrews beach mice, dunes are fragile and off-limits so they won't erode. Visitors should use beach boardwalks to cross over the dunes to get to the beach.

The region also harbors marsh and pineland habitats. Some area pine trees, such as on St. George Island, still show marks from turpentining. Opening up the tree trunk to draw out the sap to make turpentine was once a common industry throughout northern Florida. The resulting scar in the bark is called a cat face. St. George Island hikers can see examples of this along the trail to Gap Point.

Offshore, the waters along Florida's Gulf of Mexico coastline are relatively shallow because the continental shelf extends far out into the gulf. This is a perfect place for seagrass to grow. Seagrass is an important nursery to various marine life, and it's a large part of the manatee's diet. Visitors should take care not to walk in seagrass or tear it up with boat propellers.

The shallow seagrass areas in St. Joseph Bay, rich in marine life, attract flocks of migratory birds and hawks. The bay is unique in that it is the only water body here where no freshwater flows directly into it, and it is designated as a state aquatic preserve.

St. Joseph Bay was the site of the unfortunate death of 107 Atlantic bottle-nosed dolphins to red tide in March and April 2004. Many fish also died. A red tide occurs when there is a significant increase of algae that produce a neuro-toxin. Scientists are trying to learn how to predict this naturally occurring al-gae bloom. Despite the name, red tide doesn't always color the water red. The water may be a variety of colors or produce no apparent color change, according to the Florida Fish and Wildlife Research Institute.

Apalachicola Bay, along with the lower Apalachicola River, also has a special ecological distinction as a national estuarine research reserve (NERR). Such reserves throughout the United States are recognized as places where scientists can learn more about estuaries. Apalachicola NERR covers almost 250,000 acres. Florida has two other NERRs, the Guana Tolomato Matanzas in the St. Augustine area, and the Rookery Bay in Naples.

Look for wildflowers in the fall to attract migrating butterflies like monarchs and gulf fritillaries.

Where to Stay

Campgrounds

St. Joseph Peninsula State Park has 119 campsites in two campground loops. Campsites offer water and electric hookups and central restrooms with showers. The Gulf Breeze campground offers access to the beach on the Gulf of Mexico. Tent campers should reserve sites 40–46. The Shady Pines campground is better for shaded sites. Contact ReserveAmerica for details and reservations.

The park also allows primitive camping at designated sites in the wild northern portion of the park. Camping fees are $3.00 per night for adults and $2.00 for children six to eighteen. A group campground for organized youth groups is located near the cabin area. To reserve either type of camping, contact the park office directly.

Among scattered pine trees, the St. George Island State Park campground sites have electric and water hookups and restrooms with showers. There are sixty campsites, reserved through ReserveAmerica.

At the end of the park's 2.5-mile trail to Gap Point is a primitive camping area. Campers can either hike the trail to reach the camping area, or arrive by boat. Contact the park directly about staying here.

On St. Vincent Island, primitive camping is allowed only in connection with scheduled hunts.

Lodging

Eight excellent cabins line the bay at St. Joseph Peninsula State Park. All cabins feature a loft, fireplace, central air and heat, modern kitchen, and screened porch, and are completely furnished for a maximum of seven guests. The cabins are so popular that people reserve them months in advance; a two-night stay is the minimum reservation. Contact ReserveAmerica for reservations.

Lodging options in Port St. Joe range from inns (like Cape San Blas Inn: 800-315-1965; *www.capesanblasinn.com* with five guest rooms) to vacation rentals like rustic cabins (Old Saltworks Cabins: 850-229-6097; *www.oldsalt works.com* on St. Joseph Bay) or homes (try Cape San Blas Vacation Rentals: 800-720-0473; *www.capesanblasvacationrentals.com*).

In Apalachicola's historic district, there are a few bed-and-breakfast inns like Coombs House Inn (850-653-9199; *www.coombshouseinn.com*) with nineteen rooms and two suites, and Gibson Inn (850-653-2191; *www.gibson inn.com*) on the National Register of Historic Places with thirty-one rooms. Near the edge of town on US 98 is Best Western Apalach Inn (850-653-9131). Offshore, stay at the luxurious Pelican Inn (800-451-5294; *www.thepelican inn.com*) on Dog Island, reached only by boat.

On St. George Island, the main choice for lodging is a vacation rental home. Try St. George Island Vacation Rentals (800-332-5196; *www.stgeorgeisland. com*) or Collins Vacation Rentals (800-423-7418; *www.collinsvacationrentals. com*) for lists of beach homes to rent.

Nearby towns also offer small motels like Sportsman's Lodge Motel and Marina (850-670-8423) in Eastpoint and The Moorings at Carrabelle (850-697-2800; *www.mooringscarrabelle.com*) in Carrabelle.

How to Get There

St. Joseph Peninsula State Park is on the tip of St. Joseph Peninsula at the end of route 30E. Take I-10 to SR 71 (Exit #142) and follow the road southwest all the way to the town of Port St. Joe at US 98. Turn left (south) and continue south on route 30A where the road splits. At route 30E, turn right (west) onto the peninsula, following the road to the end.

St. George Island State Park is at the eastern end of St. George Island. From Apalachicola, take US 98 east across the river to Eastpoint, then look for the bridge across St. George Sound to the island. At Gulf Beach Drive, turn left (east) and follow the road all the way to the end, where the state park entrance is.

The St. Vincent National Wildlife Refuge island is reached only by boat, closest to the mainland at Indian Pass about 10 miles southeast of downtown Port St. Joe and 22 miles southwest of Apalachicola. Bring your own boat to launch here and cross the very short distance to the island, or take a ferry service mentioned under Guided Tours, above.

⊷ ⊷ ⊷

T. H. Stone Memorial St. Joseph Peninsula State Park
8899 Cape San Blas Road
Port St. Joe, Florida 32456
Phone: 850-227-1327
Admission is $4.00 per vehicle.

Dr. Julian G. Bruce St. George Island State Park
1900 E. Gulf Beach Dr.
St. George Island, Florida 32328
Phone: 850-927-2111
Admission is $5.00 per vehicle.

St. Vincent National Wildlife Refuge
479 Market Street
Apalachicola, Florida 32329
Phone: 850-653-8808
The refuge island lies offshore, but the visitor center is in Apalachicola in the John B. Meyer Harbor House, at the end of Market Street about nine blocks north of US 98 just west of the bridge over Apalachicola River. Hours are 8:00 a.m. to 4:30 p.m. Monday through Friday.

The Forgotten Coast is a good place for nature travelers to visit because it's relatively undeveloped and surrounded by natural areas. It's good for beachgoers and anglers because of the top-ranked white beaches and abundance of fish. Finally, the small-town atmosphere throughout the region makes it a peaceful place for those who just want to get away to somewhere quiet.

Nearby

Emerald Coast (chapter 3), Apalachicola National Forest (chapter 5), Apalachicola River Lands (chapter 6)

5

Apalachicola National Forest

From just southwest of Tallahassee stretching west to the Apalachicola River, Apalachicola National Forest stands as Florida's largest national forest with 564,000 acres. The Apalachicola River forms the forest's western boundary. The Ochlockonee River runs down the center. In between, the forest is dotted with lakes and swamps. Its vastness and remoteness make the Apalachicola a great place for nature travelers who want to find solitude and a true wilderness experience.

While driving the forest roads, paddling the rivers, or hiking the miles of trails, one feels the busyness of so-called civilized life passing away. Trees take over the scenery instead of buildings. Birds and other wildlife seem to be everywhere—if you look. Wildflowers bloom in unexpected places.

The Apalachicola's immense size and isolation from urban areas may be a welcoming respite to some people and a formidable challenge to others. It can be both at the same time. That's what makes a visit, even a day trip, so rewarding.

What to Do There

The good thing about national forests is that anyone, at any time, can be anywhere, exploring every inch if they like. Many people who take to this huge forest visit designated recreation areas where they can access trails, rivers, and lakes and go camping, boating, or fishing.

Apalachicola National Forest has five recreation areas, all of which charge a $3.00 day-use fee per vehicle. Camel Lake in the northwestern reaches offers a campground, picnic area, boat ramp, and hiking trail. Silver Lake in the northeast is a good "swimmin' hole" with a beach on the lake and a bathhouse with hot showers. It also has a boat ramp and trail. Wright Lake in the south has the best campground in the forest, and also offers a lake beach, bathhouse with hot showers, picnic tables, and trail.

Figure 4. Swamps are common in Apalachicola National Forest and Tate's Hell State Forest.

Close to Wright Lake is Fort Gadsden Historical Site, another recreation area and a National Historic Landmark. This recreation area preserves the site of 1800s battles and encampments, first with natives and escaped slaves fighting for the British and for their freedom, then with Confederate troops protecting the important Apalachicola River. Earthworks of the original fort are still here on the riverbank, and a covered structure houses displays of artifacts found at the fort.

Another unique recreation area is Leon Sinks Geological Area, where sinks and sinkholes of various sizes are clustered. Walking the trails to view the fragile sinks and picnicking are allowed here.

Aside from the recreation areas, there are several hunt camps throughout the forest.

Trail Tripping

Hikers can revel in the eighty-five miles of trails to explore throughout the forest. Most of those—about sixty-four miles—are part of the Florida National Scenic Trail. For maps and information, please contact the Florida Trail Association.

Other trails in the forest are usually located near designated recreation areas. A 5-mile trail loops around Wright Lake recreation area. At Leon Sinks, hikers can walk 5 miles of interconnecting trails around a grouping of sinkholes. There's a 1-mile trail loop at Camel Lake and Silver Lake. At Fort Gadsden, there's a short half-mile trail to the river and fort earthworks. The Trail of Lakes (9 miles) is a loop east of Camel Lake that connects with the Florida Trail. The trail is between forest roads numbered 121 and 105.

Off-road bicyclists get their own trails here in an area called Munson Hills, where there are a 5-mile loop and an 8-mile loop. The trailhead and parking area, complete with a bike rack and restrooms, are on State Road 363 (Woodville Highway) south of SR 263 (Capital Circle). Bicyclists are also welcome on any public forest road.

The forest is pretty wide open for horseback riders (the Florida Trail and recreation areas are off-limits), and so is camping with horses at hunt camps or any primitive areas. The forest's Vinzant Horse Trail area is considered one of the best. The interconnecting 10-, 11-, and 12-mile loops meander off forest roads in the extreme northern part of the forest. Find the trailhead just south of SR 20 on Forest Road 342.

There are no trails specifically for off-road vehicles, but the forest allows them on unnumbered forest roads.

All trail users should be aware of scheduled hunting periods. Find trail maps at forest offices or on the forest Web site.

The forest allows hikers to roam anywhere in the forest, but only experienced backpackers or orienteers should attempt to go off the designated trails. Staying on trails also protects the sometimes rare or fragile habitat in the forest.

Paddling and Boating

Canoeists, kayakers, and boaters with small watercraft can enjoy the forest's two main waterways, the meandering Ochlockonee and Apalachicola Rivers. Several boat ramps are located on these rivers throughout the forest; check forest maps for locations.

Various lakes, such as those at Camel Lake, Silver Lake, and Wright Lake recreation areas, are open to non-motorized boats and boats with electric motors.

To rent a canoe or kayak, try the Wilderness Way (850-877-7200; *www.the wildernessway.com*) on SR 363 (Woodville Highway), where you can get paddling starting at $25.00 a day. Wilderness Way also leads guided nature tours that focus on paddling, bird-watching, and other nature observation. Contact the company for a schedule of upcoming tours.

Farther away in the Big Bend region, try TNT Hideaway Inc. (850-925-6412) in Crawfordville, Riverside Café and Recreational Rentals (850-925-5668) in St. Marks, or Sopchoppy Outfitters (850-962-2020) in Sopchoppy.

Nearby Natural Areas

Tate's Hell State Forest (850-697-3734) in Carrabelle shares a border with the Apalachicola at its southern end. Tate's Hell extends the forest habitat another 185,000 acres. Although previously a slash pine tree plantation whose lands have been partly drained, the forest acts as a buffer and water-recharge area for Apalachicola Bay.

One of the forest's most unique features is its dwarf cypress swamp. A long boardwalk and observation deck area at the Ralph G. Kendrick Boardwalk lets visitors walk above the dwarfed trees and look out across the swamp. Reaching to only about fifteen feet, dwarf cypress trees are genetically identical to regularly sized cypresses. Scientists think the dwarf trees are stunted because of a lack of nutrients in the soil, according to a kiosk at the boardwalk.

The forest's unusual name comes from the local legend of a man named Cebe Tate. The story goes that around 1875, Tate went after a panther that was preying on his cattle. He got lost in the thick swamp for about a week, having suffered a snake bite and dehydration, before finding his way out near Carrabelle. There, he collapsed and announced he had just come from hell.

To get there, take SR 65 north from US 98 east of Apalachicola, and follow signs. Some signs along SR 65 point the way to the boardwalk. Another portion of the forest is closer to Carrabelle along SR 67. Visitors should request a map from the state forestry division before wandering the back roads.

Apalachicola River Wildlife and Environmental Area (850-488-5520) also continues the national forest's land to the south, following the river all the way to Apalachicola Bay. While the WEA protects marshes, river floodplains, and pinelands, it also provides several access points to the river, where there are several boat ramps. An observation tower on East Bay and hiking and biking trails let visitors get to know the varied environment. The Florida Fish and Wildlife Conservation Commission, which oversees the area, recommends visiting in spring and fall for pleasant temperatures and views of blooming wildflowers. Visitors should realize hunting is allowed here during certain times of the year; call the WEA office ahead for hunting schedules and to receive a free brochure/map. Apalachicola River WEA is on the other side of SR 65 from

Tate's Hell State Forest. The WEA office is on the river on County Road 387; take SR 71 north from US 98 in Port St. Joe to CR 387 and turn right (east), following the road to the end.

Nearby Attractions

Apalachicola National Forest is so large that the nearest towns with significant leisure attractions are Tallahassee (covered in chapter 7, Big Bend Territory) and Apalachicola (covered in chapter 4, Forgotten Coast). Please see these chapters for other places to visit.

Wildlife

While hiking, floating down the rivers, or driving forest roads, you might see white-tailed deer, American alligators, gray foxes, northern bobwhites, wild turkeys, and even Florida black bears. Warblers like pine warblers are common, and so are northern cardinals and American robins, particularly in winter. Apalachicola National Forest is also home to the endangered Bachman's warbler.

Look for . . .

Apalachicola National Forest is home to the world's largest population—or at least one of the largest, depending on whom you ask—of red-cockaded woodpeckers. Considered endangered by the federal government but only threatened by the state of Florida, these birds depend on mature pine trees (sixty-some years old and older) for their cavity nests. In some places, pine trees where the woodpeckers' nests have been found are marked with a white band of paint around the trunk.

Once living in old-growth pine forests throughout the southeastern United States, the red-cockaded woodpecker has declined because of habitat loss and forest fragmentation. According to the U.S. Forest Service and the Florida Division of Forestry, some forest management in Florida aims to help the species recover through better timber-harvesting practices, such as foregoing clearcutting. Prescribed fires also maintain their pineland habitat by preventing hardwood trees from growing there.

Like the Florida scrub jay, the red-cockaded woodpecker may live in a family group to share responsibilities of raising offspring, but not always. The woodpeckers lay from three to five eggs in mid or late spring, then care for the young for a couple of months until they are independent.

Look for red-cockaded woodpeckers on pine trees, particularly along the

Apalachee Savannahs Scenic Byway, which is the southern part of CR 379 north of where it joins SR 65 at the community of Sumatra.

Habitats

Most of the forest's vast acreage is made up of a longleaf pine and wiregrass plant community. Longleaf pines with their foot-long needles and wiregrass growing below once covered a good deal of northern Florida. Fire suppression, logging, and conversion to agricultural land or to plantations of pines that grow more quickly (like slash pines) have reduced this habitat, on which several species depend. Without fire every three to five years, longleaf pine habitats can turn into mixed forest, according to the U.S. Forest Service. Fire prevents hardwood trees from flourishing, and it can aid new growth of pines, wiregrass, and wildflowers. In fact, scientists have found that wiregrass doesn't seed except after fire during the later part of summer.

Fire aids another longleaf pine habitat plant, an endangered herb in the lily family called Harper's beauty. With a six-petaled yellow flower that blooms in mid-spring, it spreads by sending out rhizomes. According to the U.S. Fish and Wildlife Service, Harper's beauty is extremely rare. There are only three known areas where it's found, and they are all in Apalachicola National Forest along SR 65, where they like moist areas like ditches and bogs.

Other portions of the forest are bayhead swamps, floodplain forests, and prairies. Bradwell Bay swamp east of Ochlockonee River is a national wilderness area covering more than 24,000 acres. The only way to reach Bradwell Bay is to hike that portion of the Florida Trail, called "wet and rough" by the Florida Trail Association.

Where to Stay

Campgrounds

Within the forest, Camel Lake and Wright Lake recreation areas offer overnight camping at campgrounds with restrooms, showers, picnic table, and campfire ring or grill. There are twenty campsites at quiet Wright Lake, where campers get hot showers in the restrooms, for $8.00 a night. Wright Lake also has a dump station for RVs. Camel Lake has six campsites on the lake, outdoor showers only, available for $5.00 a night. Neither campground offers electricity or water hookups; generators must be turned off at 10 p.m.

Hickory Landing Boat Ramp and Hunt Camp on the Apalachicola River has twelve campsites. Mack Landing Boat Ramp and Hunt Camp on the Ochlockonee River has six sites. Sites at both areas have a picnic table and campfire ring or grill, but stand-alone toilets only. Both areas charge campers $3.00 a night.

Primitive camping is allowed anywhere throughout the forest except during deer gun hunting season in fall and winter. (Check with the forest for exact dates each year.) Primitive camping is limited to at most fourteen days in one spot during a thirty-day time period.

At Apalachicola River WEA (mentioned above), anyone may camp anywhere without a permit except where posted. Only primitive camping is available, but self-sustaining trailers and RVs are welcome.

Lodging

There is no lodging in the forest except where there are private land holdings.

The forest is so large that towns are few and far between. On the northwestern edge of the forest is Blountstown (try the Airport Motel: 850-674-8168). To the south on the Gulf of Mexico along the Forgotten Coast is Carrabelle (try The Moorings at Carrabelle: 850-697-2800; *www.mooringscarrabelle.com*). The Tallahassee area covered in chapter 7, Big Bend Territory, offers more lodging options near the eastern edge of the forest.

How to Get There

Apalachicola National Forest is so large that it may be best to start at the forest office on your first visit to get maps and speak with rangers. Take I-10 west of Tallahassee and exit at SR 12 (Exit #174). Follow the road south to SR 20. The forest office is right at this intersection in Bristol. Alternatively, take SR 20 west from Tallahassee about forty miles to SR 12 in Bristol.

✧ ✧ ✧

Apalachicola Ranger District Office
P.O. Box 579
Bristol, Florida 32321
Phone: 850-643-2282
The forest office hours are 7:30 a.m. to 5:00 p.m. Monday through Thursday and 8:00 a.m. to 4:00 p.m. on Friday.

Wakulla Ranger District Office
57 Taft Drive
Crawfordville, Florida 32327
Phone: 850-926-3561
The forest office hours are 8:00 a.m. to 4:30 p.m. Monday through Thursday and 8:00 a.m. to 4:00 p.m. on Friday.

There is no charge to drive through the forest; day-use area fees are $3.00 per vehicle. Be sure to use forest maps.

The Apalachicola is Florida's largest national forest and an important home to Florida black bears and red-cockaded woodpeckers. There is a lot for nature travelers to explore here. But the forest is so vast and towns so far from some areas that good planning is required for anything more than a day trip.

Nearby

Forgotten Coast (chapter 4), Apalachicola River Lands (chapter 6), Big Bend (chapter 7)

6

Apalachicola River Lands

On the Florida/Georgia border, the Chattahoochee and Flint Rivers join, shaking hands at Lake Seminole. From the lake, that grasp of water continues south through the Florida panhandle to the Gulf of Mexico, in the Apalachicola River. The river isn't the subject of a famous song like the Suwannee. It isn't exceptionally long like the St. Johns. But of all Florida's rivers, it has the largest amount of water flowing past its banks. It was a strategic part of the Civil War and the First Seminole War. The river actually served as a sort of highway, with 200 steamboats going up and down the channel at its peak, according to the state park service. And when you cross the river on I-10, you are crossing into another time zone. All in all, the Apalachicola is a defining river of the region.

Fortunately, a lot of land along the river has been preserved. In some places, the river's banks put on swamps, making it hard to tell just where the river ends. In other places, it dons bluffs that soar 150 feet above the river—quite a height for Florida. No matter how the Apalachicola is dressed, it reveals its unique beauty.

At its headwaters on Lake Seminole is Three Rivers State Park, a good place to begin a tour of the river. Although the river doesn't flow through this quiet park, visitors can get out on the lake and roam through the sandhills.

Farther downriver, Torreya State Park provides an amazing view of the Apalachicola from the top of a bluff—no wonder it's a National Natural Landmark. Walk down a trail to get a better look at the river up close. Take in Torreya's beautiful forested scenery, especially in autumn when the leaves change color.

Not too far from Three Rivers is another great park to explore. Florida Caverns State Park isn't on the Apalachicola but on the nearby Chipola River, an Apalachicola tributary. Florida Caverns is a National Natural Landmark known for its caves and a good example of extreme northern Florida's nature.

Together, these parks offer a lot to nature travelers who want to get to know the Apalachicola River and the northern panhandle, or who just want to see some of small-town northern Florida.

Figure 5. Young torreya trees grow in front of the Gregory House, which sits on top of a bluff overlooking the Apalachicola River.

What to Do There

The Apalachicola River is the focal point of the region, so getting out on the water is a good way to explore. The river valley's uplands are what makes a visit here so unique to Florida, however. Trails and tours provide access into this distinct part of the state.

At Torreya State Park, you may want to arrive in time for a tour of Gregory House, which sits near the edge of the river bluff. Tours run every weekday at 10 a.m., and weekends at 10 a.m., 2 p.m., and 4 p.m.

Trail Tripping

Hikers can follow the edge of Lake Seminole on the short, looping Lakeside Trail at Three Rivers. The trail begins and ends near the restrooms by the campground. At the park picnic area, the Half Dry Creek Trail is another short loop through the sandhills, where a fox squirrel might turn up.

At Torreya, hikers can explore 7 miles of trails to view the park's best features. The Apalachicola River Bluffs Trail leading from behind Gregory House is a must because it follows the river and the former site of a series of Confederate gun pits. Trail walkers should watch their step on this steep trail. From the campground area, the Weeping Ridge Trail leads to a ravine where water seeps out of the ground and tumbles into a waterfall after heavy rains.

Almost 9 miles of multiuse trails at Florida Caverns are open to hikers, off-road bicyclists, and horseback riders. The latter will appreciate the equestrian facility among the trails, including stables and a wash rack. In addition, there is a 1.5-mile nature trail that is a good way to get acquainted with the park.

Paddling and Boating

Lake Seminole is wide open for visitors at Three Rivers. A boat ramp allows access right on the lake. Paddlers can rent a canoe at the park ranger station. It is possible for paddlers and boaters to go to the northern side of the lake and be in the state of Georgia, which shares Lake Seminole with Florida.

The Chipola River is a state canoe trail that begins at Florida Caverns and runs for 52 miles, making it possible to paddle all the way to Wewahitchka at the Dead Lakes recreation area. There are several access points along the river trail from the state park to State Road 71. Along the trail, look for caves and wildlife like turtles and alligators. The park offers a boat launch, but it accommodates only small boats. Park visitors can rent a canoe at the concession.

The Apalachicola River is open for paddling and boating. For boat ramp locations, contact the Northwest Florida Water Management District or look them up in the *Florida Atlas and Gazetteer*.

Guided Tours

For a guided tour of one of the caves at Florida Caverns, sign up at the visitor center/park concession. A cave expert points out stalactites, stalagmites, and other features formed in the cave, including one cave "room" called the wedding chapel because of its ornate-looking formations. The park leads tours every day from 9:00 a.m. to 4:00 p.m. in the winter and 9:00 a.m. to 4:30 p.m. in the summer. The tour fee is $6.00 for adults and $3.00 for children twelve and under. Tour guests should be able to watch their footing and duck under short passageways.

Nearby Natural Areas

Not far from Florida Caverns is Falling Waters State Park (850-638-6130), the site of Florida's tallest waterfall. A shady walk through the damp forest leads to the fall, which descends for sixty-seven feet into a roundish stone pit. The state park service declares that it's still not known where the water goes from the falls. Be warned that the waterfall can dry up if it hasn't rained in a while. On the way, look for butterflies in the butterfly garden at the trailhead, and skinks near the waterfall. Red-headed woodpeckers fly from tree to tree in the parking lot, from where you can see rolling hills in the distance. The park is 3 miles south of Chipley. To get there, take I-10 to SR 77 (Exit #120) and go south. Watch for signs showing the way to the park on State Park Road.

South of Torreya State Park on the Apalachicola River is Apalachicola Bluffs and Ravines Preserve (850-643-2756), which is owned by the Nature Conservancy. This 6,294-acre preserve offers a scenic trail to the river for a 3.5-mile round-trip hike. At the river, there is a 135-foot-high bluff, similar to Torreya State Park. According to the Nature Conservancy, a local legend makes the area out to be the site of the biblical Garden of Eden. Watch for white-tailed deer and dusky salamanders. To get there, follow SR 12 south from the Torreya State Park turn-off. The preserve entrance is about 20 miles south of I-10 near Bristol on Garden of Eden Road.

Wildlife

The Apalachicola River area is mostly undeveloped or rural, so wildlife can roam freely in the region. White-tailed deer, Florida black bears, gray foxes, fox squirrels, and a variety of songbirds may wander the forested areas. In the river, alligators, alligator snapping turtles, and Barbours map turtles swim. Migrating waterfowl winter at Lake Seminole in Three Rivers.

Look for . . .

Bats live throughout Florida, and three species in particular live in the caves at Florida Caverns: eastern pipistrelle, southeastern, and gray bats. According to the state, it is possible to see bats during the cave tour, but sightings aren't common. The park protects roosting or maternity caves and makes them off-limits.

That's important for the gray bat, which roosts only in caves. The limited availability of undisturbed caves has led to the gray bat's endangered status. Gray bats have only one pup at a time, so the population is likely to grow slowly.

The eastern pipistrelle bat is another area resident. The smallest bat in Florida, this yellow- to brown-colored bat is full grown at 3–3.5 inches and small enough to be able to roost in even a clump of Spanish moss. The eastern pipistrelle is known for being one of the first bats to leave the roost at night in search of insects.

The southeastern bat is also a small bat. Colored from gray to orange, the southeastern roosts not only in caves, but also in buildings, tree hollows, bridges, and other places. About a hundred southeastern bats live in the large bat house on the University of Florida campus in Gainesville (known mostly for its population of Brazilian free-tailed bats), according to the university.

Bats have a bad reputation with some people, who fear them because of stories in popular culture or because of the threat of rabies. Bats are an important part of the ecosystem and are beneficial when it comes to consuming pesky insects (up to 600 in one hour). Besides that, their waste—guano—is highly prized by gardeners as a natural fertilizer. Like most other mammals, bats can carry rabies, but they aren't likely to attack people when they are infected.

Habitats

The Apalachicola River valley encompasses diverse plant communities, from floodplain forests and cypress swamps to sandhills and pine flatwoods. Florida

Caverns State Park protects the largest dry caves in the state in a magnificent display of karst terrain.

The region is beautiful in spring and summer, when flowering trees and wildflowers break out in blooms. Look for dogwoods and magnolias to display their creamy white flowers.

Another tree, the torreya, gives Torreya State Park its name. The park is one of the few places where the coniferous torreya tree grows in the wild; other species grow in California, Japan, and China. The park is propagating the tree and planting seedlings to help establish it. Visitors can see some of these young trees in front of the Gregory House.

The view from the Gregory House at one time must have included regular barge traffic along the Apalachicola River. The river was once a major shipping channel, where barges transported goods via the Gulf of Mexico. The U.S. Army Corps of Engineers frequently dredged the river in order to make sure it was clear for the large ships to pass through.

This dredging, however, was blamed for the decline in the river's water quality. Dredging pushes dirt into piles on the riverbanks, which can degrade the natural habitat and block creeks from flowing into the river. In addition, it affects marine life at the river's mouth, according to the state. In recent years, the activist group American Rivers has named the Apalachicola one of "America's most endangered rivers" because of this dredging. The group maintains that the dredging isn't necessary anymore because barge traffic has diminished, and that in addition to the environmental impact, the dredging costs the government twice as much money—$20 million per year—as the barges bring in. In 2002, the state asked Congress to put a stop to the Army's dredging.

Water usage is another issue that faces the Apalachicola. Because it begins at Lake Seminole, which is fed by Georgia rivers, its flow is affected by the other rivers' flow. If people use too much water from these rivers upstream, there is less water to flow into the Apalachicola. Florida, Georgia, and Alabama (which shares the Chattahoochee River with Georgia) have been in discussions over this water usage in the hopes of achieving a balanced, fair use agreement.

Where to Stay

Campgrounds

Campers will enjoy great views of Lake Seminole without sacrificing shade at Three Rivers State Park, where there are thirty campsites with water and electric hookups. There are central restrooms, and a dump station is provided for RVs. For reservations, contact ReserveAmerica.

The campground at Torreya State Park is situated on an Apalachicola River bluff under shade trees. Here, the thirty campsites have water and electric hookups near restrooms. For a unique camping experience, reserve the yurt— a permanent, roundish tent with air conditioning, heating, electricity, and a futon. The yurt sleeps five people and is in the main campground. For campground reservations, contact ReserveAmerica.

At Florida Caverns, there are thirty-eight campsites with electric and water hookups, and restrooms. Contact ReserveAmerica for information and reservations. The park also has two group campgrounds for organized groups. Camping in these areas is primitive, but one group camp includes full restroom facilities. Contact Florida Caverns about these group campgrounds.

Farther away at Falling Waters there are twenty-four campsites in a scenic area. The sites all have water and electricity, and a dump station is nearby for RVs. Make reservations through ReserveAmerica. Falling Waters also maintains a primitive group campground for organized groups of up to fifty people; contact the park directly for information on this campground.

Lodging

There is one cabin at Three Rivers, where guests can enjoy modern amenities in the fully furnished structure—but bring your own towels and linens. The cabin, located in the main campground, sleeps up to four people in a bedroom and loft. For more information and reservations, contact ReserveAmerica.

There are several lodging facilities in Marianna, like the Holiday Inn Express (850-526-2900) and the bungalow-style Hinson House Bed and Breakfast (850-526-1500). In Bristol, look for a couple of small motels, like the Snowbird Motel (850-643-2330).

How to Get There

Three Rivers State Park is north of Sneads on SR 271. Take I-10 west of Tallahassee to County Road 286 (Exit #158). Head north past farms to Sneads, then turn left (west) on US 90, the main road through town. At SR 271, turn right (north). The park entrance is about 2 miles ahead.

For Torreya State Park, exit I-10 at SR 12 (Exit #174) and go south through Greensboro. Continue along the hilly road toward Bristol and watch for signs to point the way to the park through an agricultural area. The park entrance is 13 miles north of Bristol.

Florida Caverns State Park is closer to Three Rivers, to the west. Exit I-10 at SR 71 (Exit #142) and go north. At US 90, turn left (west) and travel a few miles to Marianna. At SR 166, turn right (north) and look for the park entrance about 3 miles ahead.

✎   ✎   ✎

Three Rivers State Park
7908 Three Rivers Park Road
Sneads, Florida 32460
Phone: 850-482-9006
Admission is $2.00 per vehicle.

Torreya State Park
2576 N.W. Torreya Park Road
Bristol, Florida 32321
Phone: 850-643-2674
Admission is $2.00 per vehicle.

Florida Caverns State Park
3345 Caverns Road
Marianna, Florida 32446
Phone: 850-482-9598
Admission is $4.00 per vehicle, or $6.00 per horse for equestrians.

The Apalachicola River valley is lined with history and nature, a place where visitors can see a distinctly different side to Florida. The river's bluffs, and area caves and hills, lend the region a mountainlike atmosphere.

Nearby

Forgotten Coast (chapter 4), Apalachicola National Forest (chapter 5)

7

Big Bend Territory

Mention "Big Bend," and most people think of the national park on the Rio Grande in Texas. Florida also has a Big Bend, only this one is on the Gulf of Mexico, not a river. It follows the curve of the gulf waters in a bend stretching across four counties.

Because it's directly south of the state capital in Tallahassee, you might expect the Big Bend area to be a crowded place with vacation homes lining the shore. But most of the shore here has been preserved by various natural lands. Most of this gulf-front property is owned by the public.

One reason: the Big Bend lacks beaches. On a map, the shoreline appears more like the tattered edge of an old fishing cap than the smooth, rounded coast created by a sandy beach. Actually, the wetland shores, sometimes covered with marsh grasses, make it hard to tell exactly where the coastline lies.

St. Marks National Wildlife Refuge covers 68,000 acres here. Right next door is state-owned Big Bend Wildlife Management Area (WMA). A bit inland, Wakulla Springs State Park sits at the headwaters of one of the region's major rivers, one of the largest and deepest springs in the world and a National Natural Landmark. Apalachicola National Forest is close by. All are public lands—owned by all of us.

We really need to check out our waterfront property.

Established in 1931, the St. Marks refuge is divided into tracts, or units, along the shore. The main unit, St. Marks, is where you'll find the refuge headquarters and visitor center. Heading west, you find the Wakulla unit, then the Panacea unit. The Aucilla unit is toward the east. All of these tracts are on the gulf, protecting lowlands as well as uplands, and providing great opportunities for wildlife-watching, fishing, and water-based recreation.

The 6,000-acre Edward Ball Wakulla Springs park is a local favorite. Famous for being the location of the original *Tarzan* and *Creature from the Black Lagoon* movies, the actual spring bowl is three acres wide. The spring releases up to 1.2 billion gallons of 70-degree water each day. The spring run leads to the Gulf of Mexico, and the spring boil to a cave where mastodon remains and other artifacts have been discovered, but only research teams are allowed to dive here.

Figure 6. The lighthouse at St. Marks National Wildlife Refuge stands at the edge of Apalachee Bay.

Big Bend WMA, like most WMAs, is primarily a hunting land. Timber harvest also occurs here. This natural area does preserve 200 miles of coastline, however, and nature travelers are welcome. The WMA has five units—Hickory Mound, Spring Creek, Tide Swamp, Jena, and Snipe Island—so there's a lot to see. The Hickory Mound and Tide Swamp tracts are the better places for wildlife-watching and other passive recreation.

All of these natural areas belong to us, and there are a lot of ways to explore them.

What to Do There

If you haven't been to the area before, consider visiting the St. Marks refuge visitor center first. There, you can get area brochures and maps, see dioramas of the natural habitats in the region, talk to rangers and volunteers for suggestions on places to go, and see the logbook of recently sighted wildlife species in the refuge. The visitor center is in the main tract of the refuge, where a 7-mile paved road leads from the headquarters to the gulf. Trails and interesting stopping points are along the way.

At the end of the road on the water is the St. Marks lighthouse. The first lighthouse here was completed in 1831. A new tower farther inland (on the current site) was constructed in 1842 because of erosion. It was heightened to its current footage of eighty-two feet during the Civil War. In 1960, the lighthouse was automated, and it still works today. The U.S. Coast Guard currently operates the lighthouse, and it's not open to the public. However, St. Marks personnel said the refuge is attempting to acquire the lighthouse and may open it to tours in the future.

Trail Tripping

Going down trails is a great way to experience any natural area and to find wildlife. All of the Big Bend natural areas are fine places to hike or even take a short walk. Long-distance hikers can enjoy 41 miles of the Florida National Scenic Trail in St. Marks National Wildlife Refuge alone.

The refuge offers 75 miles of trails. St. Marks's main tract has seven trails, from a short walk along a levee to the longer Florida Trail. Ask for refuge trail maps at the visitor center, or purchase a Florida Trail map from the Florida Trail Association.

Behind the refuge visitor center is a good place to start: the short Plum Orchard Pond Trail, which leads around the pond. Visitors can spot birds like red-shouldered hawks at the pond right from the back porch of the visitor center.

Another notable walk at the refuge is the series of trails known as the Primitive Walking Trails. Hike a 7- or 13-mile loop along impoundments or through pine woods. Look for the sign about 1.5 miles south of the visitor center.

The refuge has a brochure for Mounds Pool Interpretive Trail, a mile-long walk where visitors can learn about the area's habitats, wildlife, and history. The trail begins at the restrooms about 5 miles south of the visitor center. Observant hikers may spot bald eagles or their nest along the trail, which can be flooded after heavy rain.

At the end of the St. Marks Unit road is the lighthouse, where a short trail and observation tower provide views of the coastal marsh. Across from the lighthouse is a parking area where impoundments allow walkers to find wading birds and wintering waterfowl.

The refuge's Panacea Unit to the west also offers trails, in 5- and 9-mile hikes. Florida Trail hikers can access the trail here, too, as well as in the Wakulla Unit. Both of these units allow seasonal hunting.

Bicycles are allowed on refuge trails, but not on the Florida Trail, which is designated as a footpath throughout the state.

At Wakulla Springs, try out three trails that offer glimpses of the true nature of the park. Just shy of a mile one way, Sally Ward Trail follows the run from Sally Ward Spring that joins the headwaters of the larger Wakulla Spring. Begin near the lodge or at the parking area near the ranger station. Running almost parallel to Sally Ward Trail, Hammock Trail takes a wider path for 1.3 miles. Visitors can request a trail map for these trails at the ranger station or inside the lodge. Another trail, a 7-mile multiuse pathway, begins at the park entrance and ends at County Road 365, where horse trailer parking is available.

In Big Bend WMA, more than 100 miles of roads and forest trams are open to hikers and off-road bicyclists. Equestrians may ride on any named or numbered roads, but in the Snipe Island Unit, only when there aren't any scheduled hunts. In fact, anyone using the trails should be aware of hunt dates; contact the Big Bend headquarters or the Florida Fish and Wildlife Conservation Commission (FWC) for information.

Nearby, the paved Tallahassee-St. Marks Trail (850-922-6007) follows the 16 miles that once was the historic Tallahassee-St. Marks Railroad line connecting the state capital with the port at St. Marks. The trail is a state park open from 9 a.m. to 5 p.m. Walkers and those on bikes, horses, or skates are welcome, and it's free. The trail can be accessed at several points. Find the main trailhead parking lot at Capital Circle (State Road 319) and Woodville Highway (SR 363).

Paddling and Boating

With all of the water throughout the Big Bend, heading out on a boat is a sure bet for getting acquainted with the area. Boat ramps are located in every unit of St. Marks National Wildlife Refuge, providing access to Apalachee Bay and the Gulf of Mexico. The boat ramp at Otter Lake Recreation Area inside the Panacea Unit is for small boats only; motorized boats are limited to motors with ten horsepower or less. The refuge prohibits airboats and personal watercraft.

The highlight of water recreation in the area has to be the 105-mile Big Bend Saltwater Paddling Trail developed by the FWC. The trail begins at Econfina River State Park near Big Bend WMA and follows the undeveloped outer coastline to the town of Suwannee, mostly through Big Bend Seagrasses Aquatic Preserve. Along the way are quiet, primitive campsites exclusively for trail paddlers, often on islands in the gulf. The wilderness nature of the trail requires paddlers to be experienced in navigation. The state sells an excellent forty-page guidebook about the trail, including maps, for $15.00. Call the state at 850-488-5520 to order the guide and to reserve campsites along the trail (reservations required for camping).

For canoe, kayak, and boat rentals, there are several places to choose from. Try TNT Hideaway Inc. (850-925-6412) in Crawfordville not far from Wakulla Springs State Park, Riverside Café and Recreational Rentals (850-925-5668) in St. Marks on the St. Marks River or Sopchoppy Outfitters (850-962-2020; *www.sopchoppyoutfitters.com*) in Sopchoppy. Shell Island Fish Camp and Marina (850-925-6226; *www.shellislandfishcamp.com*) in St. Marks rents motorboats and provides fishing guide service upon request.

There is no boating or fishing allowed in Wakulla Springs State Park.

Guided Tours

Wakulla Springs does, however, offer pontoon boat tours along the Wakulla River. There are two tours: a thirty-minute glass-bottom boat tour that gives guests a view of the spring formation and cave mouth, and a forty-minute tour down the Wakulla River. Tickets are $6.00 for adults and $4.00 for children twelve and under. Boat charters for groups are also available with a special price. Boat tours leave regularly several times a day. The glass-bottom boat tour isn't offered when weather has reduced the visibility of the water.

Fishing charters are offered at marinas and fish camps in the region.

Nearby Natural Areas

Next to Big Bend WMA on the gulf is Econfina River State Park (850-922-6007). The 3,377-acre park at the mouth of the river provides a boat launch ($4.00), river overlook, and trails for hiking, off-road bicycling, or horseback riding. The park is mostly undeveloped, and few facilities are provided. To get there, take US 98 east from the St. Marks area (or west from Perry) to CR 14, and head south. The park is at the end of the road.

On the western side of the Big Bend, Ochlockonee River State Park (850-962-2771) in Sopchoppy covers 392 acres. Visitors can hike trails along the river and through the pine forest, camp, and launch a boat ($6.00 fee) not far from the gulf waters. The entrance fee is $3.00 per vehicle. To get there, take US 319 south from Tallahassee. Watch where it joins US 98, and take the turn toward Sopchoppy, staying on US 319. The park is 4 miles south of town on US 319.

Nearby is Bald Point State Park (850-349-9146) in Alligator Point. On Ochlockonee Bay, the park offers beach swimming, nature trails, and a small launch for canoes and kayaks. Admission is free. To get there, take US 98 west, then south from the St. Marks area toward Panacea. Continue past town for about 5 miles, then turn left (east) on SR 370 and travel another 5 miles to Bald Point Road. Turn left (north) onto Bald Point Road. The park is 3 miles ahead.

Both the Wacissa and Aucilla Rivers cross through Aucilla Wildlife Management Area (850-488-5520) north of Big Bend WMA. Like most WMAs, the land is used mainly for hunting. But paddling, hiking, off-road bicycling, and wildlife-watching are also open to visitors. Both rivers are designated state canoe trails. The Aucilla's rapids and the Wacissa's springs make them both interesting to paddle, although the state recommends that only experienced paddlers attempt the Aucilla. The Aucilla Sinks Trail—a section of the Florida National Scenic Trail—leads to a series of sinks where the river disappears, then reappears again. Fat-tire bikers can explore 10 miles of old back roads. All trail users should use maps, be aware of hunt dates, and know that trails may be closed during scheduled hunts. Wildlife-watchers may spot bobcats, Florida black bears, gopher tortoises, Suwannee cooters, bald eagles, limpkins, and black-crowned night herons. There is no entrance fee. The WMA is about 15 miles south of Tallahassee and 17 miles west of Perry. To get there, take US 98 west from Perry. Entry points are located along here and to the north on intersecting Powell Hammock Road.

Nearby Attractions

San Marcos de Apalache Historic State Park (850-922-6007) is the site of a Civil War skirmish, when Confederates claimed the fort in 1861. The Spanish built the first fort here in 1679, then rebuilt it in 1718. Work on a third fort (this time made of stone) was started in 1739. Visitors can walk through the fort ruins. Admission to the park is free, but the park museum charges $1.00 for those 7 and older. The park is open from 9 a.m. to 5 p.m. Thursday through Monday. The park is on Old Fort Road in St. Marks near the southern end of SR 363 (Woodville Highway).

Nearby, Natural Bridge Battlefield Historic State Park (850-922-6007) was also a Civil War battle scene. According to the park, the five-day battle in early March 1865 ended when a Confederate militia defeated Union troops, making Tallahassee the only Confederate capital in the east that the Union never captured. Re-enactments and living history demonstrations are sometimes scheduled. To get there, take SR 363 (Woodville Highway) south from Tallahassee to Natural Bridge Road. Turn left (east) and travel for 6 miles to the park. Admission is free, but donations are accepted.

Wildlife

The Big Bend area is a favorite for bird-watchers who want to catch a glimpse of birds they're not likely to see in many other parts of Florida, particularly waterfowl species. Wakulla Springs honors its winged inhabitants by hosting the annual Wakulla Birding and Wildlife Festival, usually in April. The festival features talks and field trips focusing on wildlife—not just birds but other animals like frogs, bats, and turtles—as well as regional native plants.

In St. Marks National Wildlife Refuge, more than 300 species of birds live in or visit the wetlands and uplands. The impoundments are good for viewing any of the wintering waterfowl species, such as mallards and canvasbacks. The refuge has counted other types of wildlife, too, mentioning in its brochure fifty-two species of mammals (like Florida black bears and white-tailed deer), forty species of amphibians, and sixty-five species of reptiles.

Of its wildlife, St. Marks is home to several endangered and threatened species. Bald eagles nest here in winter. Red-cockaded woodpeckers nest in the refuge's Panacea Unit south of Sopchoppy. Wood storks show up in late spring, then leave in the fall. Manatees frequent the bay from spring to fall—look for them around the lighthouse in May, the refuge says. Loggerhead, green, and leatherback sea turtles visit refuge waters; loggerheads are known to have nested here.

One of the more famous species at St. Marks is the monarch butterfly. Thousands of monarchs visit the refuge in October as they migrate as many as 2,000 miles from northern states to Mexico for the winter. However, with the arrival of mosquito-borne West Nile virus, a warm-weather threat to people and animals, the spraying of Dibrom or other insecticides that kill mosquitoes also can harm butterflies (and other beneficial insects like honeybees). Other threats to the monarchs are loss of forest habitat in their Mexico wintering sites and possible climate change. Monarch look-alike Gulf fritillary and viceroy butterflies also come to the refuge.

At Big Bend WMA, the Hickory Mound and Tide Swamp tracts are good for wildlife-watching, particularly at Hickory Mound's observation tower on the bay and the impoundments. In winter, look for shorebirds like herons, egrets, plovers, willets, and dowitchers, and waterfowl like blue-winged teals, wigeons, mergansers, and various ducks. Summertime brings swallow-tailed and Mississippi kites.

Look for . . .

If the Florida panther is the state's most famous feline, then the bobcat is merely Florida's "other cat." Bobcats are named for their "bobbed" tail, a short three to five inches that sets it apart from most cats, which usually have long tails. Wildlife-watchers can distinguish a panther from a bobcat not only by the tail length but also by its overall size; bobcats are much smaller at about three feet long and thirty pounds. Bobcats also have small tufts of hair on the tips of their ears and a ruff of fur on their cheeks.

Bobcats range throughout the state, not just in the Big Bend area, but plenty of them are at home here in the swamps and forested areas—perhaps up on a tree limb. St. Marks refuge literature says the best time to spot a bobcat is in January in the early morning or late afternoon.

Like housecats, bobcats spend most of the day sleeping. They are more active at night, when they hunt for birds and small mammals like rodents. They also prey on young deer, according to the FWC. Although they are small, bobcats are important as predators, a necessary part of the web of life.

Habitats

Eight rivers join the Gulf of Mexico in the Big Bend area—Ochlockonee, Sopchoppy, Wakulla, St. Marks, Wacissa, Aucilla, Econfina, and Fenholloway Rivers—in addition to numerous creeks and sloughs that empty here. Some of these rivers begin in springs like the Wakulla and Wacissa, some run from lakes like the Ochlockonee, and some are born in swamps like the Econfina.

All of these freshwater inputs make the area an important estuary. The northernmost part of this bend is Apalachee Bay, directly south of the town of St. Marks and almost entirely protected by the refuge. In fact, the refuge states that 70 percent of its holdings are wetlands. In Apalachee Bay and the Gulf of Mexico, freshwater and saltwater species mingle. Food and shelter attract fish, birds, and mammals in a rich web of life.

Beyond the coastal wetlands are forested swamps, wet and dry pine flatwoods, wet and dry hammocks, and scrub communities that attract even more kinds of wildlife and act as buffers between human developments and the sea.

The presence of springs is evidence of karst, a terrain where water drains through limestone into the ground or where springs push water up from the ground. Underground caverns, caves, and sinkholes are common in karst topography. There aren't as many springs here as there are along the Suwannee River, and you won't find the caves as you do to the north around Marianna, but the springs here are so close to the gulf. Also, Florida's largest spring (in terms of water flow) is here near Spring Creek. This is a submarine spring, whose opening is under water.

Where to Stay

Campgrounds

Ochlockonee River State Park (above) has a campground with thirty campsites, all with electric and water hookups available. For reservations, contact ReserveAmerica.

Near the entrance to the main St. Marks tract is Newport Park (850-925-4530), a Wakulla County park where camping is allowed. Situated on the St. Marks River, the campground has eight sites with full hookups and thirty primitive sites. Reservations aren't required, but they are recommended in the fall when Apalachicola National Forest hunters camp here. The park has a boat ramp on the river for canoes, kayaks, and small motorboats.

Shell Island Fish Camp and Marina (under Paddling and Boating, above) allows RV camping. Econfina River Resort (850-584-2135; *www.econfina riverresort.com*) near the entrance of Econfina River State Park has sixty-five RV campsites with full hookups. There is also a tent camping area separate from the RV campground. The resort features a bathhouse, camp store, clubhouse with pool, and laundry facility in a natural setting.

In Perry, Southern Oaks RV Campground (800-339-5421) has ninety-seven campsites and a dump station. Cabins and trailers are available for rent.

Camping is allowed in designated campgrounds and throughout nearby Apalachicola National Forest. Please see chapter 5 for more information.

Lodging

The lodge in Wakulla Springs State Park, completed in 1937, is a simple but well-furnished inn with rooms from $75.00. A grand lobby with a huge fireplace and painted ceiling rafters is a nice place to relax in the evening or during poor weather (when you might not want to be outside in the park). A restaurant next to the lobby serves breakfast, lunch, and dinner at appointed hours. For more information and reservations, contact the park directly.

In St. Marks, try the Sweet Magnolia Inn (800-779-5214; *www.sweet magnolia.com*), a bed-and-breakfast with seven guest rooms. In Perry, there is a Days Inn (800-329-7466) on the town's main road, US 19. Farther down the coast in Keaton Beach, Captain's Quarters Lodge (850-578-2850; *www.keaton beach.org/lodgecq.htm*) offers furnished units on the water, along with dock access. Even farther south in Steinhatchee, try the riverfront Steinhatchee Outpost (800-589-1541; *www.steinhatcheeoutpost.com*), which rents cottages, along with canoes, kayaks, and bicycles. At Shell Island Fish Camp and Marina (under Paddling and Boating, above), there is a motel and four cabins available for rent. Econfina River Resort (above) has an inn with eight rooms and three furnished apartments to rent.

More lodging facilities are in Tallahassee and Panacea.

How to Get There

The various tracts of St. Marks National Wildlife Refuge are spread out; it's best to arrive at the visitor center for maps and directions to all of the tracts. To get there, take I-10 to Exit #217 (SR 59) east of Tallahassee and head south. At US 98, it joins with SR 59 for about 5 miles going west (turn right). A refuge sign shows where SR 59 becomes its own road again; follow it to the visitor center and on down to the lighthouse on the gulf.

To get to Wakulla Springs, take I-10 Exit #203 (SR 61/Thomasville Road) and go south through Tallahassee for about 18 miles. Turn left at SR 267, then travel about a mile to the park entrance on the right.

The Hickory Mount unit of Big Bend WMA is next to Econfina River State Park about 18 miles west of Perry. To get to the observation tower, turn south off US 98 at Cow Creek Grade. The tower is about 8 miles ahead. Cow Creek Grade is a dirt road best accessed by rugged vehicles. After heavy rain, the road can be muddy and difficult to drive. To access trails and back roads, please use a map.

The Tide Swamp unit of the WMA is located south of Perry. From the St. Marks area, take US 98 east through Perry, turning south where the highway does. At CR 361, turn right and drive 22 miles to Hagen's Cove Road. Turn right to find a parking area 1.5 miles ahead. Please refer to a Tide Swamp map when accessing trails and back roads.

❧   ❧   ❧

St. Marks National Wildlife Refuge
P.O. Box 68
St. Marks, Florida 32355
Phone: 850-925-6121
saintmarks.fws.gov
The St. Marks Unit, where the headquarters office is, charges $4.00 per vehicle. The Aucilla Unit charges a $2.00 boat-launching fee. Otherwise, the refuge is free. Like most national wildlife refuges, visitors are allowed only during day-light hours.

Edward Ball Wakulla Springs State Park
550 Wakulla Park Drive
Wakulla Springs, Florida 32327
Phone: 850-224-5950
Admission is $4.00 per vehicle.

Big Bend Wildlife Management Area
633 Plantation Road
Perry, Florida 32348
Phone: 850-488-5520

Florida's Big Bend area covers hundreds of miles of coastline on the Gulf of Mexico. State and federal natural lands protect the shore, beautifully fringed by coastal marsh grasses at the base of the important Apalachee Bay estuary. Uplands and lowlands are graced with diverse wildlife and plant species.

Nearby

Apalachicola National Forest (chapter 5), Lower Suwannee River (chapter 9)

8

Upper Suwannee River

Way down upon the S'wannee River . . .

It is the home of gators and the Gators, of Civil War and turpentining history, ranches and forests, rivers and springs, and lonely stretches of roads.

Far, far away . . .

It's the first bit of Florida that many out-of-state travelers see as they head south on I-75 in search of warmer temperatures and sunny skies.

There's where my heart is turning ever . . .

It's where pioneers settled and where displaced Native Americans ran before escaping farther away, into the Everglades.

There's where the old folks stay . . .

It's the land where the Suwannee River rolls south from Georgia's Okefenokee Swamp through what's known as the Original Florida, a part of the state that embodies the environment and history of what Florida used to be.

As the state song, written by Stephen Foster more than a hundred years ago, proclaims, this is a restful land with comforting people. Appropriately, a state park dedicated to Foster and Florida's folk history is here in the Original Florida, in White Springs. Stephen Foster State Folk Culture Center has beautiful colonial-style buildings in which you can attend classes and lectures about folk arts and crafts, and one of the best campgrounds in the state park system, right on the Suwannee. Nearby Big Shoals State Park is named for the large rocks in the river that make for a mile of Class III rapids. Farther downstream near Live Oak, Suwannee River State Park stands where the Withlacoochee River meets the Suwannee on its way to the Gulf of Mexico.

Steps away from the Foster park stands the state of Florida's headquarters for nature and heritage tourism. The Florida Nature and Heritage Tourism Center offers brochures about any kind of nature travel in the state. Visitors can stop in and ask questions about what to do and where to do it.

Chances are that a lot of what you want to do is here along the Suwannee, whether your interest is wildlife-watching, hiking, paddling, snorkeling, diving, camping, relaxing, or even history searching. There's a national forest,

Figure 7. Ocean Pond in Osceola National Forest is ringed by cypress trees.

several state parks, and enough water to turn you into a prune many times over.

What to Do There

The Suwannee River winds through 207 miles in Florida, and the upper part of this river valley covers a lot of territory. If you do visit all of these natural areas, you'll end up doing a good deal of driving. But think of it as a scenic driving tour, and you'll see a lot of the Original Florida along the way. So fill up the tank, take a long weekend and plan on seeing the back roads of Old Florida. Driving the scenic roads is more than a means to an end because of the landscape's beauty, but you'll want to get out and explore.

Trail Tripping

Hikers can traipse through many of the 1,800 acres in Suwannee River State Park on a series of trails that tell as much about the river's nature as they do its history. The park was once the site of a town called Columbus, and you can see remnants of the town, such as earthworks and a cemetery. The town was deserted after steamboats were no longer necessary for transporting goods up and down the Suwannee.

The Suwannee River Trail is a short trail that runs along the riverbank and points out the park's flora and fauna with signs along the way. Other connecting trails make for about a 1.5-mile loop. The Sandhills Trail partly traces what was once a major road between Jacksonville and Pensacola in the 1800s. The longer Big Oak Trail crosses the river and connects with the Florida National Scenic Trail. About 4.5 miles of the Florida Trail come through here. You could hike from Suwannee River State Park to Stephen Foster State Park (and beyond) if you cared to do a multiday backpacking trip. Contact the Florida Trail Association for maps and more information.

Big Shoals State Park trails intertwine over 33 miles of varying territory. High ridges, ravines, and wetland forests make hiking here—and all along the Suwannee—a real change of pace from the rest of mostly flat Florida. The trails are also open to horseback riders. Note that unlike most state parks, Big Shoals is managed by several other government agencies in addition to the Florida State Parks, and hunting is allowed here at times.

At Stephen Foster, the 4-mile Carter Camp Trail is open to hikers, equestrians, and off-road cyclists. Channeling through pines along the river, the trail connects with the Florida Trail.

The hiking is good at other Suwannee-area parks; see more under Nearby Natural Areas.

There are several venomous snakes in the area, so watch your step on the trails, particularly in summer, when snakes tend to be more active.

Paddling and Boating

The best and most popular way to explore the Suwannee River, a state canoe trail, is of course by boat. Paddle a section of the Suwannee for a day, or plan a paddling trip down the river's length for one or two weeks. Cabins and wilderness camps are planned for the length of the Suwannee River Wilderness Trail (800-868-9914; *www.floridastateparks.org/wilderness*) in a five-year project to enhance nature tourism in the area. Local outfitters and guides will help you with an excursion that fits your schedule and experience. If you prefer to use a motorboat, note that the extreme upper reaches of the river may not be deep enough for boats with a high draft, particularly during the winter dry season.

Suwannee River State Park, with the confluence of the Withlacoochee and Suwannee Rivers, is a good place to put in. Although there is a boat launch in the park, rentals aren't available here. (This Withlacoochee River is different from the one that flows through the Ocala area; there are two rivers with the same name.)

At Big Shoals where the Suwannee rapids are, paddlers have about 6 miles of the river to take in. When the water level is low, paddlers are advised to portage over the shoals rather than stay in their boats. Farther downstream is a smaller rocky outcropping called Little Shoals.

Stephen Foster focuses mostly on Suwannee history and culture, but it recognizes the calling of the river to those who want to navigate it. Rentals are available near the park.

Rentals are available at Suwannee Canoe Outpost near Suwannee River State Park (800-428-4147; *www.canoeoutpost.com*), which rents canoes for the Suwannee, the Withlacoochee, and Georgia's Alapaha River. The outpost isn't open on Wednesdays. American Canoe Adventures (386-397-1309; *www.aca1. com*), near Stephen Foster and Big Shoals State Parks, offers canoes, kayaks, and bicycles, and is closed Tuesdays and Wednesdays. Both outfitters provide shuttles throughout the area for a fee. Suwannee Expeditions Canoe and Kayak (800-961-3164; *www.canoeflorida.com*) near Troy Spring State Park is closer to the lower Suwannee, but it offers rentals for the river as well as nearby Santa Fe River, a Suwannee tributary.

As an alternative to paddling the Suwannee, you can rent a houseboat for a vacation on the river. Because of the boat's size, this trip is good for a family or group of friends. Contact Miller's Suwannee Riverboats (800-458-BOAT; *www.suwanneehouseboats.com*) for more information.

Diving and Snorkeling

It might seem funny to see wet-suited scuba divers descending on a part of Florida where the forests and cattle ranches are an hour or more from the ocean. But they visit for what you can't see, unless you go under ground: underwater caves.

In northern Florida's interesting geology, the limestone foundation gives way in many places to sinks and caves—many of them underwater. Few people can (or care to) do it, but cave diving is one of the most adventurous ways to explore nature here; many people call the area the "cave diving capital of the United States." Divers usually enter caves through springs.

In fact, one of the largest underwater cave systems in the United States is here, primarily under Peacock Springs State Park (386-497-2511) in tiny Luraville, where divers explore more than 28,000 feet of underwater caves in water that offers very good visibility. At sister state park Troy Spring in Branford (386-935-4835), the 70-foot depth of the spring attracts divers here as well. If you are interested in diving at either park, you are required to go with a buddy and be cavern certified (even divers with open-water certification aren't allowed), as a result of the deaths that have occurred here and in other underwater caves in northern Florida. Local dive shops provide equipment and lessons. If you are in the minority of Peacock Springs or Troy Spring park visitors who don't dive, you can still go to snorkel or swim and admire the springs and sinks. Admission is $2.00 per vehicle for up to eight people, and there is an extra $5.00 fee for those who want to dive.

Other nearby underwater caves to dive and springs to snorkel in are at Blue Hole Springs at Ichetucknee Springs State Park and Ginnie Springs. (See the Nearby Natural Areas section below.)

Dive shops in the area include Steamboat Dive Inn in Branford (386-935-CAVE), Cave Excursions in Live Oak (386-776-2299; *www.sidemount.com*) and Spring Systems Dive Outpost (386-776-1449) in Luraville not far from the entrance to Peacock Springs State Park.

Guided Tours

Outfitters mentioned under Paddling and Boating above also lead guided tours on the area's rivers.

Suwannee Canoe Outpost near Live Oak leads weekend-long tours of the Suwannee by reservation. All gear and meals are provided.

American Canoe Adventures in White Springs offers three-day paddling trips along the Suwannee from Fargo, Georgia, to White Springs, Florida. Paddlers can ask for custom trips all the way to the Gulf of Mexico.

Suwannee Expeditions Canoe and Kayak in Branford offers various guided day trips and canoe camping trips; contact the outfitter.

Adventure Outpost in High Springs (386-454-0611; *www.adventureoutpost. net*) also leads numerous trips on the region's waterways, including the Suwannee, Santa Fe, and Ichetucknee Rivers. Contact the outpost for a calendar of upcoming trips, or ask for a customized tour.

Santa Fe Canoe Outpost in High Springs (386-454-2050; *www.santaferiver. com*) guides paddlers down the Santa Fe and Suwannee Rivers in a three- or four-day trip. Also ask about full moon tours on the Santa Fe.

River tour guides recommend making a reservation for your trip.

Nearby Natural Areas

There are several ecologically significant areas in the Original Florida near the Suwannee River. There are also wonderful places where you can explore Florida's history.

Osceola National Forest (386-752-2577) is the smallest national forest in Florida, but it covers 200,000 acres. The forest is home to Florida black bears and red-cockaded woodpeckers, both threatened species in the state of Florida. In the winter, the forest is filled with the songs of American robins, which arrive in large flocks. One way to see the forest is to plan a route along the forest roads that go through pines and cypress swamps. Some of the roads are paved, but most of them aren't, and you could really get turned around if you don't have a map. So be sure to stop by the well-marked Osceola National Forest main office—just a few miles east of Lake City on US 90—or write or call ahead to request a free tabloid-format publication called *The Sunshine Connection*, which has articles, photos, and tips for all the national forests in Florida and includes maps of the forest roads. The maps are also essential for hiking or riding trails on horseback. The Florida Trail meanders through, and the forest offers trails of its own, like those that loop around 13,000-acre Big Gum Swamp, a nationally recognized wilderness area. Be aware that hunting is allowed in the forest in certain seasons. If you have your own boat, you may want to explore Ocean Pond, the forest's main recreation area, where a boat ramp on the southern shore attracts anglers and water-skiers alike. There is a fee for parking. To get there, take I-75 to Lake City and exit at US 90 (Exit #427). Go east about 10 miles and watch for signs. The Olustee Depot, a good place to pick up forest maps and brochures, is about 20 miles east of I-75 on US 90.

Ichetucknee Springs State Park in Fort White (386-497-4690) is the site of several springs and recognized as a National Natural Landmark. The park is known for its tubing down the Ichetucknee River (from Memorial Day through Labor Day), but here you can also snorkel, swim, paddle, hike, and dive. Diving is allowed in Blue Hole Spring from October through March for certified cave divers only. To get there, take State Road 47 south from Lake City for about 15 miles to US 27, or exit I-75 at US 441 (Exit #399), go west, and watch for signs. The park is located about 15 miles northwest of High Springs.

At O'Leno State Park (386-454-1853), something unusual happens to the Santa Fe River. It disappears, flows underground for 3 miles, then reappears again in River Rise Preserve, inside the state park. You can see where the river disappears by walking on the River Trail. There are more than 13 miles of trails for hiking, biking, and horseback riding here. You also can canoe on the Santa Fe and get rentals right in the park. To get there, take US 441 south from Lake

City for about 15 miles, or exit I-75 at US 441 (Exit #399), go west, and watch for signs.

Ginnie Springs Outdoors in High Springs (386-454-7188; *www.ginnie springsoutdoors.com*) is a veritable outdoor resort. On the bank of the Santa Fe River, the 200-acre resort's focus is on the seven springs that are 72 degrees year-round, attracting snorkelers, divers, and swimmers. Here, you'll find a lot of what state parks offer—a campground, boat ramp, picnic pavilions, equipment rentals, and volleyball courts—plus a restaurant, laundry facilities, bathhouses, and a rental cottage. Admission is $10.00 for adults and $3.00 for children seven to fourteen, which doesn't cover the cost of activities.

Nearby Attractions

Olustee Battlefield Historic State Park (386-758-0400) east of Lake City is the site of an annual re-enactment (every February) of the largest Civil War battle fought in Florida, in 1864. Monuments to soldiers from the North and the South, along with a small museum, are here. Admission is free. The park interpretive center is open daily from 9 a.m. until 5 p.m. To get there, exit I-75 at US 90 (Exit #427) and travel approximately 20 miles to the park. Olustee Battlefield is located on US 90 15 miles east of Lake City.

Florida Sports Hall of Fame in Lake City (386-758-1310) displays exhibits on Florida athletes. The museum is open Tuesday through Saturday from 9 a.m. until 4 p.m. Admission is $3.00. To get there, exit I-75 at US 90 (Exit #427) and go west for about a mile to Hall of Fame Drive. Turn right (north) and watch for signs.

Wildlife

The Suwannee River winds through a good deal of preserved land where wildlife roam. The 2002 approval of the acquisition of Pinhook Swamp north of Osceola National Forest will create what some call the Suwannee River Wildlife Corridor. The idea of a wildlife corridor is that animals are able to move through wild lands without having the interruption of cities and towns in between. Pinhook Swamp will connect the forest with Okefenokee Swamp National Wildlife Refuge in southern Georgia (and a sliver of Florida). The purchase was seen as especially good for Florida black bears, which live in the area.

Also in the forest and other area uplands, you can see many kinds of woodland birds. The Great Florida Birding Trail's River Bluffs Cluster, Flatwoods and Falls Cluster, and Warbler Woods Cluster cover the natural areas here, where the trail guide says you might see magnolia warblers, Bachman's sparrows, Acadian flycatchers, and Swainson's thrushes, particularly during the winter.

Look for . . .

You might see beavers along the Suwannee, or at least evidence of their presence: gnawed-up tree trunks or beaver dams, where they live. A symbol of Canada, beavers nonetheless do live in northern Florida.

At thirty to fifty pounds, beavers are the state's largest rodent and, like most rodents, they are most active at night. Their thick fur, webbed back feet, and flat tail make them good swimmers, while their sharp teeth make them good builders—they can chew through trees up to twelve inches in diameter. Beavers use trees for food and shelter, but their dams can cause flooding. Beavers also sometimes eat crops. Because of these two factors, some people consider beavers to be pests.

Habitats

To appreciate northern Florida's natural environment, it helps to start with its geology. A limestone foundation and the huge Floridan aquifer create the perfect environment for caves, sinks, ravines, and the like, which are crisscrossed by rivers and streams formed by swamps and springs. Although low areas like swamps are common, the elevation is generally higher here than in central and southern Florida.

Big Gum Swamp is one of the largest examples of a northern Florida swamp. According to interpretive signs at Big Gum Swamp, its water level varies throughout the year from three feet above the ground to a few inches below the "spongy mat of material" of the swamp floor. Through a series of smaller swamps, it is linked to Pinhook Swamp to the north, which in turn is linked to Okefenokee Swamp farther to the north. This swamp system is the birthplace of not only the Suwannee River but also the St. Marys River, which forms part of the Florida/Georgia border and flows into the Atlantic Ocean.

You might not know it from looking at the mature trees in the area, but turpentining and lumbering were important industries here from the late 1800s until the early 1900s. Settlers took advantage of the fact that Florida was 90 percent covered by forest, much of it pines from which turpentine could be extracted. You will still see evidence of clear-cutting in areas like the Pinhook Swamp, but most of the land has returned to a natural state.

Forests of slash and longleaf pine are prominent throughout the area, giving way to a sandhill habitat. Sandhills and a xeric (dry) hammock surround

Peacock Springs State Park, while a mesic (wet) hammock has been established at Big Shoals. Live oaks, draped with Spanish moss, are a common sight and one that says, "You are in the South."

Wildflowers bloom at different times during the year, but especially in the spring around March and April.

Where to Stay

Campgrounds

Suwannee River State Park has thirty campsites with the standard picnic table, grill, and electricity. Hot showers are in restrooms nearby, and RVs can use the dump station. The park also has two youth camping areas for organized groups. Contact the park about primitive backcountry campsites, and Reserve-America for campground reservations.

The campground at Stephen Foster has to be one of the best at a Florida state park. Not only is the park simply beautifully maintained, but the campground is laid out well and sheltered by just the right number of old live oak trees, providing some shade and yet allowing sunlight through. There are forty-five campsites. Contact ReserveAmerica for reservations and information.

There are numerous places to camp in Osceola National Forest. The campground with the most facilities is Ocean Pond, where the fifty or so sites can fill up quickly. Olustee Beach Campground on the other side of the pond is another choice. There are eight primitive campgrounds throughout the forest, some of which have drinking water and outhouses. No reservations are taken for any campsites. The east and west tower campgrounds and Hog Pen Landing Campground (near Ocean Pond) charge $2.00 per vehicle per night.

O'Leno State Park has sixty-one campsites in two loops. The Magnolia Campground is near the river, while the Dogwood Campground is closer to the entrance on US 441. The group camping area is attractive for assemblies because it offers seventeen cabins, and dining and recreation halls. (The state park says the cabins are available to individuals during the off-season, September to May.) Contact ReserveAmerica for camping information.

Spirit of the Suwannee Music Park (386-364-1683; *www.musicliveshere. com*) is a private park on the Suwannee River known for its live concerts. Whether it's blues, gospel, or folk music, Spirit of the Suwannee draws people in. It's also the site of the Suwannee Canoe Outpost (mentioned above). Horseback trail rides, dinner cruises, a café, craft village, wedding chapel, and swimming pool make this a unique park. There are various camping options here: tents, RVs, horse corrals, cottages, and even a treehouse. Besides camping fees, admission is $2.00 per person or $5.00 per vehicle.

Jim Hollis' River Rendezvous (800-533-5276; *www.jimhollis.com*) in Mayo near Peacock Springs offers camping with full hookups. It also has a lodge, cabins, and cottages. This is a good campground for divers because it holds diving classes and has a full dive shop.

Ginnie Springs Outdoors, mentioned above under Nearby Natural Areas, also offers camping. Contact Ginnie Springs for more information.

Lodging

There are plenty of chain hotels and motels to choose from in Lake City, like Jameson Inn (386-758-8440; *www.jamesoninns.com*), which is close to I-75 and includes self-serve breakfast. Le Chateau (386-294-2332; *www.southern chateau.com*) in Mayo near Peacock Springs was the Lafayette County court-house from 1883 to 1907. Since 1995, it has been an inn. It also serves dinner on Fridays and Saturdays. The Old Townsend House B&B (386-496-1187) in Lake Butler south of Lake City has four rooms.

How to Get There

Suwannee River State Park is 13 miles west of Live Oak. Take I-10 to US 90 (Exit #275) and head northwest. Watch for signs to the entrance of the park, which is on County Road 132.

The Stephen Foster park is about 15 miles northwest of Lake City. Take I-75 to SR 136 (Exit #439) and go east about 3 miles. Turn left (north) on US 41. The park entrance is on the left, across from the Nature and Heritage Tourism Center.

Big Shoals is close to Stephen Foster. Turn right (east) at US 41, then left (north) on CR 135, about a mile distance. The Little Shoals entrance is about 5 miles ahead, and Big Shoals is another 4.5 miles after that.

⊷   ⊷   ⊷

Suwannee River State Park
20185 County Road 132
Live Oak, Florida 32060
Phone: 386-362-2746
Entrance fee is $2.00 per vehicle.

Stephen Foster Folk Culture Center State Park
Post Office Drawer G
White Springs, Florida 32096
386-397-2733
Admission is $4.00 per vehicle or $3.00 for vehicles with a single occupant.

Big Shoals State Park
386-397-4331
Big Shoals is managed by nearby Stephen Foster park service personnel and several other government agencies.

The Suwannee River flows south from Georgia through what's known as the Original Florida, where sixty springs add to the flow and create a network of underwater caves. This is where the first Florida settlers came, and the history, culture, and nature of the land are preserved in several natural areas along the river and in nearby areas.

Nearby

Lower Suwannee River (chapter 9), Land of the Caves, Sinks, and Ravines (chapter 12)

9

Lower Suwannee River

For a river with such rich history and with such a prominent place in the culture of northern Florida, the Suwannee seems humble. It's homey. It runs past forests, winds on around fields, flows by small towns without any fanfare. This quiet, steadfast nature of the Suwannee adds to the character of the region. Or perhaps the region has given this character to the river, from the Timucuan natives to the explorers, pioneers, and settlers who have all been nourished by the river in some way. The Suwannee is a life force.

About midway, the Suwannee takes up the Santa Fe River and rolls with spring runs toward the Gulf of Mexico. Along the way, several natural areas stand on its banks, offering entrée to anyone who wants to take in this life.

At the river's mouth, Lower Suwannee National Wildlife Refuge claims more than 52,000 acres of land and 26 miles of gulf-front property. Because of this size, the refuge can maintain that it is one of the biggest river delta/estuarine systems in the country still in its natural state. The refuge straddles the river and several tidal creeks, protecting the rich life and beauty of the coastal marsh.

The Suwannee refuge also manages neighboring Cedar Keys National Wildlife Refuge to the south. This refuge, about 800 acres, is spread over 13 islands off the coast of the town of Cedar Key. Seahorse Key, Snake Key, Deadman's Key, and North Key are considered wilderness areas where large colonies of nesting birds gather on the protected islands. Most refuge visitors aim for Atsena Otie Key, which is just offshore from town, and the only refuge island with a hiking trail.

Upriver, Manatee Springs State Park in Chiefland is another place to encounter the Suwannee. The park's main attraction is its spring, one of Florida's 27 first-magnitude springs (more than any other state), releasing from 50 to 155 million gallons of water every day. (A first-magnitude spring is one that releases at least 64 million gallons of water each day.) The park also has several miles of trails through its uplands.

Exploring these main natural areas is a great way to experience the Suwannee's life.

Figure 8. Lower Suwannee National Wildlife Refuge and Cedar Keys National Wildlife Refuge provide sweeping views of coastal marsh.

What to Do There

The Suwannee River and its springs are the natural focal points for outdoor recreation here. The area's natural lands also include uplands that are important habitats of the river valley. Nature travelers should experience both water and land to get a feel for the area's natural character.

Trail Tripping

Lower Suwannee National Wildlife Refuge has a few designated trails. Near the headquarters (which is south of the river) is the River Trail and Boardwalk, about a half-mile walk through a swamp to the river's edge, where there's an overlook. Wildflowers bloom along the sides of the trail. Closer to the river, the swamp trail can take on a haunting look, especially on overcast days. Down the road from the headquarters is the Shell Mound Unit, where hikers will find the Shell Mound (one-third mile) and Dennis Creek (1 mile) loop trails in this area of coastal marsh and hammocks.

North of the river near the town of Suwannee, the refuge offers the short Salt Creek Boardwalk Trail (off County Road 349) and Fishbone Creek Trail (at the end of CR 357). Both trails lead to grand views of the gulf's coastal marshes.

The refuge also allows hiking and off-road bicycling on any of its 100 miles of back roads; trail trippers will want to use a refuge map. No horses are allowed.

Manatee Springs has 8.5 miles of trails for hiking and off-road bicycling. The half-mile Sink Trail near the campground leads to sinks and through a beautiful oak and palmetto hammock. The other trails are accessed from the trailhead parking area on the main park road, across from the youth camp. Here, interconnecting trails wander through sandhills and near ponds. Hikers can request a trail map at the ranger station.

For almost 32 miles, Nature Coast Trail State Park (352-493-6072) runs along the route of a former railroad. The paved trail is open to foot, bicycle, and horse traffic. The trail begins near Manatee Springs in Chiefland, heads north through Fanning Springs, then splits east to Trenton and west to Cross City. All of these communities have trailheads with restroom facilities. Contact the Florida Office of Greenways and Trails Web site for a map.

Paddling and Boating

The Suwannee River and the shallow gulf area at its mouth are favorable to canoeing and kayaking. There are several boat ramps along the length of the river.

The refuge has a designated paddling trail that follows Suwannee River as well as tributaries Shingle Creek, Rock Creek, and Demory Creek. From the boat ramp at the end of McKinney Drive in the town of Suwannee, paddlers can take in salt marshes, Indian middens, and several species of birds. Request a map at the headquarters, or find it on the refuge Web site. Of course, refuge waters are all open to paddling and boating except where posted to protect wildlife or fragile habitats. A refuge map shows the locations of boat ramps.

Manatee Springs State Park is a good place to access the river. The park is about 23 miles from the river's mouth, by water. The Manatee Spring run empties directly into the Suwannee, where a dock sits at the end of a boardwalk through the riverside swamp. (A former boat ramp area has been closed to further protect the spring run.) Canoes, kayaks, and boats are prohibited from entering the spring run during manatee season, November 30 through March 31.

The state park concession rents canoes, kayaks, and motorized boats by the hour or by the day. Visitors can also rent snorkeling equipment and fishing poles. Prices vary depending on the craft and the length of use. Reservations for rentals are recommended.

For an in-depth Suwannee River experience, paddlers can travel the river from Fort White to the Gulf of Mexico along the 207-mile Suwannee River Wilderness Trail (800-868-9914; *www.floridastateparks.org/wilderness*), developed by the state. Riverside campsites are set up along the route for multiday paddlers. Paddling the entire trail can take a week or more, but paddlers may travel any part of the river for shorter trips.

To spend a longer period of time on the Suwannee in comfort, consider gathering your family or a few friends and renting a houseboat from Miller's Suwannee Riverboats (800-458-BOAT; *www.suwanneehouseboats.com*) in Suwannee.

Check out the Upper Suwannee River (chapter 8) for more outfitters.

Snorkeling and Diving

At Manatee Springs, the springs' 72-degree water attracts swimmers, snorkelers, and divers year-round, particularly in the summer. Bordered by a paved wall and walkway, Manatee Spring appears like a swimming pool—although one with a great view in a natural setting.

Divers visit the spring and Catfish Hotel Sink just steps away. A cavern leads from the spring to the sink, then beyond. The underground cavern system has been mapped to about 26,000 feet away from the headspring. The sink is open only to divers. All divers must register with the park first and pay a $10.00 diving fee. Cave diving is limited to those with certification in cave diving, or to cave-diving instructors with students, requiring a commercial permit. Call ahead for more information.

Divers also visit private springs in nearby Williston to the east. Devil's Den (352-528-3344; *www.devilsden.com*) has a dive shop, campground, and cabin rentals. Blue Grotto (352-528-5770; *www.divebluegrotto.com*) also has a dive shop and provides picnic facilities.

See the Upper Suwannee River (chapter 8) for more springs to snorkel and dive along the river.

Scenic Driving

The refuge has a designated scenic drive north of the river. The Dixie Mainline Trail stretches for 9 miles between CR 349 and CR 357. On the road, you'll pass slash pine plantations, tidal creeks, cypress swamps, and marshes—good places to stop and look for wildlife. An interpretive guidebook accompanies the trail and is available at the refuge headquarters, at either end of the trail, or at the refuge Web site in PDF format. The scenic drive is also good for bicycling.

Guided Tours

The Manatee Springs concession Suwannee River Tours (877-362-3213; *www.suwanneerivertours.com*) leads several guided tours on the river, from two hours to two days. Tours may begin or end at Manatee Springs, or at other locations near the river for various tours.

Ancient Florida Outfitters (352-490-5830; *www.ancientfloridaecotours.com*) in Cedar Key is operated by a former national park ranger who leads paddling and hiking tours of the area. Indian mound tours are also available.

Cedar Key is also a place to find local boat tours. Captain Doug's Tidewater Tours (352-543-9523; *www.tidewatertours.com*) leads narrated tours into the surrounding backwaters to view wildlife and learn about the local environment and history. Cedar Key Island Hopper (352-543-5904; *www.cedarkeyislandhopper.com*) leaves from the Cedar Key City Marina to explore Seahorse Key and other islands in the Gulf of Mexico. Scenic sunset cruises are available.

To the south in the Nature Coast area (chapter 17) are a couple of outfitters that lead kayak tours of Cedar Keys refuge islands. Aardvark's Florida Kayak Company (352-795-5650; *www.floridakayakcompany.com*) in Crystal River and Riversport Kayaks (877-660-0929; *www.flakayak.com*) in Homosassa both offer paddling trips here.

Nearby Natural Areas

About 7 miles upriver from Manatee Springs is Fanning Springs State Park (352-463-3420). About fifty million gallons of the clear, 72-degree water bubble out of the springs each day. Here, the spring bowl is larger than Manatee Springs, and the spring run to the Suwannee River is shorter. The swimming area is impounded with a concrete wall. In season, visitors can rent canoes and kayaks at the park concession. Out of the water, park visitors can walk on a boardwalk near the springhead through a cypress swamp to the river. There is also a .75-mile nature trail through a mixed forest, where hikers might spot northern cardinals, gray foxes, white-tailed deer, and venomous coral snakes. Other paths also wind through the forested area. The entrance fee is $4.00 per vehicle, or $1.00 if arriving by water. To get here, go north about 7 miles from Chiefland on US 98 to the park entrance on the left.

Cedar Key Scrub State Reserve (352-543-5567) is an excellent example of the river valley's uplands. It's also a good example of scrub restoration, as reserve staff use prescribed fire to return the overgrown area to its natural state. Visitors can hike, bicycle, or ride horseback on the old Jeep trails, where coyotes and various woodland birds may appear. The entrance and trailhead parking area is on State Road 24 about 6 miles north of Cedar Key. To get here, take I-75 to the Gainesville area and exit at SR 24 (Exit #384). Head southwest toward Cedar Key and look for the entrance on the right. Admission is free.

The 3,500-acre riverfront Andrews Wildlife Management Area (352-493-6020) is mainly for hunting, but this bottomland hardwood hammock habitat is open to passive recreation when there are no scheduled hunts. Hike or bike along the dirt roads or nature trails; be sure to use a map from the Florida Fish and Wildlife Conservation Commission. The entrance to Andrews WMA is about 5 miles north of Chiefland, south of Fanning Springs State Park. To get here, take I-75 to the Gainesville area and exit at SR 26 (Exit #387). Head west for about 37 miles to US 98, then go west on NW 160th Street to the entrance. The day-use fee is $3.00 per person or $6.00 per vehicle.

Nearby Attractions

Cedar Key Museum State Park (352-543-5350) preserves the history of Cedar Key and early Florida. The main museum, a simple building, houses miniature dioramas of Civil War movements in the area. Visitors will learn about the town's previous location on an island offshore until a hurricane destroyed it, including the pencil factory that used the cedar trees for which the town is known. A newly restored home owned by late Cedar Key resident St. Clair Whitman invites visitors to view his personal collection of seashells, Cedar Key photographs, Timucuan artifacts, and more. The house is open from 1 p.m. to 4 p.m. Thursday through Monday. The state park is open Thursday through Monday from 9 a.m. to 5 p.m. Follow the directions above to get to Cedar Key, then watch for signs that show the way to the museum through a residential area. Admission is $1.00 for those six and older.

The town of Cedar Key itself is known for its fishing, quaint seafood restaurants, main street shops, and sunsets.

Wildlife

The Suwannee River and its surrounding habitats are home to several species of wildlife. White-tailed deer, coyotes, and even Florida black bears roam the lower Suwannee River region.

Of course, Manatee Springs is named for the manatees that visit in the winter. Manatees travel from the gulf up to the spring (and other springs on the Suwannee, including Fanning Springs), where the water is warmer. Manatees can die from cold stress, so they need to seek out warm waters. Spring runs often have patches of aquatic grasses they can eat, which is important because manatees spend several hours a day just eating. At Manatee Springs or Fanning Springs, visitors can view manatees from the docks during the cooler months, usually from November through March.

Bird-watchers can try to find as many of the 254 species of birds as they can in Lower Suwannee National Wildlife Refuge. The coastal marshes harbor wading birds like herons, egrets, and ibises. Also look for red-breasted mergansers, greater yellowlegs, spotted sandpipers, willets, dunlins, common snipes, eastern screech owls, barred owls, and chuck-will's-widows in the Suwannee area. Magnificent frigatebirds and swallow-tailed kites arrive for the summer. The refuge, Manatee Springs, Fanning Springs, Cedar Key Scrub State Reserve, and Andrews WMA—all of the natural areas here—are sites on the Great Florida Birding Trail's western section.

Look for . . .

Playfully tumbling along the riverbank or expertly diving into the water to catch a fish, river otters are fun to watch—if they would just stay still long enough. With a brown back and grayish or beige underside, they can be about four feet long and weigh up to twenty-five pounds. As members of the same family as skunks, they can spray an equally foul-smelling scent when alarmed.

Found in most parts of Florida (and throughout North America), these sleek swimmers have webbed toes to help them prey on their main food source, fish (like carp, crayfish, and catfish). Another fishing aid is their ability to stay underwater for up to four minutes. Otters may also eat reptiles, amphibians, and birds. In turn, they may become food for alligators.

Otters play and live on the water, creating burrows on the bank for their dens. Look for them at the edge of rivers, bays, and canals.

Habitats

Beginning in the Okefenokee Swamp in Georgia and winding south through northern Florida, the Suwannee River traverses different kinds of habitats before it meets the Gulf of Mexico. It cuts through sandhills, bluffs, hardwood hammocks, and even agricultural areas. Cypress swamps on the river's edge can make it hard to tell where the river really ends. Then, at the gulf, the river opens up to a wide horizon of coastal marshes softened by grasses and cabbage palms.

Along the way, sixty springs release water from the Floridan Aquifer that lies beneath northern Florida, contributing hundreds of millions of gallons of clear water to the river each day.

The Suwannee-area springs are beautiful and clear, but they are not all pure. Florida Department of Environmental Protection (DEP) water testing has shown high levels of nitrite/nitrate in Manatee Springs and Fanning Springs. According to the DEP, this is caused by "nitrogen loading," or the addition of nitrogen-based fertilizers to the region around a spring or sink (from lawn fertilizers or animal waste). Too much nitrogen in the water can increase algae and may become toxic, DEP reports have noted. Other pollutants like fuel spilled on the street can leach into the groundwater, affecting the springs' water source. Spring visitors may leave behind garbage and kick up sand while swimming, which reduces the water's clarity and can affect wildlife.

Suwannee springs' flow also has been affected. The DEP names drought and increased water consumption due to population growth as culprits, saying that people draw four billion gallons of water from the aquifer every day.

To help protect springs when visiting them, nature travelers can follow tips from the DEP. Avoid walking on the natural spring bank to help prevent erosion, stay clear of underwater plants, keep feet away from sand to prevent stirring up sediments, and take care when boating in spring runs to avoid harming plants or stirring up sediments.

Where to Stay

Campgrounds

Manatee Springs State Park has ninety-two campsites in two campground loops. All sites are situated near restrooms with hot showers, and all have electricity and water hookups. Contact ReserveAmerica for reservations. The park also has a group camping area and a primitive camping area for organized youth groups of six or more. Contact the park for more information about these campgrounds.

Shell Mound Park (352-543-6153) just north of Cedar Key is the closest campground to the refuge and is located near a refuge-protected Indian mound and mound trail. Sitting on the shore with a wide view of the coastal marshes and islands, this county park is a good place for paddlers to camp and launch their boats.

North of Fanning Springs in Old Town is Suwannee River Hideaway Campground (352-542-7800; *www.riverhideaway.com*) on the Suwannee River. Tent and RV campers can stay here, where there are laundry facilities, a bathhouse, and a general store.

Sunset Isle RV Park (800-810-1103; *www.cedarkeyrv.com*) in Cedar Key offers RV and tent campsites on or near the water.

Lodging

There are chain hotels in Chiefland, such as the Best Western Suwannee Valley Inn (352-493-0663) and Holiday Inn Express (352-493-9400). In Cedar Key, look for motels (Beach Front Motel: 866-543-5113), inns (Faraway Inn: 888-543-5330; *www.farawayinn.com*), and vacation condo rentals (Seahorse Landing: 877-514-5096; *www.seahorselanding.com*). In Suwannee, try the Pelican's Roost Bed and Breakfast (888-917-6678; *home.att.net/~fnarki*) on the gulf.

Sunset Isle RV Park (mentioned under Campgrounds, above) rents out furnished cottages, apartments, and motel rooms. Fanning Springs State Park (above) is expected to build cabins in the near future.

How to Get There

Lower Suwannee National Wildlife Refuge spans both sides of the river's coastal region. Using a boat is the best way to get from one side of the river to the other. Otherwise, using a vehicle, the nearest place to cross the river is the bridge north of Chiefland near Fanning Springs State Park. The headquarters is located south of the river. To get there, take I-75 to the Ocala area, exit at US 27 (Exit #354), and go northwest. Follow the road to Williston, then continue northwest on Alt US 27 toward Chiefland. Before you get to the downtown area, turn left (south) at CR 347 and follow it about 20 miles into the refuge to the headquarters office. Or, follow Alt US 27 into Chiefland to 4th Ave. (CR 345), following that road west, then south where it intersects with CR 347.

To get to Manatee Springs State Park, follow the directions above to get to

Chiefland. Continue on Alt US 27 as it turns north through town and joins US 98, and watch for the state park sign. Turn left (west) at Manatee Springs Road, and take the road to the end, where the park entrance is.

↩   ↩   ↩

Lower Suwannee National Wildlife Refuge
16450 NW 31st Place
Chiefland, Florida 32626
Phone: 352-493-0238
lowersuwannee.fws.gov
The refuge is open all the time. However, the headquarters office is open Monday through Friday from 7:30 a.m. to 4:00 p.m.

Manatee Springs State Park
11650 NW 115th St.
Chiefland, Florida 32626
Phone: 352-493-6072
Admission is $4.00 per vehicle.

Following Florida's famed river south to where it empties into the Gulf of Mexico, nature travelers will find riverside cypress swamps and vast coastal marshes. Paddling and boating are great ways to explore the area, but visitors should also check out the clear springs that contribute to the river. The small fishing and agricultural towns of the area make a visit here a quiet getaway.

Nearby

Big Bend Territory (chapter 7), Upper Suwannee River (chapter 8), Nature Coast (chapter 17)

10

First Coast Islands

Islands have a special place in our cultural imagination. Whether they are tropical, sun-kissed atolls or craggy isles blanketed with fog and dew—or any other kind of waterbound place—islands seem to draw people to their shores. Along the North American Atlantic coastline, islands line the sea in a peak of dunes or a swath of marsh grasses. Rivers seem to dart in and out at the water's edge. Tracing the coast south, these islands seem to get smaller and narrower, until in northeastern Florida they almost disappear on a map. The islands here may be small by some comparisons, but they are rich in nature and history.

Before Disney World, before Art Deco Miami Beach, before cow hunters and Seminole wars, before European powers fought over colonies half a world away from them, Florida was a land of native tribes who lived off the land. For 6,000 years, people lived on northeastern Florida's islands and riverbanks. They came to be called the Timucua. Mostly friendly to the French settlers who came in the mid-1500s, these people were all gone 200 years later, victims of war and European diseases for which they had no immunity.

French, Spanish, English, Confederate, and Union flags flew over the region—where some of the nation's oldest settlements were founded. If not for certain twists of fate, Florida might have been called La Floride. Jacksonville might have been called La Caroline. And certain islands might never have been preserved on this First Coast.

In a unique grouping of natural areas that includes national, state, and city parks and historical sites, the Timucuan Ecological and Historic Preserve stands to sustain the First Coast history and natural lands. This national park covers 46,000 acres of estuaries and forests just south of the Georgia border.

Two of the parks in the Timucuan preserve collection stand out as places to experience the true nature of the First Coast. Little Talbot Island and neighboring Big Talbot Island are rare undeveloped barrier islands, preserved as state parks that buffer Jacksonville from Amelia Island. The coastal scrub seems to roll on and on to the dense maritime forest. In between the islands, salt marsh grass clumps dot the water. Wide veils of clouds in various shades of gray and

Figure 9. A storm rolls south toward Little Talbot Island State Park.

blue roll in from Georgia. Visiting here, you can envision how the Timucua lived and loved their land.

What to Do There

The islands draw beachgoers to the Atlantic shore. Little Talbot Island State Park has 4.5 miles of beach. Big Talbot Island State Park also has beaches, but the beach it's known for—Bluffs Beach—is typically closed to activity because the thirty-foot drop from the picnic area to the ocean can be hazardous. The bluffs provide a unique view of the shore, not only because of the high vantage point, but also because the beach is strewn with dead trees that have fallen from the bluffs.

The island coasts are great places to explore by boat, winding through the salt marsh just as the Timucua must have done. Trails also lead to places where generations of people once walked.

Trail Tripping

At the Timucuan preserve, trails seem to be mostly near the main visitor center near Fort Caroline National Memorial. The 1-mile Hammock Interpretive

Trail leads from the visitor center along the St. Johns River to Fort Caroline. (This trail is the only way to get to the fort.) From there, the trail goes through a maritime hammock, up and down hills, and across a creek into a mixed forest before ending back at the visitor center.

Across the road from the Fort Caroline entrance is the trailhead for the 1-mile Spanish Pond Trail. It leads past Spanish Pond and Alligator Pond to a wetland overlook. At its end, it connects with the 1-mile Willie Browne Trail, crossing Hammock Creek in the 600-acre Theodore Roosevelt Area of the Timucuan preserve and ending at the trailhead at Mount Pleasant Road. These trails can be accessed off Mount Pleasant Road, too, but trail users should note that a timer-controlled gate offers access only from 6:00 a.m. to 6:00 p.m., extended to 8:00 p.m. during daylight savings time.

At Little Talbot, a 3.8-mile hiking trail loops from the park entrance through a sandy coastal hammock to the beach, then along the shore through the picnic area and back to the trailhead. Of course, hikers may walk just along the beach, or just along the interior portion of the trail, which is about 2 miles one way to the beach. The park requests that hikers check in at the ranger station first and pick up a trail map. The park's 2.5-mile paved road to the beach is also open to hikers and bicyclists. (Visitors can rent a bike at the ranger station.) There is also a 1-mile loop trail in the campground area, which is across the street from the main park entrance and guarded by a gate.

On Big Talbot Island, try the short Blackrock Trail that winds through a maritime hammock to the beach. Ask for a trail map at the Little Talbot Island State Park ranger station.

Paddling and Boating

There are several rivers and creeks around the First Coast islands, flowing through a marshy area close to the Atlantic Ocean. Watch out for shipping traffic on the St. Johns, where there is a major port.

There are so many places to launch a boat and explore by water within the Timucuan Preserve that they are beyond the scope of this chapter. From the St. Johns River to small tidal creeks, there are several places to get out on the water. The preserve has a full list of launch points and paddling trails on its Web site.

One of the more accessible launch points is at Timucuan Preserve Cedar Point on Black Hammock Island, which is west of Big Talbot Island. There are presently no facilities here, but paddlers and boaters can park and launch onto the scenic Sisters Creek. Nassau River is to the north, and St. Johns River is to the south. To get there, take I-95 to the northern Jacksonville area and exit at Heckscher Drive (Exit #358A). Head east about 6 miles along the north side of the St. Johns to New Berlin Road. Turn left (north) and continue past farms and an industrial area to a triangular stop at Cedar Point Road. Turn right (east) and go to the end, where the Cedar Point launch is on the left.

On northern Big Talbot Island, there are a boat launch, picnic area, and restrooms in a recreation area on the western side of the island. On Little Talbot Island, visitors can rent a canoe from the ranger station and launch at the boat ramp in the campground on Fort George River.

Guided Tours

Another place to rent a canoe or kayak is on Big Talbot Island, where Kayak Amelia (904-251-0016; *www.kayakamelia.com*) runs Long Island Outfitters. Here, you can book a guided tour through the islands' salt marsh. Kayak Amelia offers special tours, including sunset, full-moon and tai chi tours. Hours are 8 a.m. to 6 p.m. in summer and 9 a.m. to 5 p.m. in winter. Find them on the western side of A1A on the northern end of Big Talbot Island.

Kelly Seahorse Ranch (904-491-5166) in Amelia Island State Park (under Nearby Natural Areas, below) offers guided horseback rides on the beach. Rides are scheduled at 10 a.m., noon, 2 p.m., and 4 p.m. every day.

Nearby Natural Areas

North of Big Talbot Island is Amelia Island State Park (904-251-2320) on the southern end of Amelia Island. Known mainly for the mile-long fishing pier across Nassau Sound, the park is primarily a place to fish (redfish, tarpon, and speckled sea trout) and access the beach. A bait/tackle store and restrooms are located at the northern end of the pier. Admission is $1.00 per person. The parking area is located on the eastern side of A1A about 7 miles north of Little Talbot Island State Park.

On the northern end of Amelia Island is Fort Clinch State Park (904-277-7274), one of Florida's oldest state parks. In Fernandina Beach's historical district, Fort Clinch is also one of the older historical sites in the state, as construction on the fort began in 1847. You might arrive at Fort Clinch during a volunteer demonstration of cannon fire and learn about the fort's Civil War history. The park has 6 miles of trails for hiking or off-road bicycling where visitors might see birds or deer. The entrance fee is $5.00 per vehicle, or $3.00 per single person in a vehicle. Take I-95 to the Fernandina Beach exit (Exit #373), and follow the road (A1A/8th Street) for about 16 miles to Fernandina Beach. Turn right on Atlantic Avenue. The park entrance is about 2 miles ahead on the left.

Pumpkin Hill Creek Preserve State Park (904-696-5944) lands connect with the Timucuan preserve's Cedar Point (under Paddling and Boating, above) in Jacksonville's Northside. This preserve protects the uplands around Pumpkin Hill Creek and other waterways to improve area water quality. Although the preserve is large, only a small part is currently open to the public: 5 miles of multiuse trails through scrub and flatwoods, and an overlook on the creek's marsh where you can launch a canoe or kayak. To get there, follow the directions for Cedar Point. Before reaching Cedar Point, turn left on Pumpkin Hill Creek Road. The entrance is at the end of the road.

Huguenot Memorial Park (904-251-3335) north of the St. Johns River and Kathryn Abbey Hanna Park (904-249-4700) south of the river are City of Jacksonville parks that are part of the Timucuan preserve. Both have excellent beaches and are good places to look for birds and other wildlife; in fact, both are Great Florida Birding Trail sites (like the other Timucuan Preserve locations in this chapter). Huguenot Park has a bird observation area and is considered an important nesting area for terns and other shorebirds. Hanna Park has nice trails through the hammock, one for hiking and one for off-road bicycling. The parks are open from 8 a.m. to 8 p.m. from April through October, and 8 a.m. to 6 p.m. from November through March. Huguenot Park charges $.50 admission for everyone six and older, and Hanna Park charges $1.00. Find Huguenot Park off Heckscher Drive where A1A turns north, south of Little Talbot Island State Park. Hanna Park is off Mayport Road in Atlantic Beach. Take I-95 to Butler Blvd. (Exit #344) and head east to Southside Blvd., then exit and go north about 4 miles. At Atlantic Blvd., turn right (east), and take the road across the Intracoastal to A1A. Follow the sign for Hanna Park and take the exit ramp to Mayport Road. The park entrance is a few miles ahead on the right.

Nearby Attractions

The Timucuan preserve also encompasses Kingsley Plantation (904-251-3537) and Fort George Island Cultural State Park (904-251-2320), two sites on Fort George Island. Both are located south of Little Talbot Island State Park near the ferry landing; look for a large Timucuan sign on Heckscher Drive, and turn west, following the road to the historical sites.

Kingsley Plantation is the oldest existing plantation in Florida. The main house is there, along with the impossibly small, bare stone structures that were the slave quarters. The main house is currently closed because of structural problems, but may reopen in the future. The kitchen house is open and contains visitor exhibits. The grounds are open from 9 a.m. to 5 p.m. Admission is free.

Fort George Island Cultural State Park is the estimated location of the former Fort Saint Georges, built in 1736 by Georgia founder James Oglethorpe. Nothing is left of the fort, but the Depression-era Ribault Club there serves as a visitor center. The club's former golf course is being restored to a native landscape. Visitors can walk or bike a 4-mile trail or use the small boat launch. Admission is free. The visitor center is open Wednesday through Sunday from 9 a.m. to 5 p.m.

Wildlife-watchers will enjoy a stop at BEAKS (Bird Emergency Aid and Kare Sanctuary), where they can wander through the maritime hammock of Big Talbot Island to view outdoor facilities housing birds that have been injured. Great horned owls, bald eagles, red-tailed hawks, and pelicans are some of the residents at BEAKS (904-251-BIRD). Donations are welcome at this nonprofit facility, located off A1A north of Little Talbot Island State Park. Watch for the BEAKS sign, then turn off down the shady, dirt road to the entrance.

On Amelia Island, the city of Fernandina Beach is the main town and scene of the island's preserved history. The historic district includes some fifty blocks of homes, shops, and restaurants, some of which are Victorian homes that are now bed-and-breakfast inns. Every year, the bed-and-breakfasts dress themselves up for the holidays and invite the public for tours. (For tickets, call 866-4-AMELIA.) Here in the historic district, you can browse in antiques stores and sit down in the oldest saloon in Florida.

In Jacksonville, there is a variety of things to see and do, including museums like the Museum of Science and History (904-396-MOSH; *www.themosh.org*).

Wildlife

The Talbot islands are largely undeveloped and provide different habitats for a variety of wildlife species. Gopher tortoises are right at home in the dry, sandy uplands. Seabirds flock to the shore, while wading birds fish in the marsh. The multicolored painted bunting breeds here in the summer—one of the few places in Florida where it does so—and the bright orange summer tanager breeds here in summer as well.

Look for . . . .

With around 300 individuals, northern right whales are one of the most endangered mammals on earth. Spending summers off the northeastern coast of North America, right whale females about to give birth migrate south to the coasts of Georgia and Florida for a more favorable climate. (The colder it is, the farther south they may go, usually not farther than Melbourne.) Of all the right whale sightings that take place in Florida, many of them happen around the First Coast.

Right whales were nearly hunted to extinction. In fact, their name comes from hunting; they were considered the "right" whale to hunt because they are found close to shore, move slowly, and float when dead. Hunting right whales was outlawed in 1935, and the species was placed on the endangered species list in 1973, but the population hasn't been able to bounce back much. Getting entangled in fishing nets and fishing lines can cause injuries and death of whales. Food supply, climate, and a low birth rate may contribute to the population problem. A large cause of population decline, experts say, is collisions with ships. It's estimated that 30–50 percent of right whale deaths are caused by ships. The busy Jacksonville-area shipping lanes are calving grounds during the winter. In addition to aerial surveys by scientists, a volunteer network watches for whales from the shore each winter in order to alert the U.S. naval base in Jacksonville. The navy's Fleet Area Control and Surveillance Facility in turn alerts area ships of whale locations. According to the Florida Fish and Wildlife Research Institute, this Early Warning System has prevented ship strikes in the whale's critical habitat area.

The volunteer sightings also help researchers identify specific whales and track them in a database maintained by the New England Aquarium in Boston, Mass. Right whales are identified by the pattern of white growths called callosities on their skin. Each whale has a number and sometimes a name.

If you spot what you think could be a right whale, look for a V-shaped water spout and the absence of a dorsal fin—telltale signs of a right whale. Then call the Florida Fish and Wildlife Research Institute at 888-97-WHALE. You aren't likely to see them breach, or jump, because the female whales don't have the energy; the copepods they eat apparently don't live in Florida's warm waters, so the whales are thought to fast for the entire time they are here. Note that because of their endangered status, it's illegal to be within 500 yards of a right whale.

Habitats

The alternating open salt marsh and dense maritime hammock habitats typical of the Timucuan preserve make for a pretty drive along Heckscher Drive/A1A. These habitats, especially the marsh estuary, also make for an area of rich biodiversity. The National Park Service claims the Timucuan preserve is "one of the last unspoiled coastal wetlands on the Atlantic Coast."

Beach dunes, which are subject to erosion from human traffic, are protected with boardwalk dune crossovers. Beachgoers should use these crossovers to avoid trampling the dunes and the plants growing there. Sometimes wildlife live in these dunes, like gopher tortoises and beach mice. Sea oat grasses help stabilize the sand with their roots.

Beyond the coast, pine flatwoods, scrub, and cypress swamps cover the land. Not too far away is southern Georgia's Okefenokee National Wildlife Refuge, which spawns the Suwannee River and the St. Marys River—the boundary line between Georgia and northeastern Florida.

Where to Stay

Campgrounds

Campers will enjoy the campground at Little Talbot on the Fort George River. There are forty campsites in an oak hammock, all with water and electric hookups near restrooms with hot showers. There is also a dump station for RVs and a boat ramp. Tent campers might like to reserve campsites 4 or 38, which are shady sites near the water. Contact ReserveAmerica for more information and reservations. Little Talbot also has a primitive campground for organized groups. For group camping, contact the park office directly.

Fort Clinch State Park (under Nearby Natural Areas, above) has sixty-two campsites in two loops: near the beach and near Amelia River. Campsites have electric and water hookups, restrooms, and a dump station. A laundry facility is located in the riverside campground. Contact ReserveAmerica for reservations.

Huguenot Park and Hanna Park (under Nearby Natural Areas, above) also have campgrounds near the beach. Huguenot Park has seventy-one campsites (without hookups), a dump station, restrooms, and a camp store. Hanna Park has 293 campsites with electric, water, and sewer hookups, a camp store, restrooms, and laundry facilities. For information and reservations, contact the parks directly.

Lodging

The Talbot islands are mostly undeveloped. Hanna Park (mentioned above), which is part of the Timucuan preserve, offers four small, rustic cabins that sleep up to four people. Cabin guests may use the campground bathhouses. Contact the park directly for information and reservations.

Just 7 miles north of Little Talbot Island State Park is Amelia Island Plantation (888-261-6161; *www.aipfl.com*), a popular place to stay. Amelia Island also has several historical bed-and-breakfasts (like Fairbanks House: 904-277-0500; *www.fairbankshouse.com*) and motels (like Beachside Motel: 904-261-4236; *www.beachsidemotel.com*).

In Jacksonville close to Fort Caroline, look for large hotels (like Sea Turtle Inn: 800-874-6000; *www.seaturtle.com*) and beachside motels (like Surfside Inn: 904-246-1583; *www.jaxsurfsideinn.com*).

How to Get There

The Timucuan preserve encompasses several parks. The main visitor center for the preserve is at Fort Caroline National Memorial. To get there, take I-95 to the Jacksonville area and exit at Southside Blvd (Exit #340). Head north about 11 miles to Merrill Road, then turn right (east). The road merges with Fort Caroline Road; from there, travel 4.5 miles to the park entrance on the left.

For Little Talbot Island State Park, take I-95 to Heckscher Drive (Exit #358A) and head east for about 17 miles. The road turns north and joins A1A. The park entrance is on the eastern (right) side of the road. Although the Kingsley Plantation/Fort George Cultural State Park area is marked with a sign that includes the Talbot island state parks, don't turn at the sign, but keep heading north along the road to the Little Talbot park entrance.

Big Talbot Island State Park is to the north. Look for signs along Heckscher Drive/A1A for Big Talbot recreation areas.

When going from the Talbot islands (north of the St. Johns River) to Fort Caroline (south of the river), drivers can go by road or ferry. By road, take Heckscher Drive south and continue as it turns west. Watch for the sign for the bridge across the river, and turn left onto the ramp, taking road 9A south. Continue south to Atlantic Blvd., then head left (east). Watch for brown signs to point the way to Fort Caroline as noted above. By ferry (904-241-9969; *www.stjohnsriverferry.com*), look for the ferry sign south of the Kingsley Plantation turn-off sign. Vehicles line up in rows while they wait for the next ferry. The trip takes about ten minutes across the river, where vehicles get off on Mayport Road. From there, take Mayport Road south to Atlantic Blvd. and go west. Follow brown park signs showing the way to Fort Caroline. The ferry charges $2.75 for two-axle vehicles and an additional fee for extra axles. Motorcycles can board for $2.50, and pedestrians and cyclists for $.50. The ferry generally runs every half-hour from 6 a.m. until 10 p.m.

⊷ ⊷ ⊷

Timucuan Ecological and Historic Preserve
12713 Fort Caroline Road
Jacksonville, Florida 32225
904-641-7155
www.nps.gov/timu
The main visitor center is located at Fort Caroline and is open from 9 a.m. to 5 p.m. Admission is free, but donations are accepted.

Little Talbot Island State Park
12157 Heckscher Drive
Jacksonville, Florida 32226
Phone: 904-251-2320
Admission is $4.00 per vehicle, or $3.00 for one person in a vehicle.

Big Talbot Island State Park
12157 Heckscher Drive
Jacksonville, Florida 32226
Phone: 904-251-2320
Admission is $1.00 per person. There is a $2.00 fee per vehicle to enter the Bluffs beach picnic area and a $3.00 boat launch fee.

The First Coast islands reveal not only early Florida history, but also the natural side of the barrier island chain that extends up the Atlantic coastline. Several parks and historic sites preserve the memory of the Florida that once was.

Nearby

Matanzas River Lands (chapter 11)

11

Matanzas River Lands

There is a remarkably natural place near the Atlantic Ocean, south of St. Augustine, east of the great St. Johns River, and north of the golf-club communities that lie halfway between the Old City and Daytona Beach. The Matanzas River flows through here, and the nearby preserved lands—the Matanzas River lands—offer nature travelers a place to find peace despite the area's turbulent history.

The Timucua tribe was here first. Then the Spanish came looking for gold and the fountain of youth, founding what's considered the oldest city in North America: St. Augustine. This First Coast is the site of shipwrecks, battling nations, betrayed Native Americans, Spanish settlers, Florida crackers, and others who live on in tales that blend the Old World with the new. The Matanzas River lands saw their ownership change hands many times.

But to whom does land really belong? To those who care for and love it.

A visit to the area will show you how easy it is to "own" this land. The Matanzas River is part of the Intracoastal Waterway, but it's more than just a channel for boats to pass through. The river is wider than the waterway, and its banks undulate with the soft appearance of marsh grass where herons and egrets hide. It's a place to watch dolphins and manatees, and to paddle a canoe or kayak. Past the river are pine and hardwood forests and other great places to explore. There are a lot of preserved lands here. There are a few state parks, a national monument, county parks, and other conservation areas preserved by state agencies.

Two of these places are Faver-Dykes State Park and Washington Oaks Gardens State Park. On opposite sides of the Matanzas River, the parks do seem to be opposites: Faver-Dykes offers quiet forests and Matanzas tributary Pellicer Creek, while Washington Oaks Gardens offers a boulder-strewn beach, a rose garden, and a river view. (While you wouldn't think a garden—a place enhanced by people—could preserve a natural habitat, the majority of Washington Oaks Gardens is left in a natural state.) Together, these parks join hands in preserving the Matanzas coastal habitat. Both state parks are also in the Painted Bunting Cluster of the Great Florida Birding Trail.

Figure 10. The Washington Oaks Gardens State Park beach is strewn with large boulders.

As it is with most parks, Faver-Dykes and Washington Oaks Gardens were once privately owned lands. In this case, they were both plantations given by Spain in the 1800s to one of its generals. Washington Oaks Gardens gets its name from the land surveyor—a relative of President George Washington—who later married the Spanish general's daughter. Faver-Dykes's name comes from a more recent landowner, a St. Johns County court clerk, whose parents' last names were Faver and Dykes.

We know this about the parks because the First Coast has preserved its history so well. Hopefully, its natural areas, too, will continue to be preserved, and the Matanzas River lands stand as a place of scenic beauty, history, and wonder.

What to Do There

Naturally, a land surrounded by so much water lends itself to water activities. Paddling a canoe or kayak through the creeks and river, and splashing in the Atlantic Ocean surf, are great ways to explore this historical land. But don't miss out on the trails and pretty views offered on land.

Trail Tripping

There isn't much in the state parks for hardy hikers who like a half-day trek. However, if you can do with a few nature trails, then you'll still get the flavor of the Matanzas River lands. If you really want to stretch your legs, go across the creek to Pellicer Creek Corridor Conservation Area or a little farther north to Moses Creek Conservation Area (under Nearby Natural Areas, below).

Faver-Dykes has two short nature trail loops: one near the boat ramp and one accessed through the campground. The trail near the boat ramp takes you through the pinelands, while the other winds through a hardwood hammock. Both are close to the creek.

Washington Oaks Gardens has three and a half nature trails: the Jungle Road Hike and Bike Trail, Old A1A Hike and Bike Trail, Timucuan Hiking Trail, and a short path to the Matanzas River. All of the trails are less than a mile long, but because they're interconnected, you could have a short hike here. To access the trails, look for the trail parking lot to the north of the garden area.

Paddling and Boating

Being right on Pellicer Creek, one of Faver-Dykes's prime activities, if not *the* activity, is paddling. Pellicer Creek is an official canoe trail of the Florida Greenways and Trails department, an arm of the Department of Environmental Protection (which also runs the Florida state parks). The official trail is a 4-mile one-way trip. You can begin at the park's boat launch, follow the creek upstream to the US 1 overpass almost where the creek begins, then come back again. (You can also launch your boat at US 1 for a fee and paddle to the park.) Pellicer Creek's current is usually slow, so a round-trip paddle is enjoyable.

But you don't have to confine yourself to just the state canoe trail. The creek flows into Matanzas River, where there's more than enough for you to paddle.

You can rent canoes right at the Faver-Dykes boat launch, by advance reservation only. To arrange a canoe rental, call 904-794-0997.

Guided Tours

If it's a kayak you'd prefer to paddle, though, call Coastal Outdoor Center (904-471-4144; *www.coastaloutdoorcenter.com*). Located on the other side of Matanzas River, this nearby paddling and bait shop rents out kayaks and canoes, and it provides guided river tours and classes. One of the tours is a trip up Moses Creek in Moses Creek Conservation Area (see below). To get there from Faver-Dykes, take US 1 north to County Road 206 and turn right. Go across the Matanzas River bridge, from where you may be able to spot the lineup of kayaks on the eastern bank. Turn right at A1A, then make the first right and go all the way to the end of the road.

Gecko Latitudes (904-824-7979; *www.geckolatitudes.com*), based in St. Augustine, offers half-day and full-day paddling tours in the general area, some of them in conjunction with Washington Oaks Gardens. It even offers a women-friendly tour. Call ahead for reservations and information.

In St. Augustine Beach is Whole Earth Outfitters (904-471-8782; *www. wholeearthoutfitters.com*), which offers half-day guided paddling trips in St. Augustine and in Matanzas River near Rattlesnake Island. Customized trips throughout most of northern Florida are also available, so contact the company if you're interested.

Nearby Natural Areas

If you stand at Faver-Dykes's boat launch and look across the creek, you'll be looking at Pellicer Creek Corridor Conservation Area (386-329-4883). This area preserves a variety of habitats, including wetlands, ponds, creeks, pinelands, and hardwood hammocks. There is a web of trails for hiking, off-road biking, and horseback riding, and also a boat launch.

A part of this preserved area, called Princess Place, is the former estate of a widow who married an ousted Russian prince. A home still stands here, built by Adirondack architect William Wright, said to be the only example of Camp Style architecture in Florida and the oldest standing structure in Flagler County. If you visit here, pay attention to Princess Place's operating hours (Wednesday through Sunday, 9 a.m. until 5 p.m.), or the gates will be closed to your arrival.

The part of the conservation area that doesn't include Princess Place, near Pellicer Pond, is open any day to foot, bike, or equestrian use. To get there from Faver-Dykes State Park, head back to US 1 and go south under I-95. Turn left at Old Kings Road, and watch for signs on the left after crossing I-95 again. You'll reach the Pellicer Pond entrance first, with the Princess Place entrance farther down the road. You could also paddle across from the state park and explore the area's banks.

Moses Creek flows into Matanzas River through Moses Creek Conservation Area (904-529-2380). You can explore its scrub and forest habitats on multiuse trails, or the creek and tidal wetlands by boat. Primitive campsites are available by reservation. To get there from Faver-Dykes, take US 1 north to CR 206. Turn right and watch for signs on the left side of the road. There are two entrances, with the west entrance best suited for horseback riders.

In St. Augustine, Anastasia State Park (904-461-2033) offers a nice public beach and is listed along with Faver-Dykes and Washington Oaks Gardens as a Great Florida Birding Trail site. Old Spanish coquina rock quarries, fishing, and the beach with its sea-oat-covered dunes make this a good side trip if you're going to Faver-Dykes or Washington Oaks Gardens.

Yet another Great Florida Birding Trail site is Fort Matanzas National Monument (904-471-0116; *www.nps.gov/foma/*), a historic Spanish structure built around 1740 that stands at the river's inlet. The focus of this park is Florida's history as a one-time colony of Spain. Here, you'll hear the story of some 200 French protestants who were killed in this area because they refused to renounce their faith and accept Spain's faith in Catholicism. In fact, it is this 1565 event that gave the river its name—Matanzas—meaning "massacre." Although the park touts the area's history, its land protects several species of wildlife and preserves important coastal habitat. There's even a short nature trail. Fort Matanzas is located off A1A about 5 miles north of Washington Oaks Gardens; watch for national park signs.

Nearby Attractions

Marineland (888-279-9194; *www.marineland.net*) houses exhibits for dolphins, sea lions, penguins, turtles, and birds, and presents dolphin shows. Marineland hours are 9:30 a.m. until 4:30 p.m. every day except Tuesday. Adult tickets are $14.00, children $9.00. The aquarium is located on A1A about 2 miles north of Washington Oaks Gardens.

St. Augustine Alligator Farm Zoological Park (904-824-3337; *www.alligator farm.com*) gives visitors the chance to see alligators and other reptiles, as well as a popular bird rookery. Adult tickets are $14.95, children $8.95; discounts are offered for groups, seniors, and those in wheelchairs. The park is open every day from 9 a.m. until 5 p.m. From Faver-Dykes, go north on US 1, then east on CR 206. Head north again at A1A and watch for signs to the park.

Of course, St. Augustine itself is a great place to go, especially if you're interested in history. Tram and horse-drawn carriage tours of the city's riverfront will get you acquainted enough to explore on your own. Or just take off down the brick alleys to see what you can see: historical venues, clothing and gift stores, restaurants, and sweet shops.

Wildlife

The creek, river, hammock, pine flatwoods, and coastal habitat found at Faver-Dykes and Washington Oaks Gardens attract various wildlife.

On the Washington Oaks Gardens beach, you can see shorebirds; back on the trails, you can spot warblers and other songbirds. Alligators inhabit the river and creeks, and deer are common. Wildlife-watching tends to turn mostly toward birds and butterflies, though, which are drawn to the flower gardens and the sound of the garden fountain's running water. But sit a spell near the river to watch for dolphins and manatees, and listen for osprey calls.

Faver-Dykes's creekside boat launch/picnic area (which has a small playground) and the nature trails are good places to spot birds. Deer often appear along the gravel road that winds through a portion of the park. A few lucky visitors get to see gray foxes and bobcats, and some see river otters playing in Pellicer Creek.

Look for . . . .

The marsh rabbit is a small, brown rabbit seen near wetlands. The marsh rabbit doesn't have the long ears or huge hindquarters of the jack rabbit, and it doesn't have the puffy tail of the cottontail rabbit. But the marsh rabbit is known for something else—it can swim in order to get away from a predator. Look for marsh rabbits along Pellicer Creek at Faver-Dykes and near the Matanzas River at Washington Oaks Gardens. Other places in Florida where you might see marsh rabbits are Merritt Island National Wildlife Refuge, Big Talbot Island State Park, and Everglades National Park.

Habitats

Some say the Matanzas isn't really a river, but a sound—a body of water that happens to be on the back side of oceanfront land between two inlets. Matanzas Inlet is one of the few natural inlets on Florida's eastern coast; it has not been "improved" or dredged.

Faver-Dykes and Washington Oaks Gardens State Parks are part of the Guana Tolomato Matanzas National Estuarine Research Reserve, a collection of preserved lands in the region within a federal system of preserves that protect estuarine areas. Named after the region's rivers that contribute to the estuary, GTM protects a variety of habitats that are important to our well-being as well as that of many wildlife species, some of which are endangered or threatened. According to the state of Florida, GTM is made up mostly of pinelands, coastal salt marsh and open-water habitat, shrub and brushlands, and hardwood hammocks. At Faver-Dykes, you'll find a pine flatwoods habitat with its pines and saw palmettos, mesic hammock with its hickories and hollies, and cypress swamp with bald and pond cypresses. At Washington Oaks Gardens, you'll encounter the natural communities of beach dune with its sea oats and railroad vines, coastal scrub with its sand live oaks and cabbage palms, and xeric scrub with its rosemary and ground lichens.

The GTM general area is home to many kinds of wildlife, from reptiles and amphibians (like sea turtles and snakes), to various kinds of fish, dolphins and manatees, birds of prey, and migrating songbirds. Around 240 plant species are protected within GTM. Estuaries not only mix fresh water with salt water to provide a nursery for two-thirds of commercial fish and shellfish, but they also help prevent flooding in the uplands. And they are beautiful places.

Being within a national estuarine reserve is unique in itself, as there are only twenty-five of them in the United States. But the unique boulders that rest on the beach at Washington Oaks Gardens draw curious folks down the length of the sand where they sit. The large rocks are thought to have washed up from a submerged bar offshore.

Despite their proximity to I-95, US 1, and A1A, Faver-Dykes State Park and Washington Oaks Gardens State Park aren't overly developed, but you can see that changing. You can see signs for new housing developments promising river views and a location near the beach. You can even see the new homes themselves. But so far, that hasn't affected Faver-Dykes or Washington Oaks Gardens. In fact, in early 2003, the state purchased land to add more than 8,400 acres to Faver-Dykes, preserving what it said is the last remaining undisturbed marsh in Florida and creating a 16,000-acre conservation corridor.

Where to Stay

Campgrounds

The camping is good at the mostly shady Faver-Dykes campground. It has thirty campsites, all with picnic tables, grills, and water and electrical hookups. The sites range in price. A separate youth camping area is also available to organized youth groups. Up in St. Augustine, Anastasia State Park offers 139 campsites. There is no camping at Washington Oaks Gardens. Contact ReserveAmerica for reservations.

Primitive camping is available at Pellicer Creek Corridor and Moses Creek Conservation Areas, mentioned above.

Lodging

In St. Augustine, about a half-hour drive north from Faver-Dykes, you have a variety of lodging options, from upscale hotels (like Casa Monica Hotel: 904-

827-1888; *www.casamonica.com*) to small bed-and-breakfast inns (like Casablanca Inn Bed and Breakfast: 800-826-2626; *www.casablancainn.com*). Closer to Washington Oaks Gardens is the town of Marineland, where rental homes are available, usually by the week; try BeachCottageRent.com (888-963-8272; *www.beachcottagerent.com*).

How to Get There

For Faver-Dykes, take I-95 to US 1 (Exit #92) just south of St. Augustine and go east. Take the first right, Faver-Dykes Road, and follow it past homes to the park entrance.

To get to Washington Oaks Gardens from Faver-Dykes, take US 1 north to County Road 206 and turn right. Travel east to A1A, then turn right and go south about 10 miles to the park's entrance.

✎   ✎   ✎

Faver-Dykes State Park
1000 Faver-Dykes Road
St. Augustine, Florida 32086
Phone: 904-794-0997
Admission is $3.00 per vehicle.

Washington Oaks Gardens State Park
6400 N. Oceanshore Blvd.
Palm Coast, Florida 32137
Phone: 386-446-6780
Admission is $4.00 per vehicle or $3.00 for vehicles with one occupant.

The rivers and creeks here are natural and beautiful, in a place the state calls the last undisturbed marsh in Florida. The big rocks on Washington Oaks Gardens' beach are a unique feature.

Nearby

First Coast Islands (chapter 10), Land of the Caves, Sinks, and Ravines (chapter 12)

12

Land of the Caves, Sinks, and Ravines

The heart of northern Florida is a heart of stone: limestone. Close to the surface, it forms caves both above and below ground. Water shapes the soft stone to form sinkholes, ravines, and caverns. This is known as karst terrain, and northern-central Florida is a good place to explore it. Natural areas like Paynes Prairie Preserve State Park—whose huge prairie was formed by sinkholes—and Mike Roess Gold Head Branch State Park and Ravine Gardens State Park, whose ravines and sinkholes have been fashioned by water, are easy to visit. Not only are these parks interesting geologically, but they are great natural examples of this hilly, rocky zone.

At Paynes Prairie, nature—and life—are all around you. Overhead, there are water birds, prairie birds, and raptors. In front of you, dragonflies and bees seem to happily fill the air. Even underfoot, life is growing; sometimes it creeps across the soil in the form of a snail or an insect. Surrounded by all that life, you feel alive, too, and glad to be sharing that event-like feeling with the life around you. Paynes Prairie is a great place to feel alive. With 21,000 acres and twenty biological communities—including freshwater marsh, pine flatwoods, hardwood hammock, and wet prairie—Paynes Prairie is a National Natural Landmark, among the most significant natural areas in Florida.

Most comments about the prairie's past mention William Bartram, an American artist, naturalist, and writer who toured what is now the southeastern United States in the late 1700s. In 1774, he wrote a detailed description of the Gainesville-area prairie, calling it the "great Alachua Savannah," in his book *Bartram's Travels*.

Bartram also passed close to the Ravine Gardens area in Palatka as he traveled up and down the St. Johns River during his exploration of the state. Developed by the federal government after the Depression to spur economic growth in the region, formal gardens front the steephead ravine, with more than 95,000 azaleas planted around the perimeter. The 154-acre park is a beautiful place to walk and reflect on nature.

Figure 11. The site of the old mill is now an idyllic place to rest at Mike Roess Gold Head Branch State Park.

A similar story took place at Gold Head Branch. Developed by the Civilian Conservation Corps in the 1930s, the park plays up its steephead ravine, where a spring-fed creek bubbles up. It winds through the ravine, an area very different from the park's sandhills that surround the gully, eventually running into a lake where visitors like to swim and camp.

Any of these karst parks are good for an eco-trip for nature travelers who want to explore places that are out of the ordinary.

What to Do There

Paynes Prairie is a popular place for boating and fishing because of its access to Lake Wauberg. Its numerous trails invite hikers, equestrians, and off-road cyclists. And its observation areas lure wildlife watchers who hope to see bison, wild horses, deer, and birds. In late winter, the preserve holds the Knap-In and Primitive Arts Festival, three days of demonstrations on flint knapping, carving, basket weaving, pottery, and other arts. For dates and times each year, contact the preserve.

Ravine Gardens also has its own festival, a garden festival held at the peak of the azalea blooming season, in March. Contact the park for the festival dates and details.

Trail Tripping

Going down trails in this region can be a fascinating exploration of karst terrain. When descending into ravines and sinkholes, watch your step on the stairs, and be sure to stay on the trail.

There are several miles of trails in Paynes Prairie waiting to be explored. The most prominent is the Gainesville-Hawthorne State Trail, a 16-mile greenway between Gainesville and Hawthorne. Overlooks and creeks along the way make the trail more than your usual jogging path. Only a portion of the trail passes through Paynes Prairie, but you can take the trail to either end. Several trailheads in the area give you access: Boulware Springs City Park in Gainesville, the La Chua Trail within Paynes Prairie, the Lochloosa trailhead in Lochloosa Wildlife Management Area, and the easternmost one in Hawthorne. Cyclists, skaters, pedestrians, and equestrians are welcome on the trail.

In the same general area as the Gainesville-Hawthorne State Trail is the foot-traffic-only La Chua Trail. This is the north rim of the prairie basin, near Alachua Sink. An interpretive building stands near the trailhead. This area is open only on weekdays from 8 a.m. to 5 p.m. Another good thing to know about this trail is that you can't reach it from the main entrance of the preserve—you have to leave the park and drive through a portion of Gainesville to get to it. For the best directions, ask a ranger for a map.

To get to Bolen Bluff Trail, also, you have to leave the main part of the preserve. Just go north of the main entrance, pass the University of Florida's entrance to Lake Wauberg, and you'll see a trailhead with a parking area. About 3 miles round-trip, this is one of the more interesting trails because it takes you through a shady hammock to open marsh and a wildlife viewing deck on the dike, where you can feel as though you're part of the prairie. The trail is open from 8 a.m. to sunset, and it's free.

Wacahoota Trail is a short, shady loop near the visitor center. It will take you to the observation tower, which gives you an excellent view of the prairie and often of wildlife. If you do anything in the preserve, go to the visitor center and climb the observation tower if you are able.

Near the parking lot at the visitor center are the trailheads for Cone's Dike Trail, Chacala Trail, and Jackson's Gap Trail. Cone's Dike Trail is the one you may see from the observation tower, and it will take you close to the prairie. Jackson's Gap Trail—which leads to Chacala Trail—takes you right along the edge of the preserve's boundary. If it's still standing, a rustic building on the other side of the boundary fence on private property will give you a glimpse of Old Florida. Chacala Trail will take you to Chacala Pond, and also through a hardwood hammock and beautiful pine flatwoods. This trail, suitable for hiking, off-road biking, and horseback riding, can be flooded in some areas after heavy rains. It is also the longest trail in Paynes Prairie and meanders in many loops, so be sure to get a trail map from the ranger station or visitor center.

Lake Trail is a short trip from the restrooms at the boat launch area on Lake Wauberg to the main park road, and is open only to hiking and off-road biking.

Although not exactly a trail, a boardwalk on the eastern side of US 441 between Micanopy and Gainesville takes you to an observation deck that looks out on the marsh. You'll recognize it by the small parking lot and interpretive sign on the side of the road.

At Gold Head Branch, it's a must for visitors to go down into the ravine for the fifteen-minute Fern Loop walk along the creek, if able to take the steep concrete stairs down into the gully. Although park visitors have been observed walking up and even sliding down the sides of the ravine, this contributes to the ravine's erosion and could be dangerous for the visitor. Signs tell visitors to stay on the trail.

From Fern Loop, hikers can connect to the longer Ravine Ridge Trail, which takes about an hour to walk. The Ravine Ridge Trail takes hikers along the upper edge of the ravine and to an old mill site. The Loblolly Trail also leads in a loop from the mill site. This is the site of a former sawmill on the creek. You won't find much evidence of the mill, but you will find a bridge and a resting bench in the kind of shady, peaceful, charming spot that fairy tales are made of. Find the mill site parking area in the same paved loop as the main picnic and lake parking area.

In Ravine Gardens, visitors are free to walk throughout the gardens and down into the V-shaped ravine for a stroll along a creek. As in Gold Head Branch, steep concrete steps lead to the bottom. Two suspension bridges span the ravine at different points, allowing those who cannot walk the steps to have a view of both sides of the gardens. Visitors should go in March for the optimum view of azalea and dogwood blooms. The park's 1.8-mile road around the ravine is open to cars, bicyclists, and pedestrians, who might take advantage of the fitness stations along the route.

Paddling and Boating

At Paynes Prairie, a boat launch on Lake Wauberg gives you access to the preserve from the water. Across the lake, you'll see the Lake Wauberg recreation area for University of Florida students, who access the lake north of the preserve's main entrance.

Gold Head Branch rents canoes for paddling on Little Lake Johnson. There used to be a boat ramp on Big Lake Johnson, but the lake has dried up and the boat ramp has been removed.

For other water activities and guided paddling trips in the area, please see the Upper Suwannee River (chapter 8).

Guided Tours

From November through April, Paynes Prairie rangers offer guided activities, including an overnight 6.5-mile backpacking trip on the north rim of the prairie basin. The "prairie rim ramble" is a 3.5-mile half-day hike around the prairie's sinks. And 3-mile guided wildlife walks along the dike give you the chance to see alligators and various birds. Call the preserve to find out dates and times for these events.

Nearby Natural Areas

In northern Gainesville, Devil's Millhopper Geological State Park (352-955-2008) is a perfect example of the sinkhole territory found in northern-central

Florida. Devil's Millhopper, a National Natural Landmark, is a 120-foot sink-hole that formed when the roof of an underground cave collapsed. The sinkhole's evil name comes from the reported finding of fossilized teeth and bones at the bottom of the hole. Visitors can walk around the sinkhole's rim or descend into it on the stairs to note how the change in elevation affects the types of plants that grow there. The park is open from 9 a.m. until 5 p.m. Wednesday through Sunday. Admission is $2.00 per vehicle. To get there, take I-75 to County Road 222 (Exit #390) and drive east for about 8 miles. At 43rd Street, turn left (north), then turn left again (west) at Millhopper Road. The park entrance is ahead on the right.

Down the road from Devil's Millhopper to the west is one entrance for San Felasco Hammock Preserve State Park (386-462-7905), also a National Natural Landmark. Here, a trail winds through beautiful sandhills graced by streams that disappear into underground crevices, then reappear again downstream. Hikers can choose from the 1-mile, 4.8-mile, or 5.6-mile trails here (the longer trails start across the street from the parking area), watching for hawks, song-birds, lizards, snakes, and squirrels. The second entrance, to the north, gives access to trailheads specifically for off-road bicycling and horseback riding. To get to these trails, take I-75 to US 441 (Exit #399) and go south through the town of Alachua. Turn right onto Progress Blvd. The entrance is less than a mile ahead. Admission is $2.00 per vehicle, or $6.00 per horse for those using the equestrian trails.

South of Paynes Prairie is Lochloosa Wildlife Conservation Area (386-329-4883), where bald eagles, ospreys, and wood storks are drawn to the open Lochloosa and Orange Lakes. The northern boundary along State Road 20 runs along the Gainesville-Hawthorne State Trail. Boat ramps and multiuse trails help visitors explore the area. There are several entrances; find a trailhead in Hawthorne on CR 2082 west of US 301. The southern entrance closer to Cross Creek offers a boat ramp, primitive camping, and a trail around a penin-sula that sticks out into Lochloosa Lake. Watch out for cows in the road here, and look for bumblebees, black swallow-tailed butterflies, red-shouldered hawks, and ground doves. Find the entrance near a sign on US 301 just north of CR 325. Admission is free.

Gum Root Swamp Conservation Area (352-334-2170) offers trails through the swamp and hammock habitats. The conservation area is home to leopard frogs, bald eagles, canebrake rattlesnakes, gopher tortoises, and pileated wood-peckers. One trailhead is located at N.E. 27th Ave. and SR 26 at a flashing traffic light about 5 miles east of downtown Gainesville. The other trailhead, where a trail leads to Newnans Lake, is just a bit farther west down SR 26.

Gum Root connects with Newnans Lake Conservation Area (386-329-

4483), where animals from white-tailed deer to river otters are at home. The lake is occasionally visited by shorebirds more often associated with saltwater habitats. One trail leads from SR 26 near Gum Root to CR 234 on the eastern side of the lake, which offers another place to access the trail. South of this trailhead on CR 234 is the southern tract of the conservation area, where visitors can enjoy a short loop trail and boat launch.

Restoring pine and wiregrass habitat with prescribed fire, Morningside Nature Center (352-334-2170) is a 278-acre City of Gainesville park. Visitors can hike the 7 miles of looping trails or watch the farm animals in the living history farm. Wild animals are here, too, like box turtles, white-tailed deer, skinks, and various songbirds. Pick up a trail map at the visitor center. The park is open from 9 a.m. to 5 p.m. every day. Admission is free. The park is near Gum Root Swamp Conservation Area. To get there, take SR 26 east from the downtown area for about 3 miles. The park entrance is on the left.

Nearby Attractions

Fans of the book *The Yearling* will enjoy a visit to nearby Marjorie Kinnan Rawlings Historic State Park (352-466-3672), on the site of the Cross Creek home of the late Pulitzer Prize-winning writer, where rangers do their best to make you think you have stepped back into the 1930s. The park is open every day from 9 a.m. to 5 p.m. Tours of the house are scheduled every hour on the hour, Thursday through Sunday, from 10 a.m. to 4 p.m. except for the noon hour, from October through July. Admission is $2.00 per vehicle. A tour of the home costs an additional $3.00 for adults and $2.00 for children six through twelve. To get there from Micanopy near Paynes Prairie, take CR 346 east to CR 325, and turn right (south). The park is about ten or fifteen minutes ahead.

The Florida Museum of Natural History (352-392-1721; *www.flmnh. ufl.edu*) in Gainesville is a small but significant museum on the University of Florida campus. Exhibits include Florida fossils, interactive dioramas on northwestern Florida habitats, southern Florida's habitats and Calusa history, and traveling exhibits. A 6,400-square-foot butterfly conservatory called the Butterfly Rainforest houses hundreds of butterflies of at least fifty-five species. Admission to the museum is free, but donations are accepted. The Butterfly Rainforest and special exhibits charge for admission, generally from $3.50 to $7.50 per ticket. The museum is open Monday through Saturday from 10 a.m. to 5 p.m., and Sundays and holidays from 1 p.m. to 5 p.m. To get there, take I-75 to the Gainesville area and exit at Archer Road (Exit #384). Head east to S.W. 34th Street (SR 121), then turn left (north). Turn right at Hull Road (the third traffic light). The museum is about a quarter of a mile ahead on the right.

Micanopy, where Paynes Prairie is, is an attraction itself. With one main street and small-town charm, Micanopy was a filming site for parts of the movie *Doc Hollywood*, in which a big-city doctor (Michael J. Fox) gets stranded in a small "South Carolina" town. The real attraction here is the main street lined with antiques shops. On weekends, you'll find antiques hunters walking up and down the street, going in and out of stores, looking for treasures.

Wildlife

There are more than 400 wildlife species that call Paynes Prairie home at one time or another during the year. If you enjoy wildlife watching, you should find Paynes Prairie to be a haven. You may even want to come at different times of the year so you can see different wildlife. Look for white-tailed deer along park roads and alligators in the sinks. There are 263 bird species that have been reported in Paynes Prairie, including sandhill cranes, which you may be able to see—and hear—year-round.

At Ravine Gardens, bird-watchers might find red-tailed hawks, barred owls, northern cardinals, and hummingbirds. Other wildlife to look for are river otters, raccoons, gray foxes, and the ubiquitous gray squirrels.

In the sandhills of Gold Head Branch, visitors might come across wild turkeys, gopher tortoises, and fox squirrels, along with a variety of songbirds like Carolina wrens and white-eyed vireos.

Look for . . .

Bison once roamed a good part of North America, including Florida, where they had their own place in the ecosystem—although they weren't common here. The Florida herds are thought to have been smaller than the gigantic herds of the old American West. After about 1821, there were no more bison in Florida, according to Paynes Prairie.

Preserve rangers reintroduced bison onto the prairie in 1975, when ten bison from Oklahoma made the preserve their new home. (That was also when the preserve's rangers brought in wild horses and scrub cattle.) By bringing in these animals, rangers were hoping to preserve some of Florida's cultural history.

Longtime ranger Howard Adams said the bison population reached thirty-three when an outbreak of brucellosis—bacteria that in bovines cause fever, natural abortion, and other problems—scared local cattle ranchers. This required rangers to reduce the herd to only five bison. Now, with the bison increasing in numbers again, Adams said the preserve hopes to bring in two bulls to further aid the population. (Some wildlife experts in the eastern and western

United States say research doesn't show firm evidence that bison give brucellosis to cattle. But in Florida and in the western states, wherever bison and cattle live closely, the law usually sides in favor of the cattle.)

As you stand in the preserve's observation tower and scan the horizon for wildlife, you may realize that right below you are wild horses, snorting and communicating with one another. You might see a small group—a male with a dominant female and other females, or a male, female, and colt. The social structure of horses is fascinating, and if you're lucky enough to see the wild ones on the prairie, you may get a chance to observe their interactions.

Horses that escaped Florida's Spanish settlers ran wild on the prairie until about the 1930s. After the prairie was fenced, that ended—until rangers reintroduced them as part of the preserve's cultural heritage.

Habitats

The sinks, ravines, and caves in northern-central Florida are evidence of karst terrain. Limestone caverns seem to weave above and below ground, creating the unique geological features.

The result of several sinkholes coming together, Paynes Prairie's large basin is a unique geological and biological part of Florida. The prairie is separated into sections as a result of both I-75 and US 441 running north and south across it. From the south end of the prairie, at the top of the preserve's observation tower, you can see Gainesville buildings on the other side. Despite these distractions in the landscape, the preserve strives to retain nature's balance. This "great Alachua Savannah" is a plant community dominated by grasses, herbs, and shrubs, with trees here and there that are usually fire tolerant; fire keeps the prairie from becoming a forest. Rangers don't allow wildfires on the prairie anymore because of the proximity of private homes, but rangers do engage in prescribed burning.

While fire is a necessity, water is the element that makes the prairie so changeable. On average, the preserve gets fifty-five inches of rainfall each year. In times of drought, the prairie can develop a more brushy appearance; after a period of heavy rainfall, the prairie can become flooded. In fact, the state is working to re-create the natural flow of water across the prairie.

Gold Head Branch also shows the effect that water—or the lack of it—has on karst terrain and the general environment. Little Lake Johnson and Big Lake Johnson were once full lakes. As recently as the early 1990s, the boat ramp on Big Lake Johnson attracted trucks towing trailers with fishing boats. Even then, the water level was low, but it was enough to boat in. Today, the ramp is closed because Big Lake Johnson has nearly dried up and looks more like a prairie than it does a lake. Grasses and brush have taken over. Northern Florida experienced several years of drought from the late 1990s into the next century. During the same time, population increased, and residents drew more water from the underground aquifer. The lake's water dried up.

Where to Stay

Campgrounds

Paynes Prairie offers thirty-five RV sites and fifteen tent sites in a campground near Lake Wauberg. Sites have water and electricity and are near restrooms with showers. For more details or reservations, contact ReserveAmerica.

At Gold Head Branch, there are three campground loops: Sandhill, Turkey Oak, and Lake View. Sandhill and Lake View are primarily for RVs, and Turkey Oak (right next to Sandhill) is for tents. All RV sites have water and electric hookups, but not all tent sites have electricity. Campgrounds are located near restrooms with showers, and there is a dump station. Contact ReserveAmerica for reservations.

Gold Head Branch also offers two primitive campsites along the Florida Trail, and three group campgrounds for organized groups of up to twenty-five people. Group sites don't have electricity but have water, flush toilets, and cold outdoor showers. Contact the park to reserve any of these sites.

Lochloosa Conservation Area (under Nearby Natural Areas, above) allows primitive camping. Between Palatka and Gainesville, also try Caravelle Ranch Wildlife Management Area (904-529-2380 for camping info), 10 miles southwest of Palatka.

Lodging

Cabins at Gold Head Branch are situated near Little Lake Johnson. The older, rustic cabins sleep four people, and the more modern, newer ones sleep six in two bedrooms. All cabins come furnished with basic linens, towels, utensils, cookware, and the like. Contact ReserveAmerica for reservations.

Near Paynes Prairie in Micanopy, look for the Herlong Mansion bed-and-breakfast inn (352-383-4050; *www.herlong.com*), or head north of the prairie on US 441 in Gainesville for large chain hotels (like Marriott Residence Inn: 352-371-2101).

In Palatka near Ravine Gardens, try the Palatka Riverfront Holiday Inn (386-328-3481) right on the St. Johns River.

How to Get There

To get to Paynes Prairie, take I-75 to the Gainesville area and exit at Micanopy (Exit #374). Go east to US 441, turn left (north), and watch for the park entrance, which is on the right.

For Gold Head Branch, take I-75 to SR 26 (Exit #387) and go east through Gainesville. Continue on about 25 miles to the community of Melrose, then turn left (north) at SR 21. Follow the road through Keystone Heights to the park entrance on the right. Alternately, take I-95 to the St. Augustine area and exit at SR 207 (Exit #311). Go west through Palatka and continue west on SR 100 to Keystone Heights. Turn right (north) on SR 21, and look for the park entrance a few miles ahead.

For Ravine Gardens, take I-95 to the St. Augustine area and exit at SR 207 (Exit #311). Go west to Palatka and watch for brown signs pointing the way through a residential area to the park.

⇜ ⇜ ⇜

Paynes Prairie Preserve State Park
100 Savannah Blvd.
Micanopy, Florida 32667-9702
Phone: 352-466-3397
Admission is $4.00 per vehicle, or $3.00 per vehicle with a single person.
The visitor center, open from 9 a.m. to 5 p.m. every day, houses exhibits about the prairie's natural history and shows a short film about the park.

Mike Roess Gold Head Branch State Park
6239 S.R. 21
Keystone Heights, Florida 32656
Phone: 352-473-4701
Admission is $4.00 per vehicle, or $3.00 per vehicle with a single person.

Ravine Gardens State Park
1600 Twigg Street, P.O. Box 1096
Palatka, Florida 32712
Phone: 386-329-3721
Admission is $4.00 per vehicle.

Northern-central Florida is a terrain of rolling sandhills and karst, where ravines, sinks, and even caves make things interesting. While the caves here aren't open to the public, nature travelers can view sinkholes and other interesting geological formations throughout the region. The large Paynes Prairie takes visitors back to Florida's early days with its bison, wild horses, and scrub cattle.

Nearby

Upper Suwannee River (chapter 8), Matanzas River Lands (chapter 11), Ocala National Forest (chapter 13)

13

Ocala National Forest

Just a half-hour drive off I-75 in the heart of Florida, the city gives way to country, which gives way to the wilderness of Ocala National Forest. Some roads will have forest on one side, farms on the other. You'll see gently rolling sandhills and pine forests. Every once in a while, a cypress swamp or grassy marsh will appear out of the landscape—a pleasant surprise from Mother Nature to vary the view. Deeper exploration turns up clear blue springs that seem to glow, quiet lakes, secluded forest trails, and backroads with beautiful natural scenery. It's no wonder the Timucuan natives called it Ocala—fair land.

Perhaps one of the best things about the forest is that a place so beautiful is preserved and open to everyone. Some people find themselves driving through the forest on the way to another place. The drive through the forest certainly is scenic, but to really get to know the Ocala, you'll have to get out of the car and onto a lake or trail, or into a recreation area. You'll find some farms and a few small towns within the forest boundaries, but most of it is undisturbed, waiting for a nature traveler to revel in its views or a bear to roam through. The Ocala is a key part of a conservation corridor, a strip of preserved land, that stretches to the Georgia border. Starting to the south in Wekiwa Springs State Park and including Lake Woodruff National Wildlife Refuge and Osceola National Forest, this corridor saves the true nature of the peninsula's interior.

Despite this fact, Ocala National Forest is one of the busiest places for outdoor recreation in the heart of Florida. A mecca for off-roaders and solace-seeking hikers alike, the Ocala's abundance of lakes and rivers, and its variety of terrain, make it a popular spot. Of course, its location north of Orlando's hub helps make it a well-visited forest. And because it's the southernmost national forest in the continental United States, that adds to its appeal, too, especially in winter. The spring-based recreation areas like Salt Springs, Silver Glen Springs, and Alexander Springs can be full of people in the summer, but the Ocala's 300,000 acres of public land leave room for everyone.

Figure 12. The sugar mill at Juniper Springs Recreation Area in Ocala National Forest is the beginning of a trail through a beautiful hammock.

What to Do There

Visiting a forest like Ocala can be overwhelming because of all the recreation areas spread over so many miles. If you're a paddler or if you like to fish, you'll likely be interested in the Ocklawaha or St. Johns Rivers, which form part of the forest's boundaries, or you'll visit some of the lakes like Lake Kerr or Lake Dorr. If you're a hiker, you can trek the 67 miles of the Florida National Scenic Trail that meander through. Bird- and wildlife-watchers can stop to observe in the recreation areas or just along the forest roads. Equestrians have several trails all to themselves. Wherever your interests take you, you'll likely find a place you'll want to come back to on another visit.

Trail Tripping

Ocala National Forest gives hikers the chance to be in the wilderness without being too remote. You can hike the Florida Trail, which runs the length of the forest. It goes through Juniper Prairie Wilderness Area (north of the Juniper Springs recreation area) and past Billies Bay Wilderness Area (near the Alexander Springs recreation area), two nationally designated areas.

The forest also has plenty of its own trails for exploration. In the western part of the forest, the Lake Eaton recreation area offers two loop trails: one goes to the lake, where observation platforms provide overlooks at the water's edge, and the other to a sinkhole, where a stairway descends 400 feet to the bottom. Give yourself forty-five to ninety minutes for each trail.

At the Juniper Springs recreation area, a half-mile looping trail that starts at the main spring near an old sugar mill follows the spring run and leads you to the beautiful Fern Hammock Springs area, one of the more scenic spots in the forest. Boils provide clear blue water for fish and turtles, and a bridge provides a picturesque view of the scene.

For a quick walk around a spring head, the Alexander Springs recreation area Timucuan Trail can't be beat. You get a real sense of the thick hammock of hardwood trees and cabbage palms, yet never get too far away from the spring. An overlook on the opposite side of the spring from where you started lets you see a bigger view of the spring.

Another nice trail south of the Salt Springs recreation area makes a loop to Salt Springs Run and back to Highway 19. Here you walk through a sandhill habitat, and you are just as likely to see (or hear) songbirds as you are to see a pygmy rattlesnake. However, you may also hear the whine of airboats on the run. The Salt Springs Run observation deck offers seats where you can rest before walking back. Plan on about one hour to hike this loop.

For a beautiful view of Lake George, walk the quick trail at Silver Glen Springs recreation area. The trailhead isn't well marked, but if you follow the path from the spring, you'll find it. You'll walk through swamps and oak hammocks before reaching the four overlooks at the water's edge.

Horse riders can explore more than 100 miles of the forest on the Lake Alachua Marion, Prairie, Baptist Lake, and Flatwoods trails that are located in the western and southern parts of the forest. Parts of these trails direct riders to recreation areas and campgrounds.

For off-road bicycling, try the Paisley Woods Bicycle Trail near the forest's southern edge and the bike trail near Tishler Pond off road 155AV north of Lynne.

You can pick up a forest map and other information about the trails at the visitor centers, and request maps from the Florida Trail Association.

Paddling and Boating

The Ocklawaha and St. Johns Rivers, along with the forest's many lakes, make the Ocala a good place to explore by boat. You can rent a canoe at the Juniper Springs recreation area or Alexander Springs recreation area. The cost of a rental ranges from $10.50 to $26.00, depending on how long you have the canoe out. If you plan on canoeing all day—several miles—be sure to arrive as early in the day as possible; it can take several hours to paddle to the destination points of Juniper and Alexander Spring creeks, and canoes can get "sold out." Ask the recreation area concession about pickup times and locations.

Boat launches are located all over the forest. For a map of all of them, contact one of the forest visitor centers.

Guided Tours

Captain Tom's Custom Charter Systems (352-546-4823; *www.floridasource. com/captaintoms*) in Silver Springs offers boat trips on the Ocklawaha and Silver Rivers. Rates vary.

Sundowner Kayak Adventures (352-489-9797; *www.sundowner-kayak-adventures.com*) in Ocala offers guided tours of the Silver and Ocklawaha Rivers, among other places in this part of Florida.

In Fort McCoy—a small town north of Silver Springs near the edge of Ocala National Forest—Ocklawaha Canoe Outpost and Resort (352-236-4606; *www. outpostresort.com*) offers guided canoe and kayak tours of the river that last from a few hours to a few days.

Adventure Outpost (386-454-0611; *www.adventureoutpost.net*), based in

High Springs, periodically offers trips on the Silver and Ocklawaha Rivers. Please contact the outpost for the dates of upcoming trips in the area.

Natural Focus (352-383-9443; *www.naturalfocus.org*), based in Eustis south of the forest, offers photography tours in the Ocala.

Nearby Natural Areas

Between the forest's western edge and the city of Ocala is Silver River State Park (352-236-7148). The main feature of the park is the Silver River, which the park calls "the last uninhabited crystal-clear river in Florida." The river flows out of nearby Silver Springs and into the Ocklawaha, a tributary of the St. Johns. Two short hiking trails lead to the river (where you can launch your own canoe or kayak if you can portage it there), and two other trails wander through the sandhills, one of them past a sinkhole. All share the same trailhead at a parking lot by the on-site school and museum. The natural history museum is open on weekends, and admission is $2.00. Park admission is $4.00 per vehicle.

Not far from the park is access to the Marjorie Harris Carr Cross Florida Greenway. From the Sharpes Ferry trailhead, you can hike southeast for 3 miles through Marshall Swamp, ending at the SE 64th Ave. trailhead, where the trail becomes a paved multiuse path that ends in 5 miles at the Baseline Road trailhead. However, the Cross Florida Greenway extends beyond, with a full length of 110 miles. For maps and information, please contact the Florida Office of Greenways and Trails.

Two restoration areas on the Ocklawaha River are worth a visit if you like to hike or if you're a birder. Both Ocklawaha Prairie Restoration Area and Sunnyhill Restoration Area provide levee trails that give you views of the river. (The Moss Bluff entrance of Sunnyhill, however, isn't very scenic, so you may consider entering the restoration area from one of its other entrances.) Both also have other nonriver trails. All are shared by hikers, equestrians, and off-road bikers. You may find the trailheads of these areas just outside the forest's southwestern corner hard to find. Trail maps are sometimes located at trailheads, but not always. You can download a trail map in advance of your visit at the St. Johns River Water Management District Web site at *sjr.state.fl.us*.

Nearby Attractions

Before many of Florida's theme parks drew crowds to Orlando, the more natural Silver Springs (352-236-2121; *www.silversprings.com*) attraction, a National Natural Landmark, was already popular. Claiming to have been first with glass-bottom boats, Silver Springs offers several boat tours, a Jeep safari, live animal exhibits and shows, and occasional concerts. Hours are 10 a.m. to 5 p.m. and ticket prices vary. Next door, Silver Springs operates Wild Waters, a water theme park with slides, tunnels, and a wave pool. The park is open on varying days and times from March through September.

To some people, Ocala means horses. There are several hundred horse farms in the area, mostly west of I-75, where the landscape might make you think you're in Kentucky instead of Florida. If you want to go for a ride, visit Ocala Foxtrotter Ranch (352-347-5551; *www.ocalafoxtrotter.com*); call ahead for the ranch's ride schedule. Some of the farms where race horses are bred are open to the public, such as Bo-Bett Farm (352-591-1020), home of Rugged Lark.

Race fans of another kind may want to check out Don Garlits Museums (877-271-3278; *www.garlits.com*), which you can see from the interstate. Famed drag-racing pro Garlits's facility offers a classic car museum, hall of fame, and gift shop.

Wildlife

With so much land and so many different habitats on it, you can see that Ocala National Forest is a good place for wildlife to live.

Although the forest is a 90-minute drive from the ocean, where so many bird-watchers like to go, the region's rivers, lakes, and forested areas allow glimpses of many kinds of birds. Sandhill cranes in large flocks arrive to winter along the Ocklawaha River. You can look for them by the river and overhead. Even if you don't get to see them, you'll likely hear their loud call, which can be heard for some distance.

If you walk along the swamp trail in Silver River State Park, you'll see curious boxes attached to trees: bat houses. A park ranger said he sees bats almost every evening from the ranger station; just look up at the sky around sunset, he said. Bats common to the park are the southeastern myotis bat, eastern pipistrelle bat, and red bat.

Another curious animal at Silver River is the rhesus monkey. The monkeys are said to be descendants of those that escaped from *Tarzan* movies filmed at Silver Springs many years ago. Another story about the monkeys is that a tour operator once released the monkeys in the area so his tourists would think the area was tropical. Either way, the primates are well-established along the river and take care of themselves. If you see a monkey, don't feed it or approach it because the monkeys are wild and known to bite.

Look for . . .

Florida black bears, considered a threatened species in most of Florida, are right at home in the Ocala. Many people, especially nonresidents, aren't aware that bears live in Florida, but they do find sanctuary in places of the state where development hasn't crowded them out—Florida's national forests, southwestern Florida near Florida Panther National Wildlife Refuge, the Nature Coast area, and parts of Withlacoochee State Forest. There are an estimated 2,000 bears in Florida.

Florida black bears are considered a subspecies of the black bear found throughout most of North America. Bears here are smaller, and some may not hibernate because of the mild winters. Like most bears, Florida black bears eat mostly plants (they love palmetto berries) but supplement their diet with fish and small game. Even though they are called black bears, their color also may be any shade of brown or even blond.

The busiest of all Florida's national forests also has the state's highest concentration of black bears. Roadkill, especially on State Road 40, is a serious problem for bears; state statistics show that 43 percent of Florida black bear roadkill deaths happen here. So when traveling forest roads and SR 40, watch your speed, and watch for bears.

The number of roadkill deaths has led to a debate over whether the bear population is increasing, or just has fewer places to live. People who live near wilderness areas where bears live may be disturbed to find bears foraging in their garbage cans or eating food left out for pets. Researchers say these are likely young males looking for their own territories. Bear/human conflicts happen anywhere there are bears, but the town of Umatilla south of the forest is trying to encourage goodwill toward bears with the annual Florida Black Bear Festival every fall.

Habitats

Ocala National Forest has several distinct ecological communities. The most commonly seen are sandhill, cypress swamp, pine flatwood, and hardwood hammock. Where the Ocklawaha River flows—like the St. Johns River, north instead of south—you find floodplain forest.

Some of that floodplain forest habitat lower down the river was destroyed when the Kirkpatrick Dam went up in 1968 near where the Ocklawaha joins the St. Johns River. The dam was built to enable the Cross Florida Barge Canal, which was already under construction, to span the width of Florida. But construction of the canal stopped in 1971 because of public outcry over the damage to the Ocklawaha River. While various government agencies conducted studies and debated over what to do about the canal and the river, the reservoir that the dam created—usually known as Rodman Reservoir—became a popular recreation area, especially for bass fishing. While manatees were stopped at the locks, other kinds of wildlife like bald eagles made themselves at home on the reservoir.

Now the fate of the dam and reservoir—on the border of Putnam and Marion Counties south of Palatka—is being debated. One side, mostly government agencies and environmentalists, says the Ocklawaha has to be restored: the dam has to come down so the springs under the reservoir can reappear, so manatees can make their way from the St. Johns, to the Ocklawaha, up the Silver River again, and so habitat and water quality can be restored. The other side, mostly fishermen and people who make a living on the reservoir, says taking away the dam will do more harm than good: that a complex ecosystem many wildlife species have come to depend on has developed there over time, that it will cost more to restore and maintain the Ocklawaha than the reservoir, and that taking down the dam could affect the state's Cross Florida Greenway, which was authorized in 1990 to cover the canal's original route. The U.S. Forest Service envisions the reservoir to be gone or reduced by 2006. But some groups, such as Save Rodman Reservoir Inc., are still fighting against that, and a long process of permitting and more studies continues.

The state currently is pushing ahead to restore the river. The Ocklawaha Prairie and Sunnyhill Restoration Areas—both on the original river channel—were purchased for this purpose. More than 6 miles of the upper Ocklawaha River and 2,600 acres of marshes are being restored from farmland that had been drained. A sign at the entrance of Ocklawaha Prairie states that since restoration began in 1987, wildlife have begun returning to the area, like gopher tortoises, gray foxes, bobcats, bears, cranes, herons, egrets, and waterfowl.

While the Ocklawaha is an important feature of the area, in the southwestern part of Ocala National Forest, an area known as Big Scrub is the site of the largest sand pine scrub habitat in the world. Sand pines are found almost exclusively in Florida, and although the original range covered a lot of the state's peninsula, most of this habitat is now limited to the forest.

Where to Stay

Campgrounds

You can be a happy camper here, where there are plenty of places to camp. The biggest campgrounds in the forest (with the most facilities) are at Alexander Springs, Juniper Springs, Salt Springs, and Clearwater Lake and Lake Dorr Recreation Areas. For tent campers who want to camp without the hum of RV generators, try Grassy Pond, Hopkins Prairie, or Big Scrub campgrounds. Other campgrounds, including primitive sites, are scattered around the forest. For campground information, please call 352-625-2520.

Silver River State Park has two campground loops with a total of fifty-nine campsites. The Sharpes Ferry campground is across from the dump station and cabin loop, while the Fort King campground is farther down the road. Campsites run about $15.00 per night. Please call ReserveAmerica for reservations.

Sunnyhill and Ocklawaha Prairie Restoration Areas both have primitive tent campsites that are available by permit only; call 904-329-4410.

Colby Woods RV Resort (352-625-1122) on SR 40 is where the large RVs go when near the forest. With more than 150 full-facility sites, it's a large campground. Most of the campground is open, unshaded RV space, but you can walk down to the Ocklawaha River. A handful of cabins are also available for rent.

Tent campsites are available at Ocklawaha Canoe Outpost and Resort (mentioned above), along with camping rental equipment.

Lodging

If you aren't camping, there are few places to stay inside the forest. One you'll find near Salt Springs is Elite Resort (800-356-2460; *www.eliteresorts.com/ SaltSprings.htm*), which has a campground but also several cottages. The resort has a small grocery store and pub in the same shopping center where you'll find the Salt Springs Visitor Center.

There are many accommodations in Ocala and Silver Springs. The cabins in Silver River State Park (contact ReserveAmerica for reservations) sleep six people, and each has a modern kitchen and gas fireplace. Rates are comparable to a hotel room. Near Ocala's historical town square is Seven Sisters Inn Bed and Breakfast (800-250-3496; *www.7sistersinn.com*), where rates vary with the season. The Holiday Inn (352-236-2575) in Silver Springs is another convenient choice.

On the forest's eastern edge, the town of Astor offers a few places to stay. Riverview Cottages (352-759-2294; *www.riverviewcottages.org*) fronts the St. Johns River.

Ocklawaha Canoe Outpost and Resort (mentioned above) rents log cabins that sleep up to nine people.

How to Get There

Take I-75 to SR 40 (Silver Springs Blvd.) and head east for about 10 miles to the Ocala National Forest visitor center on the corner of SR 40 and FR 314. Alternately, take I-95 to SR 40 and travel west about 35 miles to Highway 19, a main road through the forest.

To get to Silver River State Park, turn south off SR 40 at the Wild Waters theme park on SR 35 and look for the park entrance within a mile on the left side of the road.

To get to Ocklawaha Prairie Restoration Area, take SR 40 to the town of Lynne and turn right (south) on Forest Road 314A (not 314). Where Old River Road joins FR 314A, you may see a sign that says "The Refuge." Turn up Old River Road and look for the restoration area sign on the left.

To get to Sunnyhill Restoration Area from Ocklawaha Prairie, go back to FR 314A and head south. At 464C, there should be a blinking light; turn right and look for the Moss Bluff County Recreation Area sign almost immediately on your left. From here, you can walk along the levee trail that follows the Ocklawaha River. For other entrances, continue on FR 314A to FR 89—the last right turn you can make before the road ends—and turn south. There are three entrances along this road before you reach SR 42, where another entrance is to the west.

↬ ↬ ↬

Ocala National Forest Visitor Center
17147 SR 40
Silver Springs, Florida 34488
352-625-2520

Pittman Visitor Center
45621 Highway 19
Altoona, Florida 32702
352-669-7495

Salt Springs Visitor Center
14100 N. Highway 19
352-685-3070
www.fs.fed.us/r8/florida

Entrance to most recreation areas is $4.00 per person.

The forest's springs, rivers, lakes, and gently rolling terrain, along with its location north of Orlando, make it a popular place for outdoor activities of all kinds. The forest also has the largest concentration of black bears in the state.

Nearby

Land of the Caves, Sinks, and Ravines (chapter 12), St. Johns River Country (chapter 15), Central Lakes and Springs (chapter 19)

14

Space Coast

Sticking out into the Atlantic Ocean like a diamond in its setting, Merritt Island National Wildlife Refuge and Canaveral National Seashore together are a natural jewel. These sister natural lands preserve miles of undisturbed habitat for thousands of species, some of which would be extinct if not for these adjacent conservation areas.

With more species of endangered plants and animals than any other national wildlife refuge in the continental United States, Merritt Island presents nature lovers with the opportunity for countless encounters with wildlife and infinite connections with the Earth. From Indian River to Mosquito Lagoon, the refuge offers 140,000 acres of nature's quiet beauty. Seven-mile Black Point Wildlife Drive—a self-guided tour on a mostly unpaved, one-way road—is a favorite of bird-watchers and photographers, and a great way to get acquainted with the refuge. Driving, hiking, or biking down the road, it's easy to see alligators, turtles, snakes, ospreys, herons, red-winged blackbirds, roseate spoonbills, killdeers, and marsh rats.

Canaveral National Seashore's beach stretches for 24 quiet miles along central Florida's Atlantic coast, most of it untouched by roads. This makes it Florida's longest undeveloped Atlantic beach. In fact, most people end up driving for some distance to get from one entrance of the park to the other because of the roadless wilderness in between. And the ocean stretches out in front of you all the way to Africa, larger and bluer than remembered, making you aware you're a small part of the world, the way a sky full of stars does. The beach is an amazing part of the seashore, but most of the park's 58,000 acres are taken up by Mosquito Lagoon, an important estuary that gives the park's barrier island variety and intrigue. By boat, you can explore its little islands and look for sandbars peppered with birds.

The area covered by the refuge and seashore was originally meant for the National Aeronautics and Space Administration (NASA), but the space program eventually decided it didn't need all the land. The refuge now acts partially as a buffer zone around the top-secret Kennedy Space Center. The good

Figure 13. Roseate spoonbills are at home along Black Point Wildlife Drive in Merritt Island National Wildlife Refuge.

news is this means almost certain continued undeveloped status for the island. The bad news is it's possible some fish are killed when shuttles are launched. The amusing news was when courtship-happy yellow-shafted flickers destroyed the fuel tank insulation of space shuttle Discovery in 1995, showing how nature can outdo even the best multimillion-dollar plans. The space center, refuge, and seashore all maintain that the space program and surrounding natural lands coexist with few ill effects on the environment. Because of NASA's presence, the region is known as the Space Coast.

The refuge was established in 1963 and the seashore in 1975, but people have been visiting the area for centuries. The Ais and better-known Timucuan natives lived here before European explorers came in the 1500s. Evidence of the natives' presence exists in the form of piles of shells they left behind (called middens or Indian mounds) while making meals. Later came sailing ships that wrecked off Cape Canaveral's jutting shore. Pioneers came, trying to grow citrus fruits and catch fish. Now the area is frequented by astronauts, anglers, beachgoers, and tourists.

What to Do There

Between the seashore's Apollo Beach and the refuge's visitor center, there are a number of ways to explore this land of beaches, marshes, scrub, hammock, and river.

The visitor centers are good first stops when visiting the refuge and the seashore. You'll see signs for them from the respective main park roads. At the visitor centers, you can watch a short video about the refuge or seashore and pick up maps and other literature. The refuge visitor center has some nice exhibits and a nature trail/boardwalk. Volunteers or rangers are on hand to answer your questions before you begin exploring either natural area.

As you might expect for anything labeled a seashore, the beach is the main draw for visitors there. (Swimming is allowed, but note that lifeguards are on duty only from Memorial Day to Labor Day, at parking lots #1 and #8.) While the beach is one of the best in Florida, a closer look reveals there's a lot more to the seashore than the shoreline.

Trail Tripping

Most of the trails in the seashore and refuge are short, taking an hour or less to walk and come back. There are four trails in the refuge and three trails in the seashore; to find them, just look for signs along the main park road for each area.

The refuge's half-mile Oak Hammock Trail and two-mile Palm Hammock Trail take hikers through hardwood hammock and subtropical forest. Both trails are accessible from the same parking lot. The longer Palm Hammock Trail loops around the Oak Hammock Trail.

Partway down the refuge's fabulous Black Point Wildlife Drive is Cruickshank Trail, named after naturalist and photographer Allan Cruickshank. This is a 5-mile loop enhanced by a photo blind (where photographers can hide to photograph wildlife) and observation tower. As with most of the rest of the wildlife drive, this trail is out in the open, providing wide views of marsh—and the occasional sight of NASA's large vehicle assembly building in the distance.

Near the entrance to the seashore's Playalinda Beach, yet still in the refuge, is the 1-mile Scrub Trail. This sandy loop is a place to look out for Florida scrub jays and gopher tortoises.

The first trail you'll come to after entering the seashore's north (main) entrance is Turtle Mound, named for the pile of shells left by Timucuan natives shucking oysters and other shellfish up to twelve centuries ago. The trail leads to this midden, the highest point in the park at thirty-five feet, and provides a good view of Mosquito Lagoon and the Atlantic Ocean.

After passing the seashore visitor center on the main park road, you can walk the Eldora Hammock trail. This is a small loop near the Eldora State House, a museum that preserves the memory of the town of Eldora. (See more under Guided Tours, below.)

Down the road from the Eldora State House is Castle Windy. This is a shady walk from a beach parking area to Mosquito Lagoon. Here you can walk through a maritime hammock on the barrier island. Look for citrus trees among the live oaks and cabbage palms, a remnant of the time when Canaveral was farmland.

There aren't designated horse trails in the seashore, but equestrians with their own horses may ride in the Apollo district from November through April. Riders must obtain a horse-use permit seven days beforehand; call the park office for more information.

Paddling and Boating

The seashore's wide, shallow Mosquito Lagoon with its islands is fun to explore by boat. Because the lagoon is an average of four feet deep, canoes and kayaks are perfect here. (Ask for a Shipyard Island Canoe Trail map at the seashore visitor center.) Of course, the Intracoastal Waterway goes through the lagoon's western side, where the water is deeper.

There are several boat ramps for the lagoon, both inside and outside the seashore boundary, and a few boat ramps for the refuge. For locations of all the boat ramps, request a park brochure or download a map from the seashore or refuge Web site; because the seashore and refuge are so close together, many maps and brochures include both.

Boat rentals are available at Space Coast Watercraft Rentals (321-267-7776; *www.spacecoastwatercraft.com*) in Titusville on the Indian River, from which you could access Mosquito Lagoon via the Haulover Canal, and Backwater Marine (386-427-4514) in New Smyrna Beach.

Guided Tours

The seashore offers a two-hour pontoon boat tour of Mosquito Lagoon on Saturdays and Sundays outside of turtle-nesting season. The tour is $13.00 per person, and reservations are required. Call the park office for times and availability.

Staff members also offer a tour of the Eldora State House, a museum open from 10 a.m. to 4 p.m., although you may walk through the house by yourself. The house was renovated to showcase exhibits about the town of Eldora that stood where the seashore is today. From the mid-1800s into the early twentieth century, Eldora was a small citrus-producing town with an important location on the lagoon where citrus and other supplies could be shipped. But freezing weather ruined the citrus crops, and a new railroad and the implementation of the Intracoastal Waterway on the western side of the lagoon made Eldora's location unimportant. The town fizzled and became part of the federal government's property.

Space Coast Nature Tours (321-267-4551; *www.spacecoastnaturetours.com*) in Titusville offers a variety of boat tours in the area, with emphases on nature, history, and even shuttle launches. Please contact the company for more information and reservations.

Marine Discovery Center (866-257-4828; *www.marinediscoverycenter.org*) in New Smyrna Beach offers two-hour educational boat tours of Indian River Lagoon. Tours run Tuesday through Saturday. Tickets are $20.00 for adults, $16.00 for seniors, and $10.00 for children twelve and under.

Nearby Natural Areas

Seminole Rest is overseen by the seashore but isn't exactly in the park. On the western edge of Mosquito Lagoon in the town of Oak Hill, Seminole Rest is the site of more Timucuan (not Seminole) middens and two preserved buildings from the turn of the last century. The site is open from 6 a.m. to 6 p.m. To get there from the seashore's north district, take A1A to US 1 and go south to Oak Hill, then watch for signs to lead the way.

For an almost 360-degree view of undeveloped freshwater marsh, visit Spruce Creek Park. Here, you can see egrets, warblers, mockingbirds, and white and brown pelicans, depending on the season. The park has a campground and nature trail. A bonus is the adjacent Spruce Creek Outfitters (386-763-9417), where you can get a kayak and explore the Spruce Creek State Canoe Trail from the park to past I-95. To get there from the seashore's north district, take A1A to US 1 and go north. Drive for about 7 miles, cross the Spruce Creek bridge, and look for the park on the left.

Purchased under Brevard County's Environmentally Endangered Lands program, Enchanted Forest Nature Sanctuary (321-264-5185) is a 393-acre preserve. This sanctuary has conserved land to save various ecosystems, such as mesic hammock and scrub. Enchanted Forest is open Monday through Saturday from 9 a.m. until 5 p.m. and Sunday from 1 p.m. to 5 p.m. Walk the trails on your own, or call ahead to reserve a guided tour. The sanctuary is located south of Titusville on Highway 450, a half-mile west of US 1.

Ponce de Leon Inlet, where Halifax River empties into the ocean, is preserved as a park on both sides: Smyrna Dunes Park on the south and Lighthouse Point Park on the north. A visit to Smyrna Dunes Park is a nice complement to visiting the seashore because so much of Smyrna Dunes is left in a natural state. A boardwalk loops around the park's coastal scrub, past the inlet and to the beach, while a tangent boardwalk takes you around mangroves near the river. The park, in the Scrub Jay Cluster of the Great Florida Birding Trail, is a good place to spot warblers, pelicans, sparrows, terns, sandpipers, and American kestrels. Seasonal robins fill the hammock near the end of the boardwalk. You may even spot a fox. Admission is $3.50 per car. To get there from the seashore's north district, take A1A north to Flagler Ave. and turn left. At Peninsula Drive, turn right and take the road to the end at the park's entrance.

Nearby Attractions

On the northern side of the inlet, you can visit the tallest lighthouse in Florida (the second-tallest in the nation). Ponce de Leon Inlet Lighthouse (386-761-1821; *www.ponceinlet.org*) at 175 feet tall is a National Historic Landmark. Standing since the 1880s, the lighthouse is now a museum open from 10 a.m. to 5 p.m. Admission is $5.00 for adults and $1.50 for children eleven and under. To get there from the seashore's north district, take A1A to US 1 and go north. At Dunlawton Ave., turn right and go east to A1A, then turn right and go south toward the inlet. You will see the lighthouse and signs to the lighthouse.

Despite the seashore's name, when many people hear the word "Canaveral," they think of space. Kennedy Space Center (321-449-4444; *www.kennedyspacecenter.com*) attracts visitors from around the world. The Visitor Complex is free, and it offers exhibits, educational films, displays, some of the real rockets that flew in previous space missions, and even daily appearances by astro-

nauts. To tour any other part of the space complex, however, you must purchase tickets for a bus tour of the other facilities, and prices vary. The space
center is open from 9 a.m. to 6 p.m. every day except Christmas and some
launch days. To get there, exit I-95 at State Road 407 (Exit #212) and go northeast to County Road 405. Turn left and go east to the space center.

NASCAR fans will enjoy visiting Daytona USA (386-947-6800; *www.
daytonausa.com*) to the north in Daytona Beach. Open from 9 a.m. to 7 p.m.,
this museum/attraction shows off the brands that make car racing, touches on
racing history, and gives fans a chance to tour the famous speedway on a tram.
Ticket prices vary depending on which parts of Daytona USA you want to explore. To get there, take I-95 and exit at US 92/International Speedway Blvd.
(Exit #261A). Go east a few miles and look for the speedway on the right.

Wildlife

The river, lagoon, beach, islands, marsh, and uplands provide diverse habitats
for diverse wildlife. From bottle-nosed dolphins and West Indian manatees to
peregrine falcons and reddish egrets, the area is home—if only temporarily, for
some species—to several animals that swim, fly, and run. There are fourteen
species here that are endangered or threatened, including sea turtles, the Florida scrub jay, the wood stork, and the northern right whale.

With the refuge and seashore being surrounded by water, wildlife watching
turns to the water as well. The beach is a good place to spot wintering shorebirds and year-round wading birds. In winter, too, you might be lucky enough
to spot a right whale offshore. Dolphins, manatees, and sea turtles sometimes
hang out in the lagoon or river. The lagoon islands are good places to see raccoons and cotton rats.

Astoundingly, there are 310 species of birds that visit or live in the seashore
or refuge at one time or another, drawing bird-watchers from other states and
countries to the park. Chances are good that you will find bird-watchers at the
park with whom you can share sightings.

The refuge is the scene of two birding festivals each year. The Welcome Back
Songbirds Festival held in April celebrates the return of migratory birds passing through. The day-long event is free, but some special tours are offered for a
fee. The event draws bird-watchers from all over, so if you want to learn about
birds, attending the festival is a great way to begin. Many volunteer- and
ranger-led tours and talks throughout the day make it fun. The Space Coast
Birding and Wildlife Festival held over a long weekend in November features
seminars, field trips, and competitive "birdathons." Speakers, exhibits, and so-

cial events make the festival weekend a busy and bird-filled one. For information on either festival, please call the refuge.

Look for . . .

The small Atlantic salt marsh snake, listed as a threatened species, isn't one you're likely to see. But it's worth mentioning because the Space Coast is one of the few places in the world where it's found. Living mainly on islands in Mosquito Lagoon, this marsh snake eats small fish among the grasses and isn't likely to harm people.

Habitats

The refuge and seashore have a location that gives the complex a unique mix of habitats. It holds not only a sandy barrier island beach, but also an island-dotted lagoon. It's the scene of brackish marshes, but also uplands where hardwood trees and scrub bushes dominate. Together, these natural communities support a variety of plants—1,054 species by some accounts.

The interesting thing about the seashore's beach is that only the south district's Playalinda Beach has dunes; the north district's Apollo Beach has sandy bluffs, and for most of the seashore's 24 miles of beach you won't find dunes.

Back from the beach, you'll find hardwood and palm hammocks, where the Castle Windy trail cuts through.

Beyond the hammocks in the south district, you'll find scrub habitat and pine flatwoods. But in the north district, you'll run into Mosquito Lagoon's salt marsh, where islands are alternately populated by cabbage palms and mangroves.

Farther west are the refuge's uplands north of Haulover Canal, which is a passageway between Mosquito Lagoon and Indian River. To the south, salt marshes dominate, with a few hardwood hammocks, until you reach the river.

Mosquito Lagoon is considered an Outstanding Florida Water. Even so, Mosquito Lagoon and connecting Indian River have water-quality issues that have been affecting the sea life that live there. Some sea turtles living in the waters have developed tumors on their skin, signs of a disease called fibropapillomatosis that experts attribute to the water quality. The tumors can restrict movement or even blind the turtles. Some dolphins have developed a fungal infection related to the water.

Where to Stay

Campgrounds

There is no camping in the refuge, and the only camping in the seashore is primitive. Remote campsites on islands in Mosquito Lagoon, reached by private boat, are open year-round. Some sites are better suited for groups, and some for families; call the park office or download a map of these backcountry campsites to locate the campsites on the islands. Two primitive beach campsites are available outside of sea turtle nesting season (roughly late April until September, although park staff may extend this ban as needed, depending on the presence of turtle nests). Call the park to reserve campsites.

Outside the complex, try Spruce Creek Park (mentioned above) or Riverbreeze Park (386-345-5525) in Oak Hill, which is on the western side of Mosquito Lagoon and a site on the Great Florida Birding Trail. Both are Volusia County parks, and they offer tent camping only. Prices range from $10.00 to $20.00 per night, depending on the season.

To the south, Manatee Hammock Park (321-264-5083) in Titusville offers both tent and RV sites ranging from $12.50 to $20.00 per night. Right on the Indian River Lagoon, this can be a good place to watch space shuttle launches.

Lodging

There are lots of hotels and motels to choose from in New Smyrna Beach and in Titusville. The Best Western Space Shuttle Inn (321-269-9100; *www.spaceshuttleinn.com*) in Titusville offers nature packages and has its own park. Also try the Riverside Inn (321-267-7900), a small motel right on Indian River that offers views of shuttle launches.

How to Get There

To get to the refuge and to the southern entrance of the seashore (Playalinda Beach), exit I-95 at SR 406 (Exit #220) and head east. Cross the river and take CR 402 at the fork in the road. The road ends at the Playalinda Beach entrance. This entrance may be closed during important NASA events like shuttle launches.

For the main entrance to the seashore (the north district, Apollo Beach), take I-95 to the Daytona Beach area. Exit at SR 44 (Exit #249) and go east. Take the A1A extension across the river and follow the road south. At the end of the road, you'll find the entrance.

❧ ❧ ❧

Canaveral National Seashore
7611 South Atlantic Ave.
New Smyrna Beach, Florida 32169
386-428-3384, ext. 10
www.nps.gov/cana/
The seashore is open from 6 a.m. to 6 p.m. November through March, and 6 a.m. to 8 p.m. April through October. South district access may vary depending on NASA activities. Admission is $5.00 per day per car, or $3.00 per person on foot or bicycle.

Merritt Island National Wildlife Refuge
P.O. Box 6504
Titusville, Florida 32782
321-861-0667
merrittisland.fws.gov
Visitor center hours are 8:00 a.m. to 4:30 p.m. Monday through Friday, and 9:00 a.m. to 5:00 p.m. on Saturday. The visitor center is closed on Sunday. Admission is free, but donations are welcome at the visitor center and at the entrance of Black Point Wildlife Drive. Note: the only restrooms in the refuge are at the visitor center.

This eco-trip offers the best of all nature worlds, so it's a great trip for beginning nature travelers. You'll find quiet, remote spots—and beautiful beaches and wetlands—yet it's not far from nearby towns.
Nearby
Upper St. Johns River (chapter 16), Indian River Lagoon Lands (chapter 26)

15

St. Johns River Country

Volusia County is probably best known for Daytona Beach—a destination for college students on spring break, for race cars, and for motorcycle events: Bike Week and Biketoberfest.

But go just a bit away from the coast to the western portion of the county, and it's almost another land. There are tracts of forest, large lakes, powerful springs, and the St. Johns River, one of fourteen rivers in the nation designated an American Heritage River. In fact, the river features so prominently in the area's focus that it calls itself St. Johns River Country, a fitting name. North of Orlando's bustle and directly east of Ocala National Forest, the area is easy to reach, yet close to nature.

As a destination for exploring nature, it's perfect for the nature traveler who doesn't mind—or prefers—smaller, more easily visited areas that aren't far from town. It's an especially attractive area for those who like to be out on the water: the river is a constant feature and forms the western border of the county.

Lake Woodruff National Wildlife Refuge, DeLeon Springs State Park, and Blue Spring State Park here are a trio of natural areas that sit on the St. Johns River. Each is different from the others, though, and offers its own take on the waterway: Lake Woodruff with its water-surrounded impoundments, DeLeon Springs with its large swimming area and scenic sugar mill, Blue Spring with its scrub habitat and cool-weather manatees. They all add up to a large preserved region with a lot to explore.

What to Do There

All of these areas are what they are because of water. The refuge is named for 2,200-acre Lake Woodruff (in turn named for long-ago plantation owner Major Joseph Woodruff), and the smaller Lake Dexter is also part of the refuge. The state parks are named for the springs, of course. DeLeon Springs, where

Figure 14. The Old Spanish Sugar Mill Grill and Griddle House faces the spring run at DeLeon Springs State Park.

Spanish explorer Ponce de Leon is said to have arrived looking for his fountain of youth, pumps twenty to thirty million gallons of water to the river every day. Paddling, boating, and fishing are popular activities here, and you'll find plenty of marinas and fish camps along the river.

When you're ready for a break from your exploring, you'll find the best place to eat—and make—pancakes in a state park. The Old Spanish Sugar Mill Grill and Griddle House at DeLeon Springs sits within view of the springhead, near the site of an original mill that used the spring run to process sugar. Sit at a table outfitted with a built-in griddle, and pour pancake batter made from grain ground right there to make your own hotcakes. You can also order other items from the menu. The Sugar Mill opens at 9 a.m. on weekdays and 8 a.m. on weekends and holidays, and stops serving at 4 p.m.

Trail Tripping

The 21,000-acre Lake Woodruff offers miles of walking or off-road bicycling along raised dikes that surround the wetlands, taking you through mostly open territory. An observation tower provides a good view of the marsh.

At DeLeon Springs, a short nature loop meanders through a wooded area where Old Methuselah, a 500-year-old bald cypress tree, grows. The loop looks as though it used to be a garden footpath in the state park's days as a resort—which would explain all the benches and azaleas along the trail. (Before the resort, in the 1800s, the park was part of Spring Garden Plantation. The state park system acquired the land in 1982.)

If you really want to hike, take the 5-mile Wild Persimmon Trail, which you reach from the nature loop. The Wild Persimmon Trail, named after the native tree (the fruit is edible, but please leave it for wildlife—all plants and animals are protected in state parks), is a side trail of the Florida National Scenic Trail. To hike it, you must register at the ranger station first and plan to be back one hour before sunset. The small natural history museum at DeLeon Springs displays photos of a Florida black bear that a hiker captured along this trail.

There are longer trails at nearby Tiger Bay State Forest and Lake George State Forest (below).

Paddling and Boating

Lake Woodruff and DeLeon Springs are good places to explore by canoe or kayak. In fact, because most of the refuge is water, that's the best way to explore it.

You can rent canoes and paddleboats at DeLeon Springs, and use the concession's map to find your way to the refuge via the St. Johns River. Or you can launch your own boat at the state park's ramp.

Several local marinas rent motorboats and houseboats for extended explorations of the river. Houseboats are generally rented by the week and can accommodate several people, so they're best for a group (especially if you can split the cost).

Airboats are popular on the St. Johns but aren't allowed in the state parks or refuge.

Swimming, Snorkeling, and Diving

The springhead at DeLeon Springs attracts crowds, especially when the temperature rises, because of the spring's constant 72-degree water. DeLeon is surrounded by concrete like a regular swimming pool and flows under a walkway, spilling over rocks into a run that flows to the St. Johns. While the spring doesn't look natural from this vantage point, the water is still clear and pure. Diving is limited to instructors and up to six students, and entering the underwater cave isn't allowed.

The spring at Blue Spring State Park is left in its natural state, unlike at DeLeon Springs. Swimming and snorkeling are allowed in the spring only when manatees aren't present. Divers here are allowed to enter the underwater cave, but they can't go too far because a huge boulder at about thirty feet blocks further exploration. Cave diving is dangerous and should be pursued only after earning cave diving certification—in fact, many places require this specialized certification.

Guided Tours

Both state parks have tour boat operators that provide narrated tours of the St. Johns River, where wildlife sightings are common. Reservations are recommended; prices range from $10.00 to $16.00. At DeLeon Springs, Safari River Tours (386-668-1002; *www.safaririvertours.com*) offers a couple of trips per day, lasting around two hours, and also goes into the nearby refuge. At Blue Spring, the St. Johns River Ecotours (386-917-0724) boat leaves at 10:00 a.m. and 1:00 p.m. for a two-hour tour.

Outside of the parks, consider Manatee Seeker Scenic Cruise (800-587-7131; *www.vis-arts.com/manatee*), also offering a two-hour narrated river tour, based at Pier 44 Marina on State Road 44.

Nearby Natural Areas

Hontoon Island State Park (386-736-5309) is an actual island in the St. Johns. It offers a place for river boaters to dock and stretch, and for picnickers and campers to enjoy the unique area of this small park. You can reach the island only by boat; a ferry can take you across for a small fee. The ferry runs from 8 a.m. until one hour before sundown. Once there, you can rent canoes by the hour and explore the short nature trails. The best way to get to the ferry by land is to watch for brown state park signs (starting on US 17 in DeLand) and follow them, because you'll drive for almost a half-hour past pastures and through residential areas that can make directions hard to follow. Stick with the signs.

For a more remote experience, you may want to take time to explore Tiger Bay State Forest (386-226-0250), which is between DeLand and Daytona Beach along US 92 (also called International Speedway Boulevard). You'll find entrances on both sides of the road. The south entrance offers a 2.5-mile hiking trail along the historical Tiger Bay Canal and ends at Rattlesnake Pond. The north entrance offers roads for bicyclists and horseback riders, and motorboating and fishing on Indian Lake and Scroggin Lake (although no rentals are available on site).

Another forest to explore is Lake George State Forest (386-985-7822), which lies across Lake George from Ocala National Forest. Visitors can walk or ride horses along forest roads. This state forest also is the site of ancient Indian shell mounds. To get there, go north from the town of DeLeon Springs on US 17 to State Road 40 and turn left (west). A half-mile before you get to the town of Astor, you should see a sign for St. Johns River Road, which will take you north into the forest. Another tract of the forest, Bluffton Recreation Area to the west along the same road, is a site on the Great Florida Birding Trail. Watch for the brown birding trail sign showing the turn-off, and follow the road to the end, where there's a short nature trail loop.

Nearby Attractions

Downtown DeLand, south of DeLeon Springs, is a charming place to visit. Home of Stetson University, the first private university in Florida and named for famous hat maker John Stetson, DeLand has a Southern college town feel to it while remaining small enough to stay friendly. Antiques shops, a bookstore, and an ice cream parlor are among the places you'll find downtown along the main street, US 17. The Gillespie Museum of Minerals (386-822-7330; *www.gillespiemuseum.stetson.edu*) on the Stetson campus houses a fantastic display of gems, stones, and dinosaur bones and is open Monday through Friday while school is in session.

If you like horses, then visit Spring Garden Ranch Training Center (877-985-5654; *www.springgardenranch.com*) in DeLeon Springs. Spring Garden has been a training center for more than fifty years. Some 500 horses train here, including famous Gallo Blue Chip.

The DeLand Naval Air Station Museum (386-738-4149) near the municipal airport preserves the memory of a local training base for World War II dive-bombing pilots. The museum is open Tuesday through Saturday from noon until 4:00 p.m.

And if you're daring, try one of West Volusia's most popular sports—skydiving! Skydive DeLand (386-738-3539; *www.skydivedeland.com*) offers a variety of aerial adventures.

Wildlife

Depending on what time of year you visit St. Johns River Country, you may see manatees, alligators, turtles, various woodland birds, waterfowl, and even Florida black bears.

With the river and the abundance of natural areas in the region, you can imagine that wildlife-watching is good here. Lake Woodruff, DeLeon Springs, and Blue Spring are part of the Great Florida Birding Trail's Scrub-Jay Cluster. These natural areas also are part of an important wildlife corridor that stretches from Wekiwa Springs State Park in Apopka up to the northern reaches of Ocala National Forest—and perhaps beyond, depending on whom you talk to. This corridor provides much-needed wildlife habitat and preserves ecologically sensitive lands in central Florida, where development has gobbled up a lot of natural areas, so it is a great place to see many species.

In winter, the refuge and state parks see many migratory birds that arrive from the north, looking for a warmer home. You can easily view many wading birds from the refuge's dikes as you walk around the wetlands. If you walk these impoundments, you likely will also see plenty of alligators and turtles.

The cooler months give Blue Spring the chance to celebrate the return of manatees, which travel from the Atlantic Ocean, up the St. Johns River and finally to Blue Spring for the warmer water. (It may be just seventy-two degrees year-round, but in the winter, that's much warmer than the river and the ocean.) The clear spring water makes it easy to see the manatees, which are sensitive to the cold. On warmer winter days, manatees may venture out to the river.

Look for . . .

Lake Woodruff is said to be the home of the second-largest population of swallow-tailed kites, which arrive from Central and South America to nest for the summer months. Unlike most of Florida's birds, which arrive for the winter, swallow-tailed kites are tropical birds that find Florida's summers more tolerable than those at home. These black-and-white birds of prey are named for their definitive forked tail, which is easy to identify as they soar overhead, if even for a few seconds. (Check out the rehabilitation and tracking of a Woodruff kite at Kite Site 2000: *www.adoptabird.org/kitesite*).

Habitats

Like the Nile in Egypt, St. Johns River is one of the few rivers in the world that flow north instead of south. (A few other Florida creeks and rivers, like the Ocklawaha and Silver Rivers, also flow north.) The St. Johns is Florida's longest river at 310 miles and drains a sixth of Florida's water into the Atlantic Ocean at its mouth in Jacksonville.

In 2003, a $4.6-billion river restoration project was announced. According to the St. Johns River Water Management District, the restoration will focus on improving water quality and acquiring land to preserve habitat. Details of the restoration have yet to be worked out as of this writing.

At several points along the river, there's not so much of a bank as there is an extension of the river into marshland. These freshwater marshes are important breeding grounds and habitat for many species, from birds to reptiles and amphibians.

At the refuge, there are more than 11,000 acres of marshland, mostly around the edge of Lake Woodruff. While some of the wetland has been impounded by dikes, creating large rectangles of water, this is still important habitat. Away from the dikes, there are more than 5,000 acres of hardwood swamps, along with pine flatwoods and islands thick with scrubby palm trees—a beautiful true Florida sight.

Of course, not all of the river area is wet. In DeLeon Springs, you'll find oak hammocks, particularly along Wild Persimmon Trail. Blue Spring has a sand pine scrub area near the campground.

Where to Stay

Campgrounds

Blue Spring State Park has fifty-one campsites with water and electricity. Restrooms with hot showers are nearby. Hontoon Island State Park offers twelve primitive, shady campsites. Contact ReserveAmerica for reservations.

Hontoon Island also allows you to sleep overnight in your own boat. If you'd like to consider a dock slip at the park for a small fee, be aware that slips are available on a first-come, first-served basis.

Nearby Highland Park Fish Camp (800-525-3477; *www.hpfishcamp.com*) offers boat slips, too, and a campground.

For primitive camping, try Tiger Bay or Lake George State Forests.

Lodging

Blue Spring has six two-bedroom cabins complete with kitchen, bathroom, air conditioning, and gas fireplace. Hontoon Island also offers six cabins, but they are primitive, without kitchens or air conditioning, and there are no restroom facilities. Contact ReserveAmerica for reservations.

There are plenty of lodging options in the area, especially in DeLand, where you can choose from large chain hotels (like Holiday Inn: 386-738-5200) or bed-and-breakfast inns (like Eastwood Terrace Inn: 800-613-8424; *www.east woodinn.com*). Near Lake George State Forest in Astor, Riverview Cottages (352-759-2294) rents efficiencies with a view of the St. Johns River.

How to Get There

From the north or south, take I-95 to US 92 (Exit #261), and go southwest to DeLand. At US 17, turn right (north) for Lake Woodruff and DeLeon Springs, or left (south) for Blue Spring, and watch for signs to the natural areas, all located in residential areas.

From the west, take I-4 northeast to US 17 (Exit #80) around Sanford, and then take US 17 north to the general area.

    ⊷   ⊷   ⊷

Lake Woodruff National Wildlife Refuge
P.O. Box 488
Mud Lake Road
DeLeon Springs, Florida 32130
Phone: 386-985-4673
The refuge is open sunrise to sunset. Admission is free.

DeLeon Springs State Park
601 Ponce DeLeon Blvd.
DeLeon Springs, Florida 32130
Phone: 386-985-4212
The entrance fee is $5.00 per vehicle.

Blue Spring State Park
2100 West French Ave.
Orange City, Florida 32763
Phone: 386-775-3663
The entrance fee is $5.00 per vehicle.

Just as its name sounds, this area is dominated by the St. Johns River. Natural areas along the river help preserve this nationally recognized waterway and offer nature travelers the chance to explore the river basin's springs, wetlands, and uplands.

Nearby

Space Coast (chapter 14), Ocala National Forest (chapter 13), Central Lakes and Springs (chapter 19)

16

Upper St. Johns River

Florida's longest river stretches for 310 miles. At its mouth in Jacksonville, the St. Johns is 4 miles wide, a maze of marshes, islands, creeks, shipping channels, and naval stations. Farther inland, it widens into lakes, like beads on a chain. At its headwaters, it's hard to tell exactly where it begins in St. Johns Marsh west of Vero Beach—far south of its mouth.

The river flows north, so it can be confusing to think of its upper reaches as being south. From the St. Johns Marsh heading north, Blue Cypress Lake forms. Marsh reappears, then Lake Hell 'n' Blazes. Then it's a marsh, then Little Sawgrass Lake and Sawgrass Lake before a clear river channel appears, west of Melbourne. The lakes get bigger: Washington, Winder, and Poinsett swell out of the marsh. The river continues up the coast, then turns inland in a clover of lakes near Sanford before rolling on.

The state of Florida has called the St. Johns River "Florida's first highway," indicating its importance in Florida history. Timucuan natives canoed the river, calling it Welaka, or river of lakes. Spanish and French explorers discovered the river as they both tried to lay claim to the rich land. Steamboats carried goods up and down the river, finding good stopping places that have since become towns. Seminole War raids and Civil War movements took place here. Today, the river is a great place for recreation and preservation—certainly true of the upper reaches.

Most of the river along this stretch is covered by natural areas. William Beardall Tosohatchee State Reserve, a former private hunting ground, fronts 19 miles of the river. Pine forests, hardwood hammocks, and swamps cover 28,000 acres here. Adjoining the reserve to form a large natural corridor are a national wildlife refuge, a state forest, and an assortment of conservation areas run by the St. Johns River Water Management District.

One of these areas is Seminole Ranch Conservation Area, where the St. Johns River flows for 12 miles. Most of Seminole Ranch's 6,000 acres are wetlands on either side of the river.

Another conservation area, Blue Cypress, takes us south to the headwaters. Blue Cypress Lake, marshes, and levees reveal the birth of the river.

Figure 15. Many natural areas offer access to the St. Johns River.

These and other nearby natural lands along the river allow nature travelers to go in search of the upper, southern domain of a landmark Florida river.

What to Do There

The upper St. Johns River region covers a lot of territory and encompasses several natural lands, so nature travelers will find plenty to do.

Trail Tripping

Three Florida National Scenic Trail side trails have been established in the area, at Tosohatchee, Seminole Ranch, and Canaveral Marshes Conservation Area (under Nearby Natural Areas, below). In the southern portion of Seminole Ranch, getting out on foot is the only way to explore the conservation area. For information and maps, contact the Florida Trail Association.

All of Tosohatchee's roads are open to foot, bicycle, and vehicle traffic. From the entrance, Beehead Road heads east toward the river. From here, side roads take you to the parallel Power Line Road, which actually ends at the river. Beehead Road intersects Fish Hole Road, which goes as far as the Beeline Expressway, where traffic noise interrupts the natural scene. From there, the road turns north and ends at Power Line Road, so it's possible to travel through the park in a loop this way.

Besides the roads and the multiuse trail, a hiking-only trail winds through the forest. This is the only way to access the reserve's two primitive backcountry campsites.

Horseback riders must stay on the designated multiuse trail that loops around the reserve, but this still provides several miles to ride. Horse trailer parking is located at various points along the trail and at the horse camping area.

In Seminole Ranch, hikers, off-road bicyclists, and equestrians are welcome on trails, but only foot traffic is allowed on the Florida Trail. In Blue Cypress, visitors can hike or bike the levees that cut through the marshes. Levee trails don't lead from the main recreation area at Blue Cypress Lake, but rather from parking areas along State Road 60.

Trail trippers should use trail maps, be prepared for standing water after heavy rains, and be aware of hunting dates in all of these areas.

Paddling and Boating

Tosohatchee doesn't have an official boat ramp, but people do launch onto the St. Johns River at the end of Power Line Road. Airboats are prohibited in the reserve. North of the park along SR 50, there are other boat ramps on the river.

Boaters can launch onto the river at Seminole Ranch at the end of Hatbill Road, in the conservation area's northern section. The boat launch area can become flooded when the river rises.

There are several boat launches located throughout Blue Cypress. Airboats are allowed, and they are a popular choice for getting around in the marshes. There is even a designated airboat trail through the marsh. For boat ramp and airboat trail locations, use a map from the St. Johns River Water Management District Web site or its *Recreation Guide to District Lands* booklet.

Nearby, the St. Johns tributary Econlockhatchee River is a more intimate place to paddle. Little Big Econ State Forest (under Nearby Natural Areas, below) provides several launching points along the river and also has river campsites for overnight paddlers. All forest campers need to sign in with the forest office and obtain a permit ($5.00 per night). Paddlers can rent canoes from Hidden River RV Park (under Campgrounds, below), which also provides shuttle service.

Guided Tours

Florida Outback Adventures (407-302-5550; *www.floridaoutback.com*) in Sanford leads paddling trips down the Econlockhatchee and Wekiva Rivers. Customized tours are available upon request.

Florida Eco Adventures (877-FLA-ECO1; *www.floridaecoadventures.com*) in Osteen leads pontoon boat cruises and fishing trips on the St. Johns River. Houseboat and canoe rentals are available for river trips. The company also provides all equipment needed for a backcountry camping stay in its private island reserve on the river.

Spotted Tail Guided Outdoor Adventures (407-977-5207; *www.spottedtail.com*) provides guided kayak tours of the Econlockhatchee River. The trip takes about five hours. Spotted Tail is also a fishing guide for the St. Johns and Canaveral areas.

Camp Holly Airboat Rides (321-723-2179; *www.campholly.com*) west of Melbourne sits on the St. Johns River and offers day and nighttime rides. It also rents canoes and rowboats, launched right there, and it sells snacks, cold drinks, and bait.

Grasshopper Airboat Ecotours (321-631-2990; *www.airboatecotours.com*) west of Cocoa takes guests out on the St. Johns River to view wildlife and learn about the river.

Adventure Kayaking Tours (800-554-1938; *www.paddleflorida.com*) in Vero Beach leads trips on Blue Cypress Lake, the Econlockhatchee River, and several waterways throughout Florida and the Bahamas.

Nearby Natural Areas

The St. Johns River Water Management District manages several tracts along the river that are open to the public. These consecutive conservation areas provide river access, and paddling or hiking trails. They also allow hunting, so visitors should be aware of the hunting schedule.

Close to Sanford, Lake Monroe Conservation Area (386-329-4404) allows hiking, horseback riding, and off-road bicycling on its trails. Primitive campsites are located on the trails, even near the water. But there is no direct access to Lake Monroe or the river. There is no fee for trail use or camping. To get there, take SR 46 east from Sanford to County Road 415. Turn left (north), travel across the river, and look for the parking area at Reed Ellis Road. Another parking area for another trail loop is located to the north on Reed Ellis Road.

Heading south, Canaveral Marshes Conservation Area (407-349-4972), next to both Tosohatchee and Seminole Ranch, offers trails for hiking, off-road bicycling, and horseback riding, but little else. To get there, take I-95 to the Titusville area and exit at SR 50 (Exit #215). Go west for about 3 miles and look for the parking area on the south side of the road near the Great Outdoors Resort.

Stretching from Cocoa to Melbourne along the St. Johns, River Lakes Conservation Area (321-676-6614) is excellent for overnight paddling trips because of the abundance of riverside campsites along the route. Launch from CR 520 on the river and paddle upriver to eleven campsites, mostly near Lake Winder. Day paddlers can launch from Lake Washington County Park and explore the conservation area from there. The county park is located at the western end of Lake Washington Road. Take I-95 to Eau Gallie (Exit #183) and head east to Wickham Road. Turn left (north), then left again (west) at Lake Washington Road. Continue west to the park.

Three Forks Marsh Conservation Area (321-676-6614) adjoins River Lakes to the south and continues riverside primitive camping with five sites. Access the river at the Camp Holly marina on US 192. The St. Johns River peters out toward the southern portion of the conservation area, where levees run through the marsh. Hikers and off-road bicyclists can use the levees to explore the area by land. To get there, take I-95 to the Melbourne area and exit at US 192 (Exit #180). Head west for about 5 miles to the marina. To reach the levees in the south, exit I-95 at SR 514 (Exit #173) and head west to the end of the road at the Thomas O. Lawton Recreation Area, where there is a boat launch.

Blue Cypress Conservation Area picks up the river after that, and then Fort Drum Marsh Conservation Area (321-676-6614) appears as the farthest reach of the river, now just a marsh. Florida Turnpike travelers are familiar with the name Fort Drum as a rest plaza. After visiting the real Fort Drum, it's hard to imagine that a bustling rest plaza is just a few miles away. Fort Drum is a quiet place where locals like to fish along the gravel road that stretches for about 2.5 miles. Paddlers can put in here, and hikers can take a short walk around Horseshoe Lake and Hog Island, where there are primitive campsites. Levees allow hiking and off-road bicycling around the perimeter of Fort Drum. The conservation area is located on the south side of SR 60, on the other side of the road from Blue Cypress entry points.

Lake Proctor Wilderness Area and Geneva Wilderness Area (407-665-7352) are two natural areas of Seminole County's Natural Lands Program. The 475-acre Lake Proctor area is a nice place to hike through the sandhills and hammocks, displaying the uplands of the St. Johns River basin. Hikers can take the main 2.6-mile loop trail and three shorter side trails for a total of 6 miles through the wilderness area. Access is on SR 46 just a couple of miles east of Snow Hill Road. Geneva Wilderness Area is the county's main natural lands park, with a nature center that is open the first Saturday of each month from 9 a.m. until noon. Hikers can take the trail 2 miles to the Econlockhatchee River or join the Florida Trail section that goes through neighboring Little-Big Econ State Forest. Geneva Wilderness Area is on CR 426 just south of where it meets Snow Hill Road south of Geneva.

Next to Geneva Wilderness Area is one tract of Little-Big Econ State Forest (407-971-3500). The forest covers about 5,000 acres where the Little Econlockhatchee River meets the Econlockhatchee River—lending the forest its name. The forest is a Great Florida Birding Trail site where visitors might see sandhill cranes, songbirds, wild turkeys, and hawks. The forest has two tracts: the larger, main tract between Geneva and Chuluota, and the Kilbee Tract on the St. Johns River. The main tract stretches from CR 426 east to Snow Hill Road and beyond. In between these roads, the river and a number of trails run through the pine flatwoods, prairies, and hardwood hammocks. The Florida Trail (trailhead on CR 426) cuts through the forest, and other trails are set aside for off-road bicyclists and equestrians (trailheads on Snow Hill Road). The Kilbee Tract at SR 46 on the river is mainly for hunting. The entrance fee is $1.00 per person.

St. Johns National Wildlife Refuge (managed by Merritt Island National Wildlife Refuge, mentioned in chapter 14) isn't open to the public except during special outings for organized nature groups and sometimes Space Coast Birding and Wildlife Festival field trips. It's worth noting because of its location along the river and its history as a refuge for the dusky seaside sparrow, which has been considered extinct since 1987 as a result of marsh habitat loss.

Orlando Wetlands Park (407-568-1706) is actually not in Orlando, but in the town of Christmas to the east. Close to Tosohatchee State Reserve, the park is a man-made wetland where 18 miles of dikes offer hiking and off-road bicycling. A site on the Great Florida Birding Trail, it is the scene of the annual Orlando Wetlands Park Festival in late winter. Interpretive panels in a covered pavilion near the restrooms highlight the park's birds and wildlife. It is closed from October until sometime around the end of January. The park is across the road from the southern Seminole Ranch entrance.

Nearby Attractions

Sanford Main Street (407-322-5600; *www.sanfordmainstreet.com*) is a revitalized historical district where visitors like to shop for antiques and enjoy events like street parties and parades.

You'll pass Fort Christmas Historical Park (407-568-4149) on the way to Orlando Wetlands Park. The fort here is a replica of the one used during the

Second Seminole War in the early to mid 1800s, named because construction began on Christmas Day in 1837. The park also has several restored Cracker-style houses that were moved to the location. Pioneer demonstrations and other history-related events take place here at certain times throughout the year. The park is open from 8 a.m. until 6 p.m. with extended hours during the summer. Contact the park for its schedule of fort tours.

Jungle Adventures (877-4-AGATOR; *www.jungleadventures.com*) in Christmas is a small wildlife attraction that features animal exhibits, educational shows, and a re-creation of a native village.

Wildlife

The riverside habitats are good for white-tailed deer, wild turkeys, northern bobwhites, and bobcats. In the water, look for migratory waterfowl, manatees, and wading birds like bitterns and endangered wood storks.

Bird-watchers will find several areas here along the river that are good for viewing species from tiny warblers to tall sandhill cranes. Many natural lands are on the Great Florida Birding Trail: Lake Jessup Wilderness Area, Geneva Wilderness Area, Little-Big Econ State Forest, Orlando Wetlands Park, Tosohatchee State Reserve, Seminole Ranch Conservation Area, and Blue Cypress Conservation Area. In the southernmost river basin, birders might spot endangered snail kites and crested caracaras.

Look for . . .

Found throughout Florida, the gray fox is at home along the St. Johns River. So much of the river's banks are undeveloped natural lands, where the fox can find wooded areas to live and to hunt rodents, birds, and fish. The fox, known in fables for being clever, also has found a way to live in urban areas under shrubs, porches, or decks.

Despite its name, the gray fox's coat has a variety of shades: black along the back and tail, white or yellowish underneath, and red mixed in. The red color may make some people think it's a red fox, but the gray fox is more common in the state, certainly in Florida's peninsula. In size, the fox can be three and a half feet long (almost one-third of that is the tail) and weigh up to thirteen pounds.

The gray fox is also reported to be the only member of the canine family that can climb trees, which gives it the nickname "tree fox."

You might not see a gray fox too often because it's mainly nocturnal—and good at hiding. If you do find a fox, be sure to give it the space and respect that you'd give any other wild species. Foxes can carry rabies, and the gray fox is protected by state law.

Habitats

Like the Everglades, the St. Johns River appears to be a river of grass in some places, bordered not so much by banks but by freshwater marshes. Up into the headwaters, the river begins in a marsh.

Floodplain forests also line the river. Beyond, there may be pine flatwoods and hardwood hammocks.

Like the Everglades and other areas in Florida dominated by water, St. Johns River wetlands were drained and the water flow diverted to make way for agriculture and home building. The upper river basin was once covered by 400,000 acres of marsh, but 62 percent of that was drained by the 1970s, according to the St. Johns River Water Management District.

Unlike the Everglades, there doesn't seem to be as much public awareness of the upper St. Johns restoration. Water managers have attempted to undo some of this destruction with restoration projects, which have included transforming citrus groves into wetlands, developing stormwater treatment facilities, and building impoundments, according to the district. Pollution from fertilizers and waste continues to be a problem, affecting water quality and wildlife. In 2003, the state planned to spend $2.2 million on improving water quality throughout the state.

Where to Stay

Campgrounds

Tosohatchee has two primitive tent campsites: Tiger Branch (3 miles from the trailhead parking area) and Sabal Palm (2.5 miles from the trailhead). Tosohatchee also offers a group camping area for organized youth groups, and a horse camping area with a pitcher pump and trough. Camping fees are $3.00 for adults eighteen and older, and $2.00 for minors. Camping requires a reservation, so contact the park for details.

Seminole Ranch and Blue Cypress have designated primitive tent campsites. In Seminole Ranch's northern section, three campsites are located near the main road. In the southern section, a backcountry campsite is used mainly by Florida Trail hikers. Blue Cypress's campsites are mostly remote sites used by hunters and fishermen, including the North Camp shelter. Blue Cypress County Park on the lake next to the fish camp is more accessible for regular campers (tent and RV), although there is little to no shade and no privacy. Seminole Ranch and Blue Cypress campsites are free and available by first-come, first-served basis. (Group campers should request a permit from St. Johns River Water Management District.)

The water management district offers several primitive tent campsites and shelters along the St. Johns River; request the *Recreation Guide to District Lands* by mail, or download it from the district Web site.

Hidden River RV Park (407-568-5346) on the Econlockhatchee River offers tent and RV campsites.

Lodging

In Sanford, there are large chain hotels (like Holiday Inn Express: 407-320-0845, and Best Western Marina Hotel: 800-290-1910), inns (like Rose Cottage Inn: 407-323-9448; *www.rosecottageinn.com*), and bed-and-breakfast inns (like Higgins House Bed and Breakfast: 407-324-5060; *www.higginshouse.com*).

On Blue Cypress Lake, Middleton's Fish Camp (800-258-5002; *www. middletonsfishcamp.com*), with a bait-and-tackle store, rents rustic cabins and trailers on the water. Visitors and guests can also rent kayaks and motorboats, and hire a fishing guide service.

There are more lodging options in Orlando (chapter 19) and Cocoa (chapter 26).

How to Get There

Tosohatchee State Reserve is between SR 50 and the Beeline Expressway. To get there, take I-95 to the Titusville area and exit at SR 50 (Exit #215). Go west about 10 miles, then turn south (left) on Taylor Creek Road. The park entrance is about 3 miles ahead on the left.

Seminole Ranch has two entrances. The northern entrance is on SR 46 (I-95 Exit #223) at Hatbill Road, about 5 miles west of the interstate. The southern entrance is off SR 50 at CR 420, just a couple miles west of Tosohatchee. Take CR 420 north from SR 50 to Wheeler Road, then turn right (east), where you'll find a parking area across from Orlando Wetlands Park.

Blue Cypress has several access points; refer to a map from the St. Johns River Water Management District guidebook or Web site. To get to Blue Cypress Lake, take I-95 to the Vero Beach area and get off on SR 60 (Exit #147). Follow the road west about 15 miles to Blue Cypress Road and turn right (north). This is a dirt road that ends at the lake, fish camp, and county park. Or take the Florida Turnpike to SR 60 at the Yeehaw Junction exit and go east about 7 miles to Blue Cypress Road.

◅ ◅ ◅

William Beardall Tosohatchee State Reserve
3365 Taylor Creek Road
Christmas, Florida 32709
Phone: 407-568-5893
Admission is $2.00 per vehicle.

Seminole Ranch Conservation Area and Blue Cypress Conservation Area
525 Community College Parkway SE
Palm Bay, Florida 32909
Phone: 800-295-3264

The upper St. Johns River in central Florida is a mostly undeveloped area of freshwater marshes. Natural lands run along the river and provide access for nature travelers, but with few facilities. This is an area to explore for those looking for central Florida's true quiet beauty.

Nearby

Space Coast (chapter 14), St. Johns River Country (chapter 15), Central Lakes and Springs (chapter 19), Indian River Lagoon Lands (chapter 26)

17

Nature Coast

What better place for nature travelers to go than a place that calls itself the Nature Coast?

On the Gulf of Mexico north of the Tampa Bay area, the population thins out, and nature is more evident. Coastal development defers to coastal marsh. Tree-lined streets yield to tree-filled forests. Golf course communities give way to hardwood plant communities.

As in many other parts of Florida, life revolves around the water here. Coastal springs pour their water into the gulf in a scenic estuary. Miles of the coastline are refuges for unhurried manatees, who shake winter's chill in the area's warm springs, and for graceful wading birds, who enjoy the good fishing. Inland, the Withlacoochee River sprouts its own marshes, along with flood-plain forests and lakes. With a name meaning "crooked river," the waterway wanders for 70 miles north from the Green Swamp and ends at the gulf, leaving swamps and creeks in its wake.

One of those lucky areas is Withlacoochee State Forest, the second largest in the state system. The river flows for 13 miles through the forest, which is di-vided into eight tracts. The forest is recreation friendly, with boat ramps to access the river and lakes, several campgrounds, and more than 200 miles of trails.

A lot of Nature Coast activity is focused on Crystal River National Wildlife Refuge and its sister, Chassahowitzka National Wildlife Refuge. At the head-waters of the Crystal River, the Crystal River refuge centers around Kings Bay, where thirty warm springs attract manatees, tarpon, otters, turtles, and a vari-ety of life. The Gulf of Mexico is just 10 miles away. To the south is the Chas-sahowitzka refuge, covering 31,000 acres of undeveloped gulf islands and bays. The spring-fed Chassahowitzka River flows into the middle of the refuge, whose name means "pumpkin hanging place" (referring to a species of pump-kin that may be extinct, according to the state). Colonial nesting birds roost in the refuge's mangrove islands.

Figure 16. Manatees visit the warm springs of Crystal River National Wildlife Refuge every winter.

Other ecologically significant natural areas are close by, giving nature travelers a lot to see and do on the Nature Coast. Some people consider the Nature Coast to include the Big Bend region to the north and part of the Tampa Bay area to the south. These other regions have wonderful natural lands; here they are arranged in separate chapters to make the details of smaller geographical areas easier to identify for nature travelers.

What to Do There

The Nature Coast has a dual nature of sea and forest. The Chassahowitzka and Crystal River refuges make up the gulf portion, and the Withlacoochee forest supports freshwater wetlands and uplands. Among the three, there is a lot for nature travelers to explore.

Trail Tripping

The refuges don't offer trails, but there are places to hike near the coast; see Nearby Natural Areas below.

Withlacoochee State Forest has several trails, including a portion of the Florida National Scenic Trail. Hikers have a whopping 99 miles to explore, from the half-mile nature trail in the Two-Mile Prairie Tract north of Inverness to the 19.6-mile trail at the forest's Mutual Mine Recreation Area south of the town.

Off-road bicyclists have 40 miles to pedal in the forest's Croom area, which is popular with motorized bikers and ATV riders as well.

For equestrians, the forest has 65 miles of horse trails. The Hernando Main Loop at Croom is the longest at 18.6 miles. The Bear Head Hammock Trail at Two-Mile Prairie is the shortest at 8.3 miles.

All trail trippers are welcome on the 8-mile multiuse trail in the Richloam tract off State Road 50. A complete list of trails is at the forest Web site. Contact the forest for trail maps.

Running through the forest and beyond, the 46-mile Withlacoochee Trail State Park (352-726-2251) is a multiuse rail trail—the state's longest. It traverses Hernando and Citrus Counties. The trail is paved, but portions include unpaved trails such as those for horseback riding. There are several access points along the trail. The northern trailhead is called Golf Junction, south of Dunnellon off US 41. The southern trailhead is on County Road 575 in Trilby. For other access points and a map, contact the Florida Office of Greenways and Trails. There is no entrance fee.

Paddling and Boating

Because the refuges are water based, paddling and boating are the only ways to explore them. For the Chassahowitzka refuge, boat ramps are located along CR 490 and CR 480 in the Homosassa area. Boat ramps to access the Crystal River refuge are located at several neighborhood marinas and parks; refer to a refuge map from the visitor center or Web site for ramp locations.

Once on the water, you will see the refuges' salt marsh and islands open up before you. Some areas are manatee or bird sanctuaries that are off-limits, even if just seasonally, and signs are posted in these areas. Boaters should note that both refuges border private property, and avoid trespassing; in the Crystal River refuge, homes are located right along the seawall in some parts of Kings Bay, where manatees congregate. If you're heading out on the water along the coast, you may want to request the comprehensive *Boating and Angling Guide to Citrus County* from the St. Martins Marsh Aquatic Preserve (352-563-0450).

The pièce de résistance for paddlers is the 20-mile Nature Coast Canoe and Kayak Trail (*www.citruscountychamber.com/info_tourism/canoetrail.html*). Developed by an Eagle Scout, the paddling trail winds through the salt marsh estuary from the Crystal River down to the Chassahowitzka River. Paddlers can plan a trip for the full length of the route, or take a day trip for one section of the trail. Put in at Fort Island Park along SR 44W south of the Crystal River refuge headquarters to find the start of the trail on the other side of the bridge. Or, hire a local guide (below) familiar with the paddling trail.

In the forest, paddlers and motorboaters can get out on the Withlacoochee River, Little Withlacoochee River, and Jumper Creek—all designated as Outstanding Florida Waters. For the Withlacoochee, there are boat ramps on SR 44 east of Inverness and SR 48 west of Bushnell. In the forest, find boat ramps at Hog Island and Silver Lake Recreation Areas. The forest's McKethan Lake tract allows nonmotorized boats on the lake.

Guided Tours

There are several tour guides and outfitters in the area, as well as marinas and fishing guides.

Riversport Kayaks (877-660-0929; *www.flakayak.com*) in Homosassa leads full- and half-day kayaking tours featuring wildlife-watching or fishing. It also rents canoes and kayaks.

Aardvark's Florida Kayak Company (352-795-5650; *aardvark.com*) offers guided paddling tours of the Rainbow, Weeki Wachee, and Withlacoochee Rivers, as well as the Nature Coast Canoe and Kayak Trail. Tours start at $50 per person.

Nature Coast Kayak and Canoe Tours (352-621-4972) offers a variety of paddling trips in the area.

Birds Underwater (800-771-2763; *www.birdsunderwater.com*) takes guests to snorkel near manatees when they are in Crystal River for the winter. The company also leads kayaking and bird-watching tours and offers scuba diving. Prices vary with the type of tour.

Sunshine River Tours (866-MILLSAP; *www.sunshinerivertours.com*) also offers manatee snorkeling tours, from $30.00. Call the company about guided horseback riding and scalloping (in season).

River Safaris and Gulf Charter (352-628-5222; *www.riversafaris.com*) in Homosassa offers boat tours in Homosassa from $15.00. Guests may also rent boats.

Nearby Natural Areas

Many people visit Homosassa Springs Wildlife State Park (352-628-5343) in Homosassa just to see the manatees that live there year-round. These manatees are being rehabilitated before being released into the wild. The park is one of the few places, maybe the only place, where visitors can count on seeing manatees year-round in a natural setting. An underwater observatory allows a face-to-face view of the manatees and several fish. Because the manatees are rehabilitating in the spring, no swimming or fishing is allowed in the park. Other wildlife species live here, too, in a portion of the park that used to be a private commercial wildlife attraction. Alligators, foxes, deer, various birds, and other Florida wildlife are some of the animals that live here. A visit usually begins with a narrated boat tour from the visitor center to the 1-mile Wildlife Walk, the main parcel of the park. (Visitors may also reach this section by foot or tram.) Homosassa Springs is open every day from 9:00 a.m. to 5:30 p.m.; tickets aren't sold past 4:00 p.m. Admission is $9.00 for visitors thirteen and older, and $5.00 for children three through twelve. To get there, take US 19 south from Crystal River for about 7 miles. The park's visitor center and parking lot are on the west side of the road.

The 36,000-acre Crystal River Preserve State Park (352-563-0450) stretches from the Withlacoochee River to the Homosassa River and protects some of the uplands as a buffer to aid the water quality of both rivers. Begin a visit at the office/visitor center to get trail maps and to learn about the local ecosystem with dioramas, scheduled films, and nature programs. A marina at the visitor center offers a ramp on the Crystal River. Down the street is Eagle Scout Trail, which leads to a 10-mile looping trail for hiking and off-road bicycling. This trail connects with yet another trail, the Eco-Walk. This 2.25-mile interpretive nature trail is a must-hike for any visit to the Nature Coast. Signs and benches along the way provide for thought and reflection. It winds through swamp, past ponds, through a hammock and even prairie. You can access the Eco-Walk in a separate parking area north of the visitor center instead of hiking to it from Eagle Scout Trail. The preserve is open during daylight hours; the visitor center is open from 8 a.m. to 5 p.m. Monday through Friday. There is no entrance fee. To get there, take US 19 north from SR 44 for about 2 miles. Turn left (west) on State Park Drive and watch for the preserve sign.

Another place to get out and walk near the coast is Chassahowitzka Wildlife Management Area (863-664-3203), south of Homosassa. Mostly a place for hunting, the WMA offers dirt roads through the hardwood swamp—the largest south of the Suwannee on the gulf coast, it claims. The roads also cut through pine flatwoods and sandhills, where Florida black bears, owls, turkeys, and gopher tortoises have been seen. Visitors can follow the roads by foot, off-road bike, or car to look for wildlife. Not far from the northern entrance is a parking area, kiosk, and trailhead for a pair of short loop trails: Cypress Circle Trail, which goes around a cypress dome, and Wild Turkey Trace Trail, which leads through the drier side of the WMA. Call ahead of your visit to request a map and brochure. Visitors are welcome during daylight hours. The entrance fee is $3.00 per person or $6.00 per vehicle. To get there, take US 19 south from Homosassa to the entrance, about 9 miles north of SR 50. The entrance is on the right (west) side of the road.

For even more trails, head back east to Inverness, where Potts Preserve (800-423-1476) offers 30 miles of trails that go through Withlacoochee River floodplain forest, freshwater marshes, scrub, and pine flatwoods. Hikers can choose from 3-, 5-, 12.5-, and 17-mile loops, part of the Florida Trail. The longer loops require overnight backpacking (free with a permit) at one of two backcountry sites. Equestrians can ride on 12 miles of roads. A small boat ramp at the end of Hooty Point Road (not near the main entrance) allows access to the Withlacoochee; just a short distance north of here is a primitive canoe camp. Trail users may want to call ahead to find out the hunting schedule. To get there, take I-75 to the Wildwood area and exit at SR 44 (Exit #329). Go west about 20 miles to Inverness. Turn right (north) on US 41, then right again on CR 581 (Ella Street). Turn left on Hooty Point Road, and turn right at the sign at the fork in the road.

Nearby Attractions

Crystal River Archaeological State Park (352-795-3817) near the state buffer preserve is the site of Indian burial mounds and shell middens from native peoples. A walking trail leads to six burial mounds and a view of the Crystal River in a parklike setting. Inside the small visitor center, visitors can watch a short film about the region's history. The visitor center is open from 9 a.m. until 5 p.m. every day. Admission is $2.00 per vehicle using a self-pay station. To get there, take US 19 to the Crystal River area and head west on State Park Street. The park entrance is about 1 mile ahead on the left.

Yulee Sugar Mill Ruins Historic State Park (352-795-3817) in Homosassa preserves what's left of a former plantation and sugar mill that was a big part of the region's history. Around 1,000 slaves worked the 5,100-acre plantation to grow sugarcane, citrus fruit, cotton, and other crops. Admission is free. To get there, take US 19 to CR 490 (Yulee Drive) and head west. The park entrance is about 2.5 miles ahead.

One of Florida's first tourist attractions was Weeki Wachee Springs (352-596-2062; *www.weekiwachee.com*), made famous by its mermaid shows. Young women dress up as mermaids and perform swimming routines underwater, viewable through glass. The 200-acre park also includes the Buccaneer Bay water park with water slides (open on weekends), and a cruise on the Weeki

Wachee River. Hours are 10 a.m. to 3 p.m. Monday through Thursday, and 10 a.m. to 4 p.m. Friday through Sunday; Buccaneer Bay stays open until 5 p.m. on Saturday and Sunday. Admission is $19.95 for adults and $15.95 for children three to ten. To get there, take US 19 south from Chassahowitzka to SR 50. Look for the park just south of the intersection on US 19.

Wildlife

Because the Nature Coast encompasses the gulf coast as well as the inland Withlacoochee forest, there are few Florida wildlife species you won't find here. All of these areas are part of the Great Florida Birding Trail, so bird-watching is good.

Along the coastal waters, wading birds, raptors, dolphins, marsh rabbits, river otters, sea turtles, and a variety of other marine life can be found. Chassahowitzka claims to have 250 species of birds and fifty kinds of reptiles and amphibians.

In the forest, look for white-tailed deer, fox squirrels, Florida black bears, hawks, owls, and songbirds. Alligators, turtles, and snakes live in the Withlacoochee River, along with various fish.

Look for ....

Chassahowitzka is home to an experimental flock of migratory whooping cranes. Concerned that there was only one migratory flock left in North America, in the west, wildlife biologists set out to establish this endangered bird in the eastern United States. Raising whooping crane chicks using puppets and costumes to disguise their human appearance, biologists trained the cranes to follow an ultralight aircraft the way they would follow a parent.

From their summer home at Necedah National Wildlife Refuge in Wisconsin, the cranes successfully followed an ultralight along a migration path to their winter home at Chassahowitzka for the first time in the fall of 2000. The following spring, the cranes returned to Wisconsin on their own. Every year, another small flock of young cranes is led from Necedah to Chassahowitzka, while cranes from past years make the trip on their own. Some returning cranes decide to winter in other areas nearby.

The whooping cranes at Chassahowitzka live on an undisclosed island in the refuge. While it's not likely that most refuge visitors would see a whooping crane, it's important to know their story and why they are there.

It is likely, however, that Nature Coast visitors would spot West Indian manatees, another endangered species in the region. These marine mammals travel along Florida's coasts and up into rivers. The Crystal River area may harbor the largest wintertime population of manatees in the state, where the best time to see them is from late December to mid-March.

Sometimes called sea cows, manatees aren't really cows but more closely related to elephants. Averaging 1,000 pounds and ten feet long, manatees are gentle giants that don't prey on anything (they are herbivores) and have no predators. Natives once hunted them, but today they are protected.

Despite these protections, manatees do die prematurely because of human activity. Most manatees die naturally; others die from cold stress and occasional red tides. The most controversial cause of death for manatees, however, is collisions with boats. Manatees are slow-moving creatures that don't get out of the way fast enough for some boats. If they don't die from these collisions, manatees bear distinctive scars on their backs and tails left by boat propellers; researchers have used these to identify individual manatees.

To help manatees recover as an endangered species, the U.S. Fish and Wildlife Service (FWS) and Florida Fish and Wildlife Conservation Commission (FWC) designated certain waterways as slow-speed zones for the manatees' sake. Some of these manatee zones are seasonal—in effect when manatees are more likely to be inland, from November through March. These slow-speed zones have riled boaters who, in some areas, are unable to travel far because the speed limit prevents them from reaching their destinations—say, an ocean inlet—in a given time, such as daylight hours. Restrictions on building new docks on waterways frequented by manatees is another protection the FWS set up in an attempt to reduce boat traffic. This tactic, too, has angered some waterfront homeowners and marinas who want to build docks for their boats.

These clashes over manatee protections have led to a number of lawsuits. As the number of manatees dying in boat collisions seems to rise each year, boaters-rights groups and even some counties are suing the government, asking whether the increase in deaths means the manatee population is growing. On the other side, environmentalists say the data point to a greater number of boats in the water, and they, too, have sued the federal government over what they say is a poor job of protecting manatees. While these issues are being debated, the FWC is considering whether to downlist the manatee from endangered to threatened in Florida. (This would not affect the federal status designation, which is endangered.)

Manatee protection is clearly a hot-button issue throughout the state, but especially so in areas where the majority of boat-related deaths occur: Lee, Brevard, Collier, Charlotte, Duval, and Sarasota Counties. The state of Florida has attempted to intercede between the federal government and Floridians, agreeing in 2003 to spend millions of dollars in marina gas taxes to increase the number of marine patrol officers and to increase boater education. Meanwhile, researchers are seeking ways to help boaters and manatees avoid each other using "manatee-avoidance technology"—a boat-mounted device that may signal to manatees under the water that a boat is coming so they have more time to get out of the way.

To view manatees, visit Homosassa Springs Wildlife State Park (under Nearby Natural Areas, above), take a manatee snorkeling tour, or visit the Crystal River refuge visitor center for a map of the refuge showing springs where manatees congregate so you can reach these areas with your own boat. Manatee watchers should be aware that federal fines are in effect for manatee harassment, which includes chasing, poking, grabbing, feeding, or giving water to manatees, or any other interaction that could be viewed as disturbing manatees. Visitors are advised to leave manatees alone when the animals are eating and sleeping. Some of these terms of harassment are ignored by manatee tour operators and local tourism boosters, but visitors should be aware of these rules. Manatee harassment carries a fine of $500 and up to sixty days in jail.

Habitats

The beautiful salt marsh that lines Florida's gulf coast generally starts here and continues north through the Big Bend area south of Tallahassee. Rather than the typical barrier islands found on most of the state's coastline—without much of a beach in most places—here most islands are wetlands and not suitable for development. Fortunately, most of this marshy coastline is preserved in various natural areas such as the Crystal River and Chassahowitzka refuges. The natural areas maintain the coastline's natural appearance and provide rich habitat for a variety of species: mammals, reptiles, amphibians, birds, fish, invertebrates, and plants.

This gulf area may have once been grassy prairies when the oceans were lower and Florida's land mass was larger. As the seas crept up onto the land, these prairies—far from the continental shelf where the Gulf of Mexico gets deep—became shallow underwater seagrass beds. Manatees frequent this area in the summer to eat the seagrass.

In Withlacoochee State Forest, the land is quite different. Along the meandering Withlacoochee River, the banks may be part of a floodplain forest where swamp lilies and blue flag irises bloom. Stretches of slash pines and longleaf pines cover some tracts. Other forest tracts are swamps where bald cypress, pond cypress, magnolia, and gum trees grow. In other areas, habitats run into one another in mixed plant communities where several plant and wildlife species live. The river valley includes freshwater marshes through which creeks flow into the Withlacoochee or that stand alone around lakes. All around, various wildflowers grow, like goldenrod and blazing star.

Where to Stay

Campgrounds

The refuges don't allow camping, but there are several other places to pitch a tent or park an RV in the Nature Coast.

In the Withlacoochee forest, campgrounds are located at Silver Lake, Cypress Glen, Crooked River, Hog Island, River Junction, Croom, Holder Mine, and Mutual Mine recreation areas. The Silver Lake campground is located on the lake's northern shore and has twenty-three campsites with electricity and water. Cypress Glen camping is also at Silver Lake, where forty-three sites with restrooms are open only Friday through Sunday. The Crooked River campground offers twenty primitive sites. At Hog Island Recreation Area, there are twenty primitive campsites with a dump station, along with a group camping area. The River Junction campground offers twenty primitive sites on weekends only. At the Croom Motorcycle Area, campers can choose from fifty campsites with electrical hookups. There are thirty campsites with electricity and a dump station at Holder Mine, often used by hunters during scheduled hunts. The Mutual Mine campground has thirteen primitive sites and a group camping area. Horse campers can stay at the Tillis Hill campground, where there are thirty sites with water and electric hookups, horse stalls, corral, and dining hall. All forest campers need a permit to stay overnight; contact the forest office for more information.

An excellent place to camp on the water is Chassahowitzka River Campground (352-382-2200). This is a county park on the spring-fed Chassahowitzka River. A boat launch provides direct access to the refuge, and canoe rentals are on site. The campground has eighty-eight mostly shaded sites, some with water and electricity.

Another campground to try is Camp N Water Resort (352-628-2000) in Homosassa near the Homosassa River. This campground has ninety-one campsites with full hookups, plus cabins. It also rents canoes and offers boat dockage near its boat ramp. Showers, a laundry facility, and a swimming pool are on site.

Lodging

Crystal River has large chain hotels like Best Western Crystal River Resort (800-435-4409; *www.crystalriverresort.com*) with a boat ramp, dive shop, and restaurant. Plantation Inn and Golf Resort (800-632-6262; *www.plantationinn.com*) also offers a dive shop in addition to a golf shop and course.

Paradise Found Island Retreat (352-564-1757; *www.paradisefoundisland.com*) is a unique place to stay on a private island between Crystal River and Homosassa. This is a vacation rental home surround by the gulf salt marsh.

Homosassa Riverside Resort (800-442-2040; *www.riversideresorts.com*) is on the river and has canoe, kayak, and motorboat rentals; a restaurant; marina with boat slips for rent; and a dive shop. The resort will arrange tours and fishing charters, including manatee snorkeling tours.

In Brooksville near the forest, look for Claflin House Bed and Breakfast (877-799-7299), a Greek Revival-style home on a historical street. Closer to I-75, Brooksville also has a Best Western (352-796-9481) and Hampton Inn (352-796-1000).

How to Get There

Both refuges are located off US 19 between Homosassa and Crystal River.

Chassahowitzka National Wildlife Refuge is located offshore. For access, please see Paddling and Boating, above.

To get to the Crystal River refuge headquarters, take I-75 to just north of the Florida Turnpike south of Ocala. Exit at SR 44 (Exit #329) and head west to the coast. At US 19 in the city of Crystal River, turn left (south) and look for Kings Bay Drive. Turn right (east) and follow the road through a residential area to the refuge office and visitor center.

Withlacoochee State Forest is divided into several tracts. It's best to use a forest map to find these tracts and forest trails. To reach the headquarters, take I-75 toward the center of the state and exit at SR 50/US 98 (Exit #301). Travel west to Brooksville, then turn north on US 41 (Broad Street) once in town. The office is about 7 miles ahead, before you reach CR 476.

↭   ↭   ↭

Crystal River National Wildlife Refuge
1502 S.E. Kings Bay Drive
Crystal River, Florida 34429

Phone: 352-563-2088
crystalriver.fws.gov
The refuge headquarters/visitor center is located in a former house and is open
8 a.m. to 4 p.m. Monday through Friday. From October through March (when
manatees visit the refuge), it is also open the same hours on Saturday and Sunday. This is a good place to start your trip in the Nature Coast because you can
get tips and recent wildlife sightings from helpful volunteers, and pick up maps
and brochures for the two area refuges.

Chassahowitzka National Wildlife Refuge
1502 Southeast Kings Bay Drive
Crystal River, Florida 34429
Phone: 352-563-2088
chassahowitzka.fws.gov

Withlacoochee State Forest
15003 Broad Street
Brooksville, Florida 34601
Phone 352-754-6896
The visitor center is open from 8:00 a.m. to 5:00 p.m. Monday through Friday,
and 8:00 a.m. until noon, then 12:30 p.m. to 4:30 p.m. on Saturday. Recreation
areas charge $1.00 per person.

For nature travelers, the Nature Coast is a wonderful destination, espe-
cially when endangered manatees arrive for the winter. The Gulf of
Mexico's salt marshes and a nearby forest offer several miles of natural
lands to explore in an area that hasn't yet become overdeveloped.
Nearby
Lower Suwannee River (chapter 9), Green Swamp (chapter 18), Florida's
Bay Area (chapter 20)

18

Green Swamp

Between Orlando and Tampa lies a wilderness area so large that it straddles five counties—Polk, Lake, Sumter, Pasco, and Hernando—and breaks up the sprawling development of central Florida. The reason for the Green Swamp's preservation is its importance as the birthplace of four rivers: Withlacoochee, Hillsborough, Peace, and Ocklawaha. Each river takes off in a different direction and ends in its own destination—the Withlacoochee in a quiet part of the Gulf of Mexico; the Hillsborough in downtown Tampa's bay; the Peace in southwestern Florida's Charlotte Harbor; the Ocklawaha at St. Johns River, which drains into the Atlantic Ocean at Jacksonville. Some people have even pointed to the Green Swamp's contribution to several area lakes, including the Lake Kissimmee water system, which serves as the headwaters of the Everglades.

By looking at this water flow, it's easy to see how one part of our environment affects so many other parts. In this case, it's a humble swamp, a wetland forest that provides drinking water for a booming population. In 2003, a scientific study using computer models revealed that frosts killing important crops like citrus and sugarcane might have been prevented if wetlands hadn't been drained. Fortunately for the swamp and for Florida residents, the Green Swamp was preserved in 1974 after being recognized as an Area of Critical State Concern.

Yet the Green Swamp is more than just a wetland, more than just a climate controller. In various portions of its 322,000 acres are hardwood hammocks, pine flatwoods, marshes, and even sandhills—low, wet areas next to high, dry areas. This variety of habitats is important to wildlife and a treasure for nature lovers.

Just as the Everglades ecosystem is larger than Everglades National Park, the Green Swamp is larger than the natural areas where you can explore it. Green Swamp Wildlife Management Area is the main part of the swamp and a place to find the typical swamp habitat. Divided into Green Swamp East and Green Swamp West, the wildlife management area covers more than 70,000 acres.

Figure 17. The Withlacoochee River is one of four rivers that begin in the great Green Swamp.

Lake Louisa of Lake Louisa State Park is fed by the Green Swamp. The park's swamps are as much a part of the greater ecosystem as its high, rolling hills. Other preserved areas allow visitors to explore the Green Swamp throughout the expansive five-county region.

What to Do There

Visiting Green Swamp Wildlife Management Area can be tricky because of hunt dates. In Green Swamp East, vehicles are allowed on roads only during hunting seasons. Somewhat the opposite is in effect for Green Swamp West, where only those with hunting permits are allowed to drive through during designated hunting times. (However, the Florida National Scenic Trail that winds through here is open to hikers year-round.) Before planning a trip to Green Swamp, contact the Southwest Florida Water Management District (SWFWMD) to check when you will be able to visit. Lake Louisa State Park is open all year.

Trail Tripping

Hiking is one way to explore the swamp without having to worry about whether you will be able to visit at a particular time. (Hikers are strongly encouraged to wear blaze orange vests when hiking during hunting seasons.) Almost a hundred miles of the Florida Trail wind through the Green Swamp. As you might expect, some trails are wet almost year-round. For a map of hiking trails, contact the Florida Trail Association or SWFWMD.

Lake Louisa has about 21 miles of interconnecting trails. Unlike in most of Florida, some of these trails lead through high sandhills that give visitors the chance to see central Florida's rolling terrain from up high. Some of the trails are set aside for equestrians, and some are just for hikers. Several trails are open for both hiking and off-road biking. Ask for a trail map at the park entrance.

Horse riders and off-road cyclists are welcome on Green Swamp roads during certain times of the year.

Paddling and Boating

As the birthplace of four rivers, you'd think the Green Swamp would be an ideal place to paddle. It's best to go at least outside or along the edge of the wildlife management area in order to navigate; the headwaters are either too shallow or too full of trees. A backcountry campsite on the Withlacoochee

River (which runs for 36 miles through the Green Swamp) is available by permit; contact SWFWMD.

Lake Louisa has a boat launch at Dixie Lake and Hammond Lake near the campground, but no rentals are provided in the park.

Canoe Escape (813-986-2067; *www.canoeescape.com*) in Thonotosassa offers canoe and kayak rentals for paddling the Hillsborough River. Rentals range from $8.00 to $38.00 depending on the craft and length of use; shuttle service is extra.

Guided Tours

Canoe Escape also leads guided Hillsborough River trips every Wednesday morning. Customized trips for other days are available by reservation; costs vary.

Oak Haven River Retreat (813-988-4580; *www.oakhavenriverretreat.com*) in Tampa offers guided wildlife tours and paddling trips along the Hillsborough River.

Lowry Park Zoo (813-935-8552; *www.lowryparkzoo.com*) in Tampa offers family programs centered around its Green Swamp Preserve area, where it runs a captive-breeding program for wolves with a special lease from the water management district. Programs include backpacking and guided hikes. For more information about upcoming program dates, contact the zoo.

Nearby Natural Areas

Withlacoochee River Park (352-567-0264) covers 260 acres just outside the main entrance to Green Swamp West. This is a Pasco County park that is an all-around good place to enjoy the day or to camp overnight, especially during those times when the swamp is open only to hunters. There are about 8 miles of nature trails, along with an undeveloped playing field, pavilions, and a canoe launch. Hours are 7 a.m. until dusk, and admission is free. To get there, take US 301 to Dade City. If coming from I-75, take Exit #254. Follow the truck route around the downtown area, and turn east at River Road. The park is about 5 miles ahead.

Upper Hillsborough Water Management Area (813-975-2160) adjoins Green Swamp West east of Zephyrhills. Visitors can hike the trails at any time of year on the 13 miles of the Florida Trail. The portion of Upper Hillsborough north of State Road 54 isn't open to hunting, so this area might be more attractive to hikers. Driving on the unpaved roads is allowed during hunting dates, and horseback riding is allowed outside of those dates. Upper Hillsborough is open only during daylight hours except during hunts. There are several entrances; to get to the main entrance, take US 98 from Lakeland or Dade City to SR 54 and go west for about 4 miles to the railroad tracks.

After the Withlacoochee River leaves the Green Swamp, it flows northward through Richloam Wildlife Management Area (352-754-6896), the southernmost tract of Withlacoochee State Forest. Covering more than 56,000 acres, Richloam preserves the headwaters of the Little Withlacoochee River, a tributary to the Withlacoochee. The pine flatwoods, oak hammocks, and cypress swamps are crisscrossed with several miles of trails and unpaved roads. Part of the Florida Trail winds through Richloam; hikers should note that hunting is allowed at certain times. For a map of the area, contact the Florida Trail, Withlacoochee State Forest, or the Florida Fish and Wildlife Conservation Commission. Backcountry camping is available. There are several entrances to Richloam; to get there, take SR 50 about 1 mile east of Brooksville and look for signs. Alternately, take US 98 northwest from Lakeland to County Road 471. Turn right (north) and drive through the Green Swamp to the Richloam border.

What once was a railroad that cut through the Green Swamp is now General James A. Van Fleet State Trail (352-394-2280). This 29-mile paved route goes through swamps, pine flatwoods, fields, and marshes. Open for walking, biking, and horseback riding, the trail was designated a National Recreation Trail in 2002. The trail is open during daylight hours and is free. There are several entrances along the trail: in Polk City at SR 33 and CR 665 (the southernmost trailhead), in Mabel about 1 mile west of Clermont on SR 50 (the northernmost trailhead and close to the Richloam tract mentioned above), near CR 565 about 4 miles west of SR 33, and at Green Pond Road about 7 miles north of Polk City off SR 33.

Hilochee Wildlife Management Area is a relatively small, remote area that bridges the gap between Green Swamp and Lake Louisa—in relation to both location and types of habitat. This land is more of the Green Swamp, but it also harbors sandhills typical of Lake Louisa. Visitors can drive through on a couple of unpaved roads near small lakes and must have either a hunting license or a daily use permit ($3.00 per person or $6.00 per vehicle). To get there, take I-4 to US 27 (Exit #55) and go north for almost 2 miles. At CR 474, turn left (west) and look for the Yancey Road entrance. Another entrance is off US 27 at Riddick Grove Road a few miles north of CR 474.

Nearby Attractions

The Pioneer Florida Museum and Village (352-567-0262; *www.pioneerflorida museum.org*) in Dade City displays everyday items used during Florida's early settling days. A one-room schoolhouse and other buildings are on the property as well. The museum is open Tuesday through Sunday from 1 p.m. to 5 p.m. Admission is $5.00 for adults, $4.00 for seniors, and $2.00 for children six to eighteen. To get there, go north of downtown Dade City on US 301 about a mile, then turn right (east) on Pioneer Museum Road and look for signs.

Less than a half-hour drive from the easternmost reaches of the Green Swamp are Walt Disney World's complex of theme parks and other Orlando-area attractions.

Wildlife

The Green Swamp's mix of habitats provides a home for 330 species of wildlife, according to SWFWMD, which oversees most of the natural lands here. Thirty species are endangered or threatened, like the Florida black bear, Florida scrub jay, wood stork, and gopher tortoise.

In fact, Lake Louisa calls itself "home of the gopher tortoise" because it has one of the highest concentrations of these reptiles in the state. You'll see tortoise and deer caution signs along the roads, reminding visitors to slow down for the animals that could be ahead of the blind bend.

Feral pigs are also common in the area. These animals are descendants of pigs that Spanish explorers brought to the New World for food. Boars tear up the land looking for something to eat, so they are considered a nuisance animal.

Look for . . .

White-tailed deer are common throughout Florida, including the Green Swamp. You may see deer—if only for a few seconds before they bound away—while hiking on a trail, driving along back roads, or even resting at your campsite. These graceful, shy animals seem to be interested mainly in eating plants, and they may allow you to watch them if you keep your distance and silence.

You may see deer walking in pairs or groups, wagging their tails that have white undersides. Deer use these tails to communicate to one another; raising their tails straight up to reveal the white underside usually indicates danger.

Deer are hunted in certain areas of the Green Swamp and other parts of Florida. In southwestern Florida, deer provide an important food source for the endangered Florida panther. It's estimated that a fully grown panther needs thirty-five to fifty deer each year.

People who have seen white-tailed deer in Canada or northern states may think Florida's deer are small by comparison, and they are. Key deer to the south are even smaller. Florida black bears are smaller than black bears to the north. Even squirrels in Florida are smaller. The reduced size of animals in Florida is explained by what's called Bergmann's Rule: basically, warm-blooded animals like mammals tend to be smaller in the warmer part of their natural range. Heat is dissipated more quickly by smaller bodies, but retained better by larger ones. This helps animals survive in their respective climates.

Habitats

Although the Green Swamp is a low-lying wet area, its elevation is higher than areas along the coasts toward which its rivers flow. The water table is high here. And because it's preserved, the Green Swamp aids in preventing floods.

The Green Swamp wasn't always preserved. In the 1800s during Florida's pioneer days, settlers made a living by harvesting the swamp's trees for timber (as in many other parts of Florida). The logging wiped out many of the swamp's cypress trees; those left today are relatively young.

Another kind of tree has taken hold of the general area: citrus. Settlers found that the sandhills of central Florida are ideal for growing oranges, grapefruits, and the like—trees that were introduced by Spanish explorers when Spain ruled the land. Lake Louisa State Park was once a citrus grove, and park staff members are gradually returning the rolling hills to their natural state. You may see citrus trees still in the park.

The Green Swamp is a wet place, but it can still be affected by drought. Around the turn of the twenty-first century, a few years of low rainfall left many parts of the state dry and prone to wildfires. The drought also lowered lake levels. During this time, the water level in Lake Louisa dropped to reveal a World War II–era plane that had crashed during a training exercise in 1944. It turned out to be the plane of pilot Dean Gilmore, a U.S. Army Air Corps lieutenant who went down on his twenty-third birthday. The plane was removed. During a ceremony with Gilmore's family in 2001, a monument near the lake was dedicated in his memory.

Where to Stay

Campgrounds

Lake Louisa State Park has sixty campsites in three loops, all in the same general area. The campground is relatively new, and small trees have been planted, but it likely will be some time before there is any shade or privacy here. For information and reservations, contact ReserveAmerica.

The Green Swamp has primitive campsites that are used mostly by hunters and those hiking the Florida Trail. For more information about camping here, contact SWFWMD.

Withlacoochee River Park has ten primitive campsites, and the park expects to open a few cabins in the near future. For information, contact the park (mentioned above).

Lodging

The Green Swamp is a large wilderness area, and lodging can be a half-hour or more away, depending on which section you visit.

Nearby Lakeland offers the most lodging choices, including upscale accommodations downtown (like Lakeland Terrace Hotel: 888-644-8400), large chain hotels (like Jameson Inn: 863-858-9070), and bed-and-breakfast inns (like Lake Morton Bed and Breakfast: 863-688-6788).

Lake Louisa expects to build fifty cabins in the near future. Being the closest state park to Disney World, it will be interesting to see how the addition of cabins might add to the state park's visitation.

Swann's Fly Fishing Outfitters (352-567-6029) rents out a house on the Withlacoochee River about 8 miles north of Dade City.

Oak Haven River Retreat (mentioned above) in Tampa offers vacation cottage rentals in a natural setting near the Hillsborough River.

How to Get There

There are several entrances to the Green Swamp because it is so large. The main entrance to Green Swamp East is located north of Lakeland. Take US 98 northwest from Lakeland for about 10 miles. Turn right (northeast) on Rock Ridge Road and follow it through a rural area to the entrance gate. The main entrance to Green Swamp West is east of Dade City, across the Withlacoochee River bridge from Withlacoochee River Park (directions above).

Lake Louisa State Park is located south of Clermont. Take I-4 to US 27 (Exit #55) and go north for about 15 miles to the park, watching for signs.

⊶   ⊶   ⊶

Green Swamp Wildlife Management Area
3900 Drane Field Road
Lakeland, Florida 33811
Phone: 352-796-7211
Both sides of the swamp are open from sunrise to sunset. There is no entrance fee.

Lake Louisa State Park
12549 State Park Drive
Clermont, Florida 34711
Phone: 352-394-3969
Admission is $4.00 per vehicle.

The Green Swamp is the largest wilderness area in central Florida, strad-dling five counties. The headwaters of four rivers and a recharge area for the Floridan Aquifer, the Green Swamp is an important ecological area and an interesting place to explore, especially by hiking the Florida National Scenic Trail.

Nearby
Nature Coast (chapter 17), Florida's Bay Area (chapter 20), Highland Ridge (chapter 21), Cracker Lakes (chapter 22)

19

Central Lakes and Springs

Between the St. Johns River and the Green Swamp is a land of forests, spring-fed rivers, swamp-fed creeks, and large lakes—the quieter side of central Florida, between Orlando and Ocala National Forest. The lakes, so numerous that on a map they look like holes in a sponge, seem to spill into one another. The rivers and creeks wind through wetlands and floodplain forests toward the St. Johns River. The forested lands are home to Florida black bears.

The main river here is the Wekiva, formed by runs from Wekiwa Springs and Rock Springs near Apopka. Wekiwa Springs contributes the most: forty-two million gallons of water each day. The Wekiva flows north and meets the St. Johns near DeBary, funneling water from creeks along the way.

Both Wekiva (the name of the river) and Wekiwa (the name of the spring) mean water in the Seminole language, and water seems to be everywhere here. These waters are among the clearest in central Florida; the Wekiva is designated as a national Wild and Scenic River and an Outstanding Florida Water. Swimmers and snorkelers are drawn to the cool springs, while paddlers float down the spring run and river.

Like many large springs in Florida, Wekiwa Springs was once a spa resort—1890s style. Vacationers could enjoy the springs while staying at a hotel on site. After the Depression, the attraction shut down. Today, there is nothing left of the resort at Wekiwa Springs, now a wonderful state park.

Downriver, the Wekiva flows past the 25,000-acre Seminole State Forest. The forest's pine flatwoods, sand pine scrub, and hardwoods are dotted with small springs and crossed by trails. Just a few miles away is the southern border of Ocala National Forest.

Seminole State Forest and Wekiwa Springs, together with other natural areas, are great places to explore the Wekiva River basin.

Figure 18. Wekiwa Springs attracts snorkelers and swimmers to its cool, rocky springhead.

What to Do There

In or out of the water, there is a lot to do along the Wekiva. Wekiwa Springs State Park is popular with locals, who enjoy staying at the park all day for swimming in the spring and picnicking on its sloping, grassy bank. The park can be crowded on warm days, and the parking lot can fill up. Look for swallowtails and longwings in the butterfly garden near the parking lot.

The spring floor is alternately rocky and sandy, with few shallow-water spots. There is also a strong current directly above the boil. Novice swimmers may want to use a flotation aid.

Stop in at the small natural history museum run by the park's citizen support organization. Volunteers are helpful in answering questions about the park and the area's environment.

In Seminole State Forest, many people come just to fish. Others bring their horses for a ride through nature. The forest also allows hunting during certain times of the year; trail trippers should check with the forest about hunt dates.

Trail Tripping

A 13.5-mile section of the Florida National Scenic Trail winds through Wekiwa Springs State Park. The trail includes shorter spur trails for those who don't want to hike the entire loop. Primitive campsites are located along the trail, which follows the spring run for a while; contact the park for a required campsite reservation. A 5.3-mile Volksmarch trail is another option. The short interpretive Wet to Dry Trail leads from the bridge across the spring run and points out the subtle change from hydric hammock to dry uplands. All trails are marked with blazes of different colors to help hikers stay on the path, and all trails begin at the springs.

Neither horses nor bicycles are allowed on the Florida Trail. Cyclists are welcome on the paved main park roads and service roads. Off-road bicyclists and equestrians both use the 8-mile Tram Bed Horse Trail loops. Horse camping is allowed at Camp Big Fork, a backcountry site with water for horses. Horse trailer parking is near the park's corral.

At Seminole State Forest, getting out on a trail is the best way to explore. Forest entrances are blocked to vehicles by gates; only those with a permit requested from the forest in advance may receive a code to open the gate and drive through.

There are 21 miles of the Florida Trail, in sections that measure 7.5 miles (main section), 10.6 miles (Lower Wekiva Loop), and 3.7 miles (Sulphur Island Loop). Hikers may also walk along forest roads. Backpackers can register with the forest for one of the backcountry campsites.

Off-road bicyclists can travel 25 miles of named forest roads and bike trails. A designated bike trail leads from the southern entrance and connects with a multiuse trail that starts at the northern entrance.

Equestrian trails connect the forest with the adjacent Lower Wekiva River Preserve State Park (under Nearby Natural Areas, below). There are 23 miles of horse trails, with loop trails that make for short, pleasant rides: the 7.4-mile Sulphur Island Loop, 6.9-mile River Creek Loop, 4.5-mile Paola Loop and connecting trails. Watering stations are located at various points along the trails. Horse owners can park trailers at the forest entrances' parking areas.

Trail trippers at either the park or the forest should request and use a trail map. At Wekiwa Springs, get a trail map at the ranger station. At the forest, look for a map at the trailhead kiosk, or request one from the forest office in advance.

Paddling and Boating

The Wekiva is part of a state canoe trail, the Wekiva River/Rock Springs Run Canoe Trail, considered by the state to be "the most scenic in central Florida." The 27-mile trail begins on Rock Springs Run, joins the Wekiwa Springs run at the Wekiva River, then continues toward the St. Johns. The trail leads past Seminole State Forest and Lower Wekiva River Preserve State Park, although there aren't any put-ins here. Wekiwa Springs is a fine place to access the trail and also a place where paddlers can rent a canoe from the park concession. Wekiva Marina (407-862-1500) and Wekiva Falls Resort (352-383-8055) are other places to access the trail.

Wekiva tributary Blackwater Creek flows through the forest, too. Paddlers and non-gasoline motorboaters can put in on the forest's Sand Road. To do so, call ahead to request permission and get the combination for the gate at the forest entrance. The creek is about halfway between the forest's northern and southern entrances.

West of Wekiwa Springs and the forest, several large lakes are open to boating. Lakes Apopka, Harris, Griffin, Yale, Eustis, Dora, and Beauclair all have boat ramps. For boat ramp locations, contact the St. Johns River Water Management District or look up ramps in the Florida Atlas and Gazetteer.

Guided Tours

Wekiwa Springs State Park Nature Adventures (407-884-4311; *www.canoe wekiva.com*) is the official concession inside the park. The concession rents canoes and leads a variety of tours along the river. It also provides all necessary camping equipment and gear for an overnight paddling trip.

Nearby Natural Areas

On Seminole State Forest's eastern boundary is Lower Wekiva River Preserve State Park (407-884-2008). This park covers 17,650 acres and sits alongside the St. Johns River. The Wekiva River and Blackwater Creek flow through—although there is no access to these waterways. There are no facilities at the park, but there is a short interpretive nature trail, the Sandhill Nature Trail. At the park entrance is a kiosk at the trailhead where hikers can pick up a trail guide that describes the flora and fauna of the area. Visitors can also head down the dirt road that parallels the line of the Wekiva River. There is no entrance fee. To get there, take State Road 46 west from I-4 (Exit #101C). The entrance is on the north side of the road about 9 miles from Sanford.

One of the springs that contributes water to the Wekiva River is Rock Springs, for which Rock Springs Run State Reserve (407-884-2008) is named. There are no facilities, but there are separate trails for hiking, off-road bicycling, and horseback riding; look for the trailheads along the short paved park road that ends at a locked gate. Buffalo Tram trail leads to Rock Springs Run. Paddlers may paddle the spring run through the reserve, but there are no launches here. The entrance fee is $2.00 per vehicle. The reserve is near Lower Wekiva River Preserve and Seminole State Forest on SR 46, 3 miles west of the Wekiva River.

North of Seminole State Forest is Lake Norris, where Lake Norris Conservation Area (352-343-3777) rests. The lake and Blackwater Swamp join here at the headwaters of Blackwater Creek. Visitors can launch onto the creek from the parking area near the entrance, and hike a trail to view the lake. The lake area is home to several ospreys, and the conservation area's uplands harbor scrub-loving gopher tortoises and burrowing owls. To get there, take SR 44 east from Eustis. At 44A, turn left (north), then follow the road as it turns east. Turn left (north) at Lake Norris Road and look for the entrance ahead.

Audubon of Florida's Sabal Point Sanctuary (407-539-5700) is the smallest of the region's natural areas at 600 acres, but it fronts the Wekiva and Little Wekiva Rivers just down the street from Wekiwa Springs. It also offers access to the larger Wekiva River Buffer Conservation Area, which is planned to become part of Wekiwa Springs State Park. Here, you can hike or bike the 3.5-mile trail to the Little Wekiva River while looking for wildlife like white-tailed deer and turkeys. To get there from Wekiwa Springs, go east on Wekiwa Springs Road to Sabal Palm Drive. Turn left (north) and continue on to Wilderness Drive. The entrance is at the end of the road.

Emeralda Marsh Conservation Area (352-821-2066) is a National Natural Landmark, designated by the National Park Service. The conservation area spans the isthmus between Lake Griffin and Lake Yale in a large freshwater marsh and hydric hammock. Sandhill cranes and migratory waterfowl love the site, especially in winter, when they arrive in large numbers. There are also plenty of alligators. Visitors can pick up an interpretive brochure to the 4.3-mile wildlife drive, which runs along the top of a levee through the marsh, at the southernmost entrance on Emeralda Island Road. The wildlife drive is open weekends from February to May from 8 a.m. to 5 p.m. Trails are open to hikers, off-road bicyclists, and equestrians, and boat ramps offer access to the lakes. To get there, take SR 44 west from the town of Eustis. At Lisbon Road, turn right (north), then head left at the fork in the road (Emeralda Island Road). Trailheads and boat ramps are located up and down the road.

Southwest of Emeralda Marsh on the same chain of lakes is Lake Griffin

State Park (352-360-6760). The park boasts the state's fifth-largest live oak tree, ten feet around and more than 150 feet high. A short nature trail leads to the mammoth oak. Most of the activity here is about boating, however. A boat ramp accommodates boats with trailers up to twenty-five feet long, and canoe rentals are available. While out on the water, look for alligators, river otters, bald eagles, and water birds. The entry fee is $4.00 per vehicle. To get there, take SR 44 to Leesburg, then turn north on US 441/US 27 (Citrus Blvd.). The park is 2 miles ahead.

Nearby Attractions

If you can't get enough of birds in the wild, the Audubon Center for Birds of Prey (407-644-0190) is an excellent place to see owls, hawks, kites, eagles, and other raptors. The center rehabilitates injured birds of prey. Some of those that cannot be released into the wild because of the severity of their injuries are viewable by the public. The center is open from 10 a.m. to 4 p.m. from Tuesday through Sunday. Admission is free, but donations are welcome. To get there, take I-4 to Maitland and exit at Lee Road (Exit #46). Take the first left at Wymore Blvd., then turn right on Kennedy Blvd. At East Ave., turn left, and watch for the center ahead on the left side of the road.

West of the forest on SR 46 is Mount Dora, a town known for its charming atmosphere and quaint downtown shopping district. Many people who go to Mount Dora visit the large Renninger's Antique and Farmers Market (877-385-0104; *www.renningers.com*), which is south of downtown on US 441.

To the south in Orlando, travelers can choose from a variety of things to do, from museums (like the Orlando Science Center: 888-OSC-4FUN; *www.osc. org*) to other attractions (like Henry P. Leu Gardens: 407-246-2620; *www. leugardens.org*). Theme parks are close by.

Wildlife

The Wekiva River basin is an important area for wildlife. It is part of a wildlife corridor that connects to the Ocala National Forest and other state forests as well as Lake Woodruff National Wildlife Refuge. This corridor helps threatened Florida black bears roam across their territory with few urban intrusions. Along SR 46 there are many entrances to natural areas and you'll notice caution signs for bears.

So much of this forested area is great not only for bears but also for other woodland species, like white-tailed deer, fox squirrels, and songbirds. Scrubby areas like those in Seminole State Forest and Rock Springs Run are home to

Florida scrub jays and eastern indigo snakes (both threatened). The wetlands are good places to find limpkins, wood storks, herons, and egrets.

The central lakes and springs natural areas are on the Great Florida Birding Trail, where trail literature mentions that Wekiwa Springs has thirty-four species of warblers and almost every species of woodpecker found in the state. Visit in summer to find summer tanagers, indigo buntings, and swallow-tailed kites.

Look for . . .

People might not associate Florida with turkeys, but they are common from the northern through the central parts of the state. Wild turkeys are at home in Wekiwa Springs, and you might spot them on a hiking trail, near the campground, or in other areas throughout the region. Turkeys are notoriously skittish and likely will run away as you approach.

Wild turkeys may not look like the iconic image of the turkey so commonly seen around Thanksgiving because Florida turkeys are generally smaller. Wild turkeys are smaller than farm-raised turkeys, in any case, because domestic turkeys may be fed so much that they cannot fly. Wild turkeys do fly, and they roost in trees at night.

Listen for males to start gobbling during mating season, in February, to attract mates, of which there may be several in one season. Males also show off by strutting and spreading their tail feathers.

Habitats

The Wekiva River basin includes not only the floodplain forests, marshes, and swamps you would expect to find along the river, but also hardwood hammocks, pine flatwoods, and high, dry scrub. Most of the region is a hardwood wetland, or hydric hammock, where bald cypress trees mingle with magnolias and pignut hickories. Red maples, water tupelos, water oaks, and other trees that thrive in wet habitats grow in the region.

Many rare plants grow here, including the leafy, red cardinal flower pollinated by hummingbirds, and delicate ferns like the cinnamon fern, royal fern, and hand fern. Wekiwa Springs has the state's largest population of star anise, an endangered plant, according to the St. Johns River Water Management District.

Some residents and environmentalists fear these habitats could be harmed by a planned road through the region. The Wekiva Parkway is a sign of growth, which the state Department of Environmental Protection has said poses the greatest threat to the Wekiva River basin's water quality and habitats.

The road construction project had threatened to channel traffic through the area for several years. First one state-appointed committee, then another, attempted to figure out how to get the road built while preserving as much of these quiet forests as possible. In June 2004, Governor Jeb Bush allowed the road to be built with the Wekiva Parkway and Protection Act, which provides some protection for this sensitive area while still building the connecting road through the ever-growing region.

Where to Stay

Campgrounds

Wekiwa Springs offers sixty shady campsites for tents and RVs. There are two loops of thirty campsites each, complete with water hookups and electricity, and nearby restrooms with hot showers. A dump station is available for RV users. Contact ReserveAmerica for information and reservations.

Primitive campers can enjoy four primitive campsites along Wekiwa Springs' trails and the spring run. Otter Camp and Big Buck sites are accessible to visitors on the water. Organized youth groups may want to take advantage of the park's youth camp—which includes nineteen cabins, a dining hall, and a recreation hall—or the primitive youth camp nearby. For information on these sites, contact the park directly.

In Seminole State Forest, three primitive sites stand ready for the hearty backpacker; ask about the Moccasin Springs Camp, which is indeed near a spring. Sites have fire rings and picnic tables. Contact the forest office for a camping permit.

Lower Wekiva River Preserve State Park (under Nearby Natural Areas, above) offers primitive camping for horse riders only. The camp has restrooms and a corral that holds up to fifteen horses. Contact Wekiwa Springs, which oversees the preserve, for information and reservations.

Lake Griffin State Park (under Nearby Natural Areas, above) has forty campsites, also with water and electric hookups, restrooms with hot showers, and a dump station. Contact ReserveAmerica for information and reservations.

Lodging

Wekiwa Springs is in Apopka and close to Altamonte Springs, Lake Mary, and Maitland. All of these cities have large lodging facilities (like the Hampton Inn in Altamonte Springs: 407-869-9000) as well as small inns (like Thurston House in Maitland: 800-843-2721; *www.thurstonhouse.com*). Closer to Seminole State Forest, try the Comfort Inn (352-383-3400) or the grand lakeside Darst Victorian Manor (352-383-4050), both in Mount Dora.

How to Get There

To get to Wekiwa Springs, take I-4 to Altamonte Springs. Exit at SR 436 (Exit #92) and go west. Follow the signs through a residential area to the Wekiwa Springs entrance on Wekiwa Springs Road.

Entrances for Seminole State Forest, Lower Wekiva River Preserve State Park, and Rock Springs Run State Reserve are clustered along SR 46 west of I-4 (Exit #101C). Another forest entrance is on SR 44 about 12 miles east of Eustis.

✦   ✦   ✦

Wekiwa Springs State Park
1800 Wekiwa Circle
Apopka, Florida 32712
Phone: 407-884-2008
Admission is $5.00 per vehicle.

Seminole State Forest
9610 SR 44
Leesburg, Florida 34788
Phone: 352-360-6675
The forest day-use fee is $1.00 per person. Additional recreational fees may apply.

Central Florida isn't about just theme parks, as you'll discover if you visit the region's natural areas, which reveal what the interior originally looked like—clean, spring-fed rivers, miles of forest, and large lakes. This remnant of natural Florida is just minutes from Orlando's hustle and bustle, making it a convenient trip to combine with a theme park visit or as a destination in itself.

Nearby

Ocala National Forest (chapter 13), St. Johns River Country (chapter 15), Upper St. Johns River (chapter 16), Green Swamp (chapter 18)

20

Florida's Bay Area and Gulf Islands

Many people see Florida as a subtropical paradise with warm, sunny beaches and palm trees swaying in the ocean breeze. If you can add some seashells, beach umbrellas, and a beautiful sunset to this picture, it's the ideal of bliss for many. That image is reality on many Gulf of Mexico beaches. Sandy barrier islands are places to relax and bake in the sun—and there's a string of them up and down the coast.

That chain of barrier islands is hardly broken where Tampa Bay cuts through the mainland and opens it up to the gulf. Islands at the mouth of Tampa Bay are links in the chain and protectors of the bay's ecosystem.

One of these islands is Mullet Key, where Fort DeSoto Park lies. On a map, Mullet Key looks like an old comb with most of its teeth missing and the others broken. While ruins of the nineteenth-century fort—named after Spanish explorer Hernando de Soto—do remain on the island, the park is anything but worn out. The 1,136-acre park covers the entire island, refreshingly left mostly to nature in the most densely populated county in the state. Visitors can listen for the soft sound of hundreds of cabbage palm fronds moving in the wind. The island's 7 miles of beach are among the best in the country. The park is ranked in the top-ten list by Stephen "Dr. Beach" Leatherman, a geologist at Florida International University who puts out a new list each year around Memorial Day weekend.

Another park that has won Dr. Beach's approval is Caladesi Island State Park, north of Tampa Bay up the coast. Caladesi and its sister park, Honeymoon Island State Park, offer beautiful beaches on mostly undeveloped barrier islands. And yet, Honeymoon and Caladesi are more than just beaches. Only yards from the water's edge are shady forests and thick mangroves brimming with wildlife.

The two islands were once one, a place where the Tocobaga tribe lived, fishing and collecting clams and oysters. Then Spanish explorers visited, giving Caladesi Island its name—which comes from an old Spanish dialect—meaning something like "calm bayou." The island has also been called Sand Island

Figure 19. The sun sets on Honeymoon Island State Park.

and Hog Island. After a hurricane split the island in two, Honeymoon Island (the northernmost island) was so named because of the newlyweds who were attracted by the romance of a warm island dotted with palm-thatched cottages. This resort was recommissioned by the government during World War II as a recreational retreat for those exhausted by war. The island changed hands a few times after that, and the two state parks opened in the 1970s.

These three parks, along with several other natural areas along Tampa Bay, reveal the true paradise of central-western Florida, places to rest and breathe in tandem with nature.

What to Do There

Whether you visit these parks for that ideal beach or for nature observation, you won't be disappointed. All parks offer beach areas for swimming, showers for rinsing off afterward, and concessions for drinks and snacks. Honeymoon Island and Fort DeSoto welcome furry friends to their pet beach areas. Trails through the islands' interiors and on the water reveal the gulf area's scenic beauty and a variety of wildlife, especially birds.

At Fort DeSoto, stop at the Quartermaster Museum near the gulf pier. This small building, a reconstruction of the real quartermaster housing that once stood, offers exhibits on the island's history. An interactive computer station offers more about the history and nature of the park.

Near Fort DeSoto's snack bar, visitors can tour what's left of the original fort, mainly Battery Laidley, where stark mortar pits and magazine powder rooms remain. Stairs allow climbing to the roof, where plants and trees have taken over. Because of erosion, the remains of Battery Bigelow are now under water; beachgoers may be able to spot them in the gulf. The park visitor center offers a guide to the fort and its military uses, from its construction in 1898 to the island's status as a bombing range during World War II. The fort is listed on the National Register of Historic Places.

Trail Tripping

A 6.8-mile paved trail at Fort DeSoto is one of the first things visitors see as they cross the bridge onto Mullet Key. Walk, bike, or skate along the trail to most parts of the island. In the northwestern corner of the island at the Arrow-head picnic area and Soldier's Hole, a 1-mile nature trail and a .75-mile trail go through scrubby areas. The 2,200-foot interpretive Barrier-Free Nature Trail is designed to be wheelchair accessible.

Honeymoon Island offers two short, looping nature trails: Pelican Cove Trail—which leads you along the beach and past mangroves—and Osprey Trail, which cuts through a slash pine forest and sand scrub. Osprey Trail is true to its name, and you're sure to see these birds of prey and their nests, and hear their high-pitched calls. Slight variations in elevation make the trails interesting to walk. On Pelican Cove Trail, you'll come across mangroves, and the trail may be wet or muddy—and the home of crabs that will disappear in holes underneath your feet. The two trails are connected, so you can easily walk both of them and see Honeymoon Island's various habitats. Plan at least an hour and a half to walk the trails and to stop along the beach for the view. Watch out for poison ivy.

On Caladesi Island, a 3-mile nature trail winds through the maritime hammock, pine flatwoods, scrub, and mangroves, offering hikers the chance to get off the trail at the beach on the western (gulf) side of the island. If you like to walk the beach—a lot—it's possible to walk 8 miles south to Clearwater Beach now that a sandbar has connected it to Caladesi Island. Look for the trail and the path to the beach behind the visitor center by the marina.

Paddling and Boating

Inside Fort DeSoto Park, the Canoe Outpost (727-864-1991; www.*canoeout post.com/fdhome.htm*) offers kayak rentals for paddling in the park, starting at $15.00. Open every day from 9 a.m. to 5 p.m., the outpost is located near the park's 2.5-mile canoe trail across from the dog park. Fort DeSoto also treats boaters with a continuously open boat launch area that's 800 feet long, with eleven floating docks.

Paddling at Honeymoon and Caladesi is a delight for paddlers who want to explore gulf coast mangroves and the sheltered waters of St. Joseph Sound. Caladesi Island offers a 3.2-mile paddling trail that leads from the marina through the mangroves of the island's eastern side. Paddle to the island, or rent a kayak from the park concession.

Caladesi's marina welcomes all of the island's visitors because the only way to reach the island is by boat. The marina has 108 slips, where boaters may register to stay overnight. Visitors may also arrive by ferry from Honeymoon Island.

Guided Tours

The Honeymoon Island ferry (727-734-1501) transports visitors across Hurricane Pass to Caladesi Island. More than just a way to get from Point A to Point B, the ferry ride is turned into a tour as captains relate the islands' history and share points of interest during the thirty-minute ride. Red mangroves greet you as you approach Caladesi Island and dock in the marina. The ferry runs every day, weather permitting, once an hour from 10 a.m. to 5 p.m. The round-trip price is $7.00 for adults and $3.50 for children.

At Fort DeSoto, guided tours are offered at 10 a.m. Saturdays and Sundays. Call ahead to find out what parts of the park the tours are scheduled to emphasize during your visit.

It's Our Nature Eco Adventures (888-535-7448; *www.itsournature.com*) leads guided nature walks and bird-watching tours. Other nature-oriented programs include retreats and writing workshops.

With locations in Clearwater and Ruskin, Osprey Bay Kayaks (727-524-9670; 813-645-7600; *www.ospreybay.com*) leads nature paddling tours and kayak fishing tours in the Tampa Bay area. The gear shop also offers kayak rentals and kayaking classes.

From half-day tours around Tampa Bay to a multiday trip in the Everglades, Sweetwater Kayaks (727-570-4844; *www.sweetwaterkayaks.com*) in St. Petersburg leads a variety of kayak excursions throughout the state. Kayak rentals are available by reservation.

On Tampa Bay's eastern side, Mad Paddlers Kayak and Surf Shop (877-MAD-SURF; *www.madpaddlers.com*) schedules paddling tours along the coast. Contact the shop for the current schedule.

Oak Haven River Retreat (813-988-4580; *www.oakhavenriverretreat.com*) in Tampa offers guided wildlife tours and paddling trips along the Hillsborough River. An early-morning paddle trip takes place every Saturday.

Nearby Natural Areas

The municipalities of the Tampa Bay region offer several wonderful parks that showcase the area's nature, but there are too many to mention. Here are a few chosen for their access to the water, so visitors may get to know the bay.

Just south of Mullet Key is Egmont Key, reached only by boat. The island is managed as Egmont Key State Park (727-893-2627) and Egmont Key National Wildlife Refuge. Day trippers can visit the beach to swim and look for shells. Snorkelers can view the submerged remains of Fort Dade, which—like Fort DeSoto—has, in part, succumbed to the sea because of erosion. Fort Dade was built in 1898 to defend Tampa Bay during the Spanish-American War, but by the time it was completed, the war had ended. As at Fort DeSoto, troops here never saw any fighting action. Brick pathways remain, as well as the working eighty-five-foot lighthouse built in 1858—one of Florida's oldest on the Gulf of Mexico. (The lighthouse's interior is closed to the public.) Gopher tortoises, box turtles, terns, black skimmers, and American oystercatchers are some of the wildlife that visitors might see. Contact the Egmont Key Alliance (*www. egmontkey.org*), a volunteer group, about its annual festival, when tours are offered. Visitors are allowed during daylight hours only. To get there, arrive on your own boat or kayak. Or take the ferry, which operates seasonally, leaving Fort DeSoto at 10 a.m. and 11 a.m. and returning at 2 p.m. and 3 p.m. The ferry costs $15.00 per person. There are no facilities on Egmont Key, so visitors need to take everything they need, such as water, with them.

North of Mullet Key, Shell Key Preserve (727-943-4000) on remote 180-acre Shell Key is a popular place for local boaters to visit, especially on weekends. About half of the island is off-limits to visitors so birds like American oystercatchers, black skimmers, and least terns can use the island for migrating and nesting. The birds' presence is what prompted the local Audubon Society chapter to campaign for the island's preservation. Primitive camping is allowed in designated areas on the northern and southern ends of the island. The county-run preserve is located offshore from Tierra Verde and is accessed only by private boat.

Boca Ciega Millennium Park (727-588-4882) sits on Boca Ciega Bay, one of the many bays and inlets in Tampa Bay. Although this county park is small compared to many others, it's earned a spot on the Great Florida Birding Trail, which claims the park attracts 145 bird species, including white pelicans and wood storks. The park offers access to the bay, including a canoe launch and a 35-foot observation tower. The mangroves, pine flatwoods, and wetlands are examples of the region's original plant communities, and the park makes good use of native plants in its landscaping. The park is open from 7 a.m. to dusk. Admission is free. To get there, take I-275 to State Road 694/Gandy Blvd. (Exit #28) and go west. This road becomes Park Blvd. Turn left (south) at 125th St. Then at 74th Ave., turn left (east) and look for the park entrance ahead on the right.

Facing east on Tampa Bay, Weedon Island Preserve (727-453-6506) is a 3,200-acre county park. From wet mangroves to dry scrub, the park's habitats give visitors a natural place to explore. Start at the modern-looking visitor center for Native American exhibits and maps of the hiking and canoe trails. Volunteers sometimes lead tours of these trails, so call ahead of your visit to find out what's on the current schedule. Boardwalks lead through the mangroves to overlooks at small inlets on Tampa Bay. Other trails lead past gopher tortoise burrows to picnic areas. The preserve is on the Great Florida Birding Trail, which notes ospreys, bald eagles, and mangrove cuckoos at the site. The park is open during daylight hours. Admission is free. To get there, take I-275 to SR 694/Gandy Blvd. (Exit #28) and go east about 1 mile. Before the bridge over to Tampa, watch for San Martin Blvd. and turn right (south). Watch for the park entrance ahead on the left.

Upper Tampa Bay Park (813-855-1765) gives nature travelers a chance to explore the northern reaches of Tampa Bay. Interpretive nature trails wind through pine flatwoods to Mobbly Bay and Double Branch Creek. The creek is also a place to put in your canoe or kayak to explore the county park's salt marsh and mangroves, with Old Tampa Bay being a little more than a mile to the south. At the end of the main park road, the visitor center offers exhibits and aquariums that interpret the nature and history of the bay. Behind the center, a boardwalk allows visitors to explore the watery mangrove swamp on foot. The park is open from 8 a.m. to 6 p.m. Admission is free, but donations are accepted at the visitor center. To find the park, exit I-275 at Hillsborough Ave. (Exit #47B) and go west. Follow the road through Tampa as it turns northwest toward Oldsmar. Turn left (west) at Double Branch Road and watch for the park entrance shortly ahead.

On the southeastern side of Tampa Bay, E. G. Simmons Park (813-671-7655) is a popular place for anglers who enjoy saltwater fishing. There are no trails in the 469-acre park, but there is a beach for swimming, a picnic area, and a playground. This is a good place to launch a canoe or kayak and explore the southern bay, as well as the nearby Little Manatee River and Cockroach Bay Aquatic Preserve (named after the "cockroaches of the sea," horseshoe crabs). The presence of shore birds and wading birds like reddish egrets has led to the park's listing as a Great Florida Birding Trail site. The park is open from 8 a.m. to dusk, and entrance is free. To get there, take I-75 to SR 674 (Exit #240B) and travel west. Turn right (north) on US 41, then left (west) on 19th Ave. Follow the road to the park entrance.

In southern Tampa Bay near the mouth of the Manatee River, Emerson Point Park (941-742-5923) is another place where locals like to fish, but it's also admired for its nature. In 1998, the park received a grant from the federal Environmental Protection Agency to restore wetlands and remove invasive plants. The 195-acre park stretches across the bay for 15 miles, and trails lead to overlooks at the water's edge, including a sixty-foot tower. A large Native American temple mound within the park is on the National Register of Historic Places. The park is open during daylight hours. To get there, take I-75 to the Bradenton area and exit at US 301 (Exit #224). Go west and cross US 41, then follow the road as it joins 17th St. Continue to the end of the road, at the tip of Snead Island.

Before it reaches Tampa's downtown district and the bay, the Hillsborough River first flows through Hillsborough River State Park (813-987-6771) in a beautiful natural setting. Only an hour's drive or so from the gulf shore, the park's scenery will make you think you're farther away. Pine forests and oak hammocks line the riverbanks. The park is known for its Class II river rapids, where shoals create quite a view next to cypress trees. You can rent a canoe and paddle down the river (but not over the rapids), cross the swinging bridge, hike the trails, swim in the pool (an extra $2.00 fee), or go off-road biking along the dirt roads past cow pastures. Tours of the pioneer-era Fort Foster within the park are offered Saturday at 2 p.m. and Sunday at 11 a.m.; tours charge adults $2.00 and children six to twelve $1.00. Admission to the park is $4.00 per vehicle, or $3.00 for vehicles with one person. To get there, take I-75 to Fowler Ave./SR 582 (Exit #265) and go east about 7 miles to US 301. Turn left (north) and follow the road to the park entrance, ahead about 5 miles on the left.

Nearby Attractions

Spanning Tampa Bay from St. Petersburg to the mainland is the Skyway Bridge—and there you'll find the longest fishing pier in the world, Skyway Fishing Pier State Park (727-865-0668). Even if you don't fish, go for the views or for the bird-watching. The park is located off I-275 as it goes over Tampa Bay.

The Suncoast Seabird Sanctuary (727-391-6211; *www.seabirdsanctuary.org*) is a nonprofit animal hospital that treats injured birds. The public viewing area displays birds that are too badly injured to be released back into the wild. The facility is open every day from 9 a.m. until sunset. Admission is free, but donations are welcome. The sanctuary is located in Indian Shores on Gulf Blvd. Take I-275 to Gandy Blvd. (Exit #28) and go west. The road becomes Park Blvd. Cross the Intracoastal Bridge to Indian Shores, then turn left (south) on Gulf Blvd. The sanctuary is seven blocks ahead on the right.

Spanish explorer Hernando De Soto came ashore in the Tampa Bay region in 1539, and De Soto National Memorial (941-792-0458; *www.nps.gov/deso*) commemorates his journey and arrival. At the visitor center, watch a twenty-minute film about De Soto's four-year expedition and attempted settlement in Florida, and view artifacts like armor and native pottery. A short nature trail leads from the visitor center through mangroves. This national park is open during daylight hours; the visitor center is open from 9 a.m. to 5 p.m. Admission is free. The park is located in Bradenton. Take I-75 to SR 64 (Exit #220) and go west about 5 miles. At 75th St., turn right (north) and continue about 2.5 miles to the park entrance.

In the metropolitan area of Tampa/St. Pete, there are several other attractions to visit, including Lowry Park Zoo (813-935-8552; *www.lowryparkzoo. com*), Clearwater Marine Aquarium (888-239-9414; *www.cmaquarium. org*), and the Museum of Science and Industry (813-987-6100; *www.mosi.org*). Busch Gardens in Tampa is a major theme park.

Wildlife

Because they are Gulf of Mexico barrier islands, Honeymoon, Caladesi, and Mullet Key are dominated by water. So it makes sense that most of the wildlife here are attracted by the ocean: shorebirds, sea turtles, and dolphins. But the islands also have upland areas, where you may find wildlife typically seen on the mainland: woodland birds like woodpeckers and cedar waxwings, gopher tortoises, and snakes. And if you can identify fish and seashells, there is almost no end to the wildlife you could find in these parks. Caladesi's coastal scrub is a good place to find snakes like nonvenomous black racers and venomous diamondback rattlers; park signs warn visitors about the rattlesnakes.

Around 290 species of birds have visited or make their homes on the islands. Honeymoon Island's bird observation area not far from the ranger station gives you a wide view of tidal flats, where birds sometimes look for food at low tide. Fort DeSoto is a Great Florida Birding Trail Gateway, one of the few parks on the trail where bird-watchers can pick up GFBT guides, borrow binoculars, and get general regional bird-watching information (at the visitor center). Honeymoon and Caladesi are also part of the trail.

Look for . . .

You can see Atlantic bottle-nosed dolphins, the most common dolphins in Florida waters, in the gulf area all year round. They may travel past the beach in a pod, chasing schools of mullet for a meal. Frequently, smaller groups like a dolphin with her calf are seen. Dolphins are known for the way they communicate with other dolphins with clicks and other vocalizations.

Dolphins are cetaceans, related to whales. While many people may call them porpoises, they are different species. Dolphins are distinguished by their long "beaks," which porpoises don't have, and their heads are less bulbous than the porpoise's. Porpoises usually don't travel in groups like dolphins do, and they rarely leap out of the water, the way dolphins like to play. A dolphin's dorsal fin has a curve like a hook, while the porpoise's fin is triangular.

Wildlife-watchers can use the dolphin's fin to distinguish it from a shark. Most of the time, when you see a fin above the surface of the water, it's a dolphin. Dolphins come up for air usually every two minutes (although they can stay underwater for up to ten minutes), and they move in a sort of up-and-down motion. Sharks, being fish, don't breathe air, and they move differently—side to side.

Dolphins mate throughout most of the year; in Florida, May is the busiest month for dolphin births, according to SeaWorld. Because dolphin gestation is about one year, this means May is also a common time to mate. Dolphins have one calf at a time, born in the water.

A 2004 *National Geographic* article told how researchers are looking into why so many first-born gulf coast dolphins die; less than 25 percent of first-borns live for a full year. Scientists think the reason may be that man-made chemicals and toxins stored in the mother dolphin's fat are transferred to her calf through her milk. The first-born dolphins get the brunt of these toxins, such as polychlorinated biphenyls (PCBs), leaving fewer toxins in the mother's milk for later offspring. Researchers noted that the Gulf of Mexico has a higher concentration of such chemicals than the oceans, which are bigger and have better circulation. The article concluded, however, that dolphins are complex creatures, and the toxin explanation is only a theory that researchers will continue to study.

Habitats

Honeymoon, Caladesi, and Mullet Key give visitors an idea of what all of Florida's barrier islands must have looked like before development, and it's quite varied in habitat: tidal flats like those at Honeymoon Island's bird observation area, maritime hammock like Caladesi's interior, coastal scrub like parts of Mullet Key, and mangrove shorelines common to all. Honeymoon Island boasts one of the last untouched southern Florida slash pine forests and more than 200 species of plants.

The changes in shape that these barrier islands display are typical changes among all barrier islands; consider that Honeymoon and Caladesi were once one island, and that Mullet Key has lost some of its gulf beach to erosion. Sand can gradually shift and change an island's shoreline or elevation, or be wiped out in a hurricane.

While these changes can be due to natural forces, other changes in the environment are brought on by people. One potentially hazardous man-made situation faced Tampa Bay in 2003: the possibility of a toxic spill. A phosphate fertilizer plant at Piney Point (between E. G. Simmons Park and Emerson Point Park, under Nearby Natural Areas above) had been abandoned after the company filed for bankruptcy in 2001. The Florida Department of Environmental Protection (DEP) and other agencies feared that heavy rain could cause the 1.2 billion gallons of phosphate wastewater to overflow its diked pools and spill into the region's estuary. They proposed to treat the phosphate wastewater, carry it on barges to remote areas in the Gulf of Mexico, and dump it.

The federal Environmental Protection Agency agreed, and some environmentalists considered the action to be the lesser of the two evils. Other environmentalists and residents were concerned that the treated wastewater would still contain a high level of nitrogen. Some critics blamed the DEP for not taking action on the plant before it went bankrupt, saying the state knew that the owner, Mulberry Corp., had been struggling since 1995, according to the Associated Press. Still others were concerned that the water would flow toward the Keys and harm the coral reef tract there.

The state dumped hundreds of millions of gallons of the treated wastewater into the gulf and into Bishop Harbor near the plant, according to the *Sarasota Herald-Tribune*. The dumping, along with other measures taken to clean up the Piney Point plant and a second Mulberry Corp. plant in Polk County, cost the state a reported $160 million.

A wastewater spill farther north in the bay actually did occur after Hurricane Frances in September 2004. The Cargill Crop Nutrition phosphate company's dike holding back wastewater was eroded by the hurricane, according to the Associated Press, and sixty-five million gallons of polluted water fell into Hillsborough Bay. The Tampa Bay Estuary Program said about ninety-three tons of nitrogen had spilled into the bay. There was concern for marine life and seagrass in the bay, but no fish kills were reported.

Where to Stay

Campgrounds

Fort DeSoto has an excellent campground with 238 campsites in three loops. The beauty of camping here is that the mostly shady campground is situated on a small peninsula, so most campsites are on the water, either on Mullet Key Bayou or on the interior channel where campers can attend to their boats. All sites have water and electrical hookups, and access to the restrooms with showers. The campground also includes a dump station, laundry facility, and camp store. Fort DeSoto was expecting to change its policy from accepting reservations only in person to accepting some reservations by phone; contact the park for more information.

E. G. Simmons Park (under Nearby Natural Areas, above) has eighty-eight campsites in two campgrounds. Most of the sites back up to the bay. All sites have water, and some have electrical hookups. Contact the park for more information.

Hillsborough River State Park (under Nearby Natural Areas, above), has a nice, mostly shady campground close to the river. There are 108 campsites, most with water and electrical hookups. There are full restrooms and a dump station. The park concession has a gift shop near the pool where snacks and some basic supplies are sold. For reservations, contact ReserveAmerica.

If you travel to Caladesi Island State Park in your own boat, you may register for an overnight stay in one of the 108 slips in the sheltered marina. Contact ReserveAmerica for more information.

Lodging

When it comes to lodging, visitors have a variety of options in the nearby metropolitan area, from bed-and-breakfasts (Mansion House Bed and Breakfast: 800-274-7520; *www.mansionbandb.com*) to small motels (Palm Pavilion Inn: 800-433-PALM; *www.palmpavilioninn.com*) and major hotel chains (Sheraton Sand Key Resort: 800-325-3535; *www.sheratonsandkey.com*). Minutes from Honeymoon Island at the Dunedin Marina, try Best Western Yacht Harbor Inn and Suites (800-447-4728).

How to Get There

For Honeymoon Island, take I-75 to SR 52 (Exit #285) and go west. At US 19, turn left (south). Travel to County Road 586 (Curlew Road) and turn right (west). The road ends at the entrance to Honeymoon Island State Park. To visit Caladesi Island State Park, you can take the ferry from Honeymoon Island or take your own boat.

To get to Fort DeSoto Park, take I-75 to I-275 south (Exit #274) and go north across Tampa Bay. Exit I-275 at US 19/CR 682 (Exit #17), following the road west. (Travelers can also reach I-275 via I-75 Exit #228 from the north or I-4 from the east.) At CR 679 (Pinellas Bayway), turn left (south). Toll fees altogether are $.85 (no toll for the return trip). The road ends at the park. Pass the campground; the park visitor center is ahead at a three-way stop. Most of the park's facilities are to the right.

✦ ✦ ✦

Honeymoon Island State Park
#1 Causeway Blvd.
Dunedin, Florida 34698
Phone: 727-469-5918
Admission is $5.00 per vehicle.

Caladesi Island State Park
#1 Causeway Blvd.
Dunedin, Florida 34698
Phone: 727-469-5918
Admission is $4.00 for up to eight people per private boat, or $1.00 for each person arriving by kayak.

Fort DeSoto Park
3500 Pinellas Bayway South
Tierra Verde, Florida 33715
Phone: 727-582-2267
The boat ramp and fishing piers are open twenty-four hours a day. Otherwise, the park closes at dusk. The visitor center is open from 8 a.m. to 5 p.m. every day. The museum is open from 9 a.m. to 4 p.m.

The Tampa Bay area is one of the most densely populated regions in the state, but the bay and nearby Gulf of Mexico are dotted with preserved natural areas. Shorelines are rimmed in mangrove trees or beaches that are as attractive to wildlife as they are to people. The bay is great for paddling and viewing marine life.

Nearby

Nature Coast (chapter 17), Green Swamp (chapter 18)

21

Highland Ridge

Florida's peninsula is typically flat, and at or near sea level. But there are highlands of sandhills that break up what some would consider the landscape's monotony. Ecologically, the most important of these highlands is the Lake Wales Ridge.

Rising above the rest of the peninsula by about 300 feet, this 150-mile-long area is thought to have been a desertlike sand dune island chain when the sea levels were higher and most of today's Florida was under water. This ridge, which spans five counties (Lake, Orange, Polk, Osceola, and Highlands), is now a place of citrus groves, farms, retirement communities—and endangered scrub habitat.

Although most of the ridge is covered by development, there are a few areas that show what this unique geological formation used to look like.

Lake Wales Ridge State Forest in Frostproof is made up of a couple of tracts surrounded by lakes, agriculture, and residential areas. The high, sandy, dry scrub habitat that epitomizes Lake Wales Ridge is preserved here, and so are quiet pine flatwoods. The forest offers few facilities, which is just fine for hikers, bird-watchers, and hunters.

Highlands Hammock State Park in Sebring shows another side of the ridge with its swamps and hardwood forested areas. The 9,000-acre park preserves not only the nature but also the history of the former pioneering area and offers several visitor-friendly programs and recreational opportunities.

Lake June-in-Winter Scrub State Park is a newer member of the state park system, and its lack of facilities make this a quiet park. It's also one of the best places to see the typical scrub habitat associated with the ridge. A portion of the park's 845 acres also includes wetlands, and its location on the southern shore of Lake June-in-Winter makes it popular with wildlife.

Strung together by US 27, these natural areas allow nature travelers to explore various points along the ridge and get to know this extraordinary central Florida ecosystem.

Figure 20. Lake June-in-Winter Scrub State Park is a good place to spot Florida scrub jays.

What to Do There

The Lake Wales Ridge area is a patchwork of agricultural, residential, and natural areas, dotted with lakes of all sizes. The towns of Sebring, Lake Placid, Avon Park, and Frostproof are the main jumping-off points for enjoying the region.

Trail Tripping

Lake Wales Ridge State Forest has a couple of hiking trails, Reedy Creek and Old Cabin. The Reedy Creek trail is an 11- to 22-mile loop off Lake Arbuckle Road. The Old Cabin trail is a 1-mile loop off School Bus Road. There are also 20 miles of the Florida National Scenic Trail that cut through. Horse riders are welcome in the Walk-in-the-Water tract of the forest. Trail users should be aware of designated hunting seasons. Request trail maps from the forest and/or the Florida Trail Association.

Lake June-in-Winter has a few short trails. Visitors can walk down a dirt road through the scrub, take the path past pines to the lake, or cross a stream through a hammock filled with birds. The dirt roads are open to off-road cyclists.

Highlands Hammock offers nine nature trails, each about a half-mile long. Many of them are loops that take fifteen or thirty minutes. All of them are recognized by the Florida Greenways and Trails program. Some go through the hammock, some through pinelands, and some are boardwalks over the swamps. Horse owners can ride along 11 miles of dirt roads in the park. Request a park guide and trail map to find the trails.

Paddling and Boating

The forest's Arbuckle Creek flows south from Lake Arbuckle and is a quiet spot for canoeing or kayaking. There is a boat ramp on Arbuckle Road south of State Road 64. Paddlers and boaters can also access Lake Arbuckle at the boat ramp on the northern end of the lake at the end of Lake Arbuckle Road. In the forest's Walk-in-the-Water tract, a boat ramp for Lake Weohyakapka (Walk-in-the-Water) is located off Walk-in-the-Water Road north of County Road 630.

There are numerous lakes throughout the Lake Wales Ridge area that paddlers and boaters can explore. Lake Placid, Lake June-in-Winter, Lake Istokpoga, Lake Clay, Lake Jackson, and many other lakes offer boat ramps.

Guided Tours

Highlands Hammock offers a tram tour of the park almost every day. Tuesday through Friday, the tour begins at 1:00 p.m. On Saturdays and Sundays, the tour runs at 1:00 p.m. and 2:30 p.m. Tickets are $3.00 for adults and $1.50 for children six through twelve.

The Indian Prairie Safari Eco-Tour at MacArthur Agro-Ecology Research Center (863-465-2571) takes visitors over a working cattle ranch on a swamp buggy. Covering more than 10,000 acres, the ranch offers the tour to show the research being done there in connection with Archbold Biological Station (under Nearby Natural Areas, below). Tours are offered by reservation only. Tickets are $15.00 for adults and $10.00 for children six through twelve. The ranch is located in Lake Placid on Buck Island Ranch Road. To get there, take US 27 to SR 70 and head east for about 7 miles. At Durrance Road, turn south and watch for directions to the ranch.

Nearby Natural Areas

Archbold Biological Station (863-465-2571; *www.archbold-station.org*) in Lake Placid is a scientific research facility that owns and manages more than 5,000 acres on the southern end of the Lake Wales Ridge. Archbold, a National Natural Landmark, is open mainly to researchers, but it allows visitors to watch an eighteen-minute film about the Lake Wales Ridge and hike its half-mile interpretive scrub trail. You can pick up a twenty-four-page guidebook about the trail to learn more about Archbold, the Lake Wales Ridge, the on-site weather station, and various plants and animals on the trail. Visitors are welcome Monday through Friday from 8 a.m. until 5 p.m. and must sign an application form to enter. To get there, take US 27 to the Lake Placid area. Turn west on SR 70 and travel for about a mile to CR 17 N. Turn south and look for the entrance in about 2 miles.

Avon Park Air Force Bombing Range (863-452-4254) adjoins some forest land. Despite the training exercises that take place here, the range is noted for wildlife-watching. About 12 miles of the Florida Trail pass through, and hikers can use a primitive campsite here. An observation tower overlooks Lake Arbuckle's eastern side. To get there, take US 27 to the Frostproof area. Go east on SR 64 for about 10 miles to the entrance. Contact the range office before your visit to find out whether it will be closed because of training exercises or security issues.

Tiger Creek Preserve (863-635-7506) is a 4,800-acre site owned and managed by the Nature Conservancy. Scrub, swamp, sandhill, and pine flatwood habitats are protected here, along with the creek for which the preserve is named. Visitors can hike the preserve's three trails—Jenkins, George Cooley, or Pfundstein—taking from a half-hour to six hours, depending on the trail. The preserve is open during daylight hours only. The trailheads are located in different parts of the preserve, so it's best to get a map and directions from Tiger Creek before your visit.

Jack Creek Preserve (352-796-7211) is a Southwest Florida Water Management District property of about 1,200 acres. Jack Creek connects Lake Francis with Lake Istokpoga, the fifth largest lake in the state. There are no facilities and little to do here but hike—just perfect for some people. There are no designated hiking trails, but visitors can walk along 7 miles of unpaved roads. Jack Creek is open during daylight hours only. To get there, take US 27 to Touchton Road (about 3 miles south of SR 66) and go west. Turn left (south) at Decatur Street, then right (west) on Grand Concourse Road. A parking area is located about a half-mile down the road.

Lake Wales Ridge Wildlife and Environmental Area (WEA) (863-648-3203) is a newish natural area that preserves scrub habitat and other plant communities in several tracts throughout Lake Placid. The WEA is open to hunting, but it also welcomes wildlife-watchers, hikers, off-road bicyclists, and horseback riders; these activities may be restricted during hunt dates, so contact the WEA office before your arrival. There are no facilities here, and the only paved road is on Royce Road in the Royce Unit. Hikers and bikers can access all tracts, but the only hiking trails are at the Lake Placid Scrub Unit and Royce Unit, and the only roads and firebreaks for bikers are at the Royce Unit. To get to the Royce Unit (near Lake Istokpoga), take US 27 to the Lake Placid area and head east at CR 621. At Virginia Ave., turn left (north) and go 5 miles to the entrance on the left (west) side of the road. For the Lake Placid Scrub Unit (south of Lake Placid), take US 27 to SR 70 and go west for 3 miles. At Placidview Drive, turn right (north), and look for the parking area/trailhead a mile ahead on the right (east).

Land acquisition is underway for Lake Wales Ridge National Wildlife Refuge in various tracts from the Kissimmee area to Sebring, but the refuge doesn't have any public visitation at this time. Other tracts of scrub habitat are being pursued by other agencies and organizations for conservation. The state estimates about $75 billion has been spent to preserve what's left of this unique plant community.

Nearby Attractions

Paynes Creek Historic State Park (863-375-4717) in Bowling Green preserves the memories of the Second and Third Seminole Wars. U.S. soldiers began building Fort Chokonikla here starting in 1849 in response to deadly attacks by Seminoles. The fort no longer exists, but visitors can see where it once stood. The park offers trails and picnic areas. Admission is $2.00 per vehicle for up to eight people. To get there, take US 27 to Avon Park. Go west on SR 64 for about 8 miles to CR 636. Follow that road about 5 miles to the town of Wauchula, and go north on US 17. You'll reach Bowling Green in about 5 miles; follow the signs at Main Street east to the park.

While you're in the area, you may want to check out why Lake Placid calls itself both the "town of murals" and the "caladium capital of the world." Lake Placid's thirty-odd murals on buildings downtown depict the nature and history of the area. Most of them are located on Interlake Blvd. west of US 27. As for the caladiums, more than 1,200 acres of these leafy plants grow here, and driving by the fields in summer is a popular activity for visitors, as is the annual caladium festival in August.

To some people, Sebring is best known for the Sebring International Raceway (800-626-RACE; *www.sebringraceway.com*), where the Twelve Hours of Sebring race has been held every spring since 1952. Indy cars and sports cars use the raceway for testing.

Wildlife

The scrub, sandhills, pine flatwoods, and hardwood hammocks in the Highlands Ridge area host a variety of animals. The desertlike scrub is home to gopher tortoises, eastern indigo snakes, sand skinks, and Florida mice.

In the pine flatwoods and swamps of Highlands Hammock (a site on the Great Florida Birding Trail), visitors can spot red-bellied and pileated woodpeckers, cousins to ivory-billed woodpeckers, which are considered extinct. Ivory-billed woodpeckers are rumored to have been seen in or around the park's swamps as recently as the 1960s, and researchers in Louisiana are searching remote swamps for the bird. White-tailed deer are common in the park, especially near the orange grove around sunset.

At Lake June-in-Winter Scrub State Park, the lake attracts bald eagles and ospreys. Swallow-tailed kites soar over the area in the summer.

Look for . . .

The Florida scrub jay is admired by so many people because it's relatively tame. Many people have had these blue and gray birds even land on their heads! However, that may be because they are used to people feeding them, which is against the law.

The Florida scrub jay is a special bird because it is one of the few birds that live in families. A mating pair's offspring sometimes stay with the parents to help raise their future siblings.

Scrub jays are known in other parts of the United States (like California), but the Florida scrub jay is a unique subspecies. Requiring about 25 acres per family, the Florida scrub jay is considered a threatened species because of habitat loss. They are found in many scrubby areas of Florida—even in backyards if the habitat is right—and are at home on the Lake Wales Ridge. The estimate for the number of scrub jays in Florida is around 2,000.

Look for Florida scrub jays near the entrance of Lake June-in-Winter Scrub State Park and in other sandy areas.

Habitats

Unfortunately for Florida scrub jays and other species of plants and animals that depend on the high, sandy habitat of the scrub, development has nearly pushed them out of their homes. It's estimated that 85 percent of the original ridge has been developed, according to the Nature Conservancy. Yet the highlands are home to one of the highest concentrations of endangered animals and plants in the country—especially plants.

Some of the more endangered plants in the state grow here, including the pygmy fringe tree (a three-foot-tall member of the olive family), short-leaved rosemary (an herb with delicate orchidlike flowers), scrub blazing star (a spindly flower with bushy lavender blooms), and Florida jointweed (a wiry plant with clusters of white, tubular flowers). There are twenty species of plants here that are on the Endangered Species List.

The desertlike conditions of some areas along the Lake Wales Ridge (and other scrub areas in Florida) allow the region to share desert species with the American Southwest, such as cacti, tortoises, and burrowing owls. Even though the area is high and dry, it still gets about fifty inches of rainfall each year. But the sandy soil of the scrub cannot hold the water, and it drains away quickly. Swamps like those in Highlands Hammock, and the area's numerous lakes, collect the rainfall.

Fortunately, this one-of-a-kind area is being preserved by government agencies and nonprofit groups one tract of land at a time as farms, groves, and ranches are bought and nurtured back to a more natural state for conservation.

Where to Stay

Campgrounds

Highlands Hammock is a good all-around place to camp. The park has 143 sites, including five horse camping sites, plus an area of sixteen primitive campsites separate from the main camping area. Contact ReserveAmerica for details and reservations.

Primitive camping is available in Lake Wales Ridge State Forest. One campsite is right on Lake Arbuckle. There is also a youth camp for organized groups. Campsites are available by permit only and may be used by hunters during designated hunt dates. Contact the forest for information.

Lodging

Overnight lodging on the ridge is available in Sebring, Lake Placid, and Avon Park. Choose from efficiencies and cottages (like Pratt's Resort: 863-699-1223; *www.onlakejune.com* on Lake June), resorts (like Chateau Elan Hotel and Spa: 863-655-6252; *www.chateauelansebring.com* near the Sebring International Raceway) and chain hotels (like the Ramada Inn: 863-465-3133 in Lake Placid).

How to Get There

The Lake Wales Ridge State Forest Arbuckle Tract is north of SR 64 east of US 27. To get there, take US 27 to Frostproof and turn east at CR 630. Follow the road for about five miles, then take Lake Reedy Blvd. at the fork in the road. Follow it around the eastern side of Lake Reedy to Lake Arbuckle Road. Turn right (south) at Rucks Dairy Road. Another entrance to this tract is right on SR 64. To get to the Walk-in-the-Water Tract, continue on CR 630 instead of taking the Lake Reedy Blvd. fork. There are several trailheads on this road. You can access more of the forest by driving down the road and turning left (north) on Walk-in-the-Water Road.

Highlands Hammock State Park is located off US 27 on Hammock Road in Sebring. On US 27 near Lake Jackson, watch for a sign showing the turn-off. More signs along the way lead through a residential area to the park entrance.

Lake June-in-Winter Scrub State Park also is best reached by following signs. You'll see the sign on the western side of US 27 north of downtown Lake Placid. Follow the signs along the road around Lake June-in-Winter to the entrance.

     ∾   ∾   ∾

Lake Wales Ridge State Forest
452 School Bus Road
Frostproof, Florida 33843
Phone: 863-635-7801

Highlands Hammock State Park
5931 Hammock Road
Sebring, Florida 33872
Phone: 863-386-6094
Admission is $4.00 per vehicle, or $3.00 per vehicle with a single person.

Lake June-in-Winter Scrub State Park
Daffodil Road
Lake Placid, Florida 33852
Phone: 863-386-6094
A $2.00 entrance fee is collected at an honor box.

The Florida peninsula's highlands are situated on a 150-mile-long tract known as the Lake Wales Ridge, which runs north and south through central Florida. Several endangered species live here in rare scrub habitat. Sandhills, pine forests, and numerous lakes are inviting to nature travelers looking for quiet natural beauty.

Nearby

Green Swamp (chapter 18), Florida's Bay Area and Gulf Islands (chapter 20), Cracker Lakes (chapter 22)

22

Cracker Lakes

Go through the rough wood gates of Lake Kissimmee State Park, and you enter a land of 1870s Florida. During that decade, Ulysses S. Grant and then Rutherford B. Hayes were the nation's presidents. The lightbulb, telephone, phonograph, microphone, and color photograph were invented. Women's dresses had bustles. Florida had been a state for about thirty years. And the Florida cracker—so named because of the crack of his whip, which could brush a fly off a cow without touching the cow—"hunted" loose scrub cattle for the market, driving them across the Kissimmee prairie.

It is this legacy that Lake Kissimmee State Park presents its visitors.

Situated on land that is almost an island—surrounded by Lake Kissimmee to the east, Tiger Lake to the south and Lake Rosalie to the west—the park is otherwise surrounded by open country, citrus country, cattle country. To get there, you may pass miles of rangeland and citrus groves. The era of the cow hunters may have passed, but cowboys do live on in Florida, the largest cattle-ranching state east of the Mississippi River, with an estimated 2,000 cowboys.

The area's unique open, scrubby, lake-dotted environment is attractive not only to cowboys but also to various wildlife, from those that are attracted to the water-rich environment (like alligators) to those that prefer the higher, sandy habitat (like Florida scrub jays). The area is also far enough away from the bright lights of big cities that its dark skies attract star-gazers as well.

Lake Kissimmee State Park's history and nature-rich environment make it a great place to get to know the real Florida.

What to Do There

Lake Kissimmee State Park has a unique location and history, and it makes good on this with its 1876 Cow Camp, a section of the park set up to look like a rough-hewn cattle hunter camp. On weekends and holidays from 9:30 a.m. to 4:30 p.m., you can step back in time. What was it like to be a Florida pioneer

Figure 21. A park ranger's airboat rests near the Zipprer Canal at Lake Kissimmee State Park.

and cow hunter? Find out from the Florida crackers themselves, who will wonder if you're there to buy or trade the scrub cattle if you don't speak up and ask questions of the volunteers in period dress. And what about your sunglasses? Be prepared to tell the crackers what they are, because the cow hunters will pretend not to know about such newfangled things.

Trail Tripping

There are 13 miles of nature trails within the park, all starting near the same place by the boat ramp. The trails take you through the serenity of mostly pine flatwoods, where you're likely to encounter deer, armadillos, and many kinds of woodland birds.

The 6-mile North Loop Trail takes you back to the ranger station and to the Fallen Oak Camp—one of the backcountry camping areas. The Buster Island Loop Trail, nearly 7 miles, takes you around an open field and to another backcountry camping area—the Buster Island Camp. The short Gobbler Ridge Trail takes you past the youth camping area and to the edge of the lake. Finally, a half-mile self-guiding nature trail explains the pine flatwoods and oak hammock plant communities.

To the east north of Yeehaw Junction, the Florida National Scenic Trail loops twice in the Prairie Lakes Unit of Three Lakes Wildlife Management Area. (See below, under Nearby Natural Areas.) You can access the North Loop from County Road 523 about 9 miles north of Kenansville, then reach the South Loop near Lake Marian. Both loops are about 6.5 miles long. Hikers should be aware of hunting seasons here.

Paddling and Boating

The park provides a great way to access the expanse of Lake Kissimmee's water and natural beauty. Bring your own canoe, kayak, or boat to dock at the marina or launch into the 35,000-acre expanse of the Lake Kissimmee area. Canoes and kayaks can access Lake Rosalie by the Zipprer Canal (named after the Zipprer family, from whom the park land was purchased in 1969) or access Tiger Lake by Tiger Creek. Hearty paddlers can tour all three lakes in a six- or seven-hour trip, according to the park.

Canoe, pontoon, and bass boat rentals are available at nearby Camp Mack (863-696-1108) just a quarter-mile beyond the park entrance on Camp Mack Road.

Star Gazing

The stars at night are big and bright—deep in the heart of Florida! Without the light pollution that affects the larger coastal cities, Lake Kissimmee State Park is in a prime dark spot for star gazing. If you're constellation minded, camp out with your telescope.

Guided Tours

By reservation only, a park ranger will guide you on a paddling tour of Kissimmee, Rosalie, or Tiger Lakes. You must have your own canoe or kayak. Contact the park for more information. The park concession used to operate boat tours; it may again in the future.

Camp Mack (mentioned above) offers Lake Kissimmee airboat tours, which last from one hour to an hour and a half. The price is $30.00, and there is a minimum of two people for the tour.

Nearby Natural Areas

If you've been on the Florida Turnpike south of Orlando, you probably drove right through the 62,000-acre Three Lakes Wildlife Management Area (352-732-1225) and didn't even know it. For excellent wildlife-watching and a drive in the country, consider a side trip to the Prairie Lakes Unit of the WMA, near Kenansville. As a WMA, Three Lakes is popular for hunting, but it's also known for being the best area to see bald eagles in the entire continental United States. There are more active bald eagle nests here than any other place besides Alaska. Look for the observation tower at Lake Jackson. For a scenic drive through the pinelands, ride along dirt roads labeled 5 and 19. Admission is $3.00 per person or $6.00 per car. To get there from the park, take State Road 60 and go east to US 441 (at Yeehaw Junction), then turn left (north). Take this road to Canoe Creek Road (CR 523), and follow it northwest until you see the Prairie Lakes signs. There are three entrances along the road. You can also get to the Three Lakes area via an unpaved road right off SR 60 as you're going east before you reach 441, but this isn't the Prairie Lakes Unit of the WMA. For a free brochure that includes a map, contact the Florida Fish and Wildlife Conservation Commission at 850-488-5520.

Nearby Attractions

Bok Sanctuary (863-676-1408; *www.boksanctuary.org*) in Lake Wales is known for its sixty-bell carillon tower. A National Historic Landmark, the sanctuary covers 250 acres with a garden. Admission is $8.00 for adults and $3.00 for children five to twelve. To get there from the park, take SR 60 west to US 27 and turn north, then just watch for signs pointing the way.

Wildlife

It's no wonder that Florida pioneers loved and settled this land, because the wildlife here is abundant. Covered with lakes of all sizes, this central Florida upland area attracts many species, particularly birds of many kinds: eastern towhees, sandhill cranes, wild turkeys, various warblers, and even crested caracaras and snail kites. The park is also a place to see white-tailed deer easily, along the park roads, on trails, and even near the marina.

Look for . . .

Many bird-watchers already know the area's reputation for bald eagles. You may see them flying overhead on your way to the park entrance, perching on a dock sticking out into Lake Kissimmee, or searching for prey while soaring over Buster Island. It's a source of pride for Floridians that our national symbol is right at home here along this chain of lakes.

For bird-watchers, bald eagles are a delight to encounter. Their sharp features, proud demeanor, and six-foot wingspan are more impressive in person than on television or other media. As with many species in the bird kingdom, bald eagle females are larger than males, although they look similar. Juveniles, while sometimes as large as the adults, lack the trademark white head that comes with age.

The bald eagle population across the United States was once endangered because of hunting and the use of pesticide DDT. But after DDT use stopped and the eagle enjoyed protection under the Endangered Species Act, the population rebounded. In 1995, bald eagles were downlisted from endangered to threatened in the contiguous forty-eight states, where there are about 6,000 breeding pairs.

The prairie lakes area is also where you might happen upon another large bird, the whooping crane, which stands almost five feet tall and has a wingspan of seven or eight feet. Similar to a sandhill crane, it's distinguished by its taller height and white, rather than gray, feathers. If you see one, it will likely be wearing a leg band to identify it to researchers.

The whooping cranes here are part of an experimental nonmigratory flock that was initially established in 1993. Each year, biologists add more cranes to the flock, with the hope of attaining twenty-five breeding pairs of whooping cranes. The flock roams freely throughout central Florida, with some reports of the endangered birds sighted as far away as Leesburg and near Tampa. In 2002, the experimental flock celebrated success with the first whooping crane chick born in the wild in Florida since the 1890s, a male called Lucky. Hopefully, the flock will continue to expand and re-establish a strong population in Florida.

This nonmigratory flock is separate from the more well-known migratory flock that biologists are trying to establish at Chassahowitzka National Wildlife Refuge in Crystal River. Please see the Nature Coast chapter (chapter 17) for more about this flock.

Habitats

Lake Kissimmee State Park sits on the Lake Wales Ridge, a 150-mile-long scrub environment in the center of the state. It is thought that at one time, the Lake

Wales Ridge was all there was of Florida—a small chain of islands made of sand dunes. At 300 feet above sea level, the Lake Wales Ridge is the highest point in the Florida peninsula.

This unique desertlike area is home to plants that you'd find in the American southwest—such as prickly pear cactus—and plants that are becoming harder to find, such as pygmy fringe tree, scrub plum, scrub beargrass, short-leaved rosemary, and Carter's mustard, all endangered plants. Many of the original plants of the Lake Wales Ridge are endangered because of loss of habitat to agricultural, residential, and commercial development.

Besides scrub, you'll also come across pine flatwoods, oak hammocks, and freshwater marshes while exploring the park—natural central Florida.

The third-largest lake in the state, Lake Kissimmee is really just an extremely wide portion of the Kissimmee River, which sends its water south to the Everglades. Accepting water from swamps south of Walt Disney World and channeling it to Lake Okeechobee, the Kissimmee River is an important part of the Everglades restoration.

Levees, canals, and pumps drained the river valley for cattle ranches and made the river easier to navigate and control. But this disrupted the balance of nature among the lakes and added to the Everglades' water problems. River restoration is underway, with some dams having been removed and the Kissimmee on its way to meandering through wet prairies to Lake Okeechobee again.

Where to Stay

Campgrounds

Campers will enjoy staying right at the park. There are sixty oak hammock campsites in two loops for both tents and RVs. Most campsites at Lake Kissimmee are spacious and include a picnic table, fire pit, water faucet and, if you ask for it, electricity. Clean restrooms and hot showers are located in the center of each of the two loops. The only drawback is that you can hear airboats running on the lake all night long, especially on weekends. Contact ReserveAmerica for information and reservations.

There are two primitive campsites along the park trails. A youth campsite for up to fifty people is available to organized groups. Contact the park for more information.

Primitive camping is also available at Three Lakes Wildlife Management

Area out of hunting seasons; call 352-732-1225 for a free permit. Check out Parker Hammock Camp along the Florida National Scenic Trail or Dry Pond Camp near Lake Jackson.

Camp Mack (mentioned above) offers about 150 sites for tents and RVs, but it caters mostly to RVs, with paver and concrete slabs. The campground also boasts a heated pool.

Also outside of the park, consider Harbor RV Resort (863-696-1194) on Lake Rosalie. The campground offers conveniences like full hookups, a laundry, and gas station.

Lodging

Lake Wales has a few places to stay if you're not a camper. Perhaps the most well-known is Chalet Suzanne (800-433-6011; *www.chaletsuzanne.com*), which has been around since the 1930s. The inn's restaurant is a hit with gourmets.

Westgate River Ranch Resort (866-499-9077; *www.westgateriverranch.com*), east of the park on SR 60 at the Kissimmee River, is part dude ranch, part theme park, and part timeshare, picking up on a few of central Florida's foundations. The lodge and cabins offer a place to stay, and the resort provides guests with a rodeo, horseback riding, a restaurant, petting zoo, and marina.

How to Get There

From eastern Florida, take the Florida Turnpike, exit at Yeehaw Junction (SR 60, Exit #193), and go west. Turn left at Boy Scout Camp Road, and stay to the right as you round Lake Rosalie to the park entrance.

You can also take I-4 to U.S. 27 (Exit #55) near Davenport, then travel south to SR 60 and go east to Boy Scout Camp Road.

From the Vero Beach or Tampa areas, you can take SR 60 east or west to Boy Scout Camp Road.

✎ ✎ ✎

Lake Kissimmee State Park
14248 Camp Mack Road
Lake Wales, Florida 33853
Phone: 863-696-1112
Admission is $4.00 per vehicle.

The Cracker Lakes reveal central Florida's true nature and history, with sandy ridges, an expansive chain of lakes, and open cattle country that was once home to scrub cattle hunters. The lakes and open land attract the largest population of nesting bald eagles in the continental United States.

Nearby

Upper St. Johns River (chapter 16), Highland Ridge (chapter 21)

23

Southern Prairie Lands

Few people think of prairies when they think of Florida. Up and down the state's interior, though, dry prairies once covered three million acres of land. The flat expanse of Florida's prairies was blanketed by grasses, saw palmettos, and wildflowers. Lightning started fires that kept trees from encroaching, and fires renewed the land by keeping the earth soft and ensuring fresh greenery for prairie inhabitants.

Prairies still exist in Florida—like those in Paynes Prairie Preserve State Park near Gainesville and Kissimmee Prairie Preserve State Park near Okeechobee—and Myakka River State Park is the best place in southern Florida to explore them. Myakka is one of the largest state parks in land size, at 28,875 acres (about 45 square miles). That breadth of prairie—along with its namesake river, accessed by visitor-friendly trails—makes the park one of the best in the state park system.

The Myakka River is designated a Florida Wild and Scenic River. Beginning in northeastern Manatee County, the river flows south into Charlotte Harbor on the Gulf of Mexico—a course almost parallel with the Peace River to the east. The river widens at Upper Myakka Lake, the main recreational focus of the state park. The river depth varies widely from season to season. Go in the spring, and you'll have a peaceful river. Go in summer, and not only will you have to paddle quickly, but the riverbanks and footpaths will be flooded. The four-foot-high water line on many trees tells that story.

The river was attractive to natives, who used its banks as a ceremonial ground. Later, pioneers, who called the area Big Flats, found the area a good place to raise livestock. As park staff tell it, some of those pioneers gathered Spanish moss from the trees and sold it for ten cents a pound—a good price for something that was used to stuff cushions for both furniture and early automobile seats. Settlers also used broomsedge to create—what else?—brooms to sweep the plants away from their houses. (A yard of sand was a necessary fire break around a house, as prairie fires were common.)

Figure 22. Sandhill cranes are usually easy to spot at Myakka River State Park.

Most recently, the land served as a ranch, until the state took over in the 1940s. A lot of the land in the park was once owned by Bertha Palmer Potter, a Chicago hotel magnate who decided to try her hand at ranching when she reached her sixties. Buying out another rancher, Potter built a two-story house, a one-room schoolhouse, a blacksmith shop, a barn, and a water tower that could be seen for miles. All of this supported the forty adults and children who lived on the ranch, park staff say. Some of the remains of the ranch still exist in the park today.

What to Do There

Myakka has almost everything when it comes to activities. About the only thing you can't do here is swim. It's a great place to spend a weekend or even longer outdoors.

Trail Tripping

A 1.3-mile nature trail east of the bridge over the river takes you through a hardwood hammock. Interpretive signs along the trail detail the ecology of the hammock.

The trail also leads to the Canopy Walkway, a narrow, suspended structure like a swinging bridge that gives visitors a close-up view of treetop life—airplants and songbirds—twenty-five feet in the air. Climb even higher to the top of the seventy-four-foot tower at the other end, where you can see sweeping views of the park and the river, which appears to be just a trickle from that height. Interpretive signs explain the importance of studying the forest canopy and highlight other canopy structures around the world.

If you want to stretch your legs and go deep in the woods, there are 45 miles of interconnecting hiking trails within the park. Trails take you throughout the northeast section of the park and many lead to primitive camping sites.

Most of these trails are open to off-road bicycles. Bikes are also welcome on the 7-mile paved main park road, which follows the river and provides glimpses of the water through the trees on the bank. Ask about bike rentals at the concession, Myakka Outpost.

To explore the park on horseback, take your steed on 12 miles of equestrian-only trails, which are located in the center of the park.

Before going on any of the trails in this large park, be sure to pick up a trail map from the park office at the entrance.

Paddling and Boating

Upper Myakka Lake attracts paddlers and boaters alike with its wide openness and undeveloped shores. The boat launch is right across from the concession. Bring your own boat, or rent a canoe or kayak from the park concession and explore the 11 miles of canoe trails in the park. Rentals start at $15.00.

Guided Tours

The park concession (941-365-0100; *www.myakkariver.org*) offers tours by water and by land. Each tour takes about an hour. Tours cost $8.00 for adults and $4.00 for children six to twelve. Contact the concession for departing times.

Billed as the world's largest airboats, the *Gator Gal* and *Myakka Maiden* take visitors out on Upper Myakka Lake. Unlike most airboats that can accommodate only a handful of people, these can take seventy. Also, they're covered—they look more like paddleboats than airboats—so you won't get too much sun or rain. As you blow across the lake, the boat guide will tell you about the river, its history, and the animals that depend on it.

If you prefer to stay on land, try the tram tour. Although a ride on a tram might seem a bit too "touristy," even nature snobs can get a lot out of it, mostly because of the guide's entertaining and enlightening descriptions of the park. On the tram, you'll hear about the history of the land: how natives made it their home, how pioneers settled it, and how ranchers spread across it. You'll also learn about—and clearly see the effects of—fire exclusion and what it does to a dry prairie. As the tram ventures into the park, you might see turtles, alligators, or ospreys. Tram tours run only from about mid-December through May.

Walk on the Wild Side (941-351-6500; *www.walkwild.com*) in Sarasota leads tours through the area by reservation. From half-day bird-watching and photography tours to overnight paddling trips, Walk on the Wild Side offers to help plan a variety of outdoor activities based on what you want to do.

Silent Sports Outfitters (941-966-5477; *www.adventuresinflorida.net/silent sportsoutfitters.htm*) in Nokomis offers kayak rentals and guided paddling tours in the Sarasota area. Prices vary.

Nearby Natural Areas

Myakka Prairie is a water management district conservation area across the street from the state park entrance. There are no facilities here, but you can hike or ride a horse along the trails. For information about the prairie, contact the state park, which manages the prairie.

South of the Myakka Prairie border is yet another connecting natural area, T. Mabry Carlton Reserve (941-486-2547). This quiet park preserves more of the Myakka River valley lands and offers three short nature trails through hammocks and around marshes and swamps. (Longer backcountry hiking is allowed; contact the reserve for information and a backcountry hiking permit.) The reserve covers almost 25,000 acres of dry prairie, pine flatwoods, hammocks, and wetlands, where you might find the three-toed amphiuma (a kind of salamander) or a pine woods treefrog. The entrance is located within an agricultural and residential area. To get there, take I-75 to River Road (Exit #191) and go south. Turn right (west) on Venice Ave., then right again (north) on N. Jackson Road. At Border Road, turn right (east) and look for the reserve sign.

A stopover to Oscar Scherer State Park (941-483-5956) in the city of Osprey is a nice way to complement a visit to Myakka River State Park. Florida scrub jays live here in the scrub areas, white-tailed deer wander through the pines, and alligators and otters are at home in South Creek. Rent a canoe to paddle the creek, hike or bike 15 miles of interconnecting sandy trails, or swim in Lake Osprey. The park offers 104 campsites, many right along the creek. Oscar Scherer is located on US 41. To get there, take I-75 to County Road 681 (Exit #200) and head southwest for about 3 miles. At US 41 (Tamiami Trail), turn right (north) and watch for signs to the park, about 2 miles ahead.

Nearby Attractions

Crowley Museum and Nature Center (941-322-1000; *www.crowleymuseum naturectr.org*) down the road from Myakka's northern entrance lets you see even farther up the Myakka River with a boardwalk and observation tower. You'll also see a restored Florida Cracker-style house. Hours vary with the seasons and are subject to change, so call before your visit. Admission is $5.00 for adults, $3.00 for children five to twelve, and free for members and children under five. To get there, drive north along Myakka's main park road and out the northern entrance, and follow the road to the nature center, on the right side. The northern entrance is closed on weekdays; alternately, take I-75 to Fruitville Road (Exit #210) and travel east for 11 miles to Myakka Road. Turn right (south) and go about 2.5 miles to the nature center.

The Pelican Man's Bird Sanctuary (941-388-4444; *www.pelicanman.org*) rehabilitates injured sea birds and other wildlife. Visitors can see animals that aren't well enough to be released back into the wild, and learn more about southern Florida wildlife. Admission is $6.00 for adults and $2.00 for children four through seventeen. To get there, take I-75 to Fruitville Road (Exit #210) and go west about 6 miles to US 41. Then take John Ringling Causeway (CR 789) over to Lido Key, following John Ringling Blvd. to Ken Thompson Parkway and watching for signs to Ken Thompson Park.

Springs Spa Resort and Wellness Institute (941-426-1692; *www.warm mineralsprings.com*) is a commercial watering hole and spa situated on Warm Mineral Springs, with a mineral content among the highest in the world.

People visit to swim or just sit in the spring, hoping the mineral content will be good for whatever ails them. A café is on site. The spring creek flows into the Myakka River and attracts manatees in the winter. An underwater cave exists here, but no diving is allowed; some groups have been trying to change that and to stop the commercialization of the spring. The spring is open daily from 9 a.m. to 5 p.m. Admission is $14.00 for adults, $9.00 for students, $12.00 for seniors, and $5.00 for children under age twelve. To get there, take I-75 to River Road (Exit #191) and head west to US 41, about 4 miles. Turn left (south) on US 41, and left (east) again at Ortiz Blvd., following signs.

The Mote Marine Laboratory (941-388-4441; *www.mote.org*) is a nonprofit research organization open to the public. Mote offers visitors touch tanks, a full aquarium, shark pool, and museumlike displays that provide information about marine life and what affects it. Volunteers bursting with information stand by to tell you about what you see. A gift shop and café are on site. Hours are 10 a.m. to 5 p.m. every day, and admission is $12.00 for adults and $8.00 for children from four to twelve; members visit for free. On site, Sarasota Bay Explorers (941-388-4200; *www.sarasotabayexplorers.com*) operates wildlife cruises and guided kayak tours for a fee. The complex is located at 1600 Ken Thompson Parkway on City Island. To get there, take I-75 to Fruitville Road (Exit #210), and go west about 6 miles to US 41. Then take John Ringling Causeway (CR 789) over to Lido Key, and cross over to the island from there, following the signs.

The John and Mable Ringling Museum of Art (941-359-5700; *www. ringling.org*) is part of the reason the region calls itself the Cultural Coast. Circus impresario and real estate tycoon John Ringling left his art collection open to the public here in the lavish building and grounds. The art museum offers room after room of oversize paintings, deemed to be the country's best collection of seventeenth-century Italian paintings. Visitors also have access to the Ringling family winter home, Ca d'Zan, an opulent palace right on Sarasota Bay that is an example of a mix of Italian Renaissance, Baroque, Venetian Gothic, and modern architecture. Admission also includes entrance to the circus museum, which houses historical circus costumes, posters, carved circus wagons, props, and more. In between the three buildings is a beautiful formal rose garden. Hours are 10:00 a.m. to 5:30 p.m., and admission is $12.00 for seniors and $15.00 for others over twelve; Florida teachers and students with identification are admitted free; admission to the art museum alone is free on Mondays, as Mr. Ringling declared in his will. The museum is located at 5401 Bay Shore Road. To get there, take I-75 to University Parkway (Exit #213) and go west about 6 miles to US 41. Turn left (south) and watch for signs to the estate.

Wildlife

There's a lot of room here for animals to roam, fly, or swim. To get an idea of the kinds of wildlife in the area, stop at the visitor center, where dioramas display birds, mammals, and reptiles in their natural habitats.

Bird-watchers will enjoy the park's birdwalk, a sturdy boardwalk built right over part of Upper Myakka Lake. The boardwalk ends in a wide observation area with bench seating. Interpretive signs along the way provide pictures and names of many of the birds commonly seen on the lake, such as wood storks, glossy ibises, and great blue herons. During the winter, migratory waterfowl like teals and geese visit the lake in large numbers. Note that the entrance to the birdwalk can become flooded.

One unwelcome species in the park is the feral pig, an introduced animal that has become a pest because of the way it digs up the native plants and creates ruts in the ground to look for food. If you don't see a feral pig, you might see evidence of one: large areas of ground turned up as if someone had started shoveling but changed his or her mind.

Look for . . .

It's easy to find alligators in the park, lying fat and lazy in the sun on the banks, floating alongside your canoe in the river, or resting in a wet ditch.

Alligators are common throughout Florida, although they are considered a species of special concern. The Florida Fish and Wildlife Conservation Commission (FWC) estimates there are about one million alligators in the state. Growing from a couple of inches long to thirteen feet or more, alligators prefer freshwater habitats (like Myakka River), but are sometimes found in brackish and even saltwater environments. Anywhere there's fresh water in Florida is a possible place to find an alligator. April, May, and June are courtship and mating months for alligators, which are more mobile and can become aggressive during this time.

With their strong jaws and toothsome snout, alligators are the top predator among animals. As a ranger explained, alligators are opportunistic feeders; if they see something moving, they'll go for it, no matter what it is. Typically, alligators eat turtles, raccoons, fish, birds, and other creatures found in or near fresh water.

Alligators are feared because they do attack people. The FWC reports that there are fifteen to twenty nonfatal alligator attacks each year, and thirteen fatal attacks have been reported since 1948. Some alligator attacks are blamed on the fact that an alligator lost its fear of people because people were feeding it. Feeding or harassing alligators in any way is against state law. Although the statistics show it's not likely that an alligator will attack you, and you don't need to panic if you see one, don't tease an alligator or get too close to these potentially dangerous reptiles.

Habitats

Dry prairie like the kind found at Myakka is considered one of the most endangered habitats in Florida, mainly because the unpreserved land has been developed for agricultural, ranching, or residential use. It's also because fires, which naturally prevent trees from growing on the prairies, were put out by both settlers and government workers. Dry prairies depend on fires from lightning storms. In fact, a ranger said western Florida has the most lightning strikes of anywhere else in North America. Because for many years fire wasn't allowed to do its job of cleansing the prairie of trees and promoting new grass growth, hardwood hammocks took only a couple of decades to replace much of the original prairie.

Rangers at Myakka (and in many places across the state) are trying to reverse this with prescribed burning. They deliberately set controlled fires to specific areas. The conditions have to be just right. Slowly, rangers are returning the Myakka area back to a dry prairie with prescribed fires. If you see charred trees and shrubs, that's likely evidence of a controlled burn.

The state park, Myakka Prairie, T. Mabry Carlton Reserve, and other preserved lands along the river are considered "Myakka Island," a 142-square-mile area surrounded by residential and agricultural lands. According to park literature, Myakka Island is part of a wildlife corridor through which animals like Florida black bears can roam from one part of the state to another through uninterrupted natural areas.

Besides bears, sandhill cranes, indigo snakes, burrowing owls, crested caracaras, and other animals use and depend on the dry prairie environment. Sandhill cranes are common in the park and often seen near the river along the main park road.

You may see wildflowers in the park, especially in spring. The prairie iris is especially beautiful. If you go in spring, you can easily see its purple-blue color from the park's main road as you pass the trees across from the lake. You might also see the yellow-orange-pink lantana, a butterfly favorite, in isolated clumps.

Where to Stay

Campgrounds

Myakka has two campgrounds. The Old Prairie Campground is closer to the entrance of the park and has twenty-three sites with water and electricity. This is where mostly RVs end up because of the proximity of the dump station to the campground. The Big Flats Campground is close to the river, and has gotten so flooded in the past that park rangers have closed the campground and moved everyone out after heavy rains. (However, the park has attempted to improve the campground by raising its height.) Big Flats has fifty-two sites, some with water and electricity.

Myakka also offers group camping on the south side of State Road 72, across from the entrance to the park.

Adventurous campers can register for one of the six primitive campsites within the park. Hiking with a simple map across the prairie and through the hammock will take you to your site, anywhere from 2.2 to 13.9 miles away from the trailhead. All but the most remote of the primitive sites have a water pump, but this water must be treated for drinking. It's best to bring everything you need with you—and, of course, take it all back with you when you leave.

Outside the park, try the Peace River Campground (800-559-4011; *www. peacerivercampground.com*) down the road about a half-hour away in Arcadia. The campground has a pool, playground, laundry facilities, dump station, showers, and some tent sites right on the Peace River, another good paddling spot.

Lodging

Myakka River rents out five cabins near the main park road. The cabins were built in the 1930s by the Civilian Conservation Corps (CCC), and all have air conditioning and heat, a shower in the washroom, and an electric stove in a kitchen complete with utensils. If you like it rustic, you'll enjoy these three-room cabins with fireplace and back porch. Two double beds and a double sofa bed, along with a dining table, are in the main room. Outside, you'll find a picnic table and a charcoal grill. One of the cabins is wheelchair accessible. For information about cabin rental, contact ReserveAmerica.

Outside the park, you'll find a variety of options in Sarasota. There are chain hotels (like Hampton Inn: 941-371-1900), vacation homes (like Timberwoods Vacation Villas: 800-824-5444; *www.timberwoods.com*), inns (like The

Cypress: 941-955-4683; *www.cypressbb.com*), and many other places that front the beach or bay.

How to Get There

Myakka River State Park is east of downtown Sarasota and west of Arcadia. Take I-75 to SR 72 (Exit #205) and go east for about 10 miles to the park entrance. You also can access the park through its north gate, which is open from 8 a.m. until 5 p.m. on weekends and holidays. The north gate is on Clay Gully Road, also known as Fruitville Road (Exit #210).

∽ ∽ ∽

Myakka River State Park
13207 SR 72
Sarasota, Florida 34241
Phone: 941-361-6511
Admission is $5.00 per vehicle.

Myakka River State Park and surrounding lands form a large natural area that preserves dry prairie, a rare habitat in Florida. Myakka is one of the largest state parks in Florida and allows a variety of activities near Florida's Cultural Coast.

Nearby

Florida's Bay Area and Gulf Islands (chapter 20), Highland Ridge (chapter 21), Southwestern Barrier Islands (chapter 24)

24

Southwestern Barrier Islands

Florida's peninsula is placed just so in North America, a bridge of land between the subtropics and the temperate zone. Florida stretches the Atlantic Ocean coastline down almost to the Caribbean, while creating the eastern boundary of the Gulf of Mexico on its other side. Anyone may arrive on an Atlantic beach to watch the sun rise over the ocean, then turn up in the west later in the day to watch the sun set over the gulf.

There in the southeastern gulf, the peninsula's shoreline becomes dappled with barrier islands that further extend that bridge to a subtropical environment, both geographically and culturally. Calusa natives fished here and left piles of their discarded shells in mounds, or middens, up and down the coast. When Spanish explorers arrived, they found the Calusa to be unfriendly, and they were unable to establish significant permanent settlements. Later, however, the maze of islands turned out to be a good hideout for pirates and their treasure after raids on ships in the gulf and Caribbean. Even today, treasure hunters look for gold and other riches said to have been buried on the islands or spilled in the waters. Other modern visitors just enjoy the warm, laid-back island atmosphere of the region.

For nature travelers who visit southwestern Florida's barrier islands, there are several natural areas that reveal the islands' true nature. Three stand out: J.N. "Ding" Darling National Wildlife Refuge, Cayo Costa State Park, and Lovers Key Carl E. Johnson State Park.

The Ding Darling refuge takes up more than one-third of Sanibel Island, which is known as a popular resort location. Encompassing more than 6,300 acres, the refuge preserves prime location and habitat for wildlife, especially the wintering birds that so many visitors come to see. Established in 1945, the refuge existed long before the crowds (and bridge) did. The refuge took shape after prominent editorial cartoonist Jay Norwood Darling (nicknamed "Ding" as an abbreviation of his last name) pushed for its conservation in the 1940s. Often at the forefront of conservation issues, Darling learned that a couple thousand acres of mangrove forest on the island were going to be sold for de-

Figure 23. Shorebirds face the sunset at Lovers Key State Park.

velopment, so he persuaded the U.S. Fish and Wildlife Service to preserve it as Sanibel Island National Wildlife Refuge (which was changed in 1978 to honor Darling a decade after his death).

A couple of islands north of Sanibel is Cayo Costa, a barrier island reached only by boat. While the island is lightly developed with a few homes, it is mostly natural, and Cayo Costa State Park covers its northern end. Those who make the trip are rewarded with a pristine island to explore, and a beautiful, quiet beach on which to rest.

South of Fort Myers is Lovers Key Carl E. Johnson State Park, a three-island, 1,616-acre park of mangroves, tidal lagoons, and beach. The recreation-friendly park offers plenty for visitors who are looking to spend some quality outdoor time on a pretty shore—which is really true of all of these islands.

What to Do There

The waterbound region offers a lot to do, whether out on the gulf, in the bays, or on the islands themselves.

There are several sections, or tracts, that make up the refuge. The main Darling Tract where the visitor center stands is the largest section, preserving most of the mangrove forests of Sanibel Island's northern bay side. Down the road lies the Bailey Tract, where trails take visitors around large ponds. The Perry Tract is a small portion of beach on the south side of the island, accessed through a city beach parking area (which charges a parking fee). Farther away at Captiva Island, refuge paddling trails in Buck Key preserve more mangrove areas. Together, the tracts preserve a variety of habitats and provide lots of wildlife-watching opportunities.

To begin a visit at the refuge, start at the visitor center. Here you can pick up a refuge map and wildlife checklists, get information on guided tours and canoe rentals, and ask questions. Museum-quality interactive displays give you insight into the refuge's ecological makeup as well as a hint of the wildlife and habitats you're likely to see. There are also a bookstore, restrooms, and beverage vending machines (the only facilities in the refuge).

Contact the refuge in September for information about the events planned for Wildlife Refuge Week, which takes place in October.

Many visitors come to look for shells. Shelling is popular along the gulf coast beaches and can turn into a way to learn about the gulf's sea life. Shell seekers should note that taking live shells is prohibited.

Trail Tripping

At Ding Darling, the main attraction for most visitors is the 5-mile wildlife drive, which begins at the visitor center and winds around impoundments, passes mangroves, and offers spur trails through the uplands. The paved drive—which is open to vehicle, foot, and bicycle traffic—is likely where you'll see the most wildlife, especially birds. Consider timing your visit in winter during low tide for a better chance to view waterbirds; you can get tidal charts at the visitor center.

Also leading from the visitor center is the 2-mile Indigo Trail, a hiking trail that leads past mangroves and osprey nests. Short Cross Dike Trail about halfway down the wildlife drive provides car-bound visitors the perfect place to walk between impoundments and climb to the top of an observation tower. Indigo Trail and Cross Dike Trail meet near the observation tower. A short boardwalk loop, interpretive Shell Mound Trail, takes you through a drier, forested area past a Calusa Indian mound.

In the Bailey Tract, a series of short, concentric walking trails take you around wildlife-filled ponds. The mostly open, unshaded area offers more places to view waterbirds and alligators. If you shun crowds, take note that this small 100-acre tract has far fewer visitors than the main Darling Tract—and it's free. Use a refuge map from the visitor center to find the tract, on another part of Sanibel Island.

At Cayo Costa, many visitors walk the beach, finding that the less-traveled southern end of the island is better for shelling. Paths and dirt roads crisscross the island's sandy interior. Most visitors will become familiar with 1-mile Cabin Road, the most direct route from the boat dock to the beach, and the road that rangers take to shuttle overnight guests and their gear. Gulf Trail is a nice walk through coastal scrub that parallels the gulf beach, then ends there. Across the way is Gasparilla Island. Cemetery Trail leads to a real cemetery, the final resting site of former island pioneers. Visitors can get a trail map at the ranger station. This is also the place to rent a bicycle if you want to explore the trails on wheels.

On Lovers Key's Black Island, a scenic 2.6-mile interpretive trail snakes around the maritime hammock, following the canals that are popular with anglers. Hikers and off-road bicyclists can pick up a map and guide to the Black Island Trail at the trailhead. Shortcuts allow for 1.2- and 1.8-mile treks if desired. One of the features along the trail is a hill that is one of the highest points in the county. Look for alligators, ospreys, raccoons, squirrels, wading birds, and song birds. Paved trails that connect the park's islands and which lead to the beach offer more places to hike or bike. Park visitors can rent bicycles from the park concession.

Paddling and Boating

With all of the islands in the area, getting out on a boat is a must to experience the character of the region. In fact, the chain of barrier islands here is considered a top paddling destination, so you're likely to be in good company.

The Ding Darling refuge is mostly water, so seeing it by boat is the best way to explore it. There are several miles of paddling trails in the refuge that offer excellent scenery, particularly in Tarpon Bay. Paddlers can take the 2.5-mile Commodore Creek Canoe Trail; small signs show you the way. About 7 miles west of the canoe launch, the refuge's remote Buck Key Tract at Captiva Island offers 4 miles of paddling trails. If you don't have your own canoe or kayak, you can rent one at Tarpon Bay Recreation just east of the main entrance to the Ding Darling refuge (under Guided Tours below).

Cayo Costa has ten boat slips at its dock on Pine Island Sound. Those who arrive by kayak may come ashore in a little mangrove cove; this can be mucky at low tide. The park's concession rents kayaks from here. The islands of Pine Island National Wildlife Refuge (under Nearby Natural Areas) aren't far away and could be incorporated into a paddling or boating trip.

At Lovers Key, a boat ramp on Estero Bay provides access to the Intracoastal and Gulf of Mexico. The park concession rents canoes and kayaks for those who want to explore the park's little inlets and other waterways.

For a thorough tour of the region by water, consider all or part of the Great Calusa Blueway (800-237-6444; *www.greatcalusablueway.com*), a paddling trail through Lee County. The trail begins north of Estero Island, winds through Estero Bay Aquatic Preserve (941-463-3240), and offers the option of a spur up the Estero River, then ends at the county line in the Bonita Beach area with a spur up the Imperial River. Along the route, birding hotspots and other areas of interest are marked. Lovers Key is a designated put-in site for the trail; there are several others. Use the contact information above to find maps, outfitters, and guides.

Guided Tours

Most tours in this island haven focus on the water. Located south of Ding Darling's main tract, Tarpon Bay Explorers (239-472-8900; *www.tarponbay explorers.com*) works with the refuge to provide a narrated tram tour of the wildlife drive. This is also the place to arrange guided canoe and kayak trips (or rentals) and fishing excursions. The outfitter also rents bicycles, the preferred mode of transportation on Sanibel.

Captiva Cruises (239-472-5300; *www.captivacruises.com*) runs several trips among the islands, including cruises that focus on wildlife-watching and shelling. Other companies that provide ferry service to Cayo Costa include Reliable Boat Towing and Salvage (866-298-6060; *www.boatustowing.com*) and Jug Creek Cruise Boat (239-283-9512; *www.jugcreekcruise.com*). Reservations are recommended.

Everglades Day Safari (800-472-3069; *www.ecosafari.com*) operates out of Sanibel and Fort Myers, transporting tour guests into the world of the nearby Everglades. The day-long tour includes a boat tour, tram ride, and nature walk, and includes lunch.

Gaea Guides (866-256-6388; *www.gaeaguides.com*) leads a two-hour guided paddling tour of Lovers Key State Park and a multiday, all-inclusive Calusa Blueway tour. The company also runs tours that focus on bird rookeries, fossils, and even bats.

Inquire at Ding Darling, Cayo Costa, and Lovers Key about ranger talks and other programs.

Nearby Natural Areas

There are several more islands and beaches in the area where nature travelers can get acquainted with the region. From north to south, there are a few state parks:

Near Englewood, the 245-acre Stump Pass Beach State Park (941-964-0375) sits on the southern end of Manasota Key and includes Peterson Island and Whidden Island. Visitors can enjoy the mile-long beach, hike the trail to look for coastal plants or gopher tortoises, or use the boat ramp to tour the area's islands by water. Admission is $2.00 per vehicle. To get there, take I-75 to the Port Charlotte area and exit at Kings Highway (Exit #170). Head southwest and turn right (north) at County Road 776 (Bachman Blvd.) Follow the road as it turns west, going across the Myakka River to Englewood. Cross the bridge of Lemon Bay to Manasota Key and head south, following signs to reach the park.

South of Manasota Key is Don Pedro Island, where Don Pedro Island State Park (941-964-0375) is reached only by boat. A nature trail and a mile of beach are open to crowd-weary visitors. Look for nesting bald eagles. Boat docks for day use are on the bay side, on the Intracoastal. Admission is $1.00 per person. Across the water in Cape Haze is the park's new "land base," on County Road 775 about 7 miles south of Englewood.

Gasparilla Island State Park (941-964-0375) rests on another barrier island in the chain. The island is named after Spanish naval-officer-turned-pirate José Gaspar, who is thought to have frequented the area. Other than its beach and tarpon fishing, the park is known for its wood lighthouse, used from 1890 to 1966. On the National Register of Historic Places, it was relit in 1986. Today the lighthouse serves as a museum. Admission is $2.00 per vehicle. To get there, follow CR 775 south from Englewood (above) to the Boca Grande Causeway. Go across Gasparilla Pass and follow the main road south to the park on the southern end of the island.

South of Lovers Key is Delnor-Wiggins State Park (239-597- 6196), a popular beach park. The Cocohatchee River empties into the Gulf of Mexico here, where mangroves line the shore. Wildlife-watchers may spot manatees, eagles, and ospreys. Loggerhead turtles nest on the beach in the summer. A boat ramp lets you launch onto Water Turkey Bay. Admission is $5.00 per vehicle. To get here, take I-75 to Immokalee Road (Exit #111) and go west for 6 miles to the beach.

Ding Darling manages several undeveloped island refuges in the region that are mainly mangrove islands where birds roost. Except where posted, visitors may arrive by boat, but most people don't because either there is no beach to land on or biting insects make landing unbearable. Caloosahatchee National

Wildlife Refuge is a collection of three islands covering 40 acres in the Caloosahatchee River. If you go over the river on I-75, you can look down and see the refuge islands. Near Don Pedro Island is 20-acre Island Bay National Wildlife Refuge, made of five islands. Between the mainland and Pine Island—east of Cayo Costa—is 512-acre Matlacha Pass National Wildlife Refuge, a collection of twenty-three islands. Nearby, Pine Island National Wildlife Refuge covers 548 acres over sixteen islands between Pine Island and Cayo Costa. For information on any of these refuges, contact Ding Darling.

Nearby Attractions

At CROW—Clinic for the Rehabilitation of Wildlife—(239-472-3644; *www.crowclinic.org*), injured wildlife recuperate at this nonprofit wildlife hospital. Sea turtles, bald eagles, and shore birds are some of the species that CROW has rehabilitated. The facility allows the public to learn about its work during tours at 11 a.m. every weekday. CROW is located north of the main Ding Darling entrance on Sanibel-Captiva Road.

Sanibel and Captiva Islands are attractions themselves. Outdoors, many visitors flock to the beaches for sun, shelling, and parasailing, and take to the open water for fishing and boating. Indoors, quaint shops and restaurants are tourist magnets, as well as the Bailey-Matthews Shell Museum (888-679-6450; *www.shellmuseum.org*) and The Old Schoolhouse Theater (239-472-6862; *www.oldschoolhousetheater.com*).

One popular island to visit is Cabbage Key, east of Cayo Costa. Reached only by boat, it is known for being the inspiration for Jimmy Buffet's song "Cheeseburger in Paradise." Day visitors can pull up at the marina and stop in for something to eat or drink, perhaps adding a dollar bill to the hundreds already tacked up on the walls. Or, walk the nature trails and look for wildlife. To stay overnight, check in at the Cabbage Key Inn (239-283-2278; *www.cabbage-key.com*), where rooms and individual cottages are available.

There is plenty more to do on the mainland in Fort Myers, such as touring the estates of Henry Ford and Thomas Edison (888-377-9475; *www.edison-ford-estate.com*), and the Imaginarium Hands- On Museum (239-337-2109; *www.cityftmyers.com/attractions/imaginarium.htm*).

Wildlife

The region's barrier islands and coastal areas are great places to view wildlife, especially birds. In fact, at Ding Darling, birds steal the show from the other wildlife because of their large numbers during the winter months. More than 230 species of birds live in or visit the refuge. While winter is the best time for bird-watching in the refuge, birds are visible year-round. In late spring and early summer, you might spot black-necked stilts sitting on their nests or young herons learning to fish in their juvenile plumage.

The wildlife drive offers many places to see a variety of waterbirds as well as ospreys. From the impoundments, visitors might spot alligators, horseshoe crabs, and fish. In the mangroves, nonvenomous rat snakes may appear.

Besides the wildlife drive, other areas in the Ding Darling refuge offer the chance to see wildlife. In the summer, paddlers might spot manatees in the refuge's back bay. At the Perry Tract, beachgoers might find dolphins frolicking close to shore.

Both dolphins and manatees travel up and down the gulf coast, so they could turn up near any of the region's islands. Sea turtles like loggerheads nest on area beaches.

Ospreys are right at home at Ding Darling, Cayo Costa, and Lovers Key. Listen for their high-pitched cry, or look for their large, open nests on top of dead trees or utility poles. Lovers Key is also the site of active bald eagle nests.

Look for . . .

In winter, Ding Darling attracts as many as one-third of the entire U.S. population of roseate spoonbills at one time. With their flat, rounded bills and bright pink-and-red coloring, roseate spoonbills may seem like an exotic bird. However, they are native along the southern North American coasts. A member of the ibis family, the spoonbill uses its unusual bill to sweep the water and mud to look for food, mainly insects. The state of Florida considers the bird a species of special concern.

Another wading bird found at the refuge and throughout Florida wetlands is the endangered wood stork, the only stork native to North America. Wood storks are considered an indicator species—an indicator of how well the environment is doing. Their method of fishing by touch with their long beaks is dependent on there being enough shallow ponds with fish in them. When these wetlands disappear, the wood stork's food source disappears. The draining of the Everglades led to the wood stork's decline in population, but they may now be making a comeback. However, human population expansion into wetlands may affect further wood stork success.

Wood storks range throughout southern Florida and parts of central Florida, nesting in colonies like herons and egrets. Nesting in trees above alligators ensures that raccoons and other predators won't get to the eggs and young. However, the trade-off is that sometimes, fledgling birds fall into the alligator's lair.

At almost three and a half feet tall and with a wingspan of five and a half feet, the wood stork is a large bird. It may sometimes rest on its knees, belying its full height. In flight, look for the black wing tips that aren't as visible when the wood stork is at rest.

Habitats

There are numerous islands off the gulf coast. Most of them are tree islands where red and black mangroves grow, supporting nests for waterbirds like herons and egrets—and most of those islands are protected. Other islands are rich in diverse habitats, from coastal scrub to pine flatwoods and salt marsh.

The islands are barriers to storms headed for the mainland, and storms are part of what makes the islands what they are. Captiva and North Captiva Islands were once one island. In August 2004, Hurricane Charley cut North Captiva Island in two yet again. Although mangroves and other bird nesting areas among the islands were flattened by Charley, a Ding Darling ranger expressed a positive outlook for the refuge's environment because hurricanes can have beneficial effects. Storms can take down exotic, invasive plants like Australian pines, for example, and the increased sunlight from the reduced canopy can help other plants grow.

Sanibel Island is a unique barrier island in that while it's surrounded by the ocean, it also has its own source of fresh water. (It also defies the usual long, narrow shape and orientation that most barrier islands have—parallel to the mainland.) The climate, the mix of fresh water and salt water, and the slope from low wetlands to high uplands all make the island a unique place for a spectrum of plants and wildlife. Cayo Costa, in the same chain of barrier islands as Sanibel Island, is in a similar situation.

In the refuge's Darling Tract, habitats are mainly mangrove forests and mud flats, but small portions include uplands, like the area near Shell Mound Trail. The Bailey Tract with its ponds offers visitors a good chance to see rare island freshwater wetlands. The Perry Tract, of course, consists of beach with native salt- and sand-loving plant life.

At Lovers Key, park staff are working to restore Black Island, Long Key, Inner Key, and Lovers Key with native vegetation. Park literature tells how the islands were prepared for development in the 1960s and 1970s, when mangroves were destroyed and canals were channeled. The islands later became part of the park system, in 1983.

Where to Stay

Campgrounds

Near Ding Darling, the only place to camp on Sanibel Island is Periwinkle Park (239-472-1433), with eighty RV sites and a tent camping area. There's not much shade or privacy here, but the ability to walk to the beach (slipping out the back way) and a mini zoo (the owners' collection of exotic birds, various waterfowl, and several rabbits housed near the showers) still make the campground worthwhile. There is also a dump station and laundry facility.

Cayo Costa has thirty primitive tent camping sites. Each site has a picnic table and grill. Restrooms are nearby with cold outdoor showers. Campers should bring all food and equipment necessary for the trip; the ranger station sells only ice. Rangers provide tram transportation for campers and their equipment from the boat dock to the campground on the other side of the island. Campers should be aware that checkout time is 1 p.m., which may not correspond with ferry service schedules (i.e., you could end up waiting for some time at the dock with your gear). Contact ReserveAmerica for reservations.

Lodging

Cayo Costa has twelve small, primitive cabins just steps away from the gulf beach. The cabins have no electricity and only screens for windows. Most of these were destroyed by Hurricane Charley in August 2004, then rebuilt. Contact ReserveAmerica if you're interested in reserving a cabin. Checkout time is 11 a.m., which may not correspond with ferry service schedules.

Near Ding Darling on Sanibel and Captiva, there are a number of hotels and vacation cottages. Travelers can choose from high- end resorts like South Seas Resort (800-965-7772; *www.south-seas-resort.com*) at the northern tip of Captiva Island to hotels near the beach like Sanibel Inn (239-472-3181; *www.sanibelinn.com*).

Near Lovers Key, try Lovers Key Beach Club Resort (239-765-1040; *www.loverskeybeach.com*) or Holiday Inn Beach Resort (239-463-5711).

How to Get There

The Ding Darling refuge's tracts are scattered across Sanibel and Captiva Islands. To get to the refuge visitor center, take I-75 to the Fort Myers area and exit at Daniels Road (Exit #131). Travel west to Summerlin Road, turn left, and follow the signs to the islands. There will be a toll booth ($6.00 to go over; no toll to come back) before the 3-mile causeway takes you over San Carlos Bay to Sanibel Island. (The line at the toll booth can be quite long during the busy winter season, and on weekends and holidays.) At the first main intersection, Periwinkle Way, turn right. Then just follow the signs to the refuge visitor center, where you can get a map of all the refuge tracts and information from helpful volunteers.

Cayo Costa is located about 12 miles offshore from the Cape Coral area, north of North Captiva Island, south of Gasparilla Island, and west of Pine Island. It is reached only by boat. Hire a ferry service to take you there, or use nautical charts to find the park in your own boat.

For Lovers Key, exit I-75 at Bonita Beach Road (Exit #116). Head west, then north, about 10.5 miles on this road to the main park entrance, on the left.

⇔ ⇔ ⇔

J.N. "Ding" Darling National Wildlife Refuge Complex
1 Wildlife Drive
Sanibel, Florida 33957
Phone: 239-472-1100
dingdarling.fws.gov
The visitor center is open from 9 a.m. until 5 p.m. November through April, and 9 a.m. until 4 p.m. May through October. The wildlife drive is open every day except Friday from 7:30 a.m. to 5:30 p.m. Admission to the Wildlife Drive is $5.00 per vehicle or $1.00 per pedestrian/bicyclist. There is no charge to access the other parts of the refuge.

Cayo Costa State Park
P.O. Box 1150
Boca Grande, Florida 33921
Phone: 941-964-0375
Admission is $1.00 per person

Lovers Key Carl E. Johnson State Park
8700 Estero Blvd.
Ft. Myers Beach, Florida 33931
Phone: 239-463-4588
Admission is $4.00 per vehicle or $2.00 per single-person vehicle.

Southwestern Florida's shore is scattered with numerous barrier islands whose shell-strewn beaches and mangroves fit right in with their subtropical nature. The region is a popular resort destination, but some islands remain natural and open to ecotourism.

Nearby

Southern Prairie Lands (chapter 23), Western Everglades (chapter 30)

25

Lake Okeechobee Lands

The second-largest lake wholly in the United States, the headwaters of the Everglades, the source of water for about a third of Florida's population—everything about Lake Okeechobee is grand scale. Even its name means "big waters" in a native language. On a map, the lake looks like the huge eye of Florida. If the eye is the window to the soul, then Lake Okeechobee is the window to the soul of southern Florida's environment.

The lake itself is popular with boaters, many of whom enjoy fishing for trophy bass. The lands around the lake are also attractive for recreation.

Imagine land so flat and wide you can almost see the curvature of the Earth at the horizon. Picture an area blanketed by saw palmettos, pricked with occasional live oaks, as far as your eye can see—not a building or tower in sight—where large birds soar and small birds flutter. Envision a region where bald eagles nest in tall pines and Florida panthers slink among cabbage palms. Imagine miles of grassy freshwater marsh intermingled with cypress swamps that remain in the northernmost stretch of Everglades. This is the Lake Okeechobee area.

Nature travelers can get to know this big water and surrounding big lands in areas on every side of the lake. To the north, Kissimmee Prairie Preserve State Park encloses 84 square miles of dry prairie along the Kissimmee River, which flows into the lake. The land for the park was purchased in 1997 from a rancher who had regularly burned portions of the ranch just as nature would have done before the region's wide prairies were turned into ranchland. Kissimmee Prairie is one of the few preserved dry prairies in the state. (Another one is in Myakka River State Park east of Sarasota.)

To the south, 146,000-acre Loxahatchee National Wildlife Refuge preserves the typical Everglades habitat—even if it's 70 miles or so to Everglades National Park. Here, visitors explore the wetlands by boardwalk, impoundments, or boat.

On the eastern shore, DuPuis Reserve saves the forested character of the lake next to wetlands and acres of farmland. Ponds open up among pines and cypresses over almost 22,000 acres, where visitors enjoy the roads and trails.

Figure 24. A foggy dawn comes to Sevenmile Slough at Kissimmee Prairie Preserve State Park.

To the west and even farther away, smaller natural lands are affected by Lake Okeechobee's grandeur and are still a part of the lake's reach.

What to Do There

Kissimmee Prairie is mostly flat, unshaded, and undeveloped, so you might think there isn't much to do there. But what it may lack in recreational activities, it makes up for in the abundance of wildlife you will likely see and in the peace and quiet that so many people seem to be seeking these days. Loxahatchee offers good bird-watching and paddling, and DuPuis is perfect for camping and trail riding; both are great for hiking. Look for DuPuis Reserve's 7.5-mile auto tour through the forest.

Trail Tripping

The 110-mile Lake Okeechobee Scenic Trail is part of the Florida National Scenic Trail, circling the lake along the top of the impoundment that walls it in (also known as Herbert Hoover Dike). Hikers, off-road cyclists, and horseback riders see a variety of birds here. Every year around Thanksgiving, dozens of hikers take about a week to walk around the lake on the "Big O" hike. Contact the Florida Trail Association for more information.

At Kissimmee Prairie, two unpaved park roads, Peavine Trail and Military Grade, let visitors explore 10 or 12 miles of the park. You can even follow Military Grade all the way to the Kissimmee River. You'll notice other trails on the map inside the Kissimmee Prairie park brochure, but it's best to stay on the two park roads until the park completes a separate trails map as many other state parks have done. If you really want to hike these other trails, retrace your path and don't rely on loops. The park warns trail users that the land was once used for practice bombing—Avon Park Air Force Bombing Range is nearby—and that unexploded bombs may still be around, encouraging people to stay on trails and avoid going near "suspicious objects."

At Loxahatchee, many people enjoy the Cypress Swamp Boardwalk that loops for almost a half-mile behind the visitor center. Several acres of impoundments on the open marsh provide excellent bird and alligator watching. An observation deck gives you a good view of the wetland.

DuPuis Reserve's dirt roads and trails are open to hikers, off-road cyclists, equestrians, and even scenic drivers. There are more than 25 miles of hiking trails, and horseback riders get 20 miles in this forest, well known to the equine set.

Many miles of the Florida Trail, other than the lake trail, run through the area.

Paddling and Boating

Lake Okeechobee is more a place for motorboats than canoes or kayaks, but paddlers are welcome. Find a marina in town, or take your own boat to a ramp like the one on Platt's Bluff north of State Road 70 off County Road 599. Boaters can navigate the Okeechobee Waterway and go from one coast of Florida to the other on the Caloosahatchee and St. Lucie Rivers and the lake, which make up the waterway. For a free map of the Kissimmee River and part of the lake showing boat ramps and locks, request the *Guide to the Kissimmee Waterway* from the South Florida Water Management District. (See the Resources section at the end of this book.)

At Loxahatchee, a 5.5-mile canoe trail lets paddlers explore the northern Everglades marsh. Ask for a map and information at the refuge visitor center.

Stargazing

The Lake Okeechobee area is a prime spot for amateur astronomers because of the dark skies. Far from the coastal city light pollution, Kissimmee Prairie and DuPuis Reserve often call out local astronomy clubs for regular viewings and events. Many astronomers are friendly and willing to share their knowledge with overnight campers who happen upon a stargazing party. Nights when there's a new moon allow anyone to see millions of stars and planets, and some astronomers spot deep-sky objects with their enormous telescopes.

Guided Tours

Kissimmee Prairie offers a three-hour tour of the park in a swamp buggy. Tours leave at 10 a.m. on Saturdays and cost $15.00 per person. Seating is limited, so reservations are required.

There are several fishing guides on Lake Okeechobee. Contact the Okeechobee County Tourism Development Council (800-871-4403; *www.okeechobee-tdc.com*) or a Lake Okeechobee marina.

Loxahatchee Canoeing (561-733-0192; *www.canoetheeverglades.com*) provides canoe and kayak rentals, and paddling tours, by reservation at the refuge boat ramp. Canoe rentals are $30.00 for a half-day. Single kayaks are $25.00 for a half-day, and tandem kayaks are $30.00.

Nearby Natural Areas

Fisheating Creek flows into Lake Okeechobee's western side after meandering from a swamp. Cypress trees line its banks, and quiet tannic water harkens back to a simpler time. Famed Florida photographers Clyde and Niki Butcher have said their first visit to Fisheating Creek "was the beginning of Clyde's love affair with Florida," after which he was inspired to see more of the state's natural beauty in wetlands. Nature travelers can access the stream at Fisheating Creek Outfitters (863-675-7855; *www.fisheatingcreek.com*), which rents out canoes and kayaks, and offers a campground. To get there, take SR 70 (north of the lake) or SR 80 (south of the lake) to US 27 and head toward Palmdale. Look for the Fisheating Creek sign near SR 29.

Okaloacoochee Slough State Forest (863-612-0776) is a relatively new acquisition. Covering about 32,000 acres, the forest is important habitat for Florida panthers, which are in desperate need of territory in southwestern Florida. White-tailed deer, the panther's prey, also roam through the forest. Visitors can drive along the dirt roads through beautiful country and watch for wildlife; the area also allows hunting at specified times. To get there, take SR 80 to CR 833 between Clewiston and Labelle. Head south for about 8 miles, and turn right (west) at Keri Road (CR 832). The entrance is about 7 miles down the road. Alternately, take SR 29 south from Labelle to Keri Road, and head east to the entrance.

Nearby Attractions

Okeechobee residents are proud of their battlefield on which the U.S. Army fought Seminole and Miccosukee warriors during the Second Seminole War in 1837. The battle—led by Zachary Taylor, who would become president—is considered the bloodiest battle of the war, yet a turning point for the army because it led to the unfortunate forced removal of some tribespeople under the Indian Removal Act. Okeechobee Battlefield (*www.okeechobeebattlefield. com*) is on the National Register of Historic Places but remains in private hands; if it becomes developed, the battlefield could lose this national designation. Florida Forever, the state's land-acquisition program, is currently looking to purchase the property so it will never be developed. Volunteers hold an annual re-enactment of the battle at a site near the battlefield.

Just a few miles from Kissimmee Prairie is Arnold's Wildlife Rehabilitation Center (863-763-4630; *www.arnoldswildlife.org/wildlife_index.htm*), a nonprofit facility where injured animals are treated and, hopefully, released. Some animals are housed in viewable habitats while they recuperate.

Wildlife

With the wealth of water and variety of uplands in the Lake Okeechobee area, you'll find a diversity of wildlife. You may even see plenty of wildlife, mainly birds, along the roadsides as you travel to these natural areas.

Kissimmee Prairie campers wake up to the sounds of birds singing their various songs together as one chorus. Ibises, phoebes, and killdeers make an appearance near Sevenmile Slough. Many other birds are at home on the dry prairie, such as burrowing owls, which you may see near the entrance of Kissimmee Prairie. Other birds are so plentiful that they're easy to spot, like the American kestrels (threatened) and eastern meadowlarks on area fences and utility wires. Bald eagles are known to nest in DuPuis Reserve.

The flat land full of saw palmettos and wiregrass serving as ground cover is a haven for snakes of many kinds. On the dirt roads around dusk, you may find snakes, such as ribbon snakes and pygmy rattlesnakes, soaking up the last bit of heat from the day. Most snakes are eager to get out of your way, but pygmy rattlesnakes tend to stand their ground, often in the middle of the trail. Walk off the side of the trail, if possible, to avoid stepping near these venomous snakes.

Look for . . .

Endangered Florida grasshopper sparrows live in Florida year-round, unlike the eastern grasshopper sparrows that migrate to the state. Named not for what they eat but for the sound of their song, Florida grasshopper sparrows have been in decline as a result of habitat loss.

Most of Florida's dry prairie habitat has been converted to pastures, groves, farmland, or development. Prairie habitat has been affected also by preventing fire, which is a natural occurrence and essential to keeping a prairie from being crowded out by trees and shrubs. This has affected species like the sparrow.

Scientists and volunteers, monitoring and tracking grasshopper sparrow populations, visit Kissimmee Prairie to capture the sparrows in mist nets and place leg bands on them. According to the park Web site, the Florida grasshopper sparrow population at Kissimmee Prairie is around 280. There are five other populations in southern-central Florida, adding to the total population of around perhaps a thousand.

Snail kites are another endangered bird in the Okeechobee area, ranging from Lake Kissimmee south through Everglades National Park. You might see the bird on Lake Okeechobee or at the Loxahatchee refuge.

Sometimes called an Everglades kite, this bird of prey is spotted near the water, where it hunts for freshwater apple snails almost exclusively. Snail kite populations declined along with the apple snails, which are affected by habitat loss caused by draining wetlands, invasive aquatic plants, and some water-management practices. It has been declared endangered since 1967.

Audubon's crested caracaras are found in the American southwest, which seems fitting for a bird that is a subspecies of the crested caracara, the national bird of Mexico. But the Lake Okeechobee region is the prime place to find these birds of prey in Florida. Caracaras hunt above dry prairies and pastures, so you might spot them at Kissimmee Prairie or even on your way there. When not flying or eating prey on the ground, they like to perch on fence posts, dirt piles, or low tree branches. If caracaras can't find prey, they may settle for carrion.

Caracaras are considered a threatened species because of habitat loss. Roadkill also has affected the population.

Habitats

One of the curious things to some people who see Lake Okeechobee for the first time is the dike that surrounds it. The lake was impounded in the early twentieth century, when farmers came to Florida, looking for year-round harvests. However, water naturally flowed from the lake, south through the Everglades, flooding crops. A small dike was erected to keep the water in, but it wasn't enough to protect the crops or the people when a hurricane hit in 1928. The wide, shallow lake sloshed its waters in the fury of the wind and flooded farming towns. More than 2,500 people drowned in the hurricane, according to the National Weather Service; other estimates are 1,600 to 1,800. Whatever the number, the 1928 hurricane was a tragedy as the second-deadliest hurricane to hit the United States. (The 1900 hurricane that hit Galveston, Texas, is the first with about 8,000 people dead.) Later floods promoted more discouragement, and that's when the federal government began water management to prevent loss of lives and crops, eventually building more than 1,800 miles of canals and levees, according to the South Florida Water Management District.

Unfortunately for southern Florida's environment, these water controls were the beginning of the Everglades ecosystem's decline. Instead of giving up on farming in the rocky, flood-prone lake area, residents asked for nature to be tamed. Draining the wetlands has enabled thousands of acres of farms to exist, most notably sugarcane fields, along with cattle ranches and southeastern Florida's metropolis. Today, water managers are working toward improving the water flow and water quality. But the Everglades will never be the same.

Lake Okeechobee wasn't the only water body affected. Flooding prompted the government to try to tame the Kissimmee River, too. In the 1960s, the river's 103 meandering miles were channeled into a 56-mile canal from Lake Kissimmee to Lake Okeechobee. According to the South Florida Water Management District, 43,000 acres of wetlands disappeared, and waterfowl were reduced by 90 percent as a result. In addition, because it is part of the headwaters of the Everglades, the river's unnatural flow added to the River of Grass's woes.

The river is being partially restored as a result of a multimillion-dollar long-term plan that calls for some of the river's locks and dams to be removed and for 22 miles of it to be refilled. Kissimmee Prairie and other public lands that have been acquired along the river go along with the river's restoration.

Along the river, the park can develop into a floodplain marsh habitat. Most of the park, however, is dry prairie, considered one of the most diverse in terms of the number of plant species, a habitat that was once prevalent along the Kissimmee River. In fact, the Florida Department of Environmental Protection has stated that dry prairies once covered 300,000 acres of the state. But settlers found it suitable for raising cattle and growing citrus, so the land was converted for these uses. Saw palmettos and grasses were replaced with nonnative plants. Ditches furrowed the land to prevent flooding after heavy rain.

Another part of the restoration of the area to its natural state involves prescribed burns. Dry prairies are thought to have been burned naturally by frequent lightning strikes that prevented trees from encroaching on the open land. Putting out fires was once the thing to do, but now specialists start fires on the prairie when the conditions are just right, checking first for grasshopper sparrow nests.

Shortly after a fire burns out and the land cools, new grasses and wildflowers start to grow from the ash. But you might see several kinds of wildflowers in the prairie even without a fire, like star rush, pipewort, goldenrod, pine lily, and alligator lily. Other kinds of wildflowers grow around the hammocks within the park and at DuPuis Reserve.

In Loxahatchee, the northern Everglades, scientists are watching a mini-Everglades they developed to test whether the Comprehensive Everglades Restoration Plan will work. The Loxahatchee Impoundment Landscape Assessment consists of four seventeen-acre impoundments with water controls where researchers can mimic the Everglades plan on a small scale before applying it to the larger ecosystem.

Where to Stay

Campgrounds

Campers can stay at three campgrounds along the Okeechobee Waterway. The Ortona South Campground near Labelle has fifty-one campsites. Closer to Fort Myers on the Caloosahatchee River, the W. P. Franklin North Campground is made up of thirty campsites and eight boat sites. On the eastern side of the waterway near Stuart, St. Lucie Lock Recreation Area provides nine campsites, eight boat sites, and three tent sites with no electric or water hookups. All campgrounds have restrooms with hot showers. For information and reservations for any of these campsites, contact ReserveAmerica.

There are two campgrounds at Kissimmee Prairie. Kilpatrick Hammock Campground is situated under mature oak trees and has twenty sites and restrooms with hot and cold showers. The other campground is considered a horse campground because of the paddocks around which the sites are placed, but even campers without horses may stay here. At the horse campground, half of the sites are shaded by oaks, and the other sites have no shade. Campers in this part of the park must use the restrooms at Kilpatrick Hammock. In general, none of the campsites at either campground offer privacy from your campground neighbors. Campsites cost $12.00 per night. Contact Reserve-America for reservations.

For more privacy in a beautiful setting, consider Kissimmee Prairie's primitive campsites, 3.5 miles from Kilpatrick Hammock. The primitive sites are loosely grouped in an oak hammock near a slough. Each site has a picnic table and fire ring and goes for $3.00 per person per night. Call the park office at 863-462-5360 to reserve any of these sites.

DuPuis Reserve allows primitive camping in a nice setting. Reach the campground near Gate 1, one of the reserve entrances. Primitive equestrian camping with stalls and paddocks is near Gate 3. Group camping is available with a special permit from the South Florida Water Management District. Reservations are not taken, and campsites are filled on a first-come, first-served basis. Call for more information.

Okeechobee KOA (863-763-0231) north of the lake boasts more than 700 sites, four tennis courts, two pools, and a golf course.

Lodging

Overnight options are greatest near Loxahatchee because of its proximity to populated coastal towns. Closer to the lake, however, Clewiston and Okeechobee offer some motels, like Holiday Inn Express (863-357-3529) in Okeechobee.

How to Get There

To get to Kissimmee Prairie from the north, take the Florida Turnpike south to Yeehaw Junction at SR 60. Go west to US 441, then turn south. At CR 724 (Eagle Island Road), head west. Follow signs to the park, which is at the end of the road. From the south, take I-95 north to SR 70 in the Fort Pierce area, and head west to Okeechobee. Go through downtown, then take US 98 northwest to road 700A. Watch for signs to the park, which is at the end of the road. From the west, take SR 70 or US 98 east toward Okeechobee, and follow the directions above.

To reach Loxahatchee, take I-95 to the Palm Beach area and exit at Forest Hill Blvd. (Exit #66). Go west for about 7 miles to US 441, and turn left (south). The refuge entrance is about 12 miles ahead on the right at Lee Road.

DuPuis Reserve is located south of Indiantown where the St. Lucie Canal meets Lake Okeechobee, off US 441. The reserve has four entrances. You can take SR 76/Kanner Highway from I-95 (Exit #101) all the way southwest until you reach it. Vehicles can enter at Gate 1 and Gate 6. The Gate 2 entrance offers access to hiking trails. The Gate 3 entrance is for equestrians and the nature center.

Kissimmee Prairie Preserve State Park
33104 NW 192 Avenue
Okeechobee, Florida 34972
Phone: 352-625-2520
The entrance fee is $2.00, payable at an honor box.

Arthur R. Marshall Loxahatchee National Wildlife Refuge
10216 Lee Road
Boynton Beach, Florida 33437
Phone: 561-732-3684
The refuge is open during daylight hours. The visitor center is open Monday through Friday from 9:00 a.m. until 4:00 p.m. and Saturday and Sunday from 9:00 a.m. until 4:30 p.m.; the center is closed on Mondays and Tuesdays from May to mid-October. The entrance fee is $5.00 per vehicle, payable at an honor box when a fee booth is unattended.

DuPuis Reserve
23500 SW Kanner Highway
Canal Point, Florida 33438
Phone: 800-432-2045
DuPuis is open all the time, but the nature center near the Gate 3 entrance is open only some Saturdays from 9 a.m. until noon. The entrance fee is $3.00 per person.

Lake Okeechobee's sizeable area spans many miles, and many habitats. The region's large agricultural base makes it a quiet area to roam through natural lands that surround the lake—prairies, forests, cypress swamps, and freshwater marshlands that are the northernmost reaches of the Everglades.

Nearby

Highland Ridge (chapter 21), Cracker Lakes (chapter 22), Indian River Lagoon Lands (chapter 26), Loxahatchee River Lands (chapter 27), Western Everglades (chapter 30)

26

Indian River Lagoon Lands

Along Florida's central-eastern and southeastern coast, rivers flow into a shallow estuary just this side of the Atlantic Ocean. West Indian manatees and Atlantic bottle-nosed dolphins find their way here through ocean inlets. Crabs, lobsters, and various fish join hundreds of other species under the water. Pelicans fly overhead in a straight line, casting shadows with their eight-foot wingspan. Gulls chase one another in flight just above the water's surface.

The Indian River, Banana River, and Mosquito Lagoon come together to form this estuary, the Indian River Lagoon. This is a rich ecosystem that stretches for 156 miles along the coast, at most 5 miles wide. Designated as a Wetland of International Importance—the only other one completely in Florida besides the Everglades—as well as a National Wilderness Area and a National Historic Landmark, the lagoon is a place that serious nature travelers should not miss.

To many people, "Indian River" means citrus fruit because of gift shops and highway signs promoting Indian River citrus throughout Florida. Other than oranges and grapefruits, however, the Indian River should be known for its great biodiversity. Indian River County, St. Lucie County, and Martin County make up the Treasure Coast—so called because of treasure-filled Spanish shipwrecks offshore, but also possibly relating to its richness of life: sea life, bird life, plant life, living in general.

It was the protection of life at the turn of the last century that started the Indian River Lagoon on its path toward nature conservation. Well known to many people, the story tells how birds were being hunted, some species almost to extinction, in order to fulfill the demand for feathers for fashionable ladies' hats. A small island in the Indian River, Pelican Island, was chosen as a place to protect from hunters because of the birds that nested there. President Theodore Roosevelt sanctioned the island as a reserve. The island later became the first national wildlife refuge, joining other areas the president preserved—the beginning of the refuge system that now, more than a hundred years later, includes 544 refuges across the country.

Figure 25. Wetlands stretch across Savannas Preserve State Park.

Today, Pelican Island National Wildlife Refuge encompasses several islands in the Indian River, along with land on the eastern side of the river. Visitors can view Pelican Island by boat or from an observation deck near the river.

Up the street from the refuge, Sebastian Inlet State Park rests on both sides of the Sebastian Inlet, one place where the Indian River meets the Atlantic Ocean. This recreation-friendly park is another spot where nature travelers can explore the Indian River Lagoon ecosystem, as well as enjoy 3 miles of beach.

A trip to the lagoon area should include a visit to the 5,000-acre Savannas Preserve State Park, which runs along the Indian River's western shore for 10 miles. The park claims its freshwater marsh is the largest on the southeastern coast. Savannas Preserve's location on the Atlantic Coastal Ridge means it once was an island (like the Lake Wales Ridge, chapter 21) and now harbors the rare scrub habitat that coastal development has taken away.

Inland, St. Sebastian River Preserve State Park protects part of the watershed of the Indian River's second-largest tributary. The north and south forks of the St. Sebastian River flow alongside the preserve and come together just a few miles upstream from where the St. Sebastian joins the Indian River. The St. Sebastian River is connected to a canal that is part of a system of pump-controlled waterways leading to the headwaters of the St. Johns River. Controlling floodwaters, but draining natural marshes, the canal is sometimes frequented by manatees. Trails lead to the river and through thick pine flatwoods.

These are just some of the natural areas that are part of the Indian River Lagoon ecosystem, which stretches from New Smyrna Beach to Stuart—quite a distance to cover. The northern portion of the lagoon system is covered in the Space Coast chapter (chapter 14) so smaller geographical sections will make it easier for nature travelers to identify with each area.

What to Do There

There are plenty of ways to view the Indian River, and plenty of opportunities to get out on it. The beach is a draw, too, especially for surfers who enjoy the waves around Sebastian Inlet. Sebastian Inlet State Park hosts several surfing competitions each year for surfers of all ages.

Beyond the water, there are uplands to explore, as well as nature centers and museums that interpret the region's natural and cultural history. The visitor center at Savannas Preserve includes such exhibits and is also a good place to stop and ask rangers any questions about the region's nature. Sebastian Inlet's Fishing Museum and McLarty Treasure Museum are worth a visit if you have an interest in these subjects.

Trail Tripping

Even though the region is big on the Indian River, there are plenty of places to get out on trails to explore the lagoon ecosystem's watershed.

At the Pelican Island refuge, the main trail is the Centennial Trail, a paved walkway that leads to the observation tower where you see Pelican Island and other islands in the Indian River; stationary scopes are provided for closer wildlife viewing. The Centennial Trail and its accompanying visitor facilities were completed in 2003, in time for the one hundredth anniversary of Pelican Island National Wildlife Refuge, and thus the entire refuge system run by the U.S. Fish and Wildlife Service. The boardwalk ramp to the tower is made of planks inscribed with the name of each national wildlife refuge and the date each was established, in chronological order. Even though the trail is paved, bikes aren't allowed; park your bike at the rack in the parking lot.

The refuge also has a series of trails around salt marsh impoundments. Park at the first parking lot after turning off A1A, where the trailhead is. There are two 2.5-mile loops that are good for viewing wading birds and waterfowl, especially in the cooler months.

Sebastian Inlet has a 1-mile interpretive nature trail that loops through a coastal hammock, where signs relay information about the coastal environment. The 6-mile Volksport Trail wanders from the park concession/café along the beach and onto a paved path.

The peaceful multiuse trails at Savannas Preserve lead through beautiful pinelands and scrub. Occasionally, there's noise from a neighborhood park, but trail trippers more often will hear woodpeckers, warblers, and other birds. Hikers, off-road bicyclists, and equestrians can explore the 8.5 miles of trails, which begin at the visitor center. Horse trailer parking is available. Pick up trail maps at the visitor center.

At St. Sebastian River Preserve State Park, a series of connecting multiuse trails leads through pine flatwoods, where some of the trees are marked with white bands to indicate red-cockaded woodpecker nests, and through oak scrub and swamps. While on the trail, look for climbing asters, moon vines, and primrose willow bushes with their bright yellow cup-shaped flowers. From the northern entrance, find trailheads along the main road that follows the C-54 canal; the forest is on the north side, and a high berm next to the canal is on the other. Choose from eleven trails, from the short 0.3-mile white interpretive trail to the 13.9-mile red trail. The green and red spur trails lead directly to the river's north prong. Roads and more multiuse trails lead from the park's southern entrance. Horse paddocks and watering stations are located along the trails for equestrians. There are also a few primitive campsites. Trail trippers can pick up trail maps at the park office near the northern entrance or at the kiosk near the southern entrance.

Paddling and Boating

Getting out on the Indian River is the best way to get to know this rich ecosystem. It's also the only way to get really close to Pelican Island, although landing is prohibited. (Paddlers and boaters can land at Paul's Island, which is directly west of Pelican Island.) While you can't launch from the refuge's visitor facilities, you can launch from Wabasso Causeway Park (772-567-2144) to the south at County Road 510, which is about 3 miles from Pelican Island by water.

Sebastian Inlet is boater friendly, with a marina, boat trailer parking, and boat ramps located on the Indian River not far from the inlet to the Atlantic Ocean. Paddlers, too, can launch from here to explore the river or the shore. The marina (800-952-1126) rents canoes, kayaks, motorboats, and pontoon boats.

At Savannas Preserve, a long, thin strip of freshwater marsh seems to parallel the Indian River to the east. Visitors can launch a canoe or kayak here, down the dirt road from the visitor center. On Saturdays, weather permitting, the park rents canoes and kayaks. From October through May, volunteers lead guided paddling tours of the marsh; call the park for the current schedule of tours and to make a reservation.

For paddlers who also like to hike, the Florida Trail Association maintains a trail on the St. Lucie River's south fork that is accessible only by boat. The 1-mile trail begins at the river and winds through scrubby flatwoods and a hydric hammock. To reach the trail, launch from Hosford Park (561-288-5690) south of Stuart and paddle upstream, looking for a South Florida Water Management District sign on the bank. Paddlers may stay overnight here at a primitive campsite by requesting a free permit from the water district. For more information, contact the water district or the Florida Trail Association.

Scenic Driving

Many of the region's natural areas lie along the 166-mile Indian River Lagoon Scenic Highway (772-567-3491). This national- and state-designated scenic drive forms a loop around the lagoon system and at certain points provides pretty views of the river and the ocean. To drive the highway, start from the Wabasso-area CR 510 causeway, go north along A1A, west on State Road 528 to US 1, north to Titusville and the southern entrance to Canaveral National Seashore, and back to SR 528 and US 1.

Guided Tours

Most tours here—and there are several—revolve around the Indian River. There is a variety of boat tours up and down the river.

To get close to Pelican Island, you can take a two-hour, ranger-led boat tour from the park marina in Sebastian Inlet, from November to May; call ahead for reservations.

Harbor Branch Oceanographic Institute (772-465-2400; *www.hboi.edu*) in Fort Pierce is a scientific research facility that offers tours of the Indian River and of its campus. The ninety-minute river tour on a covered boat focuses on the river's ecosystem and wildlife, such as dolphins, ospreys, eagles, and pelicans. Tours run Monday through Saturday at 1 p.m.; November through April, there is an additional tour at 10 a.m. The campus tour takes guests by bus to different parts of the HBOI campus. Guests are introduced to the facility's research programs and get to view submarine models. Campus tours run Monday through Saturday at noon, and November through April there is an additional tour at 10 a.m. HBOI also offers a gift shop and a lecture series on ocean-ography for the public. To get there, exit I-95 at Indrio Road (Exit #138) and head east about 3.5 miles to US 1. Turn left (north); HBOI is 1 mile ahead on the right.

For human-powered fun, try the Saturday canoe tour offered at the Environmental Learning Center (772-589-5050; *www.elcweb.org*) south of Pelican Island. Volunteer canoe guides lead visitors on a three-hour tour of the river, pointing out wildlife and relating the river's natural history. Commonly known as ELC, this nature center sits right on the river's edge and offers several programs—a good place to learn about the lagoon ecosystem. Fish tanks, microscopes, computer learning stations, and a boardwalk allow hands-on learning for all ages. The ELC is open Tuesday through Friday from 10 a.m. to 4 p.m., Saturday from 9 a.m. to noon (until 4 p.m. in winter), and Sunday from 1 p.m. to 4 p.m.

Florida Oceanographic Coastal Center (772-225-0505; *www.floridaocean ographic.org*) in Stuart offers boat tours in the Indian River Lagoon. The ninety-minute tour focuses on the river's wildlife and ecosystem. Reservations are required. Tours run Tuesday at 1 p.m., and Friday and Saturday at 10 a.m. The center also offers guided nature walks through a hammock and mangrove area along the river, and stingray feeding presentations. The center is open Monday through Saturday from 10 a.m. to 5 p.m. Admission is $6.00 for adults, and $3.00 for children three to twelve. Members get in for free. To get there, take I-95 to SR 76 (Exit #101) and follow the road north across US 1. Stay to the right, go over the railroad tracks, and turn right onto East Ocean Blvd. Look for the center on the river.

Dolphin Watch and Wildlife Tour (772-971-2855; *www.floridadolphin watch.com*) leaves from the Fort Pierce marina and heads on to Fort Pierce Inlet State Park and Jack Island Preserve State Park (both below, under Nearby Natural Areas). The two-hour tour focuses on the river's wildlife, especially dolphins.

If you're looking for an outfitted paddling trip on the Indian River, consider Kayaks Etc. (888-652-9257; *www.kayaksetc.com*) or Tropical Kayak Tours (772-778-3044; *www.tropicalkayaktours.com*) in Vero Beach. Kayaks Etc. leads a variety of tours, including trips to Pelican Island, moonlight paddles, tours of the St. Sebastian River, and customized private paddling tours. It also offers kayaking classes and rentals. Tropical Kayak Tours guides paddlers on waterways throughout the Treasure Coast and beyond, from the panhandle to the Everglades, and even the Bahamas. Contact these companies for their schedule of tours and reservations.

Pelican Island manages the nearby Archie Carr National Wildlife Refuge (*archiecarr.fws.gov*). This refuge mainly provides undeveloped beach habitat for sea turtles (see more below under Wildlife). The Archie Carr refuge, named after the late marine scientist who was instrumental in the refuge's creation, doesn't offer any visitor facilities or even direct public access, in order to better protect sea turtles. Wabasso Beach Park at A1A and CR 510 is one way to access the refuge's beach.

At the 340-acre Fort Pierce Inlet State Park (772-468-3985), the half-mile sandy beach is the main draw. If you visit, try out the short nature trail through the maritime hammock. Nearby Jack Island Preserve State Park is considered part of Fort Pierce Inlet State Park, but here, you'll avoid the crowds that usually come with beach parks. Jack Island preserves mangroves from A1A to the Indian River. A looping trail takes you through the mangroves and to an observation tower, where the view shows the stunning swath of green mangroves and the condo canyons beyond. Egrets, herons, and other wading birds are easy to spot here. To get to Fort Pierce Inlet, take I-95 to the Fort Pierce area and exit at SR 70 (Exit #129). Head east to US 1, then turn left (north). Watch for the North Beach Causeway (same as A1A), and travel east over the Indian River. The park entrance is ahead on the right. Jack Island's entrance is about 1.5 miles to the north on A1A.

On the western shore of the Indian River, Oslo Riverfront Conservation Area (772-567-8000 ext. 249) is a great place to visit to access the water and explore the ecosystem's uplands. While there, you might see black racers or corn snakes, anhingas or warblers. From the parking lot at the entrance, trails lead through a hammock so thick that it easily could be called a jungle—amazing, considering that busy, commercial US 1 is so close that hikers can hear the traffic. Take one path to see the largest slash pine tree in the world, about as big around as three or four adult people. Other paths lead through pine flatwoods and boardwalks through mangroves. There is a canoe landing dock among the mangroves, but at low tide the distance between the water and the dock could make landing nearly impossible. Launch at the end of the road, where there is a simple boat ramp and a parking area. To get there, take US 1 south about 5 miles from Vero Beach and turn left (east) at Oslo Road. The entrance is just ahead on the left.

Previously the site of a sand-mining operation, Indrio Savannahs (772-462-2526) is a lesser-known natural area of the region. Some people come for the catch-and-release fishing in the thirty-five-acre lake created from the sand mining. Others come to hike the 3 miles of trails through Atlantic Coastal

Ridge scrubby flatwoods to a freshwater marsh observation area. Visitors might spot scrub residents such as Florida scrub jays and eastern indigo snakes, along with wetland denizens like wood storks and white ibises. Indrio Savannahs is down the road from Harbor Branch Oceanographic Institute (under Guided Tours, above). To get there, exit I-95 at Indrio Road (Exit #138) and head east to US 1, then turn left (north). The entrance is less than a mile ahead on the left, near Tozour Road.

The remote St. Lucie Inlet Preserve State Park (772-219-1880) rests on the southern end of the St. Lucie Inlet, where a quiet, natural beach waits for those who take the effort to get there. Mangroves are also a part of this park, which offers a picnic pavilion and restrooms. Current access is restricted to those who arrive on their own boats, or who walk 3 miles north from Hobe Sound National Wildlife Refuge's beach tract (a $5.00 entrance fee). A ferry service is planned to make it easier to visit the park.

Nearby Attractions

The Lagoon House (772-567-3491) in Palm Bay acts as a welcome center for the Indian River Lagoon, providing an example to other regions in the state. Visitors can take the ramp down to the water to look for wildlife. Exhibits showcase the natural areas, history, and culture of the lagoon, and visitors can get information about the Indian River Lagoon Scenic Highway. The Lagoon House is located on the river at US 1.

The Smithsonian Marine Ecosystems Exhibit (772-465-6630) is housed at the small St. Lucie County Marine Center, where visitors can see live examples of the habitats found in the Indian River Lagoon and get acquainted with local marine life at a touch tank. A live coral reef mini-ecosystem is a major part of the exhibit. The marine center is open Tuesday through Saturday from 10 a.m. to 4 p.m., and Sunday from noon to 4 p.m. Admission is $2.00 for adults, $1.50 for senior citizens, and $1.00 for children; admission is free on Tuesdays. To get there, take I-95 to SR 70 (Exit #129). Go east to US 1, then turn left (north). At Seaway Drive, turn right and watch for the marine center turn-off on the left after the bridge, right on the water.

Almost next to the marine center is the St. Lucie County Historical Museum (772-462-1795). Visitors can learn about the area's history, from Spanish shipwrecks that happened offshore (lending the region its name, the Treasure Coast), to Seminole War history, to early settlements in the region that included pineapple plantations. Hours are the same as for the marine center. Admission is $4.00 for adults or $3.00 for county residents, and $1.50 for children six to twelve.

At the Fort Pierce city marina, the Manatee Center (772-466-1600, ext. 3333; *www.manateecenter.com*) sits at a strategic location near the inlet next to a power plant discharge area, attracting manatees to the warm water in the winter. The nonprofit center offers a manatee observation deck, butterfly garden, and gift shop. To get there, take I-95 to SR 70 (Exit #129) and go east to US 1. Turn left (north), then turn right (east) on Orange Avenue. At Indian River Drive, turn right. The Manatee Center is ahead next to the marina parking lot.

Across the street from Jack Island (under Nearby Natural Areas, above) is the Navy SEAL Museum (772-595-5845), the only museum dedicated to the Navy's "Frogmen." Displays include vessels, equipment, and the history of the training that took place here in Fort Pierce during World War II. The museum is open Monday through Saturday from 10 a.m. to 4 p.m. and Sunday from noon to 4 p.m. Admission is $5.00 for adults and $2.00 for children six to twelve.

Wildlife

The Indian River and its surrounding lands are full of life. At Pelican Island, look for—of course—pelicans, as well as ospreys, egrets, cormorants, gulls, raccoons, rough green snakes, and blue crabs.

Wood storks, herons, and other fish-loving birds frequent Sebastian Inlet, just a few of the park's 180 counted bird species. It's also a place to look for Atlantic bottle-nosed dolphins and West Indian manatees.

Savannas Preserve is a good place to find alligators, warblers, and other songbirds, along with venomous snakes like pygmy rattlesnakes and coral snakes.

The northern section of St. Sebastian River Preserve State Park is home to red-cockaded woodpeckers, which love the pine flatwoods, and American kestrels, which perch on wires near the canal berm to look for insects. Gopher tortoises burrow in the preserve's sandy areas. All the state parks here are on the Great Florida Birding Trail.

Look for . . .

Sea turtles nest all along Florida's coastline, where 90 percent of sea turtles in North America choose to lay eggs. Treasure Coast and Space Coast beaches attract a high number of nesting sea turtles, perhaps because of long stretches of undeveloped beach. Archie Carr National Wildlife Refuge, which has 20.5 miles of beach, may have as many as one-fourth of all loggerhead sea turtle nests in the country (20,000), and one-third of all the green turtle nests

(2,000). Leatherback turtles also nest in the refuge and on area beaches, but in fewer numbers.

All of these sea turtle species are on the federal endangered species list. The loggerhead sea turtle is the most common in Florida, and the only sea turtle listed as threatened instead of endangered.

Sea turtles face population threats from a number of hazards. Turtles have lost suitable nesting sites to coastal development and beach erosion. Raccoons, other wildlife, and even people raid turtle nests and consume the eggs before they hatch. Just-hatched sea turtles follow moonlight to the reflective ocean, but urban lights may make them go the opposite way—toward cities. Once in the water, they may become entangled in fishing nets, causing injuries and death. Some sea turtles, particularly green sea turtles, are subject to a virus-borne disease known as fibropapilloma, which causes large tumors to form on the turtle's body, ending in death. Although killing sea turtles (and disturbing their nests) is a federal crime in the United States, sea turtles also face hunters who kill for turtle meat and shells, particularly in the turtles' Central America and Caribbean range.

Knowing the hazards that sea turtles face, it is a joy to come across one in the wild. You might see a sea turtle while paddling near seagrass beds or while fishing off a pier. You might also see these creatures during "turtle walks" held by coastal parks (like Sebastian Inlet) and nature centers during nesting season. In the early part of nesting season—spring—turtle walks focus on finding sea turtles that are laying eggs. Toward the end of the season—late summer—these programs watch for hatchlings climbing out of their nests and crawling toward the ocean. Turtle programs are usually limited to a small group of people, and reservations can fill up quickly. To take part in a turtle walk, contact a coastal park in advance of nesting season about any upcoming turtle programs they may have.

Habitats

The Indian River Lagoon is recognized as the most biologically diverse estuary in North America with around 2,200 species, according to the St. Johns River Water Management District. A variety of sea life from plants to fish, birds, and marine mammals depend on the estuary system for at least part of their life cycles. Seagrasses help improve the water quality and provide food for several species, including endangered manatees. Mangrove trees line the shores of the lagoon in some places, creating habitat for birds in their branches and for fish among their roots under the water. Sea life such as oysters, shrimp, lobsters, flounder, grouper, seahorses, turtles, and dolphins enjoy the shallow water protected from the ocean by barrier islands.

This biological diversity is a treasure for Florida, even though its shine has been tarnished. More than 75 percent of the estuary's wetlands have disappeared as a result of drainage canals dug to make way for urban and agricultural land, according to the South Florida Water Management District. At the same time, these canals have expanded the estuary's watershed. Dirt, fertilizers, and pollutants wash into the canals, rivers, and lagoon, decreasing the water quality. This runoff is one of the lagoon's most prominent enemies, and it's something that water managers are controlling by installing underwater baffle boxes to filter the water and by constructing stormwater treatment facilities to catch and store the runoff before it reaches the lagoon.

The flow of fresh water into the brackish lagoon can affect the estuary, too—neither too much nor too little fresh water is good for the ecosystem. Freshwater flow seems to be an ongoing challenge for the lagoon. As an example of the possible problems it faces, in 2003 local residents and environmentalists protested the releases of water from Lake Okeechobee into the St. Lucie River (and the Caloosahatchee River, on the other side of the state), the Indian River's primary tributary. Releasing water from Lake Okeechobee via pumps was necessary for the lake's health, according to the U.S. Army Corps of Engineers and the South Florida Water Management District, which manage the lake's dikes and water levels. However, many people were concerned that the extra fresh water in the lagoon system would decrease the amount of dissolved oxygen in the water, which sickens and kills fish. The fast flow of water from the release also churned up the muddy river bottom, reducing water clarity. To make matters worse to some people, the water district planned to lower the water levels in central Florida's Lake Tohopekaliga, sending water through the Kissimmee River valley to Lake Okeechobee—again raising its water levels and likely prompting more lake releases. A proposed solution was to store Lake Toho's water in Lake Kissimmee, which is north of Lake Okeechobee and not connected to the St. Lucie River, in order to replenish habitat for the endangered snail kite. Lake Okeechobee water flow may always be a problem as the amount and timing of the flow has been harnessed and controlled for decades by a series of locks and pumps that prevent flooding in urban and agricultural areas.

Other problems facing the Indian River Lagoon include red tide and the spread of exotic species like the Australian spotted jellyfish. Increased boat traffic in the waterway has led to erosion on Pelican Island's shoreline, according to the U.S. Fish and Wildlife Service. The island has eroded from its original five square acres to three acres. The refuge staff is trying to build the shoreline back up and develop plans to reduce further erosion.

The refuge is also restoring land with native plants. Near the visitor facilities, visitors may notice small groves of citrus trees that have yet to be turned back into native habitat. Along Centennial Trail, saplings are staked until they can stand on their own and blend into surrounding native vegetation, much of which was planted when the trail's boardwalk was developed and opened to the public.

Where to Stay

Campgrounds

Sebastian Inlet State Park has fifty-one campsites with electricity and water. The campground includes restrooms with showers, a dump station, and a laundry. There is no shade and no privacy at this campground, but campers here do get a great view of the inlet and the river, which can be busy day and night. Contact ReserveAmerica for reservations.

For a more serene camping experience, try the primitive campsites at St. Sebastian River Preserve State Park, which offers eight campsites. Here, you can drive almost right up to the campsites, which is good for people who want primitive camping without having to hike several miles. That is especially true at Tree Frog Camp, which is next to a grassy road and is shady and protected. Nearby is Mullet Camp, open and sandy with no shade, but right next to a canoe launch canal that leads to the St. Sebastian River's south fork. Storytelling Camp, Ranch Camp, and Eagle Camp all have horse paddocks or corrals and can hold up to twenty people. To reserve a campsite, call the park directly.

Near Savannas Preserve, Savannas Recreation Area (772-464-7855) in Fort Pierce is a 550-acre county park. Campers can choose from primitive campsites, sites with electrical and water hookups, and sites with full hookups. The open, mostly unshaded campground includes showers, a dump station, and a laundry facility. There are also trails, a boat ramp, and canoe rentals for paddling in the park's canals.

Lodging

There are plenty of lodging options in the area. Choose from large hotels (like Disney's Vero Beach Resort: 772-234-2000) or independent inns (like Davis House Inn in Sebastian: 772-589-4114; *www.davishouseinn.com*). Oyster

Pointe and Oyster Bay Resort (772-589-6513; *www.oysterresorts.com*) in Sebastian offers nightly and weekly apartment rentals. Closer to Savannas Preserve, try the nearby Holiday Inn Port St. Lucie (772-337-2200).

How to Get There

Pelican Island itself is located in the Indian River near Sebastian, just west of Orchid Island. To reach the refuge's visitor facility, take I-95 to CR 512/ Fellsmere Road (Exit #156) and head east for about 2 miles. Turn right (south) at CR 510, and follow the road as it turns east. Continue across US 1 and the Intracoastal onto Orchid Island. At A1A, turn left (north), travel about 3.7 miles, and watch for the refuge sign on the left. Turn at the sign and follow the road to two parking areas: the first one for restrooms and trails, and the second one for the paved walkway (Centennial Trail) to the observation tower to observe Pelican Island. Continuing down this road (Jungle Trail) past the parking areas will lead through a golf course community and back to CR 510.

To get to Sebastian Inlet State Park, follow the directions above for the Pelican Island refuge, but continue north on A1A another 5 miles, and look for the park's entrances. Alternatively, exit I-95 in the Melbourne area at US 192 (Exit #180) and head east across the Indian River. Turn right (south) at A1A. The park entrances are about 18 miles ahead. The southernmost entrance is mainly just beach parking. The entrance just south of the inlet offers a boat launch and boat trailer parking, and is the location of the campground and fishing museum. North of the inlet is another beach parking area, along with a concession; this is where the surfing tournaments are held. The northernmost entrance is for the marina.

For Savannas Preserve, take I-95 to the Port St. Lucie area and exit at St. Lucie West Blvd. (Exit #121). Alternatively, take the Florida Turnpike to Port St. Lucie Blvd. (Exit #142). Travel east to US 1, and turn right (south). Continue on for about 3 miles, then turn left (east) on Walton Road. The main park entrance is about 2 miles ahead.

St. Sebastian River Preserve State Park is crossed north and south by I-95, and east and west by the C-54 canal that flows into the river. There are two entrances. The southern entrance on CR 512 is convenient because it's on the way to Pelican Island and Sebastian Inlet (above). After turning at the sign on the roadside, pass the county aquatic complex and continue to the covered kiosk for brochures and maps. For the main entrance, take CR 512 west instead of east at I-95, then turn right (north) after about 5 miles at CR 507. Go through the quaint town of Fellsmere, following the road as it winds through town and continues north. The entrance is on the right, on the other side of the canal.

❧ ❧ ❧

Pelican Island National Wildlife Refuge
1339 20th St.
Vero Beach, Florida 32960
Phone: 772-562-3909
pelicanisland.fws.gov
The refuge visitor facilities are open every day from 7:30 a.m. until sunset.

Sebastian Inlet State Park
9700 S. A1A
Melbourne Beach, Florida 32951
Phone: 321-984-4852
Admission is $5.00 per vehicle. The park is open all day, year-round. The Sebastian Fishing Museum is open every day from 10:00 a.m. to 4:00 p.m. The McLarty Treasure Museum is open every day from 10:00 a.m. to 4:30 p.m.

Savannas Preserve State Park
9551 Gumbo Limbo Lane
Jensen Beach, Florida 34957
Phone: 772-398-2779

St. Sebastian River Preserve State Park
1000 Buffer Preserve Drive
Fellsmere, Florida 32948
Phone: 321-953-5004
The park is open every day from 8 a.m. until sunset.

The Indian River Lagoon is a rich estuary and an ecologically significant part of Florida. There are several natural areas along the lagoon, including the nation's first wildlife refuge, Pelican Island. This area is also known for its Spanish shipwrecks, lending it the name Treasure Coast, as well as its history as a military training ground.

Nearby

Space Coast (chapter 14), Upper St. Johns River (chapter 16), Loxahatchee River Lands (chapter 27)

27

Loxahatchee River Lands

Round one bend in the Loxahatchee River, and you see a little blue heron. Round another, and you startle a small group of white ibises. Lurking in the mangrove-lined riverbank is a yellow-crowned night heron, while a submerged log supports a row of turtles. Clouds, trees, and ospreys show up in reflections in the tannic water.

The Loxahatchee, which means "river of turtles," winds its way from cypress swamps and patches of sabal palms to Jupiter Inlet. Nearly 8 miles of the river, from Riverbend Park to Jonathan Dickinson State Park, gained the waterway a Wild and Scenic River designation, in 1985 (the first Florida river to have that national title).

Jonathan Dickinson State Park is a good place to explore the river, but the park isn't about just the river. It is also about uplands. In fact, the Atlantic Coastal Ridge runs through the park and provides the elevation that supports one of Florida's most endangered habitats, sand pine scrub. Altogether, Jonathan Dickinson is a wonderful remnant of Florida's southeastern coast that is fun to explore.

The park is named after a Quaker merchant who was shipwrecked in 1696 near Hobe Sound. Dickinson chronicled his surviving party's journey from Hobe Sound to St. Augustine, the Florida settlement, providing a record of life in Florida at the turn of the 18th century.

But it's a wonder that the park isn't named Trapper Nelson State Park in honor of the man who donated this land to the state. Many people navigating the river make their way to the Trapper Nelson Interpretive Site, which is accessible only by water. This was the home of Vincent Nostokovich ("Trapper Nelson"), a true Tarzan at six feet, four inches tall and 250 pounds who often wore nothing more than a pair of shorts and a head bandana.

State park lore tells how Nelson came to the area on a train in the 1930s and decided to live along the Loxahatchee because with all the fish he saw, he figured he'd never be hungry. Squatting on the land, Nelson paid the taxes on it for three years in a row, and became the land's owner by default. He decided he

Figure 26. Blowing Rocks Preserve is usually a quiet beach.

could make money from this wilderness not only by trapping, but also by creating a junglelike tourist attraction where he grew tropical plants and kept wild animals in cages for people to see. Nelson himself was much of the attraction, as he had developed a reputation as the "wild man of Loxahatchee." The exhibit was shut down in 1966, and a bitter Nelson didn't want to have anything to do with people after that—except for one man, a friend who encouraged Nelson to leave his 800-some acres of land to the state for a park. In 1968, Nelson was found dead of a self-inflicted gunshot wound.

What to Do There

At the Trapper Nelson site, you can see where he lived and where he kept the animals (in awful cages, at least by today's standards), and take a rest in the picnic shelter after paddling. One cabin displays some of Nelson's personal items—mostly books, including a pronouncing dictionary, numerous railroad timetables, a military police field manual, and a twenty-five-cent home canning cookbook.

Trail Tripping

There are about 14 miles of hiking trails in Jonathan Dickinson. The longest one—East Loop Trail—is part of the Florida National Scenic Trail. Trails take you through pine flatwoods, cypress sloughs, and sand pine scrub. East Loop Trail is about 9.5 miles long and crosses Florida East Coast Railroad in two places. A primitive campsite is available on this trail; you have to register with the park office to camp here.

The 4-mile Kitching Creek Trail connects with the western end of East Loop Trail by way of Campsite Trail. Kitching Creek Trail goes through beautiful, open pine flatwoods and follows Kitching Creek, with some points along the way where you can stop and reflect on the creek. Numbers posted along the trail correspond with interest points in a park brochure; ask for it at the park entrance.

Off-road cyclists come to the park for 5 miles of challenging bike trails. For more information on the bike trails at the park, contact local group Club Scrub (*www.clubscrub.org*). The club holds events like night-time rides and maintains the bike trail.

Equestrians with their own horses have 8 miles of trails. Pick up a trail map at the park entrance.

Paddling and Boating

Loxahatchee River is an 8-mile state canoe trail you can access from Jonathan Dickinson or farther upriver at Riverbend Park (561-966-6600) south of Indiantown Road. Bring your own boat and launch at the boat ramp, or get a rental from state park concession Jonathan Dickinson State Park River Tours (561-746-1466; *www.floridaparktours.com*) or from Canoe Outfitters of Florida (888-272-1257) based in Riverbend Park.

While driving to Jonathan Dickinson, you'll likely see several marinas and rental shops along the road, displaying boats and personal watercraft. It's common to see all kinds of watercraft in this area because of Jupiter Inlet, which offers direct passage to the Atlantic Ocean and nearby Jupiter Island.

Guided Tours

Jonathan Dickinson State Park River Tours takes you upriver in the *Loxahatchee Queen II*, a covered pontoon boat. The tour starts at the park's concession area and docks at Trapper Nelson's, then goes back the same way. In all, it's a relaxing and educational two-hour tour.

Canoe Outfitters of Florida (mentioned above) offers tours of the upper Loxahatchee from Riverbend Park. Call about scheduled trips.

Outside of the park a few miles to the south on A1A, Jupiter Outdoor Center (561-747-9666; *www.jupiteroutdoorcenter.com*) offers ongoing tours and events, and rents bicycles, canoes, kayaks, and motorboats for better exploring Loxahatchee River, Jupiter, and the Jupiter Inlet.

Nearby Natural Areas

The mainland tract of Hobe Sound National Wildlife Refuge (772-546-6141; *hobesound.fws.gov*) a few miles to the north on US 1 isn't very big—about 232 acres—but worth the trip because the land there represents what for the most part has been lost to development in the rest of southeastern Florida. For about an hour on the mainland tract, you can explore the short pineland and scrub trails, where you might see a bald eagle or indigo snake, and watch shorebirds like least terns along the Intracoastal Waterway beach. Another tract within the refuge is a beach area on Jupiter Island, and its 735 acres preserve mangroves and coastal sand dune habitats. The beach is an important nesting area for sea turtles, and the refuge offers special programs during the summer so visitors can watch the turtles lay their eggs. To get to the refuge headquarters' main tract from Jonathan Dickinson, go just a few miles north on US 1 and watch for a sign for the entrance on the right (east). To get to the refuge beach tract, go north on US 1 and take County Road 708 east across the Intracoastal to Jupiter Island. Turn left (north) at the beach. (Watch for land crabs on the road during summer.) Travel for about a mile and a half to the end of the road, where an honor box requests a $5.00 entrance fee.

Down the street from the beach tract is Blowing Rocks Preserve (561-744-6668), a Nature Conservancy property that is mainly a research facility for native plants, but which has a spectacular beach. Previously private property where invasive Australian pine trees were allowed to take over, the preserve now flourishes with native trees like sea grapes. The preserve is named for the limestone rocks that line the shore, where high tides and strong winds sometimes force water through holes in the rock, sending plumes of water as high as fifty feet into the air. A short nature trail parallels the beach on the back side of dunes. A nature center and mangrove boardwalk are open to visitors on the opposite side of the street, facing the Intracoastal. Blowing Rocks Preserve is open daily 9:00 a.m. to 4:30 p.m. except holidays. Admission is $3.00 per person, $1.00 for Nature Conservancy members and free for children twelve and younger. To get there from Jonathan Dickinson, go south on US 1 to the inlet and head east across the Intracoastal. Follow South Beach Road north to the preserve, about 2 miles ahead.

Nearby Attractions

The Marinelife Center of Juno Beach (561-627-8280; *www.marinelife.org*) is a research and rehabilitation center that helps visitors learn about Florida's sea creatures with hands-on exhibits, a touch tank, and educational programs. To get there from the park, go south on US 1 about 6 miles. The Marinelife Center is just north of Donald Ross Road near Loggerhead Park.

Busch Wildlife Sanctuary (561-575-3399; *www.buschwildlife.com*) is a prominent wildlife rehabilitator in the area and also invites the public to visit its nonreleasable residents, including many birds of prey. The sanctuary is open Tuesday through Saturday from 10 a.m. until 4 p.m. To get there from Jonathan Dickinson, take US 1 south to Indiantown Road and turn right (west). At Central Blvd., turn left. At Jupiter Park Drive, turn right and follow the signs.

On the north side of the mouth of the Loxahatchee River, the Jupiter Inlet lighthouse stands as a red beacon not only to ships but also to Florida's history. Built during the Third Seminole War and finished in Civil War days, the lighthouse survived these events, along with many storms and hurricanes. The 115-foot structure was placed on the National Register of Historic Places in 1973. Today, it is owned by the U.S. Coast Guard, but is run by the Loxahatchee River Historical Museum (561-747-6639; *www.lrhs.org*). Everyone touring the lighthouse must be at least four feet tall. The lighthouse is open Saturday through Wednesday from 10 a.m. until 4 p.m. Admission is $6.00. On the other side of the inlet, the museum operates Dubois Pioneer Home, a reminder of what life was like for early Jupiter settlers. Built in 1898, this house sits on a shell mound. The Dubois home is open Wednesdays and Sundays from 1 p.m. until 4 p.m. Admission is $2.00 per person. An even older house—the oldest in Palm Beach County—is the Tindall House, built in 1892, not currently open to the public. The museum is open Tuesday through Friday from 10 a.m. until 5 p.m. and Saturday and Sunday from noon until 5 p.m. Admission is $5.00 for adults, $4.00 for seniors, and $3.00 for children.

Jupiter Island was once owned by the wealthy Reed family, who sold parcels of their land to wealthy friends. Today, Jupiter is still home to many of the rich and famous; residents have included singer Celine Dion, pro tennis players Venus and Serena Williams, and actor Burt Reynolds, whose Burt Reynolds and

Friends Museum (561-743-9955; *www.burtreynoldsmuseum.org*) is a local attraction that displays memorabilia of the film star and Jupiter native. The museum is at the intersection of US 1 and Indiantown Road.

Wildlife

Almost every living thing needs water to live, and Loxahatchee River is a draw for wildlife. Named for turtles, the river is a sure place to see them, although they're shy and may disappear under the water if you approach.

With about 140 bird species, Jonathan Dickinson offers good opportunities for bird-watching. It's easy to see black vultures, wading birds, and ospreys along the river, and you may even see a bald eagle overhead while paddling upriver. Along the hiking trails, look for threatened Florida scrub jays, woodpeckers, and warblers. You may even see sandhill cranes in the park.

Look for . . .

The gopher tortoise is the only tortoise native to the eastern United States. The "gopher" is often called a turtle, but its body isn't suited for the water, as turtles' bodies are. The tortoise prefers to live in high, dry environments, where it can dig burrows as long as eight feet in the soft sand.

Because tortoises live in the ground, you may not see too many of them. But while walking along a sandy trail, you may spot a tortoise out looking for a meal of grasses and other plants. Its burrow entrance is probably not far away.

Gopher tortoises are considered a species of special concern in Florida because of loss of habitat; their choice of home is also choice land for development and agriculture. Companies that want to develop on land where gopher tortoises live sometimes attempt to relocate them (or allow a local group to move them). But in case not all of the gophers are found and moved, developers in this situation often get a permit that allows them to entomb the reptiles in their burrows. The permit fee is collected and used to buy up habitat for gophers elsewhere. Many concerned citizens decry such mitigation permits.

Habitats

Jonathan Dickinson encompasses several habitats. The park's pine flatwoods sprout slash pine trees that tower over saw palmettos, shrubs, and wildflowers. The sand pine scrub area is dry and sandy, and only those plants that can withstand these conditions can grow here: the obvious sand pine trees, certain wildflowers, and even cacti.

In fact, one of the more interesting features of Jonathan Dickinson State Park is the sand pine scrub area of Hobe Mountain, which rises to a peak of eighty-six feet above sea level—the highest point in Florida south of Lake Okeechobee. This area sits on the Atlantic Coastal Ridge, a sand dune system similar to the Lake Wales Ridge, created when the sea level was slightly higher than now. Hobe Mountain and the surrounding high, scrubby area could have been an island like the Lake Wales Ridge in central Florida. Climb the steps to the top of Hobe Mountain, where a lookout tower allows you to see how big the park really is. You can also see Jupiter Inlet and the Atlantic Ocean from the top of the tower.

The Loxahatchee River begins in a freshwater marsh, winds through a cypress swamp, and eventually mingles with water from the ocean in a mangrove estuary near the river's mouth. According to a river support group, the Loxahatchee cypress swamp is the only such subtropical freshwater forest left in the world. Concerns about the practice of diverting fresh water from the headwaters—resulting in saltwater intrusion farther and farther up the river—have led to water-management projects that aim to restore the freshwater content and improve water quality.

Where to Stay

Campgrounds

Jonathan Dickinson has 135 campsites in two campgrounds: Pine Grove Camping Area and River Camping Area. River Camping Area seems shadier and more private than Pine Grove Camping Area, which is close to busy US 1.

The park has two primitive campsites, both on the Florida Trail. At 9 and 12 miles from the trailhead, these are sites for those who are interested in backpacking. For more information about the sites and for reservations, contact the park.

When you think of the word "cabin," you may imagine a rustic log structure with smoke coming out of a stone or brick chimney. But Jonathan Dickinson's cabins are more like small mobile homes. Thoroughly modern with air conditioning and comfortable furnishings, these cabins let you sleep in comfort while still giving you the feeling you're in the great outdoors. The cabins sleep from four to six people and generally cost around $85.00 to $95.00 per night. Near the River Camping Area and the boat ramp, they're also in a good location. Contact the park concession for information and reservations.

Lodging

About 3.5 miles either north (Hobe Sound) or south (Jupiter) of the park on US 1, you can find a few hotels and motels, like Best Western Intracoastal Inn (561-575-2936) and Jupiter Beach Resort (800-228-8810). There are more places to stay in West Palm Beach and Stuart.

How to Get There

Take I-95 to Indiantown Road (Exit #87A) and head east. At US 1, turn left (north). The park entrance will be about 6.5 miles ahead on your left.

⊷   ⊷   ⊷

Jonathan Dickinson State Park
16450 S.E. Federal Highway
Hobe Sound, Florida 33455
Phone: 772-546-2771
Admission is $4.00 per vehicle.

The Loxahatchee River is Florida's first Wild and Scenic River. It flows through Jonathan Dickinson State Park, which preserves rare sand pine scrub habitat and the highest point in southern Florida along the Atlantic Coastal Ridge.

Nearby

Lake Okeechobee Lands (chapter 25), Indian River Lagoon Lands (chapter 26)

28

Eastern Everglades

If you asked five of your friends what they thought of the Everglades, they would probably tell you five different things—as in the story of the blind men who examined an elephant, each talking about different parts of the elephant. One might mention the miles of sawgrass-covered marsh full of water flowing from Lake Okeechobee. Another might mention its numerous mangrove and cypress trees (more than 230,100 acres of mangrove forest, in fact). A third could talk about the wild backcountry of the Ten Thousand Islands. One would have to mention the wildlife and birds there. One might even say that he or she doesn't have much use for the Everglades because it's just a mosquito-ridden wasteland. The Everglades could be all of these.

And yet, as with so many things, the Everglades is not just the sum of its parts. That has been proven after some sixty or seventy years of engineering to make it what we wanted it to be—a dike here, roads preventing water flow there, and development and agriculture squeezing it all around—resulting in ecological disaster that has led some people to proclaim Everglades National Park the most endangered national park. The Everglades functions as a whole, each part affecting the others.

While we may be only in the beginning stages of restoring this prized landscape, it continues to be a place of ecological significance. Recognized as an International Biosphere Reserve, World Heritage Site, and Wetland of International Importance, Everglades National Park is known around the world as a place that is wild, beautiful, and in need of protection.

Each year, more than a million visitors enter the park to explore what Everglades preservation pioneer Marjory Stoneman Douglas told us in *The Everglades: River of Grass* was the only Everglades in the world. Local schoolchildren and international tourists alike come to survey this huge land and its bounty of graceful birds, unique plants, and vast wilderness. Fishermen come to the park to enjoy a day on Florida Bay. Environmentalists and nature lovers come to see what they hope won't disappear a generation after they themselves are gone.

Figure 27. Alligators along Anhinga Trail in Everglades National Park try to retain heat on a winter morning.

You may be fortunate enough already to have been among the one million visitors, or you may be so overwhelmed by the park's size (1.5 million acres) that you wouldn't know where to go first. Whatever your status, one of the best ways to get acquainted with the park—or to refresh your admiration for it—is to start at one of the park's five main visitor centers. Three of these can be accessed along the 38-mile main park road that begins at the main eastern entrance in Homestead.

What to Do There

Your first stop should be the Ernest F. Coe Visitor Center, a complex on your right after entering through the park gates. Here, you can get a free park map, talk to a ranger, shop for field guides and other Everglades-related books, and learn about the Everglades ecology with interactive displays and films. This is also where you can get your first glimpse of Everglades wildlife. Nearly surrounded by a pond, the center attracts great blue herons and other birds hoping to catch a fish.

The visitor center is named for a man who was instrumental in preserving the Everglades as a national park. Coe was a friend of Marjory Stoneman Douglas, who requested that a memorial to him be placed in the park: a bronze statue of a Florida panther, which you will see near the center's parking lot.

A little farther down the main park road, you'll come to the park entrance station, where you pay the fee to get in and have another chance to get a park map and talk to a ranger.

Soon you'll cross a bridge over Taylor Slough. This is one of the main waterways that carries water south to Florida Bay. You may not recognize it as a waterway because, after all, you are now in the River of Grass. The grass grows up through the slough's bottom, making it hard to see the water. Look for birds flying overhead.

Within minutes, you'll see a brown sign pointing the way to the Royal Palm Visitor Center, to the left. Unlike the visitor center near the park entrance, this one is actually less center and more nature. There are some great trails in this area of the park (see below), which used to be Royal Palm State Park before Everglades National Park came into being in 1947.

The park road takes you past a campground and some trailheads, then the Pahayokee Overlook, a place to stop and get a scenic view of the grassland. Several more miles of scenic driving go by before you reach Mahogany Hammock, a boardwalk trail through mangroves.

Now you're in the southern part of the park. You'll see roadside ponds for canoe launches and paddling trails before you reach the Flamingo Visitor Center, which sits on Florida Bay—the destination of all the water in the Everglades and which separates mainland Florida from the Keys. Flamingo is a large area with a marina, lodging, restaurant, campground, museum, and plenty more trails. This is where you'd pick up rentals and take guided tours.

Trail Tripping

There are plenty of hiking trails in the eastern portion of Everglades National Park.

While at the Royal Palm Visitor Center, take the two nature trails there, Anhinga and Gumbo-Limbo. The main attraction at the visitor center is Anhinga Trail, a half-mile boardwalk above a portion of Taylor Slough. Because of its location on the water, you can easily see alligators, turtles, and wading birds. You'll also likely hear the pig frog's occasional rhythmic grunt. The boardwalk winds through mostly sawgrass marsh, but you'll also see mangrove and pond apple trees. This is one of the most popular trails in the park because of the abundance of wildlife, and you could spend a lot of time here.

When you've seen all you can along Anhinga Trail, head back toward the Royal Palm Visitor Center and take the third-mile paved Gumbo-Limbo Trail. Winding through a shady subtropical hammock that was just about flattened by Hurricane Andrew in 1992, the trail offers you a chance to see the nonwatery side of the Everglades. The trail is named for the native gumbo-limbo tree, but you'll also see royal palms and lots of ferns.

The Royal Palm area's two trails aren't enough for the serious hiker who longs to walk miles into the wilderness, but just a mile or so west of there, south of the main park road, are the Pineland Trails. More than 28 miles of connecting paths allow you to explore the lakes, sawgrass prairies, hammocks, and pinelands of Long Pine Key.

Long Pine Key Nature Trail runs 7 miles west of Long Pine Key Campground to Pine Glades Lake and is one of the trails where you can ride your bicycle. The other bike-friendly trail is the 11-mile Old Ingraham Highway, which will take you to two backcountry campsites: Ernest Coe and Ingraham.

Pineland Trail is among the trails in this group, but it is on the north side of the main park road and only a half-mile loop. While short, the trail does give you the experience of hiking through typical Florida flatwoods full of pines and palmettos.

Farther west along the main park road, the quarter-mile Pahayokee Overlook boardwalk isn't really a hike, but its observation tower will give you a good view of the marshland. Pahayokee is a Seminole word that means "grassy waters."

Mahogany Hammock and West Lake Trails are both half-mile boardwalk loops through mangroves.

The connecting Snake Bight (1.5 miles) and Rowdy Bend (2.5 miles) Trails go through a hammock and end with a boardwalk at Snake Bight, a kind of mini bay of Florida Bay. These trails are good for bird-watching and biking, too. The one-way 1.8-mile Christian Point Trail to the south also leads to Snake Bight. All of these trails are just a few miles north of the Flamingo Visitor Center.

Eco Pond near the Flamingo parking lot is a good place for bird-watching. A short trail circles the pond, and you can see anything from a great egret to a bald eagle. Climb to the observation deck for an overview of the pond.

The 7.5-mile Coastal Prairie Trail is the longest in the Flamingo area, and its destination is a small, primitive beachfront campsite called Clubhouse Beach. True to its name, the trail goes through a coastal prairie along Florida Bay.

If you go out of the park the way you came in and go north on Krome Ave., you'll find another small area of nature trails in the eastern portion of the park. Located just west of the park boundary off Richmond Dr. (SW 166th St.), the

Chekika area offers a campground, restrooms, and picnic area. Chekika is often closed because of flooding, so call the park ahead of your visit to find out whether it's open.

Paddling and Boating

The Everglades is a watery wonderland perfectly suited for exploring by water. Besides Florida Bay, there are several canoe trails along the main park road where you can launch a canoe or kayak. Motorized boat launches are at the Flamingo marina, West Lake, and off US 1 near Little Blackwater Sound. Boat launch fees are $3.00 for nonmotorized boats and $5.00 for motorized boats, and they're good for seven days.

Nine Mile Pond Loop about 11 miles north of Flamingo is actually about 5 miles; the number nine refers to the pond there, not the length of the canoe trail. Here, you paddle through coastal marsh and mangroves.

To the south, enjoy more mangroves on Noble Hammock Trail, a 2-mile loop. Nearby is the launch for Hells Bay Trail, which leads to a few primitive backcountry campsites. The closest, at 3 miles, is Lard Can campsite. Another half-mile puts you at the Pearl Bay chickee, one of the covered platforms above the water that are fairly prevalent in the Everglades backcountry. About 5 miles out is another, the Hells Bay chickee. The Hells Bay area is named for the navigational difficulty created by an abundance of mangroves.

The 8-mile West Lake Trail gives you a chance to see alligators and maybe crocodiles up close and personal across some small lakes and along creeks. West Lake is known to be a hazard for paddlers on windy days because of its openness.

Mud Lake and Bear Lake Trails connect with the Wilderness Waterway, a paddling trail that meanders through the Ten Thousand Islands backcountry. You can paddle Mud Lake in a 7-mile loop via Buttonwood Canal near Flamingo. Bear Lake Trail makes use of a series of canals, too, and ends at Cape Sable, about halfway between primitive backcountry campsites Clubhouse Beach and East Cape. But it's a long paddle, 11 miles to the end.

The Wilderness Waterway is covered in the Western Everglades, chapter 30.

If you'd like to spend a lot of time paddling the Everglades, definitely check out *A Paddler's Guide to Everglades National Park* by Johnny Molloy, which covers the subject in depth.

Flamingo is the place to rent canoes, kayaks, skiffs, pontoon boats, houseboats, bicycles, fishing poles, binoculars, and even ice chests from the park concession for your adventures on or near Florida Bay. Rental fees vary by the size of the boat and the length of time you use the equipment; check with the concession.

Guided Tours

At Flamingo, the concession offers a few daily guided boat tours. The ninety-minute Florida Bay tour takes visitors out on the water to see this other side of the park. The two-hour backcountry tour takes passengers along the mangroves and gives them the chance to see crocodiles and manatees in the shallow water. Tour prices range from $7.00 to $18.00, depending on the tour.

Florida Bay Outfitters (305-451-3018; www.kayakfloridakeys.com) in Key Largo offers kayak tours that last from a few hours to several days. The three-hour Dusenberry Creek tour near the park offers a good chance of seeing manatees and bottle-nosed dolphins. The Flamingo Triangle tour lasts three days and is highlighted by camping on remote islands. Other tours, and rentals, are available.

Everglades International Hostel (800-372-3874; www.evergladeshostel.com) in nearby Florida City organizes park tours by canoe, bicycle, and foot. Some of the hostel's tours go into Crocodile Lake National Wildlife Refuge, which shares a border with Everglades National Park. Crocodile Lake is mainly water; there are no public viewing facilities on land. The hostel also provides canoe, kayak, camping gear, and bicycle rentals, if you want to tour the area by yourself.

Rangers offer talks and lead a number of guided walks and canoe trips from late fall to early spring. For a schedule of these activities, ask at a visitor center, or call ahead.

The Flamingo Marina offers fishing charters; contact the concession about availability and prices.

Please be aware that there are no banks or ATMs anywhere in the park.

Nearby Natural Areas

Right in Homestead is another national park, Biscayne National Park (305-230-7275; www.nps.gov/bisc). The park preserves the uppermost section of Florida's reef, the third largest reef system in the world after Australia's Great Barrier Reef and Belize's Mesoamerican Barrier Reef. It's also the beginning of the Florida Keys, and a tremendously popular area for local boaters. Because the park is 95 percent water, it helps to have a boat—or access to one—so you can explore Biscayne Bay and its islands. That's no problem because the park concession offers glass-bottom boat tours, snorkel tours, and canoe and kayak rentals; fees vary. If you decide to try the primitive camping on Elliot Key, there is boat transportation for you and your equipment, for a fee. Elliot Key, an agricultural area before the park service took it over, has some nice hiking trails. The much smaller Boca Chita Key is the site of a small stone lighthouse and chapel built when Honeywell company founder Mark Honeywell owned the island in the 1930s and 1940s as his private getaway. The lighthouse wasn't approved, so it didn't really get a chance to function, but it provides a nice view of the little island and other nearby islands if a park service employee or volunteer opens it up for you. Boca Chita serves mainly as a marina where local boaters can dock and relax, especially on busy weekends. You can camp here, too, but there's no shade or privacy.

John Pennekamp Coral Reef State Park (305-451-1202) in Key Largo is the most popular state park in Florida, partly because of the easy access the park provides to the calm, shallow waters of the Keys, where you can access the reef. About a 40-mile drive from the entrance of Everglades National Park, Pennekamp also offers boardwalk trails through mangroves and a small beach. Like Biscayne National Park, the Pennekamp concession offers glass-bottom boat tours and snorkeling tours, where you may see the famous Christ of the Deep, a nine-foot bronze statue standing in about thirty feet of water. The park concession also rents power boats.

Nearby Attractions

About 8 miles from the entrance to Everglades National Park is Everglades Alligator Farm (305-247-2628; *www.everglades.com*), a private company offering airboat rides, alligator and snake shows, and the chance to see crocodiles and other animals. Admission is $17.00 for adults and $10.00 for children older than four.

Homestead Main Street (41 N. Krome Ave.) is a revitalized historical downtown area that dates to the 1917 construction of the original town hall. Now a place for museums, antiques shops, and cafés, Homestead Main Street dedicates the second Saturday of each month to showing off and viewing classic cars.

Speaking of cars, Homestead is also the home of the Metro-Dade Homestead Motorsports Complex (305-230-5000; *www.racemiami.com*) where races are held. With a track that's 1.5 miles long, the structure really stands out on the drive to Biscayne National Park.

Although perhaps not an attraction, a large produce market named Robert Is Here (305-246-1592; *www.robertishere.com*) makes for a nice stop on the way into Everglades National Park or after several hours there. You can't miss the place: situated at an intersection of roads bisecting agricultural fields, the open-air shop has the words "Robert Is Here" painted on the roof in large white letters. (Robert himself said he painted the roof back when he opened the store to let people know he was in business.) Here you can buy not only local produce, but also the specialty, Key lime shakes.

Metropolitan Miami is an easy drive from the park, and you can find plenty to do and see there, including the Miami Museum of Science and the nearby Vizcaya Museum and Gardens (a National Historic Landmark Italian Renaissance-style structure on Biscayne Bay), Fairchild Tropical Gardens, and the beaches.

Wildlife

The Everglades is known for its wildlife. Alligators immediately come to mind, as they are often called the "keepers of the Everglades" because their habit of creating "gator holes" in the marsh helps provide a habitat and food source for other animals. But the park is home to so many more species that you might spot—if only for a fleeting moment.

The park says there are several endangered species at home in the Glades: Cape Sable seaside sparrow, red-cockaded woodpecker, snail (Everglades) kite, wood stork, American crocodile, Atlantic hawksbill turtle, Atlantic leatherback turtle, Atlantic Ridley turtle, green turtle, Florida panther, Key Largo cotton mouse, Key Largo wood rat, West Indian manatee, and Schaus swallowtail butterfly.

Everglades National Park is known around the world for its birding. Go during the dry season (approximately November through April), and you'll likely be comparing binoculars with visitors from Canada, Japan, Germany, Britain, and France.

There are 347 different species of birds that spend at least part of their lives in the park. Some are migratory, just passing through, and many others spend their winters here. As many birds as there are, it is overwhelming to consider that the number of birds you can see in the Everglades today is just 10 percent of what it used to be before its ecological downfall. Hopefully, bird populations will rise as the ongoing restoration process heals the River of Grass.

Look for . . .

Southern Florida is the only place in the world where crocodiles and alligators live together in the wild. Crocodiles are mostly saltwater creatures, while alligators prefer fresh water. But in and around Florida Bay, fresh water and salt water mix.

Scientists estimate there are between 500 and 1,200 crocodiles in the wild in North America, and they are all in southern Florida. Crocodiles are federally endangered as a result of hunting and habitat loss. Some reports suggest the fluctuation of salinity levels in the Everglades region also affects crocodiles, which can live to be sixty years old.

Crocodiles are known to be reclusive, but you might see these reptiles around the marina at the Flamingo Visitor Center near Florida Bay, and at Biscayne National Park. Many crocs like to hang out in the water around the Turkey Point nuclear power plant near Biscayne National Park. Crocodile Lake National Wildlife Refuge, which spans the area east of US 1 between the mainland and Key Largo, is another croc haven.

You can tell crocodiles and alligators apart in several ways, but perhaps the easiest way is to compare the shape of their heads. Crocodiles have narrower heads and rather pointy snouts compared with alligators. Crocodiles also show their bottom teeth even when their jaws are closed, unlike alligators.

Habitats

As you travel south on the main park road from the eastern entrance to Flamingo, you'll go from freshwater to saltwater areas. In between are tree islands and brackish areas.

Taylor Slough near the entrance sports sawgrass—it is a river of grass. Soon, though, you reach the upland area of Long Pine Key, an island with a slight elevation that is all the advantage trees need to grow in this otherwise watery habitat. The surrounding marsh is just inches lower, but in the Everglades and in the rest of flat southern Florida, mere inches make all the difference. The elevation of Long Pine Key is the reason hardwood hammocks and pine flatwoods were able to develop in the middle of a marsh. This slight change in elevation allows visitors to see several habitats in one place, at Royal Palm Visitor Center, Long Pine Key Campground, and the Pinelands trails. Many of the animals and plants in the eastern portion of Everglades National Park are there because of Long Pine Key.

South of Long Pine Key, you'll see cypress and freshwater prairie, dotted with ponds. As you get closer to Flamingo and Florida Bay, you'll travel through mangroves until you reach the coastal prairie.

This diversity of habitats contributes to the Everglades' distinctiveness. The Everglades' location at the edge of the subtropics further adds to its uniqueness; there are plants and birds from the tropics as well as the northern part of the country.

As beautiful and rare as it is, Everglades National Park is considered the most endangered national park by some people.

Water demands from neighboring urban and rural areas, flood control management, and pollution over the years have wreaked havoc on the natural flow of water south from Lake Okeechobee, through the Everglades, and into Florida Bay. The natural sheet flow of water has been manipulated by levees, canals, water pumps, and roads to accommodate the cities and farms that have sprung up in southern Florida. The result is that when the Everglades would normally be dry (late fall and winter), it can be flooded; when it would normally be wet (late spring through early fall), it can be dry. Lawn and crop fertilizers, pesticides, and herbicides get into the water from runoff. Sometimes, this polluted stormwater is pumped directly into the Everglades or the ocean after heavy rains to prevent cities from flooding. The current system of canals and pumps wastes water, flushing 1.7 million gallons into the ocean every day, according to a government document.

This pollution and the natural water cycle's interruption have affected animals and plants throughout the Everglades. Just a few examples:

• The National Park Service estimates Florida Bay has lost more than 68,000 acres of seagrass habitat as a result of poor water quality. Seagrass is important to the endangered manatee, which eats seagrass, and to other marine life like small game fish and blue crabs.

• Because of unnatural water retention, tree islands—where many of the Everglades' wildlife species live—have died off because of the flooding. According to a *Miami Herald* report, 250 acres of tree islands disappear each year because of water retention, and 60–85 percent of tree island habitat already has died. Along with the tree islands, some animals like white-tailed deer drown for lack of solid ground.

• Unnatural water flow has also been blamed for the reduced populations of many birds, including endangered species like the wood stork and snail kite. For both birds, the interrupted water cycle has meant less food for them to eat, which in turn has meant fewer nests.

• The reduced freshwater flow from Lake Okeechobee has allowed salt water to creep into the Everglades. This increased salinity level may be affecting crocodiles, seagrass, and the coral reef tract that lies south of the Keys on the other side of Florida Bay.

To address the Everglades' environmental problems, the state of Florida and the federal government have developed the Comprehensive Everglades Restoration Plan, considered the largest environmental project in the world to date.

There are sixty major components of the restoration plan, which covers sixteen counties and 18,000 square miles. The restoration plan is expected to take at least thirty years to be carried out and will cost an estimated $8 billion. Water quality is a major issue of the plan, and so is water waste. At the current time, various lawsuits involving organizations such as the state, the Miccosukee Tribe, sugarcane farm corporations, and landowners who risk losing their property for the sake of the plan are trying to influence the plan through the courts. We will know the outcomes of these legal challenges in time.

Although the damage to the Everglades has reduced the area to half of what it once was and endangered many species of wildlife and plants, it's to our environment's benefit that we began to notice these detrimental effects after only fifty years or so of harmful water management. While so much damage was done in so short a time, we have learned that our water control methods were destructive and have set about trying to repair some of that damage. Some improvements have already been made, including a reported reduction in toxic levels of mercury in fish, birds, and Florida panthers, and culverts that have been built along Tamiami Trail north of the park to improve water flow. Everglades National Park will benefit from the restoration by having improved water quality and a more natural water sheet flow, among other enhancements that are expected to help the park wildlife populations as well as the local economy.

Where to Stay

Campgrounds

Just miles from Royal Palm Visitor Center (7 miles from the main entrance) off the main park road, the Long Pine Key Campground is a natural choice for camping. It has 108 tent and RV sites and one group site. There aren't any electrical hookups. However, there are restrooms (without showers), telephones, and a dump station. There is also a fishing pond and an amphitheater for ranger programs.

Another campground in the park is located near Flamingo Visitor Center, a thirty- to forty-minute drive from Long Pine Key. With nearly 300 sites, some with bay views, this is the place to camp if you want to be near the hustle and bustle. Here you get showers with your restrooms (but with cold water), two dump stations for RVs, and an amphitheater. You're closer to supplies at the concession if you run out or forget something.

Neither campground provides much shade or privacy. Sites are $14.00 per night.

In the backcountry, Everglades National Park has a staggering forty-seven campsites, each requiring a permit. Some are chickees—simple roofed structures—raised above the water where there is no dry land along canoe routes, and others are on the ground. Although they are in the backcountry, some campsites have toilets.

For park campground reservations and information, please call 800-365-CAMP.

Lodging

Flamingo Lodge (800-600-3813; *www.flamingolodge.com*) is the only place to stay in the park, with 103 rooms and twenty-four cottages. The word "lodge" may make you picture a rustic stone or wood structure, but actually, Flamingo Lodge looks more like a motel. Room rates vary from season to season, but they are comparable to most motels in Florida.

Everglades International Hostel (mentioned under Guided Tours, above) provides beds ranging from $13.00 to $35.00. Budget travelers also enjoy a laundry, communal kitchen, garden, and Internet access here.

Redland Hotel (800-595-1904; *www.redlandhotel.com*) is a renovated historic inn and offers thirteen reasonably priced rooms. About 10 miles from the park entrance, the Redland Hotel also has a restaurant.

There are plenty of other hotels and motels to choose from in the southeastern Florida metropolis.

How to Get There

From the north, take the Florida Turnpike until it ends in Homestead. (While driving, be sure to watch for the Turnpike extension turn-off south of Hollywood. This extension goes west and then south to Homestead. If you miss the turn-off, you'll end up in North Miami.) Turn right at the first traffic light (Palm Drive or SW 344th St.), and follow the signs to the park entrance.

From the west, take I-75 (Alligator Alley) to US 27 in Ft. Lauderdale and go south. Get onto the Turnpike and go south, following the directions above. Alternatively, take US 41 (Tamiami Trail) east to Krome Ave. and turn south. Turn right on Palm Drive, and follow the signs to the entrance.

❧   ❧   ❧

Everglades National Park
4001 State Road 9336
Homestead, Florida 33034-6733
305-242-7700
www.nps.gov/ever/

Ernest F. Coe Visitor Center
Open 8:00 a.m. to 5:00 p.m.
305-242-7700

Royal Palm Visitor Center
Open 8:00 a.m. to 4:15 p.m.
305-242-7700

Flamingo Visitor Center
Hours vary with the season
239-695-2945
Entrance fees are $5.00 per pedestrian or cyclist, and $10.00 per vehicle. Save your receipt; it's good for seven days.

Everglades National Park is the top nature tourism destination in Florida. The park gives visitors the chance to explore the world's largest freshwater marsh and view many kinds of wildlife, including many that are endangered.

Nearby

Western Everglades (chapter 30)

29

Big Cypress National Preserve

Driving down Loop Road in Big Cypress National Preserve, it still looks dark even though the sun has just come up. The tree canopy over the road gives it a tunnel effect. Large birds fly just ahead, their wings spanning the lane. A pig frog grunts, a woodpecker rattles, and a heron cries. You hear water splash, then the heavy-sounding beating of wings. In between are the sounds of small songbirds and crickets. The place is as noisy and busy as ever, and yet you're deep in southern Florida, distant from any city.

Although situated between greater Miami and Naples, Big Cypress is far removed from the mindset of either city. This is a place where cypress swamps ring grassy prairies and cumulus clouds rise vertically for miles into the sky. Miles of back roads lead to surprises: round a corner, and a pond will shake with the flutter of startled endangered wood storks; stay until nightfall, and a chuck-will's-widow will murmur the sound of its name; watch the sun rise over the flat horizon, and see it cast a pink glow like a sheer blanket over a pond.

The stiff prairie grasses point toward the sky. Cypress trees stretch out their moss-draped arms as a resting place for birds, while their knees rise out of the water like tarnished stalagmites in a cave. Narrow strips of canals full of black water follow the roads almost everywhere they take you; without them, roads would be impossible in this land consumed by water. Alligators sometimes appear as toothsome ghosts when the mud on their ridged backs dries to a white powder. When it's been dry, vehicles on gravelly back roads roll yellow-white dust into the air.

The most beautiful thing about Big Cypress, besides the fact that its 1,100 miles are free to the public, is its wide openness. Traveling north on Turner River Road, you get to a point where the trees on either side stop crowding and recede, giving visitors a savanna-like view of what a lot of Florida looked like originally: tall grass stretching across the land studded with clusters of native cabbage palms. Another really beautiful place is on western Loop Road, where the road turns for the first time and becomes really just a bridge between noth-

Figure 28. Cypress trees are a common sight at Big Cypress National Preserve.

ing but water and trees on either side of you. With alligators in the water below, birds in the trees up high, wildflowers growing along the banks, and nothing mechanical, automated, or computerized in sight, you feel as though you're really someplace special.

What to Do There

Big Cypress is open to a lot of outdoor activities. Because most of the preserve is far from developed areas, you will need to bring plenty of water with you, plus snacks or meals, depending on how long you plan to stay—and remember to pick up/pack out your trash. Also note that there are only a few restroom facilities in the preserve: at the Big Cypress National Preserve Oasis Visitor Center, Monument Lake Campground, and Midway Campground.

Hunting is allowed in Big Cypress, and some people may want to call ahead to check on hunting season dates before planning a backcountry trip that could be disturbed by the sounds of gunshots. Dates, locations, and weapons allowed vary.

Scenic Driving

If you travel Tamiami Trail (US 41) between Naples and Miami, you can't help but see scenic beauty because the two-lane road goes right through the preserve. You could be satisfied with driving just this road, but to see more wildlife and get better acquainted with the preserve, also take Turner River Road and Loop Road, both unpaved for the most part.

Turner River Road is a 20-mile lane that stretches from Tamiami Trail north to just beyond the east/west I-75 stretch known as Alligator Alley. With the Turner River canal its constant companion, the road takes you past cypress swamps, prairies, and pinelands—plus a few private homes and the Big Cypress Wilderness Institute, an organization that helps at-risk young people through work projects. The intersecting Wagonwheel Road will take you to Birdon Road, where you can turn south and go back to Tamiami Trail, or go farther west to State Road 29.

Loop Road is a 26-mile lane going through mostly cypress swamp habitat, beginning and ending at Tamiami Trail. The eastern section of the road that begins at the preserve boundary is paved, and here you'll pass private residences and remnants of an old service station—an old settlement called Pinecrest that existed before Tamiami Trail was built. You'll also pass the Loop Road Education Center, used by groups of students from elementary school through college.

Trail Tripping

If you don't mind getting wet, you'll enjoy hiking Big Cypress's trails. Allowing you to pass through pinelands, hammocks, and prairies and past cypress stands, most of the trails are recommended for hiking only during the cooler, drier months—roughly late November through mid-March. Some trails can be flooded with waist-high water during the summer and fall.

However, the Fire Prairie Trail and Concho Billy Trail are mostly dry year-round because they used to be roads before the preserve was created in 1974. Both are located off Turner River Road, and both are 5 miles round-trip. Be prepared to share the trails with mountain bikers. The Concho Billy Trail is also open to off-road vehicles (ORVs).

For a short walk, try the Tree Snail Hammock Nature Trail, located across from the Loop Road Education Center. As its name suggests, the trail winds through an area dense with trees and other vegetation. One-page trail guides may be available at a kiosk on the road if they're stocked. On the trail, look for an old 1920s moonshine still. Another short walk—a half-mile—is on the new

Kirby Storter boardwalk between Monument Lake Campground and H. P. Williams Roadside Park.

Big Cypress is where you'll find the end—or the beginning—of the state-wide Florida National Scenic Trail; 31 miles of the trail wind through the preserve. The trail is sort of broken up into sections by Tamiami Trail and Alligator Alley. Contact the Florida Trail Association for trail maps and tips for hiking the trail.

Experienced hikers can strike out anywhere through the backcountry; here is a place where you can actually create your own trail if you really know what you're doing. A compass and GPS device are recommended.

Big Cypress requires all daytime and overnight hikers to register for a free permit before hiking. You can get permits at the visitor center and at major trailheads.

Paddling and Boating

Although most visitors probably use Big Cypress's roads and trails, canoeing or kayaking is another way to explore the preserve. There are two canoe trails in Big Cypress. Both lead south from Tamiami Trail through coastal marshes and mangroves, and end in Everglades National Park's Ten Thousand Islands area.

The Turner River Canoe Trail launch site is a half-mile from H. P. Williams Roadside Park on Tamiami Trail, marking the southern end of Turner River Road—about 6 miles east of SR 29. The National Park Service recommends leaving your boat at the launch site, driving to Williams Park to leave your vehicle, and walking back to the launch site. The trail takes you to the town of Chokoloskee (estimated to be about a five-hour paddle), where you can continue to the Everglades National Park Gulf Coast Visitor Center in Everglades City (another hour).

Or you can take the long way home through the Wilderness Waterway (a week or more) in Everglades National Park. The trail ends at the Everglades National Park Flamingo Visitor Center. If you choose this route, it is recommended that you go with a guide or a friend who has traveled the Wilderness Waterway before, at least your first time out. This is a backcountry trip that requires preparation, planning, skill, and navigation knowledge.

But to come back to Big Cypress on the Turner River Canoe Trail, instead join up with the other canoe trail in the preserve, Halfway Creek, to paddle a loop in the southwestern portion of Big Cypress (and a little of Everglades National Park). The estimated time for paddling the loop is four hours.

If you want to start at Halfway Creek Canoe Trail, launch at the end of

Seagrape Drive, about 3 miles east of SR 29 on Tamiami Trail, where parking is available. From here, you can paddle to Chokoloskee or the Gulf Coast Visitor Center (about four hours), or do the Halfway Creek/Turner River loop.

It's also possible to paddle these trails in the opposite direction, starting at the Gulf Coast Visitor Center or Chokoloskee.

Guided Tours

Unlike nearby Everglades National Park and Biscayne National Park, Big Cypress doesn't have concessions that offer tours. However, from December through April, park staff members lead guided walks and canoe and bicycle trips in the preserve.

Several outfitters in nearby Everglades City offer tours through Everglades National Park, leaving from the area of the park's Gulf Coast Visitor Center.

Nearby Natural Areas

Everglades National Park Shark Valley Visitor Center (305-221-8455) is just a few miles east of the Miccosukee Indian Village on Tamiami Trail. The main attraction here is a 15-mile paved loop that allows hikers, bicyclists, and tram riders a view of the vast Everglades grasslands, punctuated by an observation tower at the halfway point. There are also two short nature trails. This is an excellent spot for wildlife-watching. There is a fee for bicycle rentals (or bring your own bike) and the tram tour. The parking area can fill up during winter; some people park on the shoulder of the road on Tamiami Trail when this happens. Another possible setback is that the park may close if the water gets too high. Admission is $8.00 per vehicle, good for seven days.

Fakahatchee Strand Preserve State Park (239-695-4593) adjoins both Big Cypress and Everglades National Park. Mainly a cypress swamp, this 74,000-acre state park features a slough through which water flows into the Ten Thousand Islands estuary to the south. However, it may be better known for its native orchids, which were made famous by the Susan Orlean book *The Orchid Thief* and the resulting movie *Adaptation* starring Meryl Streep and Nicolas Cage. There are two main ways to explore the park. One is on a dirt road (Janes Scenic Drive) reached from SR 29 about 5 miles north of where it intersects Tamiami Trail. Drive down this road far enough, and you'll reach adjacent Picayune Strand State Forest, a planned housing development that went bankrupt before any houses could be built; removing the eerily empty rows of roads is part of the Everglades restoration. The second way to explore Fakahatchee is on a short boardwalk through a cypress swamp reached off Tamiami Trail about 8 miles west of SR 29; look for parking next to a tall fence around a tribal housing area. Admission is free.

Nearby Attractions

Just a half-mile east of the Big Cypress visitor center on Tamiami Trail is the home and gallery of Clyde and Niki Butcher. A small Florida cracker-style structure, Big Cypress Gallery (888-999-9113; *www.clydebutcher.com* or *www.nikibutcher.com*) showcases the photography of both Clyde and his wife, Niki. Clyde's large-format black-and-white landscapes—whose subjects are often the Everglades—cover the walls. Small prints and calendars are also available if you aren't prepared for the size or expense of Clyde's photographs. Niki's black-and-white photography includes Florida landscapes but also features people and buildings, and she paints her photos by hand with a small cotton swab. Big Cypress Gallery's hours vary; call before your visit to check for times and special events like the annual Labor Day swamp walks.

Florida's two Native American tribes, the Seminole and Miccosukee, both offer insight into their heritage as well as nature tours.

The Miccosukee Indian Village (305-223-8380) is on Tamiami Trail, about 18 miles east of the Big Cypress National Preserve Oasis Visitor Center. For a small fee, you can go on a guided tour of a working Miccosukee village and learn about the tribe's history and modern-day life. There are airboat tours, alligator-wrestling shows, and a gift shop, as well as a restaurant that serves traditional food for breakfast and lunch. The village is open every day from 9 a.m. until 5 p.m.

Big Cypress Seminole Indian Reservation (800-617-7516; *www.seminoletours.com*) is actually not in Big Cypress, as you might imagine. It's farther away, located north of Alligator Alley, which parallels Tamiami Trail some 20 miles to the north. To get there from the preserve, follow SR 29 north from where it intersects Tamiami Trail to Alligator Alley and go east; look for the Snake Road exit about 25 miles later, and follow posted signs. The Billie Swamp Safari here offers day and overnight packages, with airboat and swamp buggy tours to view wildlife and learn about the Everglades, and the chance to sleep in the traditional lodging, a chickee. The Ah-Tah-Thi-Ki Museum (open Tuesday through Sunday from 9 a.m. until 5 p.m.; tickets are $6.00 for adults, $4.00 for students and seniors) is also a draw for people wanting to experience Seminole history and culture. At about 25 miles from the edge of Ft. Lauderdale, the reservation is the only place to buy gas and food along Alligator Alley, although two rest plazas offer restroom facilities along the way.

Wildlife

There are a lot of species here to see—including nine species considered federally endangered or threatened—but some of the more exciting ones like the Florida panther and the Florida black bear will likely elude you. (Congratulate yourself if you do get to see them!) Your chances of seeing these two will increase the farther you get away from the main roads. If you hike or travel the paths and trails, that's probably where you would see them. But you never know—so always keep your eyes and ears open.

Bird-watching is another story, especially during the fall and winter when avian creatures soak up the warmth of southern Florida. The canal alongside Turner River Road is a place where you can see wading birds like herons and egrets any time of the year.

It's also a great place to see reptiles and amphibians. You can always find alligators and turtles on the banks of the canal or swimming in the water. As you drive, bike, or hike in the preserve, watch out for snakes so you don't step on them or run over them. Roads are warm spots that attract these cold-blooded creatures. Snakes are fascinating, but always keep your distance while you watch them. The federally threatened eastern indigo snake makes its home in Big Cypress. With shiny black skin and length of up to eight feet, this snake may appear intimidating, but it is nonvenomous. However, there are four venomous snakes found in Big Cypress: the eastern diamondback rattlesnake, pygmy rattlesnake, water moccasin (cottonmouth), and coral snake, which is small and pretty but dangerous nevertheless.

Note that Big Cypress doesn't allow wildlife-watching with artificial lights (spotlighting).

Birds once lived here by the tens of thousands, especially wading birds, whose populations have taken a 95 percent hit since the 1930s. Many people are hopeful of a comeback, however, especially now that the Comprehensive Everglades Restoration Plan is underway.

Five birds on the endangered species list make their home in the preserve: the snail kite, wood stork, Cape Sable seaside sparrow, and red-cockaded woodpecker.

Look for . . .

Big Cypress and neighboring Florida Panther National Wildlife Refuge are the main home of the Florida panther, a subspecies of the cougar—also known as puma or mountain lion—that once ranged throughout eastern North America. With fewer than a hundred Florida panthers left, they are considered one of the most endangered mammals. Panther numbers dwindled at first because of previous government incentives to kill them. Today, the population is affected by a lack of habitat in which to live; they have been crowded out by human populations that grow every day. Wildlife officials are considering moving some panthers to other states where there may be more room for them to live, but some of these states are against introducing this predator to their communities. According to the state, there has never been a reported Florida panther attack on a person, and the U.S. Department of Agriculture states that more cattle are killed by wild dogs than any other predator. Despite these facts, the Florida panther may have an increasingly hard search for habitat.

Many panthers are tracked via radio collars by state and federal biologists, who can monitor not only the panthers' whereabouts but also—when they can be temporarily captured—their weight and general health.

Roadkill also affects panthers. Although underpasses along Alligator Alley have reduced vehicle collisions there, panthers are struck along Tamiami Trail. Although wildlife caution signs line Tamiami Trail, the speed limit may be too high to help prevent collisions with panthers.

A much smaller mammal, the weasel-like Everglades mink, is considered threatened in the state of Florida. Found in a few places only in southern Florida, the minks live mostly near the water around vegetation, where they can hide from larger predators. Like other similar animals, Everglades mink like to swim and can hold their breath for a long time while they look for a meal.

Another species specific to the area is the smallest subspecies of fox squirrels, the Big Cypress fox squirrel. Loss of habitat and roadkill have earned this squirrel a threatened designation in the state of Florida. The U.S. Fish and Wildlife Service had considered listing it as threatened on the federal Endangered Species List, but stated in February 2002 that "the squirrel still occupies most of its historic range in southwest Florida and has shown itself to be adaptable by residing in altered habitats such as golf courses and residential areas where native habitat is preserved."

Habitats

Water is the main force here. The shallow, riverlike sloughs slowly flow through the cypress stands and prairies toward the estuaries to the south. The sloughs' presence is important to the overall health of the Everglades. Although Tamiami Trail allows people to access the preserve, its construction in the late 1920s disrupted the natural flow of water. Road runoff and pollution from the surrounding communities have been threatening the life of the Everglades and have contributed to the downfall of Florida Bay. News of a low-oxygen "dead zone," dubbed the Black Water Phenomenon, in the ocean stretching from

Naples to Marathon in the Keys caused alarm in 2002, but scientists say they aren't sure yet whether the cause is unnatural runoff from the Big Cypress basin.

Most of the land in Big Cypress is under water for many months of the year. Even when you can't see the water, it can still be there, under what looks like solid ground but is really a kind of organic carpet. This is marl, which sits on top of limestone just under the surface.

The preserve's official brochure/map issued by the National Park Service tells readers that Big Cypress wasn't named for big cypress trees; it was named after its big size—about 1,500 square miles (or 729,000 acres).

When you view a grouping of cypress trees from a distance, you may see why it's called a dome—the outline of the grouping is rounded. The tallest cypress indicates where the deepest water is in the dome. Inside the dome, the trees are so thick that the sun can seem to disappear. The land under your feet will be mucky, and more than likely, your feet will disappear from view under the water.

About a third of the preserve is covered with cypress swamps. In fact, Big Cypress holds the largest known stands of dwarf cypress. Most of the cypress trees are dwarf cypress, although there are a few tall bald cypress trees, some said to be up to 700 years old. Most of the bald cypress trees have been logged.

Another significant habitat is the marl prairie. Here you'll see sawgrass and other grasses and wildflowers that enjoy standing in fresh water and require periodic fires to keep trees from taking root and crowding the prairie.

Scattered pinelands—endangered slash pine forests that were logged to just a percentage of what they used to be in southern Florida—and small islands of hardwood hammock round out the rest of the preserve, with some mangrove areas to the south where Big Cypress adjoins Everglades National Park.

These mineral-rich habitats still show proof of the oil extraction that was allowed from the early 1970s, resulting in some 20 million barrels of oil. Although the National Park Service had declared that 10 percent of the preserve could be used for oil extraction, many people were upset in 2002 when Collier Resources, a company with oil rights to the area, requested permission to use dynamite to look for oil in the preserve. The U.S. Department of the Interior, which operates the National Park Service, stepped in and announced in May 2002 that it had reached an agreement to buy from Collier Resources the mineral rights to the preserve, Florida Panther NWR, and Ten Thousand Islands NWR so no new oil and gas development could take place in the three adjoining areas.

Besides mineral rights, another sore point with environmentalists has been the use of ORVs in the preserve because of the damage they can cause to soil, vegetation, water quality, and wildlife. In 2000, Big Cypress finalized specific guidelines for ORV use, including speed limits, vehicle size, and hours and locations of operation. The preserve requires all ORV riders to register for a yearly $50.00 permit—of which 2,000 are given out—and to stay on specific ORV trails, which are shown on a map available at the visitor center. These trails avoid marl prairies and other sensitive habitats.

Where to Stay

Campgrounds

Campers have several campgrounds to choose from, although some are closed during the wet season (summer and early fall). Most are primitive, and none offer electrical or water hookups. All campers need to register for a permit before camping in the preserve and to recognize designated quiet times. Campsites are first-come, first-served.

Monument Lake Campground off Tamiami Trail offers several sites around a borrow pit (where rocks were scooped out and now there is water). Both this and the Midway Campground offer a dump station and restrooms. A $16.00 fee is collected from December 15 through April 30.

Primitive campgrounds Bear Island (a secluded spot at the northern end of Turner River Road), Mitchell's Landing (a clearing off Loop Road), and Pinecrest (near and similar to Mitchell's Landing) provide little more than space. Backcountry campsites also exist.

Lodging

There's nowhere to stay in the preserve, so if you're not a camper and you don't like driving long distances (from certain parts of the preserve) to get to a hotel, you're better off making Big Cypress a day trip. Miami to the east and Naples to the west offer loads of lodging options.

The closest places to stay are in Everglades City to the west and Miami to the east. Everglades City offers bed-and-breakfasts, rental villas, and motels (like Ivey House Bed & Breakfast: 941-695-3299; *www.iveyhouse.com*). Toward Miami, the closest place to stay is Miccosukee Resort and Convention Center (877-242-6464; *www.miccosukee.com*) on Tamiami Trail that also has restaurants, a casino, and spa.

How to Get There

From western Florida, take I-75 south to the Naples area and get off at the last exit before it turns into Alligator Alley (a toll road). Head west and watch for signs directing the way to Tamiami Trail. Follow Tamiami Trail south and east to the preserve. Alternately, take Alligator Alley ($1.50 toll) east to SR 29, then exit. Travel south to Tamiami Trail, then east to the preserve.

From eastern Florida, take the Florida Turnpike (a toll road) south to the Broward/Miami-Dade county line, then follow the Turnpike extension west. Exit the Turnpike at Tamiami Trail and head west toward the preserve. Alternately, take US 27 south to County Road 997, continuing southwest. Turn west at Tamiami Trail and follow it to the preserve.

↤ ↤ ↤

Big Cypress National Preserve
HCR 61, Box 110
Ochopee, Florida 34141
Phone: 239-695-1201
www.nps.gov/bicy
The Oasis Visitor Center is open daily except Dec. 25 from 8:30 a.m. to 4:30 p.m.

This eco-trip shows you the real wilderness of southern Florida. There are few facilities, and "civilization" is distant, but you'll be in a land where rare Florida panthers roam.

Nearby

Lake Okeechobee Lands (chapter 25), Eastern Everglades (chapter 28), Western Everglades (chapter 30)

30

Western Everglades

Tucked away behind major highways, cypress swamps, and mangroves, you'll find Everglades City and its neighbor, Chokoloskee. These towns in the Ten Thousand Islands symbolize both a beginning and an ending.

This is the place to begin an Everglades backcountry water trip—whether for a day or a week. It's also where you can begin to understand what the Everglades meant to settlers only a few generations ago: a rough country, a place where life is a struggle for survival, where the land and water compromise with the tides to reveal or hide fish, crabs, birds, and other wildlife.

Everglades City and Chokoloskee are an ending: the end of the road before reaching the Gulf of Mexico and miles of Everglades backcountry, the last place to see the end of a time when the Everglades was a wild frontier.

This area is full of lore of the early settlers. Many people are well acquainted with Florida legends Loren "Totch" Brown and Edgar J. Watson, men whose lives were defined by the remoteness of the Everglades. Totch Brown recalls his life here as an alligator hunter and drug smuggler in his memoir, *Totch: A Life in the Everglades*. Before him, Edgar Watson was a farmer accused of killing his workers on payday, so a town mob set out to kill him, as recounted in *Killing Mr. Watson* by Peter Matthiessen. These characters and their Wild West–like lawlessness are still remembered today by many people. Their stories just make visiting the western Glades that much more interesting and serve to remind that the Glades reveals itself in so many ways: through its nature and history, through its wildlife, and through its people.

The Everglades is so varied that your sense of awe and respect increases with each mile. Most of those miles in the western Everglades are salt water and brackish water, the destination of the water flowing through the River of Grass. The water opens up before you, though seemingly closed off by the mangrove islands. The sky also opens up above you, even larger than the water you float on. The clouds roll across like an Impressionist painting that is constantly changing: it's cerulean with white, puffy clouds; it's pink with gray cirrus wisps; it's the color of steel thick with mountain-shaped billows.

Figure 29. A bottle-nosed dolphin plays in the wake of a tour boat in western Everglades National Park.

One park guide says it is a shorter distance to Key West by boat than by car, and that is very telling. This is a land of water. The only way to see the western Everglades is to get out on a boat.

What to Do There

Everglades National Park is so expansive that it has five visitor centers. The western entrance, about 40 miles southeast of Naples, is just one. Although the national park covers about 1.5 million acres, don't expect the Gulf Coast Visitor Center to be large. (One uneducated visitor was overheard saying, "This isn't very big for a national park.")

About one-third of the park is a water body of some kind, and this is where you'll find most of that third. This is the saltwater portion of the park, so, naturally, exploring this part of the Everglades is focused on the water.

Trail Tripping

The western Everglades isn't really a place to hike because of its watery nature. The Gulf Coast Visitor Center doesn't have any trails. You can walk the nature trail at Sandfly Island on the other side of Chokoloskee Bay, if you can get there by boat.

For longer hikes, you'll find trails at Collier-Seminole State Park (below) and in the nearby Big Cypress area (chapter 29).

Paddling and Boating

From Chokoloskee Bay, through the Ten Thousand Islands, into the Marjory Stoneman Douglas Wilderness Area that skims the Gulf of Mexico, the watery world of the Everglades stretches on and on.

Bring your own canoe, kayak, or boat—or get a rental—and explore Chokoloskee Bay for the day. Other day trips include paddling 2 miles to Sandfly Island (which takes about one hour) and the Halfway Creek Canoe Trail (detailed in chapter 29).

For an overnight trip, there are several backcountry campsites within a few miles from the visitor center: Tiger Key (beach site), Picnic Key (beach site), Kingston Key (chickee), Rabbit Key (beach site), Lopez River (ground site), and Sunday Bay (chickee). Staying at any of these campsites requires a backcountry camping permit from the national park, which can help you plan a route.

The more adventurous wilderness seekers attempt to navigate the Wilderness Waterway, a 99-mile route between the Gulf Coast and Flamingo Visitor Centers that spans the Marjory Stoneman Douglas Wilderness Area. This shallow inland route is probably the most remote area in Florida, so it requires a lot of planning, including requesting backcountry permits and filing a trip report with the park. The National Park Service estimates it takes paddlers eight or nine days to cover the route; motorboaters with a draft of two feet or less can manage it in seven hours. Larger motorboats can certainly travel between the two visitor centers, but not through this route because of the shallow depths. If you haven't done a lot of paddling before or if you're not familiar with nautical charts, it's best to go with someone who has paddled the Wilderness Waterway before, like a tour guide. This is a place with names like "Lostmans Five Bay," "Camp Lonesome," and "Buzzard Key," so it's not for the faint of heart.

To plan a Wilderness Waterway trip or any Everglades paddling excursion, check out *A Paddler's Guide to Everglades National Park* by Johnny Molloy, which details all the trails and campsites in the Everglades backcountry.

Boat rentals are available from many local marinas, such as Glades Haven Marina (239-695-2073; *www.oysterhouserestaurant.com/marina.htm*).

Guided Tours

Everglades City and Chokoloskee exist on tourism and fishing, so finding a tour is easy. You'll see several signs for tours along State Road 29 as you drive through.

Boat tours of the park leave every half-hour from the Gulf Coast Visitor Center (239-695-2591). While you wait for your tour to begin, you can visit the natural history displays on the second floor of the visitor center, have a snack from the concession, or watch for birds and dolphins near the marina. Tours last from one and a half hours to one hour and forty-five minutes, and prices vary from $10.00 to $16.00.

There are several airboat tour operators in the region. One of them is Totch's Island Boat Tours (866-MANATEE; *www.airboateverglades.com*), run by the legendary settler's family. The airboat tour goes through the backcountry well-known to guides.

Note that airboats aren't allowed within the national park, so these tours go just outside the park. Some local airboat tour operators were fined in 2004 after an undercover investigation revealed they were feeding alligators and other wildlife, which is illegal—and dangerous! Make sure your tour guide respects wildlife and laws.

North American Canoe Tours (239-695-3299; *www.evergladesadventures. com*) offers a variety of tours in the Everglades, from half-day sightseeing trips to longer backcountry paddling tours. Prices vary. Tours are organized at Ivey House bed and breakfast inn just a few miles north of the visitor center on SR 29. (See below, under Lodging, for more about Ivey House.)

Nearby Natural Areas

Collier-Seminole State Park (239-394-3397) is just down the road from Everglades City—not quite in Naples, yet not quite in the Everglades. The main feature of this park is the access to the Ten Thousand Islands. You can take a boat tour from the park concession or rent your own canoe here and paddle down the 13-mile-long Blackwater River canoe trail. A small museum houses documents, photos, and displays of Collier County history, including that of Barron Collier, a New York advertising executive who bought up more than a million acres of land in southwestern Florida in the 1920s. A good portion of that land is now preserved in the various natural areas of the county, although the Collier family still owns a lot of land. Hike or bike your way through a network of upland trails in another area of the park along US 41 that you have to reach by leaving the park entrance; it's best to ask the ranger on duty how to get there. Once there, you'll find a quiet mixed forest that can sometimes be flooded. To get to the park from Everglades City, go north on SR 29 to US 41 (Tamiami Trail). Turn left (west) and travel for about 12 miles to the park entrance.

Corkscrew Swamp Sanctuary (239-348-9151; *www.audubon.org/local/sanctuary/corkscrew*) is a prized Audubon Society nature preserve well known to Florida nature seekers and avid bird-watchers. A National Natural Landmark, the swamp preserves more than 11,000 acres of bald cypress stands and slash pine forest. Although the boardwalk through the swamp is only 2.5 miles long, you could spend all day making your way around the loop because of all the wildlife there is to see and the peaceful natural beauty you'll want to take in, including orchids, barred owls, alligators, red-shouldered hawks, and wood storks. (You can also opt for a shorter mile-long loop of the boardwalk.) A modern nature center with displays and a gift shop are at the entrance. Prices range from $4.00 to $10.00, and children six and under get in free. The sanctuary is open daily during daylight only, so hours vary with the seasons. To get there from Everglades City, travel north on SR 29 for about 40 miles to the town of Immokalee. At County Road 846 (Immokalee Road), turn left (south) and look for signs showing the way to Sanctuary Road.

Rookery Bay National Estuarine Research Reserve (239-417-6310; *www.rookerybay.org*) preserves the northernmost of the Ten Thousand Islands mangrove forests. Mostly a facility for scientists to study the estuary, the 110,000-acre reserve does allow some public visitation. The visitor center houses displays about the estuary and offers volunteer-led tours among the islands to look for birds, sea turtles, and other wildlife. The visitor center is open from Wednesday through Sunday from 9 a.m. to 4 p.m. Admission to the visitor center is $5.00 for adults and $3.00 for children six through twelve. To get there, take Tamiami Trail to the Naples area. Turn south at CR 951. About a mile down the road at the intersection of Tower Road, look for Rookery Bay on the right (west) side of the road.

Not far from there is Tigertail Beach, a Marco Island city beach. This is a good spot for bird-watching, as you might find reddish egrets, pelicans, plovers, and other shorebirds, especially in winter. A native plant garden attracts butterflies. Parking is $3.00. To get there, follow Tamiami Trail to CR 951, all the way south to Marco Island, and watch for signs leading the way.

Ten Thousand Islands National Wildlife Refuge (239-353-8442) is 35,000 acres of marsh and mangrove island wilderness. Although it borders Everglades National Park, Big Cypress National Preserve, and Collier-Seminole State Park, the only way to visit the refuge is by boat, as most of it is water. The refuge is a good place to see manatees, herons, and egrets. Sea turtles nest here in the summer.

Nearby Attractions

Everglades City preserves its history with a couple of small museums.

The Museum of the Everglades (239-695-0008) was a laundry during the days when the Tamiami Trail was being constructed, in the late 1920s. Today, it offers exhibits that preserve the area's history. The museum is open Tuesday through Saturday from 11 a.m. until 4 p.m. Donations are suggested.

In Chokoloskee near the end of SR 29, Smallwood Store Ole Indian Trading Post and Museum (239-695-2989) stands on stilts at the water's edge. A site on the National Register of Historic Places, the small structure was the main gathering spot in town about a hundred years ago when it was the only place to get supplies and mail in this remote agricultural area. The Smallwood Store is also the scene where Edgar Watson is believed to have been killed.

Wildlife

This is not the place where you're likely to see a lot of so-called typical Everglades wildlife, like alligators, which prefer freshwater habitats. But you might see Atlantic bottle-nosed dolphins, West Indian manatees, roseate spoonbills, ospreys, and bald eagles.

Look for . . .

While out in a boat, you could see some of the various shark species that live near Florida's shoreline. However, many sharks head toward deeper waters in the winter, which is the best time to visit the Everglades, so there's a chance you won't see these feared finned fish. The most common sharks in Florida include blacktip, blacknose, nurse, lemon, bonnethead, and Atlantic sharpnose sharks.

Bull, tiger, and hammerhead sharks are also common, and are considered more aggressive in regards to attacks on people, according to the Florida Fish and Wildlife Research Institute. In addition, tigers and hammerheads can grow to eighteen feet, supporting their menacing reputation. While Florida is the site of the majority of shark attacks in the United States—perhaps the world—scientists who study sharks say attacks are rare given the number of people entering sharks' territory, and fatal attacks are even more rare. Scientists say shark populations have been in decline and that more sharks are killed by people than people killed by sharks.

Habitats

Perhaps one of the most famous habitats in Florida, the Everglades actually contains eight distinct natural communities. On this side of the park, you'll wander in mostly marine, coastal marsh, and mangrove environments.

In fact, the Ten Thousand Islands area is one of the largest mangrove estuaries in North America, according to the U.S. Fish and Wildlife Service. Mangroves are important to birds, which nest in the trees because they grow near their food source, and to fish, which use the root systems as nurseries. There are three kinds of mangroves in Florida: red, black, and white. It's the red mangroves that appear to be walking on the water with prop roots that hold the trees above the surface. These salt-tolerant trees also harbor crabs and oysters.

Some of the marine areas of the park contain seagrass, which helps filter the water by creating oxygen and is a food source for manatees, turtles, and other marine creatures. Seagrass is hurt by pollution and by boats whose propellers tear up the grass. Boaters should avoid shallow seagrass areas if possible.

Most of the backcountry and the Wilderness Waterway is in what's known as the Marjory Stoneman Douglas Wilderness Area, designated in 1978. Named after the late activist and writer of *The Everglades: River of Grass*, this is the largest nationally designated wilderness area in Florida.

For information about the Everglades restoration, please see the Eastern Everglades (chapter 28).

Where to Stay

Campgrounds

The only camping in this side of Everglades National Park is primitive, on remote islands in the backcountry. Camping on these sites requires a permit, and there is a fee. There are three types of campsites in the backcountry: ground sites, beach sites, and chickees, which are covered, raised platforms over the water. "Chickee" is the word Seminole and Miccosukee tribes use for this open-air kind of shelter. Contact the park visitor center for more information.

Collier-Seminole State Park has 137 campsites for tents and RVs. The sites are near US 41, which can be noisy at night because of traffic. Contact Reserve-America for information and reservations.

Outdoor Resorts of America (239-695-2881) operates a campground in Chokoloskee for RVs only. With 283 sites, this campground boasts swimming pools, tennis courts, and a health club, and it also provides boat rentals.

Lodging

The western Everglades is a wilderness area, but you'll still find places to stay. The facilities in Everglades City are mostly small inns (like Ivey House: 239-695-3299; *www.iveyhouse.com*) and vacation rentals (like River Wilderness Waterfront Villas: 239-695-4499). The Rod and Gun Lodge (239-695-2101) is a longtime landmark that has received several U.S. presidents and has heard many years of fish stories.

For hotels and resorts, you'll have to go to Marco Island or Naples.

How to Get There

From western Florida, take I-75 south to the Naples area. Exit at CR 951 (Collier Blvd.), just before the Alligator Alley toll plaza. Take that road south for about 7 miles to US 41 (Tamiami Trail) and head southeast. At SR 29, turn right (south) and travel toward Everglades City. The national park Gulf Coast Visitor Center is about 3 miles down the road.

From eastern Florida, take the Florida Turnpike extension south to the Miami area. Exit at Tamiami Trail and travel west for about 49 miles to SR 29. Turn left (south) there, and follow the road 3 miles to the visitor center.

↦ ↦ ↦

Everglades National Park Gulf Coast Visitor Center
815 SW Copeland Ave.
Everglades City, Florida 34139
Phone: 239-695-3311
www.nps.gov/ever

The western Everglades is an entrance to the largest wilderness area in Florida. The backcountry marshes and mangrove islands on Florida's southern tip can be explored on a day-long boat trip or in more detail over the course of a week.

Nearby

Eastern Everglades (chapter 28), Big Cypress National Preserve (chapter 29)

31

Lower Keys

Situated as far south as you can go in the continental United States, if you count islands, the lower Keys are a unique part of Florida. The island chain's culture appears part Caribbean, part quaint fishing town, perhaps even part Hollywood. The Keys' history as outpost, backwater, and pirate hideaway has contributed to the culture as much as songs by Jimmy Buffet and the Beach Boys, real-life stories of finding Spanish treasure, and tourism advertisements.

Tourists are attracted to the Keys mainly for their climate and waters. With Florida Bay to the north, the Straits of Florida to the south, the Atlantic Ocean to the east, and the Gulf of Mexico to the west, the Keys are surrounded by a wealth of water. They are also protected by a barrier reef that contributes to their popularity, especially among divers and snorkelers in search of corals, pretty fish, or shipwrecks.

Once only accessible by boat—and later, by train—the Keys are bound together by US 1, the main road in and out of the Keys. This 126-mile stretch of road can take three hours or more to traverse, but many travelers believe it's worth it. (Of course, many people reach the Keys by sea or air.)

Many of them are lured by the beaches or waters of Bahia Honda State Park on Bahia Honda Key. Meaning "deep bay," Bahia Honda is named for its naturally deep channel, one of the few in the Keys. Visitors may come for the beach or boating but, hopefully, many travelers take the time to explore the state park further, whether along trails, in the water, or even along the main park road. While not a large park, its preserved nature and location in a quiet part of the island chain make it a great park to visit.

It's also a good point from which to plan a visit to nearby National Key Deer Wildlife Refuge on Big Pine Key. Another island of preserved nature, Big Pine Key nonetheless is a more urban environment in which the animals the refuge is known for must survive. Here, scenic points of interest lie on the same road as houses and shopping centers. The Key deer the refuge protects are more easily seen on homeowners' lawns and on the streets than they are near the

Figure 30. A Key deer roams one of the more natural areas of Big Pine Key.

mangrove trees whose leaves they like to eat. They are a one-of-a-kind species, however, so the visit is worthwhile.

Both of these places are beyond the 7-mile bridge that separates the lower Keys from the rest of the islands. Once you cross that expanse of blue-green water with brown pelicans and magnificent frigatebirds flying overhead, you are close to experiencing the more natural, less commercial, sometimes quiet part of the Keys.

What to Do There

Because the Keys are surrounded by water, a lot of activities focus on Florida Bay, the Florida Straits, or the Gulf of Mexico. But there are plenty of things for landlubbers to do, too.

Trail Tripping

Bahia Honda has two short nature trails. The interpretive Silver Palm Nature Trail is a loop that goes through a mangrove and along the beach. It's named for the silver palm tree, and there are more here than any other place in Florida. Pick up a trail guide to learn about points of interest along the way, such as land crabs and sea oats. Another trail—which isn't really much of a trail—is near the concession and leads to Old Bahia Honda Bridge, which gives you a great view of the park and surrounding waters.

In the refuge, a 0.7-mile nature trail cuts through pine flatwoods and gives you the chance to see Key deer and various birds and butterflies. Visitors can also walk around Blue Hole, where an observation deck over a borrow pit provides glimpses of wading birds, turtles, and alligators. Both trails are located on Key Deer Blvd. toward the north end of Big Pine Key.

Florida Keys Overseas Heritage Trail (305-451-3005) will span from Key Largo to Key West when it's completed. The multiuse trail will make use of the abandoned railroad that was once the only way to get through the Keys by land. Parts of the trail are already open to the public.

Paddling and Boating

With its shallow, typically calm waters, the Keys are an ideal place for paddling and boating. On nearly every island, it seems, you'll see a marina or a boat retailer, proving the popularity of water-related activities.

The Bahia Honda concession, Coral Reef Park Company (305-872-3210; *www.bahiahondapark.com*), rents ocean kayaks by the hour ($10.00 for a single or $18.00 for a tandem) or half-day ($34.00 for a single or $45.00 for a tandem).

The concession also oversees the park's marina, which includes two boat ramps and nineteen boat slips. Boaters can stay here overnight and have use of the bathhouse and sewage pump. Reservations are recommended.

There are many other marinas, boat ramps, and outfitters located throughout the Keys.

Guided Tours

The state park concession sells tickets for guided snorkeling tours to Looe Key, a patch of reef about 12 miles south of the shore. Looe Key is the site of the HMS *Looe* wreck and the focus of Looe Key National Marine Sanctuary. Snorkelers can expect to see different kinds of corals. Depending on the season, tours leave Bahia Honda two or three times a day. Snorkelers have an hour and a half in the water. Tickets are $27.95 for adults and $22.95 for children under eighteen. Snorkeling equipment rental is extra.

Looe Key is a popular snorkeling and diving spot, but Western Sambo Ecological Reserve may not be as crowded. The reserve is an important marine nursery in the Keys, and the reef portion harbors star and brain corals. Adventure Charters and Tours (888-817-0841; *www.keywestadventures.com*) in Key West takes snorkelers to Western Sambo by sailboat and provides equipment. The tour leaves three times daily and costs $30.00.

Reflections Nature Tours (305-872-4668; *www.floridakeyskayaktours.com*) on Big Pine Key leads a variety of daily kayak trips throughout the lower Keys. Sunset, full-moon, and custom tours are available. Tour prices vary.

Many other dive shops and tour guides in the rest of the Keys provide trips to the reef areas and Florida Bay backcountry.

Nearby Natural Areas

Florida Keys National Marine Sanctuary (305-743-2437; *www.fknms.nos.noaa. gov*) comprises 2,800 square nautical miles of the Keys. In fact, the islands of the Keys are surrounded by the sanctuary. This is a prime area for boating, fishing, swimming, snorkeling, and diving.

The sanctuary also harbors uninhabited islands and mangrove forests, some of which are part of National Key Deer Wildlife Refuge, Great White Heron National Wildlife Refuge, and Key West National Wildlife Refuge. These are mostly backcountry areas of the Keys that are accessible only by boat or seaplane. For more information about these refuges, contact the Key Deer office, which oversees all of them.

Dry Tortugas National Park (305-242-7700; *www.nps.gov/drto*) is isolated from the rest of the Keys because it is not connected by US 1. (Neither are the Marquesas Keys, in between Key West and the Dry Tortugas, connected.) Although Key West is the end of US 1, the actual island chain continues to the southwest. The Tortugas, 70 miles west of Key West, were named for the turtles that explorers saw there, and later became known as the Dry Tortugas because of the lack of fresh water. Fort Jefferson on Garden Key is the main visitor attraction and offers the only facilities on the islands. Bird-watchers visit throughout the year, but especially during April and May, when they can see pelagic birds. To get there, book a day trip on the *Yankee Freedom II* (800-634-0939; *www.yankeefreedom.com*) or with Sunny Days Catamarans (800-236-7937; *www.sunnydayskeywest.com*). Both tour boats leave at 8:00 a.m. and return to Key West by 5:00 or 5:30 p.m., and offer breakfast and lunch. The boats take about two hours each way. For a quicker trip, try a seaplane that leaves out of Key West International Airport, offering transportation to the Dry Tortugas in about thirty-five or forty minutes.

Curry Hammock State Park (305-664-4815) is a relatively undeveloped park near Mile Marker 56 in Marathon. The ocean side of the park (the main entrance) offers beach access, a playground, and restrooms, while the northern side of the park (across US 1 from the main entrance) offers little more than a photo blind. The significance of the park is its excellent location along the migration route for migrating hawks. Each fall—usually in October—the Florida Keys Birding and Wildlife Festival (*www.keysbirdingfestival.com*) holds an event here. Field trips, classes, and talks about birding and birds of prey are part of the festival program. Visitors who arrive during hawk migration may also happen upon university students performing studies on migrating birds of prey. An honor box requests $2.00 per vehicle.

Nearby Attractions

The lower Keys are generally less commercialized than the upper or middle Keys, and you'll find fewer attractions around Big Pine Key. However, less than an hour's drive southwest, you're in Key West.

Here, nature lovers will enjoy Key West Butterfly and Nature Conservatory (800-839-4647; *www.keywestbutterfly.com*), where 1,200 native and exotic butterflies flutter in an atrium garden with flowers, waterfalls, streams, and colorful songbirds. Visitors begin with a short film about butterflies, then proceed down the brick paths in the garden, where a butterfly might even land on them. Hours are 9:00 a.m. until 6:00 p.m.; tickets are sold until 4:30 p.m. Admission is $10.00 for adults, $8.50 for seniors and active military personnel, and $7.50 for children four through twelve. To get there, take US 1 into Key West. Turn left at Duval Street and follow it almost to the end of the road. The conservatory is one block north of the Southernmost Point marker.

Fort Zachary Taylor Historic State Park (305-292-6713) features a lighthouse and stronghold that date back to before the Civil War. Although Florida was part of the Confederacy, Union troops occupied the fort for the duration of the war. The fort was used during the Spanish-American War as well. Park staff lead tours of the fort every day at noon and 2 p.m., and Civil War reenactors turn out for the annual Heritage Festival every January. Some visitors come just to swim or snorkel along the beach, however. Fort Zachary Taylor is located at the end of Southard Street on Truman Annex in Key West.

The Audubon House and Tropical Gardens (877-281-2473; *www.audubon house.com*) was the home of a ship captain during the nineteenth century. Many of naturalist John James Audubon's paintings are housed here to commemorate his trip to the Florida Keys in 1832. Visitors can tour the one-acre garden and buy Audubon art in the gift shop. Hours are 9:30 a.m. until 5:00

p.m. Admission is $9.00 for adults and $5.00 for children. Audubon House is located south of the intersection of Greene and Whitehead Streets. To get there, take US 1 to the end (Mile Marker 0) and continue on Whitehead Street to the house.

Just down the street from the Audubon House is the Ernest Hemingway Home (305-294-1136; *www.hemingwayhome.com*), which attracts thousands of fans of the late adventure author. Visitors can tour the house and see where he wrote *A Farewell to Arms* and where he gathered character ideas for *To Have and Have Not*. Many visitors are charmed by the sixty or so cats that are free to roam the property, descendants of Hemingway's pets. Hours are 9 a.m. to 5 p.m. Admission is $10.00 for adults and $6.00 for children five years and older. The Hemingway house is located at 907 Whitehead Street.

There are many other attractions and points of interest in Key West, including just the streets themselves, which reveal the local color.

Wildlife

The lower Keys islands' unique location lends itself to unique wildlife.

In the Keys' marine areas, dolphins, whales, and sea turtles make use of the warm waters. Driving along US 1 through the Keys, you'll see marine mammal research facilities and even a turtle hospital. Pygmy sperm whales are often rescued in the Keys.

Hawk migration peaks in October, when these birds of prey usually arrive in the Keys on their way to Central or South America for the winter. (Of course, some of them stay in Florida.) Peregrine falcons, sharp-shinned hawks, and merlins are among the birds counted flying through.

Another bird of interest in the Florida Keys is the endangered white-crowned pigeon. Native to the Caribbean islands and Florida Keys, the pigeon eats the fruit of tropical hardwood trees like poisonwood and strangler figs. The bird lives in the Keys from April to September.

Another endangered species in the Keys is the Miami blue butterfly, found exclusively at Bahia Honda. The Miami blue once ranged throughout southern Florida but declined in numbers because of habitat loss and use of pesticides against mosquitoes and other insects. For a few years, butterfly enthusiasts knew the small, bright blue butterfly lived here in extremely small numbers (currently about twenty to fifty) but attempted to keep the location secret for fear of the butterfly's extinction. Then the news of their location broke in a local publication. The attention may have prompted the Florida Fish and Wildlife Conservation Commission to grant the Miami blue emergency endangered status in 2002, bypassing the agency's usual lengthy process. Now a captive breeding program may help the population rebound. If you happen to see the Miami blue while visiting Bahia Honda, be careful to watch from a distance, as this butterfly is now protected by law. There are many other interesting butterflies throughout the Keys, such as the atala and endangered Schaus' swallowtail butterfly.

Look for . . .

Although they're about the size of a large dog (twenty-four to thirty-two inches high and forty-five to eighty pounds in weight), Key deer are a subspecies of the white-tailed deer common throughout North America. They are thought to have once lived from Duck Key to Key West, but now live in scattered areas from the Johnson Keys to Sugarloaf Key. Big Pine Key and No Name Key are the likeliest places to find them. The best time to see the deer is just before sunset, when they come out to forage on lawns and trees. Look for them along roads and on trails, particularly toward the northern ends of the islands.

Key deer, which number about 700 or 800, are endangered because of previous overhunting and habitat loss. Although the refuge provides the deer with protection from hunting and further habitat loss, roadkill is still a serious problem because of the area's urban environment, and is the main cause of premature death in Key deer, at about 50–70 percent of all deaths. Refuge literature cites hurricanes, stomach worms, and brain abscesses as other threats to the deer.

Visitors are warned not to feed Key deer. Some people have done that from their vehicles, and now the deer approach cars, adding to the roadkill problem. Federal and state laws against feeding Key deer and other wildlife are in effect to protect them.

Habitats

National Key Deer Wildlife Refuge protects mangrove forests, hardwood hammocks, and pine rocklands on Big Pine Key and No Name Key. The rocklands typify the rocky nature of the Keys, and many people visiting the Keys for the first time may be surprised by the lack of beaches they saw in travel brochures. Most of the Keys' shoreline is lined by mangrove trees, not beaches.

Bahia Honda has been recognized as having one of the best beaches in the Keys, if not Florida. And it truly is one of the few natural large beaches in the Keys. Bahia Honda also protects tropical hardwood hammock habitat.

Although several tropical plants can grow in the Keys and southern Florida, the state isn't tropical, despite the common misconception. ("Come visit our tropical beach!") With the Florida Keys being just 70 to 90 miles north of the Tropic of Cancer, which marks the tropical zone, southern and central Florida are in a subtropical area. This in-between place makes for an interesting mix of temperate and tropical habitats.

This complex area is also key to the development of the Florida reef system. The reef tract begins south of Miami and follows the Keys toward the Gulf of Mexico. The reef is the largest barrier coral reef in North America and supports a variety of marine life. It also supports the Keys economy, as commercial and sport fishing, diving, and tourism all depend on the reef. The National Oceanic and Atmospheric Administration (NOAA) has reported that the 82,000 Keys residents depend on the reef for 8,000 jobs and $106 million in income, and that the reef's economic value (if you could place one) is $7.6 billion.

The value of the reef is more than what it can provide for people, however. The uniqueness of having this expansive coral reef is a treasure. Yet as we recognize its importance, we recognize that the Florida reef, like reefs around the world, is in decline. Divers and snorkelers in the Keys might notice areas of dead coral. Scientists continue to study coral reefs to discover what is causing them to die and become unhealthy. Some factors scientists have uncovered include:

• poor water quality as a result of sewage dumped from boats and coastal cities, fertilizer runoff from coastal lawns, and gas and oil spills—causing algae to grow in the corals;

• direct damage to coral from divers, fishermen, boaters, and storms;

• overfishing;

• reduced freshwater flow from Florida Bay (likely the result of reduced freshwater flow through the Everglades), which has led to plankton blooms and fish die-off, according to NOAA;

• coral-killing diseases whose cause still isn't fully known; some scientists believe dust carried on the wind from Africa, which settles on Caribbean-area coral and deposits a fungus, is believed to affect sea fans especially hard, according to the U.S. Geological Survey;

• rise in sea levels (thought to be caused by an increase in carbon dioxide in the environment, prompting global warming), which takes sunlight farther away from corals.

• bleaching, which the National Aeronautic and Space Administration (NASA) says is a direct result of greenhouse gas emissions that warm the surface of the ocean.

The good news is that people are becoming more and more aware of the ocean as an ecosystem that needs to be protected for the overall health of the Earth.

Where to Stay

Campgrounds

Bahia Honda offers excellent camping with eighty campsites. The Sandspur Campground faces the ocean and provides beautiful beach views and privacy from your campground neighbors. You'll also be able to hear the gentle surf all night long. (Ask for campsites 64–72 for sites right across from the water.) The Buttonwood Campground is located on the western/northern side of the island and is usually populated more by RVs on the open, paved sites. The nearby Bayside Campground is a small area (eight campsites) with no electricity. For information and reservations, contact ReserveAmerica.

Big Pine Key Fishing Lodge (305-872-3868) offers RV and tent sites, and cabins.

Lodging

Bahia Honda rents out three duplex cabins (for a total of six units) that are more like vacation homes, on stilts facing the bay. Each side of the modern duplex sleeps six people and includes all linens and utensils. Cabins are popular and can be booked nearly a year in advance. Contact ReserveAmerica for reservations.

The Big Pine Motel (888-872-9191; *www.bigpinekeymotel.com*) offers boat parking and a pool.

The next closest place to stay is Marathon, which requires going back over the 7-mile bridge. There, you'll find independently run motels and efficiencies (like Hidden Harbor Motel: 800-362-3495; *www.hiddenharbormotel.com*) and chain hotels (like Best Western Marathon Resort: 877-743-9009; *www.marathonsbest.com*).

About a thirty- to forty-minute drive from Big Pine Key is Key West, where there are many more lodging options, including several houses that have been converted into inns (like Banyan Resort: 800-985-3993; *www.banyanresort.com*), chain hotels (like Hilton Key West Resort: 877-317-4600), and vacation home rentals (like Key West Hideaways: 888-822-5840; *www.keywesthideaways.com*).

How to Get There

Take the Florida Turnpike extension to its end near Homestead and continue on US 1 south through the chain of islands in the Keys. Bahia Honda State Park is located near Mile Marker 37; watch for signs along US 1. The Key Deer refuge is located on Big Pine Key near Mile Marker 30. The refuge headquarters office is located in a shopping center on Key Deer Blvd. (County Road 940). Trails and observation areas are located on or near this road in a residential area.

➦ ➦ ➦

Bahia Honda State Park
36850 Overseas Hwy.
Big Pine Key, Florida 33043
Phone: 305-872-2353
Admission is $5.00 per vehicle.

National Key Deer Wildlife Refuge
28950 Watson Blvd.
Big Pine Key, Florida 33043-0510
Phone: 305-872-0774
nationalkeydeer.fws.gov
Refuge facilities are open during daylight hours. There is no entrance fee.

The lower Keys are a more natural, less commercial part of the island chain. Here, endangered species found nowhere else live among the residents, and the world's third-largest coral reef system attracts a variety of marine life—not to mention divers, snorkelers, and fishermen.

Appendix 1. Resources

Natural Areas

National Park Service, Southeast Region
100 Alabama Street SW
1924 Building
Atlanta, Georgia 30303
Phone: 404-562-3100
www.nps.gov

National Forests in Florida
325 John Knox Road, Suite F-100
Tallahassee, Florida 32303
Phone: 850-523-8500
www.southernregion.fs.fed.us/florida/

National Wildlife Refuges, Southeast Region
1875 Century Blvd., Suite 400
Atlanta, Georgia 30345
Phone: 404-679-4000
southeast.fws.gov/maps/fl.html

Florida State Parks
3900 Commonwealth Blvd., MS 535
Tallahassee, Florida 32399
Phone: 850-245-2157
www.floridastateparks.org

Florida Division of Forestry
3125 Conner Blvd.
Tallahassee, Florida 32399-1650

Phone: 850-488-4274
www.fl-dof.com

State Wildlife Management Areas (WMAs)
Florida Fish and Wildlife Conservation Commission (FWC)
620 S. Meridian Street
Tallahassee, Florida 32399-1600
Phone: 850-488-4676
www.wildflorida.org/nbr

Florida Office of Greenways and Trails
Florida Department of Environmental Protection
3900 Commonwealth Blvd., MS 795
Tallahassee, Florida 32399-3000
Phone: 850-245-2052

Northwest Florida Water Management District
81 Water Management Drive
Havana, Florida 32333-4712
Phone: 850-539-5999
www.state.fl.us/nwfwmd
Ask about guide *Exploring District Lands*

Suwannee River Water Management District
9225 County Road 49
Live Oak, Florida 32060
Phone: 386-362-1001
www.srwmd.state.fl.us
Ask about the recreation guide, or publications about boat ramps and canoe
    launches, or springs of the Suwannee River.

St. Johns River Water Management District
4049 Reid Street
Palatka, Florida 32177
Phone: 386-329-4500
sjr.state.fl.us
Ask about *Recreation Guide to District Lands*

South Florida Water Management District
3301 Gun Club Road
West Palm Beach, Florida 33406
Phone: 561-686-8800
www.sfwmd.gov
Ask about *Guide to the Kissimmee Waterway, Lake Okeechobee Recreation
    Guide,* or *Public Use Guide*

Southwest Florida Water Management District
2379 Broad Street
Brooksville, Florida 34604-6899
Phone: 352-796-7211
www.swfwmd.state.fl.us
Ask about *Recreation on District Lands*

The Nature Conservancy Florida Chapter
222 S. Westmonte Drive, Suite 300
Altamonte Springs, Florida 32714
Phone: 407-682-3664
www.nature.org

Florida Trail Association
5415 SW 13 Street
Gainesville, Florida 32608
Phone: 877-HIKE-FLA
www.florida-trail.org

Rails-to-Trails Conservancy
2545 Blairstone Pines Drive
Tallahassee, Florida 32301
Phone: 850-942-2379
www.railtrails.org

Also, many counties in Florida manage ecologically significant parks. For more information on them, try a Web search for "(name of county) parks."

Camping

ReserveAmerica
800-326-3521
www.reserveamerica.com

Kampgrounds of America
PO Box 30558
Billings, Montana 59114
406-248-7444
www.koa.com/where/fl

Visitor Information

Tourism development councils, convention and visitor bureaus, and chambers of commerce provide information about visiting their respective areas. If you are planning a visit to a specific part of Florida, contact these visitor services for brochures, tips, and even discounts.

Alachua County Visitors and Convention Bureau, 352-374-5231

Amelia Island Tourist Development Council, 904-277-0717

Baker County Tourist Development Commission, 904-259-1999

Bradenton Area Convention and Visitors Bureau, 941-722-3244

Bradford County Chamber of Commerce, 904-964-5278

Central Florida Visitors and Convention Bureau, 863-298-7565

Charlotte Harbor and The Gulf Islands Visitor's Bureau, 941-743-1900

Citrus County Tourist Development Council, 352-527-5223

Clay County Tourist Development Council, 904-264-2651

Cocoa Beach Area Chamber of Commerce/Convention and Visitors Bureau, 321-454-2022

Columbia County Tourist Development Council, 904-758-1312

Daytona Beach Area CVB/Volusia County, 386-255-0415

Emerald Coast CVB/Okaloosa County Tourist Development Council, 850-651-7131

Flagler County Palm Coast Chamber of Commerce, 386-437-0106

Greater Fort Lauderdale Convention and Visitors Bureau, 954-765-4466

Greater Miami Convention and Visitors Bureau, 305-539-3040

Gulf County Tourist Development Commission, 850-229-7800

Hamilton County Tourism Development Council, 386-792-6828

Hernando County Tourist Development Council, 352-540-4323

Highlands County Convention and Visitors Bureau, 863-385-8448

Indian River County Chamber of Commerce Tourism Division,   772-567-3491

Jackson County Tourist Development Commission, 850-482-8061

Jacksonville and The Beaches Convention and Visitors Bureau, 904-798-9111

Kissimmee/St. Cloud Convention and Visitors Bureau, 407-847-5000

Lake County Convention and Visitors Bureau, 352-429-3673

Lee County Visitor and Convention Bureau, 239-338-3500

Leon County Tourist Development Council, 850-488-3990

Madison County Tourist Development Council, 850-973-2788

Martin County Tourist Development Council, 772-288-5434

Melbourne-Palm Bay Area Chamber of Commerce, 321-724-5400

Mexico Beach Community Development Council, Inc., 850-648-8196

Monroe County Tourist Development Council, 305-296-1552

Naples, Marco Island, Everglades CVB, 239-403-2384

Okeechobee County Tourist Development Council, 863-763-3959

Orlando/Orange County Convention and Visitors Bureau, Inc., 407-363-5872

Palm Beach County Convention and Visitors Bureau, 561-233-3000

Panama City Beach Convention and Visitors Bureau, Inc., 850-234-0607

Pasco County Tourism Development Council, 727-847-8990

Pensacola Bay Area Convention and Visitors Information Center, 850-434-1234

Putnam County Chamber of Commerce, 386-328-1503
Santa Rosa County Tourist Development Council, 850-939-2691
Sarasota Convention and Visitors Bureau, 941-955-0991
Seminole County Convention and Visitors Bureau, 407-665-2900
South Walton Tourist Development Council, 850-267-1216
Space Coast Office of Tourism/Brevard County TDC, 321-637-5483
St. Johns County Visitors and Convention Bureau, 904-829-1711
St. Johns River Country Visitors Bureau, 386-734-0575
St. Lucie County Tourist Development Council, 772-462-1535
St. Petersburg/Clearwater Area Convention and Visitors Bureau, 727-464-7200
Suwannee County Tourist Development Council, 386-362-3071
Tampa Bay Convention and Visitors Bureau, 813-223-1111
Taylor County Chamber of Commerce, 850-584-5366
Wakulla County Tourist Development Council, 850-984-3966

Nature Festivals

Spring

Florida's First Coast Birding and Nature Fest (800-653-2489;
   www.visitoldcity.com/events), in St. Augustine
Pelican Island Wildlife Festival (772-562-3909; *www.nbbd.com/npr/pips/*), in
   Sebastian
Suwannee River NatureFest (352-493-6736; *www.originalflorida.com*), various
   locations
Suwannee River Valley Birding Festival (877-635-3655), in White Springs
Wakulla Wildlife Festival (850-561-7278; *www.wakullacounty.org*), various lo-
   cations
Welcome Back Songbirds Festival (352-754-6722;
   www.floridaconservation.org), in Brooksville

Fall

Florida Birding Festival (727-464-7217; *www.pcef.org*), in St. Petersburg
Florida Black Bear Festival (407-323-1298; *www.flblackbearfestival.org*), in
   Umatilla
Florida Keys Birding and Wildlife Festival (305-743-7124;
   www.keysbirdingfestival.com), in Marathon
Panhandle Birding and Wildflower Festival (850-229-9464;
   www.birdfestival.org), in Port St. Joe
Space Coast Birding and Wildlife Festival (321-268-5224; *www.nbbd.com/fly*),
   in Titusville

Winter

Big "O" Birding Festival (863-946-0300; *www.bigobirdingfestival.com*), various locations
Charlotte Harbor Nature Festival (239-995-1777;
   www.charlotteharbornep.org), Port Charlotte
Orlando Wetlands Park Festival (407-568-1706), in Christmas

Books

50 Hikes in Central Florida by Sandra Friend. Countryman Press, 2002.
50 Hikes in North Florida by Sandra Friend. Countryman Press, 2003.
50 Hikes in South Florida by Sandra Friend. Countryman Press, 2003.
A Hiker's Guide to the Sunshine State by Sandra Friend. University Press of
   Florida, 2005.
A Paddler's Guide to Everglades National Park by Johnny Molloy. University
   Press of Florida, 2000.
A Paddler's Guide to the Sunshine State by Sandy Huff. University Press of
   Florida, 2001.
Diving and Snorkeling Florida Keys by William Harrigan. Lonely Planet, 2001.
Florida Camping by Marilyn Moore. Avalon Travel Publishing, 2003.
Mountain Bike: Florida: A Guide to the Classic Trails by Steve Jones and
   Dennis Coello. Menasha Ridge Press, 1997.
National Audubon Society Field Guide to Florida by Peter Alden. Knopf, 1998.
Sea Kayaking in Florida by David Gluckman. Pineapple Press, 1998.
The Best in Tent Camping Florida by Johnny Molloy. Menasha Ridge Press,
   2000.
The Everglades: River of Grass by Marjory Stoneman Douglas. Pineapple Press,
   1997.
The Florida Atlas and Gazetteer. DeLorme Publishing Company, 2001.
The Springs of Florida by Doug Stamm. Pineapple Press, 1994.
The Wild Heart of Florida: Florida Writers on Florida's Wildlands edited by Jeff
   Ripple and Susan Cerulean. University Press of Florida, 1999.

Emergencies

To report a wildlife violation or suspicious activity concerning wildlife, call toll-free 888-404-3922, or *FWC or #FWC on a cell phone.

To report an injured or dead manatee or sea turtle, call toll-free 888-404-FWCC (3922).

Appendix 2. Common Florida Wildlife

Florida's location between the tropics and the temperate zone makes for interesting wildlife watching. Subtropical southern Florida is the only place in the world where crocodiles and alligators mix, for example. Geography also contributes to bird-watching. Thousands of northern birds migrate to or through Florida every fall as they look for warmer winter homes. Migrating raptors stop along the eastern coast down through the Florida Keys on their way to Central America or South America, with October being the peak time for hawk watching in the Keys. Southern birds like swallow-tailed kites do the same in reverse, flying to Florida for the summer.

Wildlife watching is an important part of Florida's economy that people seem to have begun recognizing just within the past decade. The Florida Fish and Wildlife Conservation Commission (FWC) funded a research report noting that in 2001 Florida attracted more out-of-state wildlife watchers than any other state. Residents and visitors spent $930 million that year on wildlife-watching (everything from bird seed for back yards to travel expenses like food, lodging, and entrance fees)—five times the amount of money collected on the Florida Turnpike, the report found. The FWC performed a study in 2000 that showed wildlife-related activities generated $5.5 billion in retail sales, resulting in a $7.8 billion overall economic impact.

Wildlife-Watching Tips

When traveling through Florida's natural areas, it's helpful to have a field guide handy so you can identify the animals and plants you see. Some field guides include a checklist (or "life list") so you can record which species you have identified. If you are interested in maintaining a list of birds, consider joining the Wings Over Florida program run by the FWC, which awards certificates of increasing levels to bird-watchers based on how many species they've identified. For more information, contact the Wings Over Florida (*www.wildflorida. org/wof*) headquarters at 3900 Drane Field Road, Lakeland, FL 33811-1299.

Some species are more easily identified by sound than by sight because of their nocturnal or reclusive nature. For this reason, wildlife-watchers may consider investing in software or audio recordings to learn what various wildlife species sound like. Examples include the audio guides published by Peterson Field Guides.

The Great Florida Birding Trail (850-922-0664; *www.floridabirding trail.com*), managed by the FWC, is a good resource for finding bird-watching spots. (Trail sites are often good places to see other wildlife, too.) The trail is laid out to recognize existing natural areas that are good for bird-watching, organized by geographical location and species. Currently, the eastern, western, and northwestern portions of the trail have been marked, while the southern portion has yet to be developed. Contact the Great Florida Birding Trail office or Web site for guides to the developed portions of the trail.

The Web site includes a printable page of bird-watcher calling cards, which bird-watchers and/or nature travelers can leave at the businesses they patronize while traveling. The idea behind the calling cards is to help the business community recognize that people are visiting the area because of the local natural lands, with the hope they will further protect and preserve them if only because it's good business.

Other Tips:

Be quiet and still. Many times, people don't see wildlife because they are making too much noise or walking too quickly. Try this: find a quiet spot and stand silently for five minutes. Listen to the sounds around you. See whether you can catch movement out of the corners of your eyes. Look in the dirt for tracks or scat. Examine trees for nests or dens. Make a mental note of all that you notice. Then go to another spot to observe.

Watch at the right time. Most wildlife are active just after sunrise and just before sunset. Nocturnal animals, of course, are more active at night. That's not to say you won't see any wildlife at noon, however. But the more interesting discoveries will happen when animals are most active.

Keep your distance. Most wildlife have a natural fear of people and will flee if you get too close. That's why binoculars are a handy tool for wildlife watchers. Also, studies have shown that some species become stressed in the presence of people. For some species, it's against federal or state laws to approach or harass animals, such as manatees and alligators.

Don't feed wildlife. There are many reasons for this:

• Animals that are fed can forgo their natural diet in favor of handouts, and that can make them malnourished because the food being offered by humans is not the food they need and normally eat.

• Animals that become used to people feeding them lose their natural fear of people. This can make animals aggressive, which can be dangerous when it comes to predators like alligators. Neighborhood waterfowl have been known to attack children if they are used to children feeding them. It can also simply be annoying when, for example, a sandhill crane destroys property to get attention and ask for its regular snack. In many cases, wildlife officials have no choice but to destroy aggressive wildlife. Relocation works for some animals, but not all of them.

• Losing fear of humans also makes animals easy targets for people who want to harm wildlife, because they have become too trusting.

• Finally, federal and state laws are in effect against feeding several species, with fines and jail time as consequences.

Wildlife are able to find food on their own, so, lastly, they just don't need handouts.

Common Species

The following is a list of only common or well-known Florida species; it's not exhaustive. If a species has a designation on the federal endangered species list, it's noted. If a species isn't on the federal list but is on a separate list kept by the state of Florida, then that is noted. (In many cases, the state's designation differs from the federal list.)

Birds

Bird-watching is so popular because birds are typically the easiest wildlife to see. The variety and number of bird species also make bird-watching interesting. There are an estimated 480 species of birds in Florida.

Birds of Prey
American kestrel (threatened—Florida)
Bald eagle (threatened—U.S.)
Cooper's hawk
Crested caracara (threatened—U.S.)
Osprey
Peregrine falcon (endangered—Florida)
Red-shouldered hawk
Red-tailed hawk
Snail/Everglades kite (endangered—U.S.)
Swallow-tailed kite
Barn owl
Barred owl

Burrowing owl (species of special concern—Florida)
Great horned owl
Screech owl
Black vulture
Turkey vulture

Water-Oriented Birds

American bittern
Black-crowned night heron
Common egret
Great blue heron
Great egret
Great white heron
Green-backed heron
Least bittern
Little blue heron (species of special concern—Florida)
Reddish egret (species of special concern—Florida)
Snowy egret (species of special concern—Florida)
Tricolored heron (species of special concern—Florida)
Yellow-crowned night heron
Glossy ibis
Roseate spoonbill (species of special concern—Florida)
White ibis (species of special concern—Florida)
Wood stork (endangered—U.S.)
American oystercatcher (species of special concern—Florida)
Black-necked stilt
Caspian tern
Dunlin
Greater yellowlegs
Herring gull
Killdeer
Laughing gull
Least sandpiper
Lesser yellowlegs
Ring-billed gull
Royal tern
Ruddy turnstone
Sandwich tern
Semipalmated plover
Snowy plover (threatened—Florida)
Willet
Wilson's plover
Sandhill crane (threatened—Florida)

American coot
Clapper rail
Common moorhen
Limpkin (species of special concern—Florida)
Purple gallinule
Blue-winged teal
Green-winged teal
Mallard
Mottled duck
Pied-billed grebe
Ring-necked duck
Wood duck
Anhinga
Brown pelican (species of special concern—Florida)
Double-crested cormorant
Magnificent frigatebird
White pelican
Belted kingfisher

Woods-Oriented Birds

Ruby-throated hummingbird
Chuck-will's-widow
Downy woodpecker
Hairy woodpecker
Northern flicker
Pileated woodpecker
Red-bellied woodpecker
Red-cockaded woodpecker (endangered—U.S.)
Red-headed woodpecker
American crow
American robin
Barn swallow
Black-whiskered vireo
Blue jay
Blue-gray gnatcatcher
Boat-tailed grackle
Brown thrasher
Brown-headed nuthatch
Carolina chickadee
Carolina wren
Common grackle
Common yellowthroat
Eastern meadowlark

Eastern phoebe
Eastern towhee
European starling
Fish crow
Florida scrub jay (threatened—U.S.)
Gray catbird
House sparrow
Loggerhead shrike
Northern cardinal
Northern mockingbird (state bird of Florida)
Painted bunting
Palm warbler
Pine warbler
Prairie warbler
Purple martin
Red-winged blackbird
Spot-breasted oriole
Summer tanager
Swamp sparrow
Tree swallow
Tufted titmouse
White-eyed vireo
Yellow-rumped warbler
Yellow-throated warbler
Common ground dove
Eurasian collared dove
Mourning dove
Northern bobwhite
Wild turkey

Reptiles and Amphibians

Note: * designates venomous species
American alligator (species of special concern—Florida)
American crocodile (endangered—U.S.)
Gopher tortoise (species of special concern—Florida)
Broadhead skink
Brown anole
Eastern glass lizard
Florida scrub lizard
Green anole
Southeastern five-lined skink
Chicken turtle

Common cooter
Florida redbelly turtle
Florida softshell turtle
Red-eared slider
River cooter
Snapping turtle (species of special concern—Florida)
Kemp's ridley turtle (endangered—U.S.)
Green turtle (endangered—U.S.)
Leatherback turtle (endangered—U.S.)
Loggerhead turtle (threatened—U.S.)
Bullfrog
Cuban treefrog
Giant toad
Green treefrog
Pig frog
Pine woods treefrog
Squirrel treefrog
Southern cricket frog
Southern leopard frog
Black racer
*Canebrake rattlesnake
*Copperhead
Corn snake (species of special concern—Florida)
*Cottonmouth/water moccasin
*Eastern coral snake
*Eastern diamondback rattlesnake
Eastern ribbon snake
Indigo snake (threatened—U.S.)
Pine snake (species of special concern—Florida)
*Pygmy rattlesnake
Rat snake
Ring-necked snake
Rough green snake

Mammals

Florida panther (endangered—U.S.)
Bobcat
Florida black bear (threatened—Florida)
Common gray fox
Coyote
Red wolf (endangered—U.S.)
Key deer (endangered—U.S.)

White-tailed deer
Common raccoon
Opossum
Marsh rabbit
Eastern cottontail
Big Cypress fox squirrel (threatened—Florida)
Eastern fox squirrel
Eastern gray squirrel
Sherman's fox squirrel (species of special concern—Florida)
Southern flying squirrel
Everglades mink (threatened—Florida)
Northern river otter
Florida mouse (species of special concern—Florida)
Nine-banded armadillo
Brazilian free-tailed bat
Seminole bat
Southeastern myotis bat
Eastern red bat
West Indian manatee (endangered—U.S.)
Atlantic spotted dolphin
Bottle-nosed dolphin
Humpback whale (endangered—U.S.)
Northern right whale (endangered—U.S.)
Pygmy sperm whale
Risso's dolphin
Striped dolphin

Wildlife Calendar

When do alligators mate? When do migrating hawks appear in Florida? What can you do in your back yard to help wildlife? Check this list, courtesy of the FWC, for wildlife happenings. You may consider using this wildlife calendar to plan trips. For example, if you want to see specific species, you can find out when and where they are likely to be.

January

This is a great time to watch overwintering ducks and geese in wetlands.
    Ospreys, hawks, owls, sandhill cranes, great blue herons, and roseate spoonbills begin breeding and nesting.
    Carolina yellow jessamine blooms in northern and central Florida woods.
    Observe hawks and kestrels along highways.

Manatees congregate around springs, seeking the warmest water.

Otters, bobcats, and foxes breed in January and February.

Clouds of tree swallows roost at sunset over large marsh systems.

February

Purple martin scouts look over northern Florida nesting sites. Make sure houses are up!

Look for trilliums and dogtooth violets in rich panhandle ravines.

Alligator snapping turtles begin mating, followed by nesting throughout spring.

Clean and repair eastern bluebird nest boxes.

Greater sandhill cranes migrate from Florida northward to Michigan and Wisconsin.

Bald cypress trees leaf out in Big Cypress Swamp.

Ospreys return and begin nesting at Paynes Prairie.

Wood storks are nesting in Corkscrew Swamp.

Watch for manatees in spring runs.

Screech owls begin nesting in central Florida.

Opossums and armadillos give birth this month.

March

Carolina wrens begin nesting. Hang a gourd or open basket under your eaves.

Migrating birds, in full breeding plumage, arrive in waves each week.

Swallow-tailed kites return to southern Florida wetlands.

Male frogs and toads move to ponds, streams, or ditches to breed during rainy nights.

Lake Kissimmee shellcrackers bed on the full moon.

Look for red foxes emerging from remote beaches.

First mangrove cuckoos return to the Keys.

Listen for newly returned chuck-will's-widows calling after sunset.

Bromeliads start to flower in southern Florida swamps.

Great blue herons may be seen on their nests.

Largemouth bass spawn throughout central Florida.

Last chance to see congregations of manatees until next winter.

April

Neotropical migratory birds, including swallow-tailed kites and purple gallinules, return.

Migrant warblers concentrate on coasts after cold fronts.

Gray bats arrive mid-month from Alabama to summer caves.

Courtship for most snakes occurs in April.

Adult crocodiles dig nest sites; male alligators bellow in the marshes.

Beginning of sea turtle nesting season on Florida's beaches.

Alligator snapping turtles commence laying eggs.

Pine barrens tree frogs start calling.

Purple gallinules arrive from Latin America to nest.

Plant extra parsley for black swallowtail butterfly larvae to forage.

Set out coral honeysuckle, trumpet creeper, coral bean, red buckeye (northern Florida), or geiger tree (southern Florida) to nourish hummingbirds all spring and summer.

Most wild turkey hens are nesting.

Pitcher plant bogs in the panhandle are in full bloom.

Larval mole salamanders mature and leave ponds.

May

Tropical birds arrive in Dry Tortugas.

The first of the month is the height of crocodile nesting in the Keys.

Loggerhead sea turtles lay eggs.

Flathead catfish congregate below Jim Woodruff Dam and the Apalachicola River.

Courting male alligators are bellowing in wetlands.

Peak flight period for Schaus' swallowtail butterfly in Keys.

Last cedar waxwings and goldfinches head north.

Painted buntings nest through summer in northeastern Florida.

White swamp lilies dot wet prairies and sloughs in the Everglades.

Least terns and snowy plovers nest on beaches and sandy flats.

Celebrate International Migratory Bird Day.

June

Gopher tortoises are breeding, as are manatees.

Laughing gulls and black skimmers hatch young on beaches.

Most animals—including alligators, southern flying squirrels, black-necked stilts, and red-cockaded woodpeckers—are nesting.

Peak month for wildfires, which rejuvenate many Florida plant communities.

Red bats and Seminole bats are born.

Blooming tarflowers in flatwoods signal the beginning of summer.

Black-necked stilts are nesting in southern Florida.

Cicadas emerge and begin the song of summer.

Sea turtles crawl ashore to lay eggs on dark nights.

Male alligators bellow during courtship rituals.

July

Scrub morning glory and butterfly weed bloom in July.

Sea oats are flowering on Atlantic beaches.

Shorebird migration starts mid-July and peaks mid-August.

Purple martins and tree swallows begin to gather to migrate south for the winter.

Buck deer in new velvet can occasionally be spotted.

Swallow-tailed kites begin gathering in communal night roosts before migrating.

In southern Florida, young crocodiles are hatching, and magnificent frigatebirds may be seen flying overhead.

Mulch your garden to conserve water, but leave patches of soil exposed for dusting by birds.

August

Alligators hatch from mid-August to mid-September.

Yellow warbler migration begins.

Black bear cubs begin to wean from their mothers.

Purple martins and tree swallows begin staging in large flocks, preparing to migrate.

Young sea turtles hatch and flee to the sea during summer months.

First flocks of blue- and green-winged teal arrive to winter on Florida wetlands and lakes.

September

Warblers migrate southward.

In late September, gray bats migrate to northern Alabama for winter hibernation.

Manatees begin to concentrate in rivers and bays and near power plants.

First signs of leaves changing color; blazing star, rabbit tobacco, and blue curls abloom.

Peak of hurricane season: watch for unusual bird sightings following tropical storms.

Bald eagles return to nest sites and begin courtship.

Blue crabs migrate to deeper water for the winter.

Hawk migration begins at St. Joseph Peninsula in Gulf County.

Peak blooming period for water-spider orchids in central Florida.

October

Early October is peak migration for warblers.
    Monarch butterflies migrate along the Gulf coast.
    Turkey vultures return mid-month to Miami courthouse.
    Migratory sandhill cranes arrive, and chimney swifts leave.
    Indigo snakes breed in gopher tortoise burrows.
    Black bears are on the move, gathering food.
    Gray foxes begin mating this month.

November

Sandhill cranes and bald eagles arrive to winter.
    Watch for northern harriers gliding low over the marshes.
    Peak month for roadkills of black bears, their movement probably due to food gathering.
    Peak of deer rutting in central and northern Florida.
    Cedar waxwings come south for the winter.
    Florida manatees migrate to freshwater springs during winter.
    Ornate chorus frogs begin calling.
    Indigo snakes breed in tortoise burrows.
    Winter rains, shorter days, and cooler temperatures present the perfect time for adding plants to your yard that provide food for wildlife.

December

Annual Christmas Bird Count begins mid-month.
    Buy live Christmas trees for later planting; red cedar, holly, and pine are nice.
    Great horned owls are courting (loud, deep hoots), as are barred owls. Listen for the latter's "who cooks for you, who cooks for you all?"
    Manatees concentrate near springs.
    Bears are still on the move. Watch out for them in Lake, Collier, Marion, Highlands, Jefferson, Gulf, Volusia, and Hernando Counties.
    Belted kingfishers become more common as winter migrants join resident populations.
    Look for downy, hairy, red-bellied, and red-headed woodpeckers at your feeders, also goldfinches and evening grosbeaks.
    Overwintering ducks and geese flock to wetlands like Paynes Prairie, St. Marks National Wildlife Refuge, and Tommy Goodwin Waterfowl Management Area.
    Snail kites are nesting in southern Florida.
    Goldfinches are plentiful in northern Florida.

Appendix 3. Activity-Based Destination Recommendations

Sometimes you know exactly what you want to do, and are just looking for a place to do it. Try these suggestions for the top places to explore natural Florida with your favorite activity in mind.

Hiking/Backpacking

Apalachicola National Forest (chapter 5)
Blackwater River State Forest (chapter 2)
Mike Roess Gold Head Branch State Park (chapter 12)
Myakka River State Park (chapter 23)
Ocala National Forest (chapter 13)
Paynes Prairie Preserve State Park (chapter 12)
Tosohatchee State Reserve (chapter 16)
Wekiwa Springs State Park (chapter 19)
Withlacoochee State Forest (chapter 17)

Nature Trails

Arthur R. Marshall Loxahatchee National Wildlife Refuge (chapter 25)
Crystal River Preserve State Park (chapter 17)
DeLeon Springs State Park (chapter 15)
Grayton Beach State Park (chapter 3)
Highlands Hammock State Park (chapter 21)
Honeymoon Island State Park (chapter 20)
Lake Kissimmee State Park (chapter 22)
Lake Louisa State Park (chapter 18)
Lovers Key Carl E. Johnson State Park (chapter 24)
Manatee Springs State Park (chapter 9)
Merritt Island National Wildlife Refuge (chapter 14)
Savannas Preserve State Park (chapter 26)
St. Marks National Wildlife Refuge (chapter 7)
T. Mabry Carlton Reserve (chapter 23)
Weedon Island Preserve (chapter 20)

Bird-Watching and Wildlife-Watching

Big Bend Wildlife Management Area (chapter 7)
Corkscrew Swamp Sanctuary (chapter 30)
Crystal River National Wildlife Refuge (chapter 17)
Everglades National Park (chapter 28 and chapter 30)
Homosassa Springs Wildlife State Park (chapter 17)
J. N. "Ding" Darling National Wildlife Refuge (chapter 24)
Kissimmee Prairie Preserve State Park (chapter 25)
Lake Kissimmee State Park (chapter 22)
Lake Woodruff National Wildlife Refuge (chapter 15)
Merritt Island National Wildlife Refuge (chapter 14)
Myakka River State Park (chapter 23)
Ocala National Forest (chapter 13)
St. Andrews State Park (chapter 3)
St. Marks National Wildlife Refuge (chapter 7)
St. Vincent National Wildlife Refuge (chapter 4)
The Keys (chapter 31)
Three Lakes Wildlife Management Area (chapter 22)
Timucuan Ecological and Historical Preserve (chapter 10)

Paddling

Big Bend Saltwater Paddling Trail (chapter 7)
Blackwater River (chapter 2)
Calusa Blueway (chapter 24)
Everglades National Park (chapters 28 and 30)
Indian River Lagoon (chapters 14 and 26)
Matanzas River (chapter 11)
Loxahatchee River (chapter 27)
Nature Coast Paddling Trail (chapter 17)
Peace River (chapter 23)
Suwannee River Wilderness Trail (chapters 8 and 9)
Tampa Bay area islands (chapter 20)
Timucuan Ecological and Historical Preserve (chapter 10)

Camping

Bahia Honda State Park (chapter 31)
Blue Spring State Park (chapter 15)
Fort DeSoto Park (chapter 20)
Grayton Beach State Park (chapter 3)

Kissimmee Prairie Preserve State Park (chapter 25)
Manatee Springs State Park (chapter 9)
Shell Mound Park (chapter 9)
Silver River State Park (chapter 13)
Stephen Foster Folk Culture Center State Park (chapter 8)
Topsail Hill Preserve State Park (chapter 3)

Horseback Riding

Amelia Island State Park (chapter 10)
Apalachicola National Forest (chapter 5)
Cape San Blas (chapter 4)
Florida Caverns State Park (chapter 6)
Ocala National Forest (chapter 13)

Scenic Driving

A1A (chapters 10 and 11)
Apalachicola National Forest (chapter 5)
Big Cypress National Preserve (chapter 29)
Emeralda Marsh Conservation Area (chapter 19)
Fakahatchee Strand Preserve State Park (chapter 29)
J.N. "Ding" Darling National Wildlife Refuge (chapter 24)
Lower Suwannee National Wildlife Refuge (chapter 9)
Merritt Island National Wildlife Refuge (chapter 14)
Pensacola Bluffs Scenic Highway (chapter 3)
Scenic Highway 30A (chapter 3)
Three Lakes Wildlife Management Area (chapter 22)
US 1 (chapter 31)
US 98 (chapter 4)

Snorkeling and Diving

Biscayne National Park (chapter 28)
Florida Keys National Marine Sanctuary (chapter 31)
Northern Florida (chapters 8 and 9)
Panama City Beach (chapter 3)
Wekiwa Springs State Park (chapter 19)

Index

Since 2000, Holly Ambrose has published and edited *EcoFlorida: Your Guide to Exploring Natural Florida*, a monthly publication that she began after working in print, online, and multimedia publishing. *EcoFlorida* has taken her traveling across Florida with her husband, Jim, who takes many of the photographs in its pages. Holly holds a degree in journalism and since 1994 has written freelance articles for regional publications as well as sites online. Holly and Jim live about a mile from the Everglades.